www.ingramcontent.com/pod-product-compliance
Lightning Source LLC
Chambersburg PA
CBHW050242010526
44107CB00032B/1382/J

TRAMPLING UNION TERROR

"Breaking Through" by Claiborne Duncan Gregory

TRAMPLING UNION TERROR

Riders of the Second Alabama Cavalry

"Charge Them Boys, Kill the Damn Thieves"

Dr. Jeffrey F. Addicott
Lt. Colonel (US Army, Ret.) BA, JD, LLM (2), SJD

with David E. Gould

Illustrations by Livia Lavender

This book is dedicated to the courage, spirit, and sacrifice of our kinsmen:

Dr. John A. Baldwin
Acting Assistant Surgeon
Company F, 2nd Alabama Cavalry Regiment
Confederate States of America

Private James A. Gould
Company B, 2nd Alabama Cavalry Regiment
Confederate States of America

Private Thomas M. Mosley
Company E, 2nd Alabama Cavalry Regiment
Confederate States of America

Trampling Union Terror:
Riders of the Second Alabama Cavalry

Copyright© 2024 by Dr. Jeffrey F. Addicott

ALL RIGHTS RESERVED. No part of this publication may be reproduced, distributed, or transmitted in any form or by any means, including photocopying, recording, or other electronic or mechanical methods, or by any information storage and retrieval system without the prior written permission of the publisher, except in the case of very brief quotations embodied in critical reviews and certain other non-commercial uses permitted by copyright law.

Produced in the Republic of South Carolina by
SHOTWELL PUBLISHING LLC
Post Office Box 2592
Columbia, So. Carolina 29202
www.ShotwellPublishing.com

Cover Art: "Breaking Through" by Claiborne Duncan Gregory

ISBN: 978-1-963506-03-7

FIRST EDITION
10 9 8 7 6 5 4 3 2 1

Contents

Introduction
War Crimes and Warriors i

Part I
The Rebel Cavalry

Chapter One
Structure of the Force 1

Chapter Two
General Themes for the Cavalry 15

Part II

Chapter One
Second Alabama Cavalry Regiment 105

Chapter Two
Patrolling the Florida/Alabama Line 115

Chapter Three
Sham Fighting in Northeast Mississippi 147

Chapter Four
Glory at Last 179

Chapter Five
In Ferguson's Brigade 201

Chapter Six
Meridian: Prelude to Terror 273

Chapter Seven
The Dalton/Atlanta Campaign 305

Chapter Eight
Terror March to the Sea 401

Chapter Nine
Davis' Cavalry Escort 433

Conclusion
The End & The Beginning 463

Endnotes 484

About the Author 529

Introduction

WAR CRIMES AND WARRIORS

"The object of terrorism is terrorism. The object of oppression is oppression. The object of torture is torture. The object of power is power. Now do you begin to understand me?"[1] — George Orwell

THIS WORK IS A COMPANION to the 2023 book, *Union Terror: Debunking the Justifications for the Union's Use of Terror Against Southern Civilians.*[2] *Union Terror* explored not only the legal and policy implications of the Lincoln Administration's decision to employ a merciless scorched-earth campaign against large segments of unresisting Southern noncombatants, but also proved as absolutely false all of the so-called justifications for its use of terrorism with particular emphasis focused on the 1864 Union terror operation from Atlanta to Savannah, colloquially known as the "March to the Sea." Although Sherman's formidable army of approximately 60,000 infantry enveloped by another 5,000 cavalry was supplied with 2,500 new commissary wagons holding ample provisions and rations to last for the expedition's 30 day march, the Federal general allowed his men to pillage and destroy the foodstuffs and homes of defenseless women and fatherless children in blatant violation of the laws of war as they then existed, not to mention

disregarding the laws of humanity. To those who care to educate themselves on the depth and breadth of the premeditated Union atrocities, this cowardly picture of criminality is not overdrawn.[3]

Tested by the Union's own rules of warfare set out in General Order 100,[4] the outrageous conduct of Federal military forces against an unresisting civilian population was intentional and to ensure maximum suffering on the noncombatants, in addition to burning down their homes, all agricultural implements were broken, all personal articles of value stolen, and all horses, cattle, hogs, and chickens either butchered, driven off, or killed and left to rot. Coupled with a parade of vile insults and other acts of depredation, the crimes have too long been covered up by apologists for those directly responsible — Lincoln and his generals. If we as Americans unhesitatingly and rightfully object to human rights abuses and violations of the law of war by other nations, by what standard, human or Divine, can the United States stand mute in the face of its own deplorable record of terror? Indeed, the old saw is valid: Those who ignore the past are doomed to repeat it.

While most mainstream writers about the American Civil War obfuscate and/or fail to condemn the raw atrocities committed by the Lincoln Administration, it is interesting to note that our enemies do not — they often make reference to the wide-spread Union war crimes for their own propaganda purposes. For instance, in 1944, the magazine *Signal*, a widely distributed German publication of the Nazi regime published in German, French, and Spanish, boasted a full length photo of General Ulysses S. Grant on its cover to introduce the reader to the main article called: *The Method of Warfare of the Americans*, which spent five full pages detailing the terror tactics of Grant and Sherman against innocent civilians, just 80 years prior. With the arrival of U.S. troops in Europe, the Germans hoped to frighten Europeans into believing that they could expect the same treatment![5]

As the title of this work suggests, the prism employed to further explore the matter of Union terrorism centers around a storied Confederate cavalry command, the 2nd Alabama Cavalry Regiment.

Not only did the 2nd Alabama actively contest numerous Federal terror raids in Mississippi and Alabama, the gray horse soldiers had the unique distinction of witnessing first-hand the crescendo of Union savagery during Sherman's march across Georgia as they vigorously resisted the wrongdoers every step of the way. In fact, while serving both independently and under various commands, to include General Ruggles and General Ferguson, the 2nd Alabama Cavalry had the unique distinction of fighting Union terror raids — Sherman and others — more than any other cavalry regiment in the entire Confederacy!

As such, this book is divided into two related parts. Part I sets up the historical backdrop of the War to include a general review of the Confederate cavalry and Part II is about "war crimes and warriors." The *war crimes* recount the horrendous outrages on non-combatants which occurred during Union military strikes in the western theater of combat to include General Sherman's notorious Meridian foray in Mississippi in early 1864, followed later that year by his infamous March to the Sea. The *warriors* describe the hard riding troopers of the Confederacy's 2nd Alabama Cavalry Regiment, Southern men who valiantly defended their families, State, and country from the miscreants.

— Tom and John —

I am a proud 20-year veteran of the United States Army who not only spent most of my career as a senior legal advisor responsible for ensuring compliance with the law of war, but also had the good fortune to serve as the Staff Judge Advocate to the United States Army Special Forces Command (Airborne) — the Green Berets. That said, my interest in the 2nd Alabama Cavalry is certainly not unconnected with the fact that I am the great-great grandson of two young men that served honorably in the regiment, one as a "high private" in Company E and the other as an acting assistant surgeon, assigned to Company F.

It is also certain that my childhood summers spent in south Alabama in the 1960's on the old homestead of my great-grandparents, Minnie (Mosley) Baldwin and Ira Baldwin, left an indelible impression about the value of our shared Southern heritage. I was particularly enthralled by the fact that I had only to reach back one person from Minnie and Ira (who I vividly recall) and I would be standing face-to-face with their respective fathers — two hard-fighting Southern cavalrymen.

In stark contrast to the one-dimensional thought police who self-righteously patrol our social media and school systems on a crusade to denigrate all things Southern, most Southerners of my generation were told that our Rebel forebearers were great heroes who took up arms against overwhelming numbers of ruthless invaders, risking everything to defend their communities. Sadly, as bright as these memories are, conformism to a visceral hatred of all things "Confederate" presents a powerful negative in the modern tunnel vision world of *woke* culture which seeks only to suffocate rather than facilitate an understanding about objective reality — the good, the bad, and the ugly. In short, with an unrelenting abandonment of critical thinking skills accurate historical interpretation is sacrificed on the altar of political correctness. For example, while it is certainly a correct observation that the evil of slavery was a festering national wound and an outrage to the democratic norms and values set by the Founding Fathers, the vast majority of white Southerners did not own slaves and few viewed themselves as fighting to perpetuate the vile institution. They fought because they were invaded.[6]

While tangible evidence of my Confederate roots evoke images of a black slouch hat ripped by a Yankee bullet hole, a coarse corduroy covered Federal "bulls eye" canteen, strange looking green colored eye glasses, and a war-time medical book from the Atlanta Medical College, I am convinced that the experiences my kinsmen faced are valued additions to the national fabric. At the very least, it is my earnest hope that intolerance and ignorance will not forever masquerade as the new *reimagined* reality of our nation's true history.[7]

John Augustus Baldwin and Thomas M. Mosley resided in adjoining counties in central Alabama and willingly answered the call to arms of their new country, the Confederate States of America. Both were single men in their twenties when they left their homes in the summer of 1862, to join the freshly minted 2nd Alabama Cavalry Regiment. Three long years later, in May of 1865, the two veterans came limping back to what remained of their homes, one without an eye and the other wrecked by disease. Times were desperate and the State government had no resources to assist either the returning veterans or the displaced former enslaved Southerners that also sought to create new lives for themselves and their families. Along with facing the physical challenges posed by destitute communities, the sufferings and memories associated with the War would long define what it meant to be a Southerner.

Like so many post-War Confederate veterans, Baldwin and Mosley breathed deep the horrors of conflict and yet they did not abandon themselves to despair. Ironically, the War was lost but they were not defeated in spirit — rugged individualism and the desire to be left alone still pulsed through their veins. The two men picked up the pieces, worked hard, and in 1867, married two local Alabama girls.[8] Both were soon thereafter blessed with a great number of offspring to include respectively my maternal and paternal great grandparents, Minnie Mosley and Ira Baldwin. So it was that the two Confederate veterans who rode side-by-side would share a common progeny when Ira and Minnie united in marriage on July 22, 1898, in Butler County, Alabama.[9]

— Through Their Eyes —

The 2nd Alabama Cavalry Regiment was recruited from the fertile farmlands of south and central Alabama in the Spring of 1862, a year after the War began. The men that made up the regiment were homogeneous in their backgrounds and all embraced an unfaltering commitment to the instilled virtue of duty. Since no literary source exists to preserve the heroic accomplishments of this hard fighting regiment,[10] this work attempts to pull the riders

back from the vortex of time so that their service may be properly honored and hopefully assist in renewing a commitment by future generations to celebrate the essential qualities of duty and honor that have long formed an integral part of the American mosaic.

When properly lead, the 2nd Alabama was a brave and extremely capable force with many skirmishes and battles to their credit. Participants in some of the key events of the Civil War, the men logged thousands of miles on horseback over inhospitable terrain, often in conditions of broiling heat and bone chilling cold, boldly confronting Federal cavalry terror raids in Mississippi, Alabama, and Georgia.

While the 2nd Alabama cut their combat teeth blunting Union cavalry strikes in Mississippi and Alabama in 1863, their most demanding service occurred during Sherman's Meridian raid, the Dalton-Atlanta campaign, and the March to the Sea. They also saw action in the evacuation of Savannah and served as part of the final escort of President Jefferson Davis in 1865, as he fled into Georgia following the fall of Richmond.

Of course, this study is penned based on what resources remain as most of the original sources and relics have vanished into the vast ocean of time. On the other hand, those primary sources that have survived, particularly the letters, diaries, reports, newspaper articles, and military documents are often tainted with exaggerations, inaccuracies, misleading information, and even, on occasion, contradict one another. For instance it is not uncommon to read about a particular combat action contained in separate Union and Confederate "after-action reports" found in the *Official Records of the War of the Rebellion*,[11] and conclude that both sides emerged victorious! Also, many subsequent tellings of various particulars about the regiment relied on earlier accounts so that an initial error in the first was carried on into others, such as the grossly inaccurate rendition by one historian that 450 troopers of the 2nd Alabama Cavalry surrendered at Forsyth, Georgia, in May 1865,[12] when in fact by that date in the War there weren't even 1,000 troopers left in the entire brigade of which the 2nd Alabama was only one regiment.

Ira Baldwin and Minnie (Mosley) Baldwin, circa 1915.

Furthermore, since only the literate left letters or diaries much contemporary information and discourse is simply unknowable. In turn, some of the veteran's post war recollections found in such valuable references as the *Confederate Veteran*, were recounted years after the events took place when memories tended to highlight the humorous and gallant and mute out the horrific and base.

Still, enough details can be marshaled to both chronicle the regiment's history and to also offer intimate snap-shots of various "behind the scenes" experiences and accomplishments — some reflecting poorly on the regiment and others cloaking it with

amazing approbation. As such, the firsthand accounts contained herein come from various members of the rank and file, with particular attention to a treasure trove of wartime letters penned by Harden Perkins Cochrane (1843-1925),[13] who rose to the position of the sergeant major of the regiment, and the wartime diary and post-War memoirs of the regiment's brigade commander, Brigadier General Samuel Wragg Ferguson (1834-1917).

Finally, while the workings of the eternal clock sweeps clean the tears of men, it is hoped that this work will provide a window through which the reader can get a feel for what it was like to be a Southern cavalryman. In this light, the 2nd Alabama Cavalry Regiment served to the very end, not because they viewed themselves as part of a great Greek tragedy "where you know what the outcome is bound to be,"[14] but because they believed that they were in the right, fighting to ward off vicious invaders who terrorized the innocent.

Part I
The Rebel Cavalry

Chapter One

STRUCTURE OF THE FORCE

"A horse must be a bit mad to be a good cavalry mount, and its rider must be completely so."[15]
— Steven Pressfield

THERE WERE MANY acrimonious tenacles of grievance, real and imagined, that contributed to the departure of 11 Southern States to form the Confederate States of America. However, one thing was always certain, the Lincoln Administration would never recognize the Confederacy's bid for independence. Upon being sworn into office in early 1861, Lincoln took immediate steps to form a massive army to invade the new nation and force it back into the United States at the point of the bayonet. Interestingly, the slave-holding States of Virginia, Tennessee, North Carolina, and Arkansas initially refused to join the Confederacy, only doing so in direct response to Lincoln's call for violence, although Maryland, Delaware, Kentucky, and Missouri, other slave-holding States, elected to stay with the Union to fight with the North to preserve the United States (West Virginia, a slave-holding State, was admitted to the United States mid-way through the War, in 1863, bringing to five the number of slave-holding States that fought to keep the Union intact).

The stage was set. Like the 13 American colonies that had likewise declared their independence from Britain 85 years prior, if the Confederacy was to survive it would have to fight. Following the organizational system of the United States military, the nascent country divided its ground forces into infantry, cavalry, and artillery. The basic fighting unit for both the infantry soldier and the cavalry trooper was the *regiment* which on paper consisted of ten *companies* of about 100 men each (the cavalry company is also called a *troop*), including enlisted and officer. The military organization for infantry and cavalry followed a similar hierarchy with artillery units assigned to each beginning at the regimental level.

Company: 100 men.

Regiment: 10 Companies.

Brigade: 3-5 Regiments.

Division: 2-5 Brigades.

Corps: 2-4 Divisions.

Army: Variable Number of Divisions or Corps.

The Confederacy drew the vast majority of its fighting men from the small localities and farms all over the South. The typical Southern Soldier — about 65 percent of the rank and file — was an uneducated non-slave owning farmer, though the various units held non-slave owning laborers, clerks, bankers, college students, and merchants as well, all previously dependent on their own labor to make a living for themselves and their families. They were young men, almost a quarter in their late teens and over ninety percent under the age of thirty. While modern American males stand around two inches taller and are far heavier than the average Civil War soldier, it is a stretch to assume that people were drastically shorter during the 1860's. The average height was five foot eight inches.

With few exceptions the companies and regiments were formed exclusively from the men who resided in their individual States and the regiment received its designation accordingly. In fact, in rural America with its far-flung towns and villages, young men and women found it most practical to marry their neighbors. Thus, as one would suspect, the company rosters were filled with kinsmen bearing the same last name — brothers, cousins, sons, and fathers. Related by blood and in keeping with their Scottish/Anglo-Saxon heritage these men camped together, marched together, fought together and died together as family.[16]

This purity of allegiance to the community remained firm at the regimental level. For example, out of the original 119 members of Company E of the 2nd Alabama Cavalry Regiment, 76 had direct familial relations sharing the same last names, and probably another two dozen or so were indirectly related as cousins.[17] Thus, Company E's Private Thomas Mosley, served right alongside with his two brothers in the same company, Reddick Mosley and Mathew Mosley.

Each company was identified by an alphabetical letter from A to K (based on long standing military tradition the letter J was never used). Each company was also further divided into four or five squads, led by a senior enlisted man or a junior lieutenant. Companies were commanded by officers of the company grade rank of captain and often times referred to by the name of their original or current captain and/or by a nickname that the company might give themselves.

The regiment itself was commanded by a field grade officer with the rank of full colonel. Company grade ranks were lieutenant and captain and field grade ranks were major, lieutenant colonel and colonel. The regimental level staff officers included: adjutant, commissary officer, ordnance officer, quartermaster, surgeon, assistant surgeon, and chaplain, and the senior enlisted support side included sergeant, the sergeant major, and regimental bugler. The three grades of lieutenants assigned to each company oversaw the running of the company to ensure that all standards were met

when it came to drill, quarters, latrines, stable duty, paperwork, roll calls, and inspections. Other regimental jobs held by lower enlisted soldiers were waggoneers, farriers, blacksmiths, and saddlers.

The military designation for the regiment would be numerical, rather than alphabetical, and coupled with the State identifier and type of force, such as: *2nd Alabama Cavalry Regiment.* Like the practice of companies, the regiment might also be known by the name of its original or current regimental commander. Thus, during its first year in service the 2nd Alabama Cavalry Regiment was sometimes known as Hunter's Alabama Cavalry Regiment, after its first regimental commander, Colonel Fountain Winston Hunter. Later, it was sometimes referred to by the name of subsequent regimental commanders.

During the early part of the War the men of each company and regiment elected their own officers and non-commissioned officers, a process that sometimes led to the favorite, not the competent, serving in positions of leadership. Usually, the long standing practice was to elect pre-War militia officers for command slots and in many cases the men would vote with their feet by simply gathering around the candidate of their choice.

Over the course of the War, Alabama gave many State identified regiments of her sons to the Confederacy to include sixty-one regiments of infantry (plus two smaller battalions of infantry), twenty-seven batteries of artillery, and fourteen regiments of cavalry (plus two smaller sized battalions of cavalry), about 120,000 white males in total. In addition, the State produced one regiment of infantry and four regiments of cavalry with Confederate national identification. Curiously, the strong Union sympathy in the northern counties of Alabama spawned two regiments of cavalry to the United States. The Union regiment that saw the most service was designated as the First (1st) Alabama Cavalry Regiment Union,[18] with the Second (2nd) Alabama Cavalry Union,[19] formed late in the War, seeing little real action.

— Black Confederates in the 2nd Alabama Cavalry —

White Southerners have good reason to protest vehemently against the disgraceful manner in which their Confederate history is vilified by fact denying commentators and historians. In turn, a true record of that time must also recognize the contributions of black Southerners, the majority of which were still held in human bondage yet who also supported the Confederate war effort. While most historians might correctly acknowledge with little criticism that "large numbers of slaves chose to fight with their *colonial masters* instead of accepting British offers of freedom during the American Revolution," the thought of even larger numbers of "black men and women serving the Confederacy seems beyond comprehension and reason, and is a vexation."[20]

Accordingly, it would be disingenuous to disregard the valued participation of the many black Southerners that served in and with the 2nd Alabama. Like most other Confederate cavalry regiments, the 2nd Alabama had significant numbers of black Americans functioning in a variety of vital support roles, with some armed and engaged in scouting, guard duty, and even combat at the front right alongside their white counterparts.[21] In most cases, their names were never listed on company records but a growing body of scholarship and research is slowly bringing many of their stories to light.[22] The impressive Civil War museum at the Atlanta History Center provides a low-ball figure of 50,000 for the number of black Southerners who served in the Confederate military. Their museum placard reads:

> As many as 50,000 [blacks] may have served in the Confederate Army, occasionally as soldiers, but usually as cooks or forced laborers [emphasis added].[23]

To be sure, most black Southerners were there as servants to their masters or as teamsters, cooks, blacksmiths, and caretakers for the animals.[24] Much to the consternation of Frederick Douglass

Confederate Veteran Reunion.

and others in the Union, it was quite natural and not uncommon to see large numbers of black Americans wearing gray and butternut uniforms marching and riding right along with white Rebels, many of them armed to the teeth, most enslaved, but some as freemen.[25] Douglass wrote in late 1861:

> It is now pretty well established that there are at the present moment many colored men in the Confederate army, doing duty not only as cooks, servants and laborers, but as real soldiers, having muskets on their shoulders, and bullets in their pockets, ready to shoot down loyal troops, and do all that soldiers may to do..."[26]

After the War, marble monuments were erected in several Southern States to honor individual black Confederates by name for their combat prowess, and black Southerners dressed in grey uniforms were always encountered at Confederate veteran reunions. Even today, the heritage group Sons of Confederate Veterans celebrates its black members with great respect.

For the uninformed, the sometimes complex interactions and close relationships between white and black Southerners in the old South will ever remain in the shadows. For example, it is inconceivable to some that a white Confederate soldier could ever close a letter to his mother expressing love to the enslaved people that remained at home,[27] like Private Alex K. Hall, 2nd Alabama, who in August 1863: "Give my love to all, Darkies included of course. Yours affectionately, Alex."[28] While both Northerners and Southerners alike might employ banal language that is rightfully jarring to modern readers, the context is always key to gauge the degree, if any, of actual animosity or racism suggested.

As in many countries of the past, the framework of societal and cultural interaction in the antebellum South was set in the disturbing and vile practice of human bondage. Yet even in this barren soil one could observe in many instances the existence of a genuine

reciprocal affection between master and slave, which often resulted in the slave finding his path to manumission. Interestingly, the States loyal to the United States had about 430,000 slaves while the Confederate States had about 260,000 free blacks in their general population. Free or enslaved, many Southern blacks identified themselves with their own families and country[29] and those that did not serve in the field with the Army stayed on the home front and sustained the farms, a war-time development in which the majority of the white population accepted with confidence.[30]

It is not surprising, for instance, to discover that the 2nd Alabama Cavalry boasted quite a few black "Confederates" amongst their numbers. The surviving writings of Private Harden Cochrane, Company D, 2nd Alabama, provides some revealing insights about the role of black Southerners who served with the regiment. His numerous letters speak affectionately about his body-servant, Claiborne, who accompanied him throughout most of his military service. Without question, the unique fraternity of military life in Confederate units extended to men like Claiborne who were viewed as integral parts of the outfit.

Born and raised in Tuscaloosa, Alabama, Cochrane was an 18-year-old student at the University of Alabama and a member of the University Cadet Corps when the War broke out. Because of his experience in military drill, Cochrane and his fellow cadets were sorely needed as drill masters to turn the unskilled green recruits flooding into boot camps all across the South into infantrymen. Not unexpectedly, Cochrane was immediately assigned as a drill instructor at Camp Shelby, Alabama. The work was grueling and the hours long,[31] and Cochrane was quick to resign his position in the spring of 1862, to join the 2nd Alabama Cavalry, where he served first as a private in Company D and then in late 1864, as the regiment's highest ranking enlisted man — the sergeant-major.[32] For over three years in active service with the regiment Cochrane was never far from his faithful body-servant, Claiborne.

Structure of the Force

*Sergeant Major Harden Perkins Cochrane.
1925 Confederate Veteran Reunion.*

57th Georgia Mess Group with Scott, an Enslaved Black Southerner.

As noted, the use of servants in the field was common and not just restricted to the officers, particularly for the 2nd Alabama, which was composed of many well to do members. In fact, quite a few of the lowest ranking enlisted men in the 2nd Alabama had servants living with them in camp. Although the troopers and their servants were under military jurisdiction, the servants were only responsible to their masters and not to orders given by the normal chain of command,[33] much in the same manner that modern day civilian contractors who accompany American armed forces in overseas operations are not subject to military orders.[34]

In the letters Cochrane wrote back home to his relatives and friends he often referred to both Claiborne and other black Southerners in the regiment as they performed a variety of tasks, mostly for their owner/Soldier or four-person mess group. Apparently, out of the four enlisted men in Cochrane's mess group, three of them were accompanied by their own personal servants. Cochrane cataloged Claiborne's duties as follows:

> Claiborne curries and waters our [the four mess-mates] horses and washes for us and cooks every other day. Willie Sander's [Cochrane's mess mate] negro cooks one day and Claiborne the next and Bostic [another black servant] brings water all the time.[35]

An earlier letter written on November 11, 1862, describes in detail how the mess constructed their winter log cabins and how a separate wooden house was built for "Claiborne and William and Bostic to stay in."[36] Reflecting the unique position of servants in camp, the same letter notes that Captain J.J. Pegues, the company commander at the time, requested on several occasions the temporary use of Claiborne.

> The Captain [from Tuscaloosa] expects his wife this week [the trip from Tuscaloosa took about three days] and is having his house put up today. He asked me to

let Claiborne help him and of course I consented as I had nothing particular for him to do.[37]

Indeed, Claiborne and others had numerous "opportunities to earn money by doing odd jobs for other members of the command,"[38] as suggested in an amusing story of how Claiborne was able to outsmart three very shrewd members of Company D by selling one of them a broken-down abandoned Yankee mule that Cochrane himself had "captured" while out on a patrol.

> I picked up a Yankee mule that has the worst sore on its back that I ever saw …. I intended to … either sell or turn loose the mule that I had picked up. Claiborne said he could sell him. A man in the company said he would give me one hundred and fifty on credit …. Yesterday he came up to me with the most sorrowful countenance I ever beheld and said, "Oh, Harden! I came up to get off of that trade. I'm sick and tired of it [the mule]. I will give you ten dollars to take him off my hands" …. He went on finding fault with the mule, had not examined him, etc. etc., said that two men had advised him to buy the mule. He was angry with them, wanted to shoot the mule …. I was so much amused at Claiborne cheating the three most conceited horse traders in the company.[39]

Running like a red thread throughout all his correspondence is the undeniable story of a very personal relationship/affection between Claiborne and Cochrane. For instance, a June 23, 1862, letter describes with pride how Claiborne cared for and rode Cochrane's mount and confirms that Claiborne also had his own personal horse.[40] A July 5, 1862, letter playfully describes how the two young men carried, distributed, and then ate watermelons together;[41] a December 27, 1862, letter recalls how Claiborne eagerly traveled up and back from the cavalry camp near Brewton,

Alabama, to Tuscaloosa, with much needed personal supplies;[42] and a November 26, 1863, letter describes how Claiborne brought Cochrane a large sum of money and a Confederate issued overcoat from home traveling through a freezing storm to do so. Cochrane writes how he "caught up with him [Claiborne] on a freezing night" and warmed him "up by my overcoat and gloves."[43]

Based on myriad stories that seem to transcend the servant/master relationship, there is little reason to suspect that Cochrane's affection and admiration for Claiborne was insincere or constituted an isolated case. A revealing letter of July 21, 1862, written from Bluff Springs, Florida, shows that this black Southerner, Claiborne, was considered a trusted part of the regiment and on very familiar terms, even with Private Cochrane's commanding officer.[44] It reads:

> To Miss Henrietta Williams
> Tuscaloosa, Alabama
>
> Claiborne sends howdy to Ma and all, and his love to all his family. Tell Myra [that] Claiborne says he is well and doing well and is much better pleased than he was when he first came [to the camp of the 2nd Alabama Cavalry Regiment]. He wants to see you all very much. Claiborne says if Captain Pegues is there [Captain Pegues was Private Cochrane's company commander who was then on furlough back home in Tuscaloosa] please send his [Claiborne's] best overcoat if Captain Pegues will bring it. If Captain Pegues has gone, there is a Mr. Blocker who overseered [sic] for Mr. Rufus Clements who I think will bring it to Claiborne.

Other references to black Southerners in the Cochrane collection include the following: (1) letter from Camp Stone in Montgomery, dated June 1, 1862, which refers to a "Hortentius, Mr. Beard's

servant,"[45] that carried soldier mail back to family members in Tuscaloosa; (2) letter of July 5, 1862, where Cochrane spoke of two blacks he was assigned to stand guard over that were confined in the regiment's stockade but did "not belong to anybody in the regiment;"[46] (3) letter dated September 6, 1862, describing the death of Sergeant Bissel's servant "with camp fever;"[47] (4) letter of November 30, 1862, where Cochrane again mentions Bostic who had been left behind with Claiborne when a scouting party rode out of their camp to go "on a seven day scout ... to Milton [Florida]."[48]

Chapter Two

General Themes for the Cavalry

"No man could ride with [General] Shelby for four years and be worth his salt at anything afterward. I did it and I know it."[49] — *Confederate Cavalryman*

THE AMERICAN CIVIL WAR was the last large conflict in the history of warfare in which men on horseback played a significant role. But this final hurrah for the mounted soldier was also dramatically different from previous wars where cavalry had been employed as a sword wielding shock force slamming full speed into fixed infantry, trampling and scattering them about as so many dominos. With the advent of rifles which could kill at 1,000 yards, that wild and exciting tactic was suicide and commanders who attempted it were fools.

Rebel cavalry quickly adapted to the times. Playing largely on its mobility factor the cavalry proved extremely useful in five new ways: (1) reconnaissance, to scout out the movements of enemy forces and develop their size and direction of travel; (2) screening, to protect the flanks and front of friendly infantry from surprise enemy attack; (3) guarding, to ensure supplies and points of special interest, like bridges, were secured; (4) harassing and raiding behind enemy lines, to strike suddenly and disrupt supply and transportation systems;

and (5) fighting, sometimes against other cavalry (dismounted or mounted), but most of the time dismounted and fighting limited skirmishes on foot to delay advancing enemy infantry.

If necessary, a good cavalry regiment could easily "march" (the term march was used for the cavalry as well as the infantry, even though the men rode horseback) 40 miles a day so that both in the tasks of reconnaissance and screening, troopers served efficiently as the eyes and ears of the army. Without real time cavalry reports, infantry commanders might well be able to hear the noise of enemy columns on the march, but they were unable to know the significance or purpose of the sounds. Accurate cavalry dispatches could reveal the types, strengths, or dispositions of opposing forces. In this case the cavalry was not fighting for a battlefield victory, but for actionable intelligence to allow the infantry to succeed. Robert E. Lee utilized his cavalry in this manner and often remarked that the cavalry commander for the Army of Northern Virginia, the trusted J.E.B. Stuart, was his eyes and ears.

Because practically every Southern boy learned how to ride and shoot at an early age, the Confederacy had the workings of a ready-made mounted force, yet one that knew nothing about organized warfare. As one might expect in the case of a fiercely independent people, the biggest hindrance to transforming these men into effective cavalrymen was their disdain for uniformity and discipline. Without question, the successful Rebel cavalry commander was one who could instill strict discipline in his men without breaking that spirit of aggressiveness and independence which often paid high dividends when it came to hard combat.

It is no surprise that the Confederate cavalry started the War with better mounts, better horsemen, better tactics, and better leadership. Though frequently lacking in basic necessities and hardened by the labors of campaigning across hundreds of miles in all sorts of weather, Rebel cavalrymen were ragtag in appearance but always performed at a higher level of efficiency than their Union counterparts. In this regard, General William T. Sherman respected the Southern riders far more than his own numerically

superior cavalry. He called them the "best cavalry in the world."[50] "War suits them," Sherman noted, "and the rascals are brave, fine riders and dangerous subjects in every sense."[51]

When a full cavalry regiment rode out for duty the metallic jangle and rattle of sabers, tin cups, and pans would fill the air as hundreds of horses kicked up large dust clouds which hovered above the landscape. This daunting sight signaled that a fighting force of great effectiveness was ready for action, even if the greater struggle was always one of "beans and bullets." The War would be won or lost on the battlefield, but failure was inevitable if the men lacked the weapons, equipment, and supplies to sustain them and their mounts in the field. Unfortunately, as the War progressed and deprivations of every kind set in, the Confederate cavalry was unable to maintain its superiority. Losses and shortages in the materials of war so decimated the Confederate horse regiments that by 1865, they were all used up.[52]

The turning point in the initially lopsided balance in favor of the Rebel horsemen began in mid-1864. Even then, however, the Union had great difficulties putting its vastly superior number of splendidly-equipped horsemen to good use. They may have been better armed, better fed, better mounted, and better equipped, but they were never better led and almost always outfought. It was not until the very last year of the War, when Southern resources were depleted, that Union cavalry was able to strike out at will all across the Confederacy.

— Early Warning System —

Given that a primary mission of the cavalry was to act as an early warning system, regiments were often obliged to dispurse their individual companies (also known as troops) and station them in separate camps at great distances apart to stand watch over large areas of territory. In turn, once the outlaying companies were situated at a particular spot, they would then "picket" squadrons of troopers at smaller semi-permanent outposts. The purpose

of outpost duty or "heavy picketing" was to assist in blocking enemy infiltrations as well reporting on hostile movements.[53] This reconnaissance mission also greatly assisted in providing the necessary fresh forage for the many horses and mules as well as comforting the local communities that friendly forces were close by to blunt Union terror raids.

Each cavalry company also had a number of specially selected men designated as "scouts" who were given the very risky job of ranging out even further than the picket outposts, to ascertain the disposition of enemy forces. The scouts usually rode at night and hid in the daytime either in dense thickets or with friendly civilians. However, they were always extremely careful to stay attired in their full military uniform bearing their arms openly, since if caught behind enemy lines in civilian clothes they could lawfully be executed as spies.

— Shielding the Regiment —

Moving out as a single regimental body required order of action so that the men traveled in columns of four abreast, terrain permitting. At full strength, this might take up ¾ of a mile of road from front to rear. Regimental scouts and other mounted "skirmishers" roamed in front and on the flanks to warn of ambush or other trouble. At evening camp, pickets were placed at stationary positions 400-500 yards from the main body and could be on duty for up to 24 hours, which meant keeping their horses saddled in order to sound the alarm back to the regiment at a moment's notice. In front of these picket posts, there were also roaming "videttes" which consisted of small numbers of cavalrymen scattered out another 400-500 yards in front of the pickets. They too were on the lookout for enemy forces.

If camped for lengthy periods, each morning mounted patrols of a half dozen men or so were sent out several miles beyond the videttes.[54] These scout patrols reported on all conditions from terrain features to enemy movements. Longer patrols might extend scores

of miles into the countryside lasting from five to ten days before returning to camp. Again, all scouts and advanced skirmishers were careful to dress in their gray military uniforms to avoid accusations, if captured, of being a spy.

Finally, the regimental commander had a special body of hand-selected troopers to serve both as his personal escort squad and as a quick reaction force to aggressively probe out ahead of the regiment when required. This group was led by a trusted and energetic junior officer, held directly responsible for responding to the commander's directives.

— Skirmishing Up Front —

In reviewing the historical reports, letters, and memoirs the term "skirmishing" or "skirmishing up front" is a constant description given to characterize cavalry fighting. Sometimes this entailed nothing more than meeting engagements consisting of running gunfights with small enemy scouting parties, but it also referred to all out brawls between larger bodies of horsemen and even engaging in the deadly cat and mouse dance of dismounting for combat to conduct shooting matches with superior bodies of advancing enemy infantry. Depending on the particular mission and circumstances, the cavalrymen took on these fights in regimental, company, or even smaller group formations, sometimes with the support of one or two light batteries of artillery.

Hundreds of times the 2nd Alabama Cavalry skirmished up front along narrow winding roads and railroad tracks, in swamps, forgotten valleys, hills, river crossings, and forests in Florida, Alabama, Mississippi, Tennessee, Georgia, North Carolina, and South Carolina. In the mounted combat actions, of one sort or the other, the casualties were generally not too heavy. Most of the pistol or rifle shots simply missed even though practiced hands turned black and grimy from gun powder residue reloaded and fired as fast as practicable. Of course, some of the slugs would hit with a resounding "thud," tumbling the rider to the ground. If the wound

was not fatal, perhaps a hit to the leg or arm, comrades would quickly spirit him away to seek medical attention while the rest of the troop continued the fight.

In the larger engagements, the close nature of the fighting could turn particularly vicious, with no real objective other than to kill or "drive" the enemy. Rarely, however, would the men experience a mounted saber-waving horse charge across open ground where Yankees and Confederates smashed head to head. Rarer yet was a thundering cavalry charge against massed infantry, due to the absolute devastation on the horse soldiers wrought by long-range rifled muskets. The only exception might be those occasions when a demoralized enemy was fleeing in hasty retreat and the cavalry commander might be emboldened to "keep the scare up" in hot pursuit. This too could be very dangerous should the enemy reorganize somewhere out of sight at a secondary prepared defensive line and wait for the pursuing horsemen to gallop out into the open.

A firsthand account of an Alabama horse Soldier speaking to the rigors of cavalry life to include "skirmishing up front" appeared in the *Mobile Register and Advertiser* of April 19, 1863:

> Many of the noblest and bravest spirits of this war have thus fallen: but no halo of battle glory brightens their names — they fell "skirmishing up at the front." Between outpost, picket and mount duty, precious little rest does the cavalryman see. If no skirmish requires his aid, there is the tiresome and stealthy ride through the thickets, over the hills and down the valleys, or the weary, silent waiting at the deserted cross road or lonesome hill top; through sunshine and darkness, through all weathers; no tent to shelter them from the drenching rain, no fire to thaw their numbed fingers or warm their scarce, scanty rations.[55]

— Fighting On Foot —

In addition to the traditional cavalry functions of scouting, guarding, and skirmishing, the major innovation in cavalry employment during the War consisted of dismounting the troopers at strategic points of contact and temporarily using them to fight as ground troops. The South was the first to fully understand that horse soldiers (dragoons) could be used to maneuver quickly to a particular point of need, dismount, and then fight as infantry to either impede the progress of advancing enemy forces, spearhead the movement of friendly infantry, or simply develop the strength of the enemy. The last mission, developing the size of the enemy, was by far the more dangerous component of the three as it obligated the cavalry to fight for longer periods, thereby sacrificing the lives of the men for the indirect result of gathering intelligence.

In fighting dismounted, the role of the "horse-holder" was critical. In order to take up positions and fight on foot an officer or senior non-commission officer in each company would first require the mounted men to count out by fours, with the "number 4 man" left behind at least a half a mile or so back to hold the reins of the four saddled and waiting horses, while troopers 1, 2, and 3 moved forward to combat.

If the verbal command to "count off by fours" signaled that fighting on foot was imminent, generally this tactic would be of short duration and the men up front would either return to the point of departure to remount and move out as directed, or wait for the horse-holders to come up to them for a quicker departure. For the cavalryman, who was very much averse to walking anywhere when he could ride, the position of number 4 was often a source of great sport. One Rebel anecdote on the matter captured it perfectly:

> Therefore, when the command was given, "count fours," it was usually obeyed as follows: "One," "two," "three," "bully"; "one," "two," three," "bully," etc. This had become a little monotonous to one of the commanding

officers, so one day, after the usual "one," "two," "three," "bully," had come down the line, he commanded: "Two," "three," and "bully" will dismount and advance; number one will hold the horses.⁵⁶

Nevertheless, this novel and practical use of cavalry was hazardous work given the disparity in arms. Because cavalrymen carried mostly short ranged weapons — pistols, shotguns, and carbines — they were not suited for prolonged stands against superior infantry who possessed long rifles, particularly when fighting on open ground. In addition, fighting on foot meant that a full twenty-five percent of the troopers would be out of the fight!

Still, cavalrymen fighting on foot could be very effective, particularly in heavily wooded terrain where the enemy infantry was obliged to march in close order file on or beside a single dirt road. Properly dismounted and deployed, a much smaller body of cavalry could cause a superior force of enemy infantry to dramatically decrease its rate of advance. When fired upon by dismounted troopers concealed in the woods or behind hastily thrown-up breastworks the opposing infantry would have to halt, fall out of formation, fan out in strong parallel skirmish lines, and then move forward to flush the Rebels out. Then, after some sharp exchanges of gunfire the cavalry would simply abandon their positions, fall back to their horses, and gallop a few miles down the road to some other good defensive ground where both sides would repeat the process all over again.

Where the tactic would not work particularly well was when dismounted cavalry were expected to act as regular infantry for long periods of duty in fixed positions. For example, throughout the tactical retreats of the Army of Tennessee in the 1864 Atlanta campaign, the duration of horse-holding could last for a day or longer causing great suffering for the animals who were required to remain saddled and waiting behind with little access to forage or water.

Designed only to supplement the fire-power of friendly infantry, the cavalry could only accomplish just so much. Without question,

at the desperate fight to hold the strategic ground called Bald Hill outside of Atlanta in July 1864, the 2nd Alabama Cavalry showed that dismounted cavalry might well hold against vast numbers of infantry, but only for a while.

— Raiding —

Cavalry would not only guard wagon trains, supply depots, bridges, and outposts, they would also raid them. While watching their own points of interest was monotonous, attacking the enemy's in a hit-and-run raid was absolutely sublime. Indeed, the much-vaunted Rebel cavalry was feared for its ability to make spectacular forays behind enemy lines disrupting rail transportation, burning supply depots, and gobbling up isolated military outposts to the tune of millions of dollars of loss.

Due to their ability to strike quickly and move away just as fast, these cavalry strikes were quite successful and a source of great delight to the troopers. Not only did it raise morale, but large stores of Yankee government booty was scooped up and carted away for both official and "unofficial" use.

— Weapons —

The Rebel cavalry used a dizzying variety of carbines and pistols manufactured from many sources to include a few Southern made. Some of the rifles were breach-loading, but the vast majority loaded from the muzzle with paper cartridges. Ideally the cavalryman was armed with multiple pistols carried in holsters or belts and a carbine (with ample ammunition to use them). He also carried a crudely made saber, but as the War progressed this item fell into disuse.

Although the War Department was supposed to provide the cavalryman with his arms and accompanying equipment such as waterproof cartridge boxes to hold ammunition, it was more likely that any given trooper would be equipped with weapons brought from home, purchased from private vendors, or captured

Confederate Cavalryman with Colt Revolver and Bowie Knife.

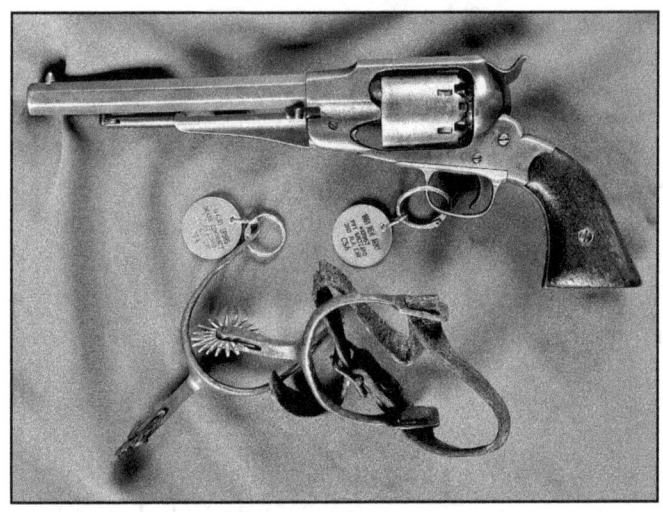

Remington New Model Army 1858 Revolver, Serial Number 13967 and Cavalry Spurs. Private Joseph Gizzard, Co. K, 2nd Alabama Cavalry. Jeffrey Addicott Collection.

from the enemy, to include long arms, carbines, shotguns, pistols, derringers, and wicked looking "bowie" knives made by some village blacksmith. Of course, a good pistol was an absolute necessity for close quarter combat and each trooper desired at least two, with some, like Private James A. Gould of Company B, 2nd Alabama Cavalry, who carried six!

For all practical purposes, the Rebel cavalryman "depended on obtaining Northern-made revolvers as his main handgun."[57] The most common pistol was the six-shooter cap and ball .36 caliber 1860 Colt Army revolver, though the similar in design eight-inch barrel .44 or .36 caliber Remington was greatly prized. Foreign made pistols from Britain, Italy, and France, or ones manufactured in the Confederacy itself, like the beautifully crafted Spiller & Burr, were also carried.

Because the "bullets" in all of these weapons were still based on cap and ball technology, reloading the firearm involved a messy and time-consuming process. For this reason, most of the troopers were keen on carrying along as many extra pistols as possible, carefully sealing the loaded cylinders with a layer of grease, for quick backup in a firefight. The Remington revolver's patented lever release push-out cylinder was probably the most useful — and durable — for rapid reloading, particularly if the trooper was lucky enough to have an extra prepared cylinder in his pocket.

Besides the challenge of getting weapons into the hands of the cavalrymen, the other obstacle for the quartermaster was supplying the proper cartridges. Confronted with so many different models and calibers of guns carried by the men (lead slugs for the pistols were round while most rifles used conical slugs), procuring the proper ammunition was a nightmare. In addition, since the Confederacy had no factories that produced the superior metallic cartridges, the captured Yankee Henry or Spencer repeating rifles were no better than attractive clubs once their accompanying rim-fire bullets were depleted.

At one point, Major General S.D. Lee ordered his brigade commanders to collect all "irregular" guns, causing General Fer-

guson to issue the following order to his cavalry regiments (an order that was clearly not enforced[58]), which included the 2nd Alabama Cavalry.[59]

HdQrts Cavalry Brigade
Calhoun Station, Miss March 26, 1864

I. In obedience to orders from Department HdQrts and to secure uniformity of arms in the different commands, Regimental Commanders will turn over to Lieut. I. West Thompson, ordnance officer at these HdQrts tomorrow morning at nine o'clock a.m. the arms in the respective Regiments as follows:

The 2nd Alabama Regt. All their guns except Enfield Rifles, artillery carbines and N.S. Springfield muskets Cal 577.

The 56th Alabama, all their guns except Austrian Rifles.

Col. Miller's Reg. [11th Mississippi] All their guns.

12th Miss Regt. All their guns.

Ordnance sergeants with a sufficient detail will be present to attend to the execution of this order and will bring with them all arms herein ordered to be turned over.

II. Lieut. Thompson, ordnance officer, will hereafter personally distribute the arms so as to secure the desired uniformity. Private arms will be appraised & paid for if turned over.

III. No soldier will be allowed to carry arms other than those of the kind or caliber distributed to his Regiment or company except his Company Commander forwarded through the proper

channels. Any officer authorizing or permitting a violation of this order will be arrested and tried for disobedience of orders.

By Command of

Brig Genl Ferguson

In turn, the issue of wasting ammunition was always of great concern to the Confederacy, where everything was in critically short supply. In the spring of 1864, General Ferguson issued strict orders to his regiments about the matter.[60]

HdQrts. Cav. Brigade
W. Elyton, AL April 22, 1864

Commanding officers of Regiments will see that the men are supplied at once with ammunition to suit their guns, sufficient to fill their cartridge boxes. If the necessary ammunition is not on hand it will be supplied by the Brigade Ordnance Officer.

The attention of the officers and men of this command is called to the shameful waste of ammunition which has been constantly going on in this Brigade since its organization [July 1863]. Since Oct. 7th, 1863, this Brigade has destroyed two hundred thousand rounds of ammunition and upwards and we all know well how very few of the enemy we have disabled in comparison with this enormous .... The excuse has been made that the men have been forced to waste their cartridges on account of the want of cartridge boxes. This excuse no longer exists and the men will be henceforth held to strict accountability.... All allowances will be made for the inconvenience of

marches and campaigns, yet officers as well as men will be hereafter required to attend to this important part of their duties strictly & faithfully.

By Command of
Brig Genl Ferguson

As with all his fellow cavalrymen, Private Cochrane was constantly looking to acquire surplus pistols. On one occasion he wrote, "I have bought a good pistol, a five shooter, [a] little larger than Uncle Claudie's."[61] Another time he apologized for not sending money home due to buying another handgun, "I did not send any money home this last time because I bought a pistol for $25."[62]

Pistols were important, but the real dominator in weaponry by the Northern over the Southern cavalryman was the repeating carbine which the Union introduced midway through the conflict. At the start of the War, the heavy .52 caliber Sharps carbine single shot was a favorite of the cavalry. With a barrel of 22 inches, opened at the trigger guard and loaded by inserting a paper or linen cartridge into the breach, a practiced trooper could load and fire perhaps six times in a minute. As impressive as the Sharps and even the British Enfield muzzle-loading carbine proved to be, they were no match for the Union cavalry when armed with the new repeating rifles like the splendid Spencer seven-shot carbine which would easily outperform anything the Rebels had.

The seven-shot Spencer rifle held eight rim-fired metallic cartridges, seven in a spring-loaded tubular magazine located in the stock and one in the chamber, and could spit them out as fast as the soldier could work the loading lever, pull the hammer back, and squeeze the trigger. Just over three feet in length and costing about $35 dollars, they were extremely popular with Union cavalry and many of the Yankees, like Wilder's Lightning Brigade, purchased them in droves.[63] Wilder believed that the Spencer was more reliable than either the Henry repeater or the Colt revolving rifle (which was really the Colt pistol set out on an extended wooden stock) and

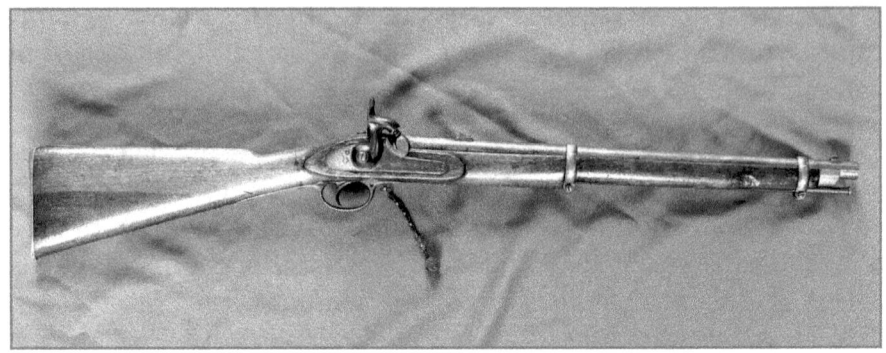

British Enfield Carbine, J S Anchor Mark. Imported by Blockade Runners and Issued to Confederate Cavalry. Jeffrey Addicott Collection.

used his own funds to purchase many of them for his men. When these superior weapons were introduced to the field, the Southern cavalry quipped with their usual gallows humor that the Federals could load on Sunday and shoot all week.

For the most part, one way or the other, the men of the 2nd Alabama stayed fairly well armed by "Confederate" standards. Lt. Colonel J.J. Pegues recalled that the "2nd Alabama [Cavalry] regiment was first armed with double barreled shot guns [these were privately owned] which were gradually replaced with carbines and long range rifles, acquired mostly from the enemy."[64] One chronicler of the regiment wrote:

> [The] Second [Alabama] Cavalry were armed with shotguns and pistols. The occasional cavalryman who sported a captured Federal Enfield or Springfield rifle was envied by all his comrades.[65]

Next to his mount, working firearms were essential to survival and only if both were serviceable would the trooper be classified as "effective" for service. A sharp regiment became proficient with their weapons and endeavored to keep them in prime condition, particularly when under the watchful eye of sergeants and junior

officers who were required to conduct daily inspection of arms and ensure that each man maintained the prescribed amount of ammunition.

Finally, no discussion of cavalry arms would be complete without touching on the heavy cavalry saber. While greatly romanticized, the steel saber was an item that became less and less useful as the War progressed, particularly for the western theater of operations where dismounted fighting became a regular course of business. Except in very rare cases, saber-waving cavalry charges were only pertinent when fighting enemy forces who were also mounted. In such an environment, sabers wielded up close could do gruesome damage, chopping off limbs and opening skulls.

Known by collectors as the "Dog River" saber, named by Confederate sword collector William Albaugh and taken from a letter written by Private Cochrane who noted that he received his Confederate manufactured saber at a place on the Dog River near Mobile, Alabama,[66] Southern horsemen were issued a crudely made heavy cavalry steel saber sheathed in a seamed metal scabbard.[67] Patterned after the U.S. Army Model 1840 saber, dubbed "Old Wrist Breaker," thousands of these unmarked "by the maker" weapons were produced in Southern foundries.

In 1862, practically all members of the 2nd Alabama possessed a serviceable saber used for drills, contests in camp, or parades, but by 1865, probably only one out of forty still had one.[68] In the serious business of combat every trooper preferred a good pair of six-shooters in his hands.

While the trooper was provided his edged weapon by the government, the cavalry officer was expected to supply his own saber by private purchase. The officer's sword served as his symbol of authority and rank, but was also an important tool in combat where the mounted leader used the weapon to inspire his men and gesture out commands. The size and style of the officer cavalry saber was not proscribed and several sword-makers in the South produced some exceptionally beautiful blades, to include the well-known James Conning factory in Mobile (Conning was also under

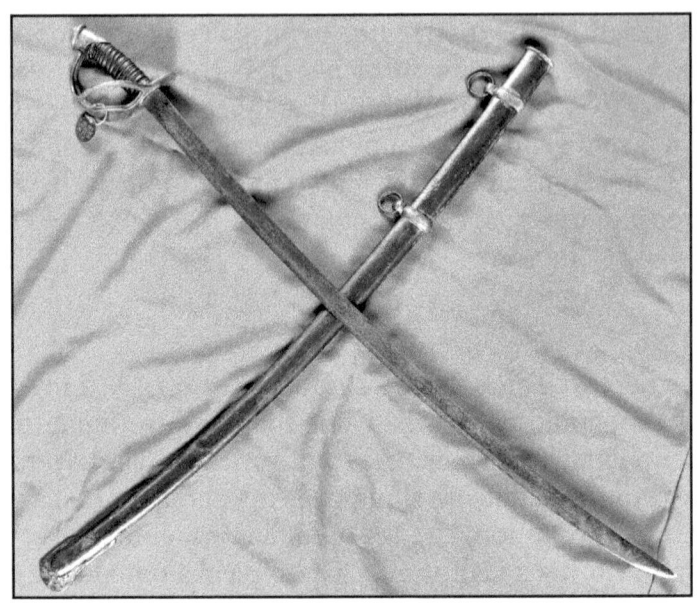

Dog River Cavalry Saber. Private Joseph Grizzard, Co. K, 2nd Alabama Cavalry. Jeffrey Addicott Collection.

Wooden Canteen. Private N.R. Reid, Co. A, 2nd Alabama Cavalry. Jeffrey Addicott Collection.

contract with the State of Alabama to furnish enlisted troopers with a marvelously sturdy version of his officer saber). Similarly, like the troopers they commanded, the line officers also discarded their swords in favor of additional guns causing upper level commanders, like General Ferguson, to order his officers to keep their sabers, even if most of the troopers did not.[69]

— Equipment —

When deployed away from a stationary camp, the things besides weapons that could be carried while mounted were limited to the bare essentials such as a haversack and a canteen. The haversack was either tied to the saddle or slung over the shoulder and contained food, extra ammunition, change of undergarments, socks, cooking utensils, and other small items. The typical Confederate canteen was wooden, constructed by civilian firms using the same methods for making larger barrels of the time and the men would often carve their name and outfit on the canteen for easy identification.

Most important of all was the matter of dry ammunition. Since wet ammunition was worthless, each trooper had to have waterproof boxes to carry both the paper cartridges and metallic caps to prime his weapons. These small boxes were attached to a belt or hung over the shoulder in a sling.

Finally, a good saddle was critical. The most popular style was the Confederate copy of the Federal's McClellan saddle and Southern factories strained to produce them. In many instances, Rebel cavalry looked forward to fighting Union cavalry if for no other reason than to take their excellent horse equipment.

— Uniforms & Clothing —

At the beginning of the War, Richmond expected the individual States to provide soldiers with all the necessary items required to sustain them. This included food, uniforms (to include undergarments), blankets, shelter, wagons, weapons, ammunition, fodder,

and horse gear. The State would then present the bill to the Confederate government for which they were often paid late, or little, or not at all. Along with State supply depots, the Confederate central government also set up its own depots and factories to produce uniforms and equipment, contracting out to private companies as well to help cope with the overwhelming demand. For instance, the State run depot in Montgomery was not able to provide each company of the 2nd Alabama Cavalry with the required regulation military uniforms before they departed out of that city for their first assignment to Florida.

Nevertheless, once deployed into service, each regiment, brigade, and division had its own specialized officer appointed as a quartermaster, responsible for commissary and ordnance. To accomplish the herculean task of supplying the soldier with basic needs, the quartermaster served as a purchasing agent with authority to draw on government supplies kept in prepositioned warehouses and depots. Under certain conditions, he could also requisition items of need directly from private persons or businesses.[70]

The issued yellowish gray coats and pants were usually made of Southern cotton (sometimes a mixture of wool was included) and very coarse. According to dress regulations, cavalry would get either a tunic or more often the "roundabout," a short waist-length shell jacket with a single row of buttons and yellow stripes on the collar. The pants had the same yellow stripe running down the leg on the outside seam. That said, the trousers had no belt loops and were held in place by a tie string or suspenders. Of course, since the pants were the first thing to wear out, it was standard fare to see troopers with a plethora of patches and/or civilian garb of every description to include the popular captured Federal wool blue pants.

Sadly, due to deficiency in every sphere of the manufacturing process, many of the uniforms were shoddy and ill-fitting so that probably half the force ended up wearing some sort of homespun clothing colored with dyes made from walnuts or logwood.[71] By 1863, if one were to encounter the "average" Rebel cavalryman he would probably be clad in blue Union trousers with a butternut

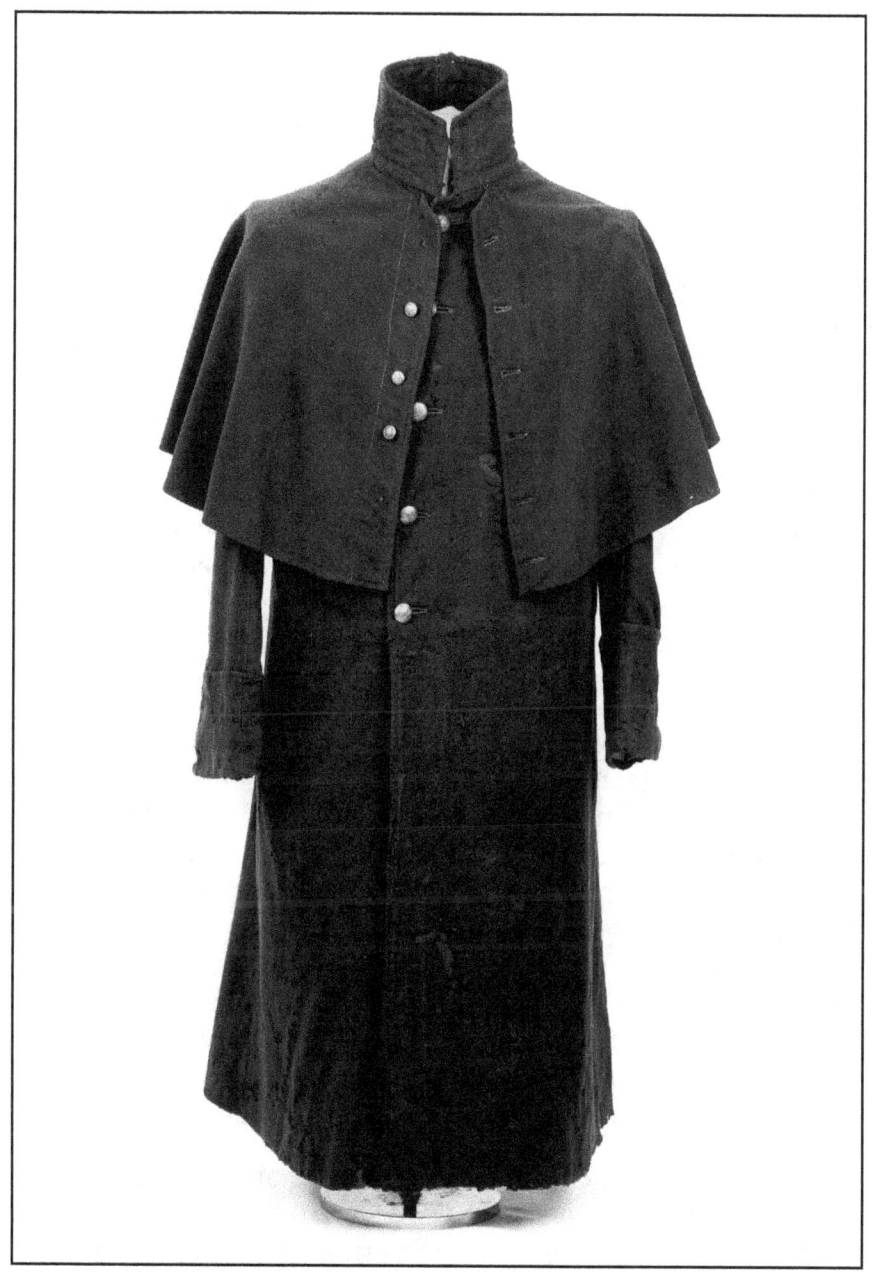

Union Great Coat Dyed Brown.
Private W.E. Englehardt, Co. K, 2nd Alabama Cavalry.
Photo Courtesy of Alabama Department of Archives & History.

short jacket and a slouch hat, all completely worn and stained with sweat and dirt.

As was the case with their side arms, all officers were required to purchase their own uniforms and some were rather resplendent being sewn by private tailors from rich gray broadcloth and the rank designated on the collar in bright gold thread. The finished product was as elaborate as the purchaser's pocketbook permitted.

Good footgear was also greatly coveted, particularly the high leather boots so essential when navigating through thick brush or heavy woods, with metal spurs of every variety strapped onto the heels to facilitate movement. Well accustomed to the saddle, many of the men already possessed knee high riding boots when they joined and to ensure longevity, wore them only when on field duty. In camp, they would slip on lesser footgear, or go barefoot. As riding boots were a premium, those troopers who died with their boots on rarely wore them into the afterlife!

All cavalrymen were particularly keen to get a heavy overcoat and oil-cloth. The oil-cloth, also called a gum-blanket, was a marvelous item that provided state of the art protection from the elements. Nothing more than a large piece of canvas with an India rubber coating applied to one side to make it water-proof, these rubberized blankets were in use since the 1840's and ideal not only for sleeping on damp ground but also to shelter the men from rain, especially when they were on guard duty. By 1863, the majority of the 2nd Alabama either had some sort of an improvised rubber poncho or heavy overcoat. Cochrane described their usefulness:

> Willie Inge and Walter Guild were on guard last night. There is a large pine tree by the guard tent and Willie said he went away from it and stood with his [rubber] blanket in an opening. Walter did not get wet either, because he had on his blanket. You have no idea how useful a [rubber] blanket is in rainy weather. It is nearly as good as a tent if you stand up.[72]

Whenever the Confederates captured Union uniforms, such as the popular great overcoat, they were expected to dye them brown in order to avoid confusion with the enemy. For instance, discovering that such was not taking place in his command, in December 1864, General Nathan Bedford Forrest ordered:

> All men & officers belonging to this command who have blue Yankee overcoats & clothing and who do not have them dyed by the 20th Inst The Coats Especially will be taken from them ... and turned over to the Qr M [Quarter Master] of The Division.[73]
>
> Gen. N.B. Forrest

Along with the uniform came the head gear. In the beginning of the War, Confederate depots provided gray "kepi" hats for the troopers. As a practical matter, the kepi, adopted after the French style, was generally rejected outright or discarded fairly soon afterward. Most cavalrymen preferred the more suitable slouch hat, which was a medium-brimmed, brushed felt cowboy-styled covering that the men acquired on their own. Usually dark in color, slouch hats were far more suited to the elements and provided shelter on the head and neck from sun and rain. Private Cochrane wrote home to his cousin:

> I would like very well to have my ... hat if it is not a white foundry one. I never wish to wear another of those hats. The one I have is not worn out but dirty. I would like a nice hat if Ma has it bought but if not write me word and I can get a [hat] made in Mobile.[74]

Troopers also needed underwear of some sort, especially necessary to help reduce chaffing from the rubbing friction of the saddle. Most undergarments of the day extended from the hip to the ankle and were made from cotton. Although this item of clothing

was also supplied by the government, like their fellows in other regiments of the Confederacy, the men of the 2nd Alabama sought homemade clothing, "both for comfort and durability"[75] and would regularly send home for such. In a letter to his mother, Cochrane described how appreciative he was for the extra shoes and pants shipped from home.

> Dr. Venable got to camp yesterday [and] brought my drawers and they fit me exactly. They are the coarsest but the most comfortable pair I ever put on. The weather is damp now and in the winter they will just suit. Make the other pair just the same size. Don't make the legs any tighter or looser, if anything a little looser. Dr. Venable said he brought over the shoes and they all were needed.[76]

Many women made hazardous trips from their small dog trot cabins to the nearest rail station to mail out boxes of clothes to their men folk. Another source of new clothing came from the innumerable women's organizations that sprang up all across the South. These charitable groups would raise money to purchase bolts of cloth and other materials and then make clothing for the soldiers.

Indeed, particularly in the first couple of years of war, the men were constantly receiving boxes from home consisting of all sorts of clothing items to include socks, shirts, underwear, hats, gloves, overcoats, and blankets. In one unusual letter to his brother, Cochrane asked for someone at home to send him a sheep skin which he could use as both a saddle blanket and night bedding. He also noted, "a great many of our men know how to make their own shoes and their wives know how to make most any kind of cloth, even flannel."[77]

> If there is a large sheep skin at home I wish you would wet it and rub it about and make it soft and send it

by Claiborne [the body-servant]. I want one with the wool tolerable short. I wish it to put under my saddle in the day and to sleep on at night.[78]

— Paperwork —

Then as now, there was an incredible volume of army paperwork that went into running the regiment and a steady stream of written documentation followed every soldier from the time he enlisted until the time he was released from service. Many of the forms set out in the regulations were preprinted templates by State and Confederate offices set out in a fill-in-the blank format with a signature block, allowing for uniform and quick recording of pertinent information. There "were more than 19 forms for the Medical Department; 25 for the Subsistence (Commissary) Department; 29 for the Ordnance Department; and 64 for the Quartermaster and Pay Department."[79]

The company clerk was responsible for safeguarding all the logs and the mundane day-to-day paperwork, with the daily "morning report" being of utmost importance. Each morning the men were assembled by their individual lettered company and a senior non-commissioned officer would then record with pencil and paper the status of each member. The soldier was either marked present or absent for duty. If absent, the reason was listed which could include furlough (leave), hospital, absent without leave, in the stockade, on extra-duty, police duty, or detached on special duty. Most importantly, only those present for duty that possessed a serviceable mount and adequate weapons of war were categorized as "effective."

— Discipline —

George Washington understood that "discipline is the soul of an Army" and that only firm protocols of required conduct could turn the agrarian minded civilian into a soldier kept to his proper duties. Thus, the two primary concerns for both enforced and genuine

discipline: (1) learning the military system of doing things; and (2) abiding by the civilized rules of warfare, particularly when it came to interacting with civilians and their private property.

Discipline requires leadership. Whether in camp or in the field, the quintessential element for any fighting unit is finding a capable leader who possesses equal quantities of self-discipline and personal courage. Like all armies, a portion of the confederate rank and file contained the coarse and arrogant members of society, who, left to their own devices, could cause great harm to both themselves and the *esprit de corps* of the organization. Without proper leadership accompanied by the imposition of a regimen of strict discipline, trouble was sure to follow. So, while the Rebel cavalry had its share of the brave and the not so brave, every man was expected to pull his weight and enforcing strict and reflexive obedience to orders was essential.

In the summer of 1863, just after the 2nd Alabama Cavalry was assigned to the brigade of General Samuel Ferguson, the very capable division commander, Major General S.D. Lee, issued a series of precise orders of behavior for all his cavalry,[80] per the Confederate Articles of War.[81]

HdQr Cavalry in Miss

General Order No 13   Canton Sept. 27th, 1863

I. The following order of the late Maj. Genl Earl VanDorn is adopted for the guidance of the Cavalry in Mississippi.

II. Any soldier on the march found galloping his horse without orders or permission will be dismounted and made to walk to the next camp. Commander of Brigades will see that there is a distance of about a mile between their Brigades and the Brigade which precedes them and they will endeavor to keep a steady pace at the head of

their columns. There may be a distance of about one hundred fifty yards between Regiments unless otherwise ordered for the occasion. Regiments will however be well closed up and in good order.

III. Brigade Commanders will be notified when to water horses on the march or the Bugle will sound for that purpose.... The Bugle will be rapidly repeated from front to rear. A half of fifteen minutes will be made every two or three hours according to circumstances: when the whole command will dismount the men being allowed to fall out of ranks on foot and readjust their saddles.

IV. The discharge of fire arms in camp or on the march is positively forbidden unless ordered .... All guards will be ordered to apprehend any person violating this paragraph wherever he may be or to whichever he may belong.

V. Private property of citizens must be respected under all circumstances and no impressment will be made by any person in this Command except upon written orders from the Gen. Comdg. Division or authority of the Gen. Commanding. Anyone found violating this order will be tried by court martial and punished according to the articles of war.

VI. Regimental or [Quarter] Masters must be present at the distribution of forage to their Regiment. Twelve ears of corn is allowed to a feed and two bundles of fodder when it can be got. Masters will make payment for forage ... all under the supervision of Brigade Commanders

who will cause a just and accurate settlement for everything purchased.

VII. When private property is destroyed and the actual perpetrators cannot be found, it will be taken as evidence that the command encamped nearest the property destroyed it, and the commanding officer will be held personally responsible. He would therefore be prudent to pay strict attention to the requirements of good discipline and keep the necessary Regimental guards.

VIII. On the march there will be a guard placed in the rear of each Regiment whose especial duty it shall be to prevent men from falling out of ranks and to keep order in their Regiments....

IX. Any officer misbehaving before the enemy will be disgraced in Genl orders & sent to the rear.

X. Any Regiment, Battalion or section of artillery misbehaving will be returned to duty in the rear with the baggage, and their colors taken from them.

XI. Any Regiment, Battalion or Company faltering in a charge will be disgraced. Cavalry knows no dangers: Knows no failures; what it is ordered to do it must do. Brigade Commanders will be particular therefore to be plain and explicit in giving orders in action, as to what is expected of their commands.

XII. After every action in which this command may be engaged the name of the most conspicuously brave Soldier of each company & officer of each Regiment will be published in General orders ....

Official By Order of Maj. Genl. Lee

— Camp Life & Field Duty —

The typical soldier's life was divided into two broad categories — life in camp and life on the move (in the field). Field duty could be described using a variety of adjectives from exciting to extremely hazardous, but only one word was required to sum up camp life — dull. Still, the cavalry regiments had it far better than their brothers in the infantry as they trended towards mobility, fulfilling their multifaceted roles of scouting, raiding, and protecting the flanks of infantry.

Detailed in Part II, the 2nd Alabama found itself in camp for almost a full year before seeing real combat action. Interacting in camp with large numbers of people was an exacerbating experience for the troopers and far from the glamorous life they had expected, especially in the early months, when many found themselves on "police duty" or in the regimental stockade for various infractions of military protocols.[82] While few would dare desert or go on a self-granted "holiday" home, all longed for the pleasures and independence of their former civilian lives and tragically, a handful of the most despondent chose to escape military life by committing suicide. Private Cochrane described one such poor fellow in a letter written just after the regiment had been sent to its first duty assignment in Florida.

> I forgot to write ... about a man in our company killing himself. His name is Obey Slate. He lives 4 miles from town [Tuscaloosa]. He had just got here [camp at Bluff Springs, Florida] and was not very well. He got to thinking about being in the army and of being sick away from home. He left a child 11 days old at home and his mess was broken up here [the other men in his living group]. He was troubled generally and went down to the branch where there is a round hole about 12 feet in diameter, very deep in the middle. This man took off his hat and his boots

and socks and was found standing straight up with his head about 2 feet under the surface. So this is another case of a drowned man standing in the water [reference to another suicide in the regiment]. This one had been missed about two hours.[83]

In short, life in a static cavalry camp consisted of regulation and routine with particular emphasis on mastering a myriad of key skills, called the "drill," necessary for uniformity of action. Typically there were four "roll calls" each day with lots of drill and care for the horses in between. A standard schedule would consist of the following:[84]

Reveille — call of the company roster   Daylight

Stable Call — care and inspection of horses

Sick Call — (for the men)

Breakfast   6 AM

Boots & Saddle — drill practice with horse   7 AM

Water Call (for the horses)   9 AM

Dinner — call of the company roster   12:30 PM

Guard Mounting — e.g., picket duty   1:30 PM

Water & Stable Call (for the horses)   4:00 PM

Retreat — call of the company roster   6:00 PM

Tattoo — call of the company roster   8:00 PM

Taps — sleep

All of these multifarious daily activities were announced by the company or regimental bugler. Indeed, most verbal orders were transmitted from officers directly to their assigned buglers who would then make the appropriate sounds to alert the command. In most cases, the regimental commander's senior bugler heralded the initial command which was then echoed across the field by the various company buglers.

In fact, there were 20 or so distinct bugle calls which announced almost everything to be done, both in the field and in camp. Learned by repetitive exercises, the individual noises became so reflexive to man and beast alike that even years later the old veterans could easily identify them all. Ironically, it was often observed that the horses would "learn these [bugle calls] quicker than the men!"[85]

Along with ordering "Dismount," and "Horse-Holders to the Rear," the most important bugle calls on the battlefield included:

> "Forward," "Trot," "Gallop," "Charge," "To the Left," "To the Right," "Come About," "Halt," "Disperse," "Commence Firing," "Cease Firing," and "Rally on the Officer."[86]

After mastering the rudimentary aspects of these maneuvers in a "camp of instruction," the men of the 2nd Alabama practiced them with their horses over and over, to the point that they (and the horses) could do it in their sleep — quickly and uniformly. They learned how to properly mount up and dismount; how to walk, how to gallop, or charge; how to retreat; how to regroup; how to move to the right, or move to the left; how to advance in column, or advance in line; and how to fight on foot. Furthermore, the horseman had to be proficient with his pistol, shotgun, or rifle while mounted. He also learned to use the saber and practiced different variations of the "strike," the "thrust," the "parry," and the "block."

In a letter written shortly after the regiment arrived on the Florida/Alabama line, Cochrane revealed how the entire regiment responded to their first bugle call to action.

> We had a little excitement in camp the other night, on the night of the 3rd [July 3, 1862]. We have pickets stationed every night 2 miles from camp and on Thursday night (3rd) we heard guns fired in the direction of our pickets. It was about 10 1/2 o'clock at night. The guard heard this firing and reported it to headquarters [the regimental commander's tent]. The Col. soon had us out. We were ordered by our company officers to saddle our horses and let them stand in their accustomed places. We did that. Then they marched us on foot to the back of our encampment where we were put in lines of battle with our sabers on and shotguns in our hands. We were given the "Watch Word" [a secret phrase to employ as a challenge] and told if the enemy advanced we would be wheeled a little to the right and would have to fight them were we were. But after a while a picket came in and said something to Col. Hunter [the regimental commander], I don't know what, but our officers were ordered to march us to our tents and to tell us to be ready in case of alarm and not to unsaddle our horses until the horn blew. After a while the horn blew and most of us unsaddled and went soundly to sleep and I did not dream of the Yankees or anything else that night.[87]

Once the cavalryman and his horse were thoroughly "broken in" the tendency in most Rebel cavalry commands was to loosen up significantly on drill. The new recruits and replacements learned on the job.

— Horses and Mules —

In 1860, railroads were still few and far between in the South. Mules and horses were the backbone of public and private transportation, particularly in the western regions where animal labor pulled everything from barges to wagons.

The War took a heavy toll on the animals with the infantry particularly hard on them, moving tons of supplies and equipment across rugged landscape. When the War began, there were about 2.5 million horses in the South, when it ended half had been destroyed,[88] used up by shear exhaustion, disease, or battle wounds. The average useful life of a working horse or mule was only seven months.

Cavalry duty was also strenuous and a good cavalry horse was invaluable. The properly trained mount must not only be accustomed to gunfire, but know how to strike the various speeds and pace of the column in order to maintain an even gait — the speed of the troop in motion is not set by the fastest horse but by the slowest. The rates of movement were 4mph at the walk, 6mph at the trot, and up to 16mph at the full gallop.

Perhaps the greatest drawback for those wishing to join the cavalry was the requirement to supply a decent war horse. Unlike Union cavalrymen, the Southerner was required by law to provide his own horse and initial riding gear upon enlistment receiving in return a stipend of forty cents per day "for the use and risk of their horses"[89] with additional compensation if the animal should be killed or disabled in action. Thus, only the better-off sections of society could afford to join and then hope to maintain their status, as each man also had to provide for replacement mounts when their horse died or became unserviceable. All other horses or mules brought into Confederate service by the government were branded with a pronounced "CS" on the hind quarters.

The requirement for the Southerner to provide his own steed proved very unsatisfactory. Replacements were expensive, hard to

acquire, and the promised government compensation for mounts injured or killed (at the appraised value on the date of muster) was seldom provided. In turn, those troopers without a working horse (sick, crippled, or lame) were relegated to what the men jokingly called Company "Q," also termed the "slow train," which meant that they remained back with the regiment's supply wagons, hitching a ride or walking. Q Company was also composed of shirkers as well as other good soldiers who, for some reason or another, were not fit for duty.

Once a horse was disabled or killed, the trooper was obligated to replace it within forty days or, according to regulations, be subject to transfer to an infantry unit from his home State. To this end, special passes were regularly granted for the men to go home to secure replacements from their farms or neighbors. The possibility for abuse in this regard was great and near the end of the War the practice was halted altogether due to skyrocketing rates of desertion. For example, when the 2nd Alabama was first assigned to Ferguson's brigade, the general issued orders for each company commander to ensure that the men who went home to procure new mounts were of good character and intent.[90] By April of 1864, General Ferguson further restricted the practice.[91]

HdQrts. Cavalry Brigade
Clements Mills 18 miles East
Tuscaloosa, Ala. April 19th, 1864

I. The privilege heretofore allowed men to go home after horse having been abused to the determent of the service will be discontinued in the future except in extreme cases and the applications in these cases must be accompanied with a certificate on honor from the captain of companies that the applicants are good soldiers, careful with their horses, never straggle, or gallop their horses in camp or on the march unless under orders & have not for six months prior to the filing of the application sold or exchanged horses

without the consent of the company & Regimental Commanders.

II. The names of all soldiers whose horses become unserviceable will be reported to the Regimental Quarter Masters and the times at which their horses become serviceable again such soldiers will draw infantry pay during the interim.

III. Soldiers becoming dismounted from any other cause than the accidents of the service unavoidable will be sent to the rear to serve with the infantry or regularly transferred to the infantry or artillery ....

IV. Regimental Commanders are eager to give their personal attention to the grooming of horses at least twice a day and are directed to have daily inspection of the horses in each command. Delinquents will be compelled to groom their horses at least two hours more than is absolutely necessary.

Official By Command of

Brig. Genl. Ferguson

The other manner in which the Confederate cavalry replenished mounts, particularly in the last year of the War, was to requisition them from the local civilian community, a practice that even when properly enacted caused extreme displeasure, but when wrongfully performed spelled outrage from the farmers and communities so affected. With little hope for real compensation, the lucky civilians were those who were given in exchange for their good animal a used up "Confederate" horse, too injured or malnourished to continue. Thus, commanders took great pains to both ensure that civilians were treated as fairly as possible and to punish renegade troopers who "impressed" animals without proper authority.[92]

In the spring of 1862, the Confederate army had just over 250,000 men under arms with an estimated 90,000 horses and mules in the field. These animals required adequate forage and grain, and iron horseshoes which ideally were changed out every 30 days. At the start of the War, Army regulations required that each horse was to be fed 14 pounds of "long forage," e.g., hay, and 12 pounds of grain, e.g., corn, each day.[93] This was later reduced to 10 pounds of long forage and 10 pounds of grain. In other words, it would require well over 30,000 pounds of grain per month to sustain the horses and pack mules of only a single company of cavalry, with probably another 10,000 pounds on top of that during the winter months.[94] In addition, the horses were allowed to graze whenever possible since along with their normal rations of rough feed, each animal needed at least two to four acres of editable grassland per day.

The quartermaster was responsible for procuring grain and long forage which were brought in by train or wagon from various government depots. From the very start it was a system that never keep up with the needs. As early as June 1862, Theodore Moreno, Inspector and Muster Officer for the 2nd Alabama Cavalry, observed that "the horses in this company [Company F] are in miserable condition, [with] complaints throughout the regiment of insufficiency of forage."[95] Company F's commander, Captain William Allen agreed. "In consequence of the heavy scouting duty and the inefficiency of the A.Q.M. [Quarter Master] of this department," he wrote his superior, "I beg leave to state that all of my horses are unfit for service for want of sufficient forage."[96] By September 1862, Captain Allen's horses were in such desperate straits that he was obliged to shift camp several times just to find suitable grassland and/or grain. He reported:

> The company [F] moved from Camp Lee, Fla on the 17 of Sept for … Pollard, Ala. Left Camp Lee near Pollard on the 14th of October for this place [Camp Hunter, Alabama]. Owing to its failure of the A.Q.M. to furnish feed for our horses. Have been unable to do much scouting for the last two months.[97]

Similar to the impressment of civilian horses, individual regiments were often obliged to impress forage directly from local farms and plantations. Again, when properly performed it was distasteful for the civilians, but when miscreants used the process to steal, it was disastrous to home front support. Given temporary command of Ferguson's Brigade in March 1864, 2nd Alabama's Colonel Richard Earle, issued the following order regarding the taking of forage for the horses.[98]

HdQrts. Cavalry Brigade
Calhoun Station, Miss March 21st, 64

I. Hereafter wagons will, as far as practicable, be sent out after forage. Whenever it becomes necessary for details of mounted men to go instead of wagons, a Company officer will accompany each detail from the several companies composing the Regiment. A field officer will be put in charge of all the details from the command and will be held responsible for all damage done by the troops of his Regiment.

II. The field officer in charge of the details from each Regiment will personally superintend the measurement and issue of forage and will see that all necessary guards are posted around the premises of citizens to prevent depredation & that the men are kept together.

III. Lists of these forage details will be handed to the Field officers in charge. The Rolls will be called on leaving and arriving in camp and all absentees will be arrested and tried at once.

By Command of Col. R.G. Earle Cavalry Brigade

During the fighting in Georgia in 1864, impressment of forage from the locals became the primary means for cavalry regiments

to survive. Serving along with General Wheeler's corps of cavalry, the 2nd Alabama saw heavy fighting protecting the flanks of the Army of Tennessee and as the Yankees closed in and destroyed the rail systems in Georgia, it became increasingly difficult to bring in sufficient corn by rail to feed the thousands of horses. In fact, the regular issue of corn ceased altogether and the emaciated animals had to live off the immediate countryside. For instance, in a July 7, 1864, message to Headquarters, General Wheeler bristled about the drop in government supplied feed for his cavalry horses: "I have the honor to report that for the last three days I have received but thirteen pounds of corn per horse for this command."[99]

Not only was feeding a necessity, but stabling, watering, managing, grooming, and exercising the horses were of paramount importance. Since foul air and dampness were the causes of many diseases of the horse, maintaining clean, dry, and spacious stables was imperative. Glanders, a contagious respiratory disease transferred when horses affectionately rub noses, plagued the cavalry and the only solution was to shoot the infected animal and spread out the others. Hence, when in a stationary camp setting, horses were assigned to individual stalls and/or specific spots on a picket line established near the stables according to the platoon of their riders and/or place in the march. Stable sergeants assisted by stable orderlies were assigned to the stalls to both work themselves and also oversee those unfortunates detailed to "police duty." Such duty included cleaning up manure (as soon as it was dropped during the daytime) and moving it to the manure pile, rotating out old bedding straw, fixing equipment, feeding and watering, grooming, caring for sick or injured horses, and generally doing whatever was needed.[100]

On the march or in camp, horse care was always foremost for each of the men. The "first thing in the morning is to feed, water, and curry the horses," wrote Private Hall of the 2nd Alabama, "then one of the mess goes to town, and gets the morning papers and all read.[101] When on the march each man would carry a day or two worth of hard grain in saddlebags, apart from what the wagons would haul, to ensure that his mount was fed three times

Lantern. Private Joseph Grizzard, Co. K, 2nd Alabama Cavalry. Jeffrey Addicott Collection.

a day, dividing up the rations equally. When halted for the night, the horses were fed and combed before the men collected wood for the campfires and the animals were never far away from where the cavalryman slept. The men might sleep on blankets laid on waterlogged ground, but the horses were always picketed on the better ground so that when it rained the animals were on the highest and most sheltered ground.

Concern for the safety of the horses required rotating "fatigue" duty both day and night to guard them from harm. Requiring a good lantern for such night duty, Cochrane explained the process in a letter to his father back home in Tuscaloosa.

> We have had lately only one man detailed to go out on picket every night which is four miles [out from the main camp], and a few to go on fatigue duty and three at night to mind our own horses. When I am on that camp duty guarding our horses I keep a light [lantern] and sit most of the time on my bench in front of our tent and occasionally make my round to see if any horses have broken loose. From actual experience I have seen horses lie down and snore like people, only a little louder. Some of them lie down soon after supper but just before day you can go up the line of horses and more than half will be asleep.[102]

In addition to feeding and guarding the horses there was the constant need for obtaining or fixing saddlery of all sorts. From saddles to stirrups to reins, all manner of leather equipment were in line for repair or replacement and if the quartermaster could not supply these essentials, the men made do with whatever was at hand. In this, the troopers of the 2nd Alabama became quite adept, making a wide array of necessities from self-cured leather both for themselves and their mounts to include shoes, cap boxes, belts, bridles, and even saddles.

Finally, maintaining a properly shod horse was an absolute. Not only did the hoofs require the standard care of being cleaned and trimmed but horseshoes were a necessity. To keep the animals in fit condition, each horse's "U" shaped iron horseshoe was supposed to be removed every five weeks, the hoof reshaped with a file, and then a new shoe nailed in place. Trained farriers were on hand to perform the necessary tasks and portable forges were carried on the march so that skilled horseshoers in each company could shod any horse that needed care.

As was the case for every member of the regiment, Private Cochrane owned several different horses during his tenure with the cavalry and he was always on the lookout for an opportunity to trade up for a better horse, or to purchase a backup animal in case

his main mount was killed or injured. On one occasion, Cochrane noted that his mess mate had made a great deal.

> Willie Inge made a trade yesterday and bought a fine mare for one hundred and seventy-five dollars. It is a beautiful animal. It belonged to a man in our company named [Private] Crossland. He is now employed by the Government to make shoes as he had the rheumatism and was not fit for a Soldier. I expect Willie will send his other horse home.[103]

In June 1864, Private Alex Hall wrote his father concerning how to best get his younger brother still at home into the 2nd Alabama cavalry by juggling the horses then on hand between the needs of the family and his sons.

> In a few months, Charley will come into the army, and if he joins cavalry will want a horse. Now my advice is that if Father can afford it to buy a horse for C. and let Tecumseh [horse] stay home, until next winter; when I will bring Fanny [Private Hall's horse] home, and get him. Thus leaving a horse at home for any emergency that may arise. The one left at home can be made useful working crop, or in any other way most advisable. If it is to be had, C. had better get a saddle tree on the Texas order [type], no matter for looks so it will not hurt a horses back.[104]

The cavalryman and his horse formed a close bond and it was not uncommon when troopers on the march stopped to catch some shuteye on the ground, with their horse tied by a line to the wrist, that the animal would crop all the grass around as far as the tether would go without harm to their master. One Rebel trooper noted:

> The cavalryman and his horse got very close to each other, not only physically, but heart to heart. They ate together, slept together, marched together, and often died together. Frequently a wounded horse would be seen bearing his wounded rider back from the front.[105]

For many veterans of the Rebel cavalry their "recollection of some of the horses of my comrades is more distinct than is of the men who rode them."[106] One such horse named "old Sorrel" belonged to a Private "of D company, ___ Alabama cavalry."[107] The Private in question was always willing to loan "old Sorrel" to any of his fellow troopers that had a broken-down horse so that they could then avoid reassignment to the slow train. Herein, is the true story of "old Sorrel" as told by a fellow Alabamian cavalryman that had the misfortune to "borrow" him.

> Now old Sorrel was a horse with points but he had only one good one to counter-balance many bad ones. His one good point was bottom, and as service under [General Joseph] Wheeler essentially required "critters" with bottom, this was a very strong recommendation. His bad points were his being about as rough-gaited as a camel, his indisposition to lope as long as he could torture his rider by trotting, a mouth so tough that no mortal could hold him when he took a notion to run away, and his total lack of discretion — being as apt to run towards or into the enemy's lines as away from them. I rode this idiot once, and am not likely ever to forget the experience. First he seemed to try to dislocate every bone in my body by trotting for about five miles while the other horses were in an easy canter; then getting on a shelving rock, let all four of his feet go from under him and came down in a heap — the horses behind jumping over us, and

narrowly missing my head with their hoofs. The next day I and two others were on picket, sitting quietly on our horses .... Suddenly there appeared from a crossroad the advance guard of a regiment of Federal cavalry, not over fifty yards from us. Throwing our guns hastily to our shoulders we fired, and about a dozen of the enemy returned the compliment. Old Sorrel had apparently been asleep, but as one of the enemy's bullets grazed his flank, he suddenly became one of the widest awake horses ever seen. He jumped, I think, about fifteen feet, and proceeded to run away in the most approved fashion. Fortunately he was headed away from the road, and right into the woods he went. I knew I could no more hold him than I could a locomotive, but I did try and guide him to keep him from killing me and himself by contact with a tree. I soon saw a fence ahead and a man throwing off the rails. I yelled to him to get out of the way, knowing that the fool horse would run over anything that was in this road. The man evidently misunderstood my motives, for the only reply I received was to "go to hell." He had just time to duck his head when Sorrel cleared him fence and all.[108]

Along with his comrades, Cochrane was constantly comparing his own mount to others, as well as commenting on any new horses that were brought into the company. Cochrane's favorite was a reliable gray named "Dock." Just before New Year's Day of 1863 he wrote home:

Lawley's brother got here [cavalry camp at Brewton, Alabama] last night. He brought a horse to [Private] Lawley as his old one does better for a family horse than a charger. My Gallant Gray [named Dock] is in fine order and health. He is fatter, freer, livelier and

better than when I left home and can walk 4 miles an hour with the greatest ease. I met with two men on the scout who wished to swap. One wanted to swap his for which he said he was offered $300. I told him I would not take $300 for him. In fact there is not but one horse in the company I would give mine for and that one is Captain P's [Pegues] cream, which he has been offered $800 for, so you see I like Dock pretty well.[109]

Interestingly, in a letter dated June 14, 1864, written during some of the hardest fighting that the 2nd Alabama would see during the entire War, Cochrane was deeply concerned with the health of Dock whom he had sent back home to Tuscaloosa by way of Claiborne.

Please Mam [Cochrane's mother] don't have Dock worked nor let the negroes gallop him so when you send them on errands.... I should not write about a horse at such a time but it is highly important that he is kept in a condition for me to ride at all times, for if we stay up here [fighting Sherman's advance towards Atlanta] two months longer and Darby [his current horse] is able to carry me to Tuscaloosa without my walking he will do well. He [Darby] is not gone up [worn out for service] quite yet but he is so old and inactive he tires himself as he goes and tires me for he keeps me spurring almost all the time.[110]

As stated, about one million Southern horses and mules perished during the War, the majority from disease and hard service, but many from the horrible effects of battle[111] — the horse was naturally the biggest target and tens of thousands suffered ghastly wounds from bullets and shrapnel. Cochrane often lamented the plight of the wounded horses. Commenting

on a fight the 2nd Alabama had with a brigade of Union cavalry at Kingston, Georgia, in June 1864, he wrote:

> Our list [of wounded for Company A] shows we have fought. We have had seven wounded horses and three wounded men, two of them severely. But this was done at Kingston some time ago .... I did not mention some time back when I wrote that Larry, my horse, was one of the seven that was wounded. The wound was slight. The ball struck him on the top of the head, passed through the headstall and halter and came out the right ear. The bullet sounded like it hit the bone but it did not injure him, he is well now. The horses of the two [brothers] Mr. Hills were wounded badly.[112]

Sam Watkins, Confederate infantryman in the Army of Tennessee, recalled the sad spectacle of the dead, wounded, and dying horses that accompanied battle.

> And then to see all those dead, wounded and dying horses, their heads and tails drooping, and they seeming to be so intelligent as if they comprehended everything.[113]

To help with the effects of disease, wounds, and hard service, the government established dedicated "horse hospitals" to provide care for sick and disabled horses and return them to duty as quickly as possible. One such typical camp in Virginia "employed 83 whites and 179 blacks (19 free and 160 slaves)."[114]

Shortly after the fall of Atlanta, General Wheeler ordered Red Jackson's division to establish a Recruitment/Convalescence horse camp at nearby Newman, Georgia, for the treatment of sick and injured mounts.[115] Other horse camps sprang up as well to include large ones at Carthage and Eufaula in Alabama.

Sadly, many horses were rendered unfit due to "sore backs" caused by improper riding by the trooper, e.g., sitting wrong in the saddle, slouching down, or not resting the animal at intervals. One cavalryman in Robert E. Lee's army also recalled the effects of heavy riding in wet conditions:

> Our horses' backs were raw with ulcers one and two inches deep and full of maggots. The green flies had put up a big job on us, our blankets were full of maggots and rotten, our saddles had from a pint to a quart of maggots in them and we had to run them out with hot water and soap and it was months before the horse's backs were cured.[116]

Apart from all the hardships and sufferings of the animals, the most horrific threat to the well-being of these innocent creatures came with Lincoln's policy of total war in which the Union intentionally targeted all horses and mules to include even plow animals for death. In mid-1863, Union Quartermaster General Montgomery C. Meigs explained the cruel and twisted policy.

> No horses of any kind should be left in possession of residents [civilians] in the rebel country. A horse is as much contraband of war as a barrel of gunpowder, and, being used by a guerrilla, a spy or a messenger, more injurious to us. Even in the plow they relieve the men from the necessity to digging for a living, and leave them free to plot mischief.[117]

— Camp Life —

On those occasions when all the companies were billeted together the regiment was like a small portable village, fixed in place but ready to move at a moment's notice. Everything necessary to sustain man and beast was set out in a structured system according to military manuals prescribing the standard operating procedures (SOP) for a cavalry camp.

Though each company camped separately from one another, there was no common kitchen at the regimental or company level. Instead, the men in each company divided up into informal groups of four called a "mess-mate." Each mess was chosen by the men themselves and a close family-like bond naturally attached holding them tightly throughout all the exigencies of military life — they slept together, ate together, rode together, and fought together.

In the first year of their war service, when the 2nd Alabama was disengaged from real combat, Private Cochrane and his mess-mates more or less enjoyed an easy life. Cochrane, however, admitted the downside. "I like camp life pretty well," he confided in a letter home "but I don't see how in the world a Soldier manages to be smart when he goes home, for in camp he may sometimes be called on for a good deal of work but generally he has nothing to do and then it is the laziest life I ever led."[118]

What would the cavalry camp look like? The first thing the outside observer would spot were the housing accommodations consisting of long files of dirty white canvas tents of varying sizes with the "tents opening on the [dirt] street facing the left of camp."[119] Whenever possible, the floors of the tents would be covered by wooden planks drawn from the closest lumber mill. Attached onto or near the tents themselves one would next see that small trees had been cut to construct awnings for shade and that a variety of logs and mismatched hand-crafted furniture was scattered about the grounds.

Typical Confederate Summer Camp.

The animals were corralled in paddocks or wooden lean-to type barns set out near the supply wagons and portable forges, where blacksmiths worked to keep them shod and ready for duty. When on active campaign, however, the horses were held in place by rope in a single file so that they faced the opening of the tents about three to six paces from where their masters were billeted. Forage and water were placed between the tent and the animal.

Ideally, camp sites were located on high ground to mitigate the untoward effects of torrential rains and flooding. On those occasions, dripping men huddled miserably in their canvas tents cursing the elements, louder whenever someone slipped and fell or a tent blew down and was flooded out. Private Cochrane wrote home about one such episode of flooding near Pollard, Alabama, in the fall of 1862. Fortunately, his company had camped on slightly higher ground than some of the others.

> It has been raining almost incessantly for three days. We have been kept in our tent without even the

opportunity of cooking our provisions. We only ate two meals yesterday and today we ate our breakfast at twelve o'clock. Our tent leaked a great deal and this morning there was scarcely a dry plank in our tent floor .... The worst of it was that nearly half of the regiment was under water. You ought to have seen the men wading out from their tents. The floors [wooden planks] of most of them are floating. In our commissary tent the water was half way up the barrels.[120]

Set out at least 150 paces in front of the tents or cabins and concealed in bushes or by a mound of dirt, separate sanitary sinks were dug for the men and the officers. Shovels and loosened soil were available to be thrown back into the hole as necessary.

While there often existed a rather casual standard of personal hygiene, most of the men soon learned that staying clean was essential to good health. For instance, the only way to rid their clothes of the number one infestation that plagued them all — the "grayback" or lice — was to boil the garments in salty water. For this they employed the larger mess kettles. Like death itself, lice was no respecter of persons. According to one veteran, "it preyed alike on the just and the unjust."[121]

The other sight that would impress the observer about a cavalry camp, besides the great number of horses and mules, was the surprising number of parked wagons. Not only did the regimental headquarters have sturdily built wagons to haul ammunition, food, forage, tools, furniture, medicine, and other baggage, each company also possessed its own allotment of dedicated wagons and quite a few pack mules. These wagons would carry things specific to each particular company from large cooking pots to an assortment of personal items.

Above the camp would hang a thick layer of gray smoke emanating from hundreds of campfires which permeated food,

water, skin, hair, and hide. Not only were the wood-fed fires necessary to cook the greasy slabs of bacon and purify questionable water sources, but the heavy smoke mercifully covered the horrid body odors of man and beast that might otherwise cause even the strongest stomach to turn inside out. The sour musk of a sprawling cavalry camp was part and parcel of the fabric of life.

Active smoke was also an essential blessing to help stave off the ever present mosquitoes and flies. Attracted by the horseflesh, there were all types of pesty insects to include the house fly, the green fly, the blue tail fly, and the horse fly.

One of the most tedious of duties required from the men were the numerous "police" duties and those guilty of minor military infractions were always first on the work list to "volunteer." Such would include cleaning horse stalls, digging latrines, moving heavy equipment, extra guard duty, or other needed activities. Cochrane wrote of three occasions when he was on police duty:

> I was detailed on police duty and had to cut down pine trees to make a lot [corral pen] to put the Confederate mules, which work our wagons. I had a hard day's work.[122]

> I had, however, to help put a cannon on the cars [railroad flatbed] which weighed over 5,000 pounds without the wheels. The tire on the wheels was five inches round. We had right hard work but your humble servant did not hurt himself.[123]

> I was detailed to go to Pollard yesterday and help load the wagons with commissary stores. I regarded it as pretty light work. Four of us had to load and unload two wagons with about thirty sacks of meal, some molasses, sugar and rice.[124]

During the winter months the armies on both sides went into semi-hibernation, though the cavalry might occasionally stay more active on scouting and raiding missions. Around the October-November time frame commanders selected a locale with ample water and timber and easy access to transportation to set up "winter quarters." Each mess-mate built their own crude log cabin or hut in accordance with a master plan set out by the engineers, so that the men and animals could move about with ease along the paths or wooden plank streets in-between. The small structures were generally comfortable and well-sealed with mud and straw stuffed between the chinks of the logs. The furnishings were improvised from wooden boxes, leftover lumber, or whatever was available so that some were quite elaborate with small rock chimneys and even bunk beds. Covered lean-to barns were also thrown up for the animals.

Cochrane fondly described to his family back home the winter quarters he helped construct in the winter of 1862-1863, when companies D and H were detached from the main body of the regiment (then spread out a distance of about six miles in various cavalry camps from Pollard, Alabama, to their main camp at Bluff Springs, Florida). The two companies were ordered to go about 18 miles north from Camp Lee near Bluff Springs in order to guard a vital wooden bridge over the Escambia River located about seven miles from Brewton, Alabama. They were also ordered to watch for deserters and pro-Union draft dodgers. In fact, a fairly large "deserter camp" had sprang up in the dense swampy woods of the Florida panhandle in November 1862.

If the Yankees came in force up from Pensacola, they were ordered to burn the bridge and fall back. In mid-October 1862, Cochrane detailed the company's anticipated winter camp as follows:

> We expect to spend the winter there and build houses and stables and scout about. We will have hard work at first but you see we will be well situated in a warm climate in warm log houses and in seven miles of the

railroad. We will be in seven or eight miles of Brewton but you must direct all your letters to Brewton, Ala. in care of Captain Pegues [the company commander] and not Col. Hunter's 2nd Ala. cavalry. We will not be in the 2nd regiment [at Pollard and Bluff Springs] but in Captain Pegues company.[125]

By the second week of October 1862, Cochrane proudly described the almost completed project as a little village.

It deserves the name of village for we have fourteen houses with a space between where we have a long shelter with stalls for 108 horses. Besides, there will be three more houses built for the officers [and another for the servants]. It would do you good to see how well we are fixed in our new log cabin. Instead of the cold ground we sleep on beds of straw. Instead of a smoky fire in the open air we have a chimney and various other comforts too numerous to mention.[126]

— Food —

One thing for sure about the Confederate soldier, he was always hungry.[127] Dreams of freshly baked bread, sweet corn, ripe watermelons, and roasted pork were never far from mind. What foodstuffs the government's commissary did not issue, the soldiers supplemented with extras obtained by barter, trade, purchase, packages from home, hunting, fishing, or captured goods.

Most certainly, Rebels were keen on shooting wild game at every opportunity. Squirrels and wild turkeys were always popular food sources and practically everyone learned how to prepare squirrel stew.

Skin squirrels very carefully, so as not to allow the hair to touch the flesh; this can be done by cutting a slit under the throat, and as you pull it off, turn the skin over, as to enclose the hair. Cut the squirrel in pieces (discard the head), and lay them in cold water; put a large table spoon of lard in a stew pan, with an onion sliced, and a table-spoonful of flour; let fry until the flour is brown, then put in pint of water, the squirrel seasoned with salt and pepper, and cook until tender. When half-done put in some strips of ice puff-paste and a little butter.[128]

Noting that the cavalry could range about the countryside soliciting food off the locals, the infantry would derogatorily call them "buttermilk rangers," but in reality the troopers much preferred gathering "applejack" or other alcoholic spirits. On occasion, it was not uncommon that sweet potatoes, peanuts, corn, coffee, sugar, alcohol, and tobacco might also find their way into camp.

Early on in the War, adequate amounts of food was generally available and men were allowed to go home or into the local communities in order to carry back large orders of donated foodstuffs. Private Cochrane often commented on this practice. For example, he wrote:

> Wm Wade left for home yesterday, on twelve days leave [of] absence to bring some potatoes (100 bushels I believe), which were donated to this company by the citizens of Pleasant Hill.[129]

Given that the four-man mess was the standard set up for living and eating, the camp process became routine. Each morning, one member would go for water, another would prepare the food, a third would pack up any equipment, and the fourth would check on the welfare of the horses. Whether by drawing straws or otherwise, the

men rotated these duties, with each member of the mess cooking for a full week in his turn.

Private Cochrane's mess-mates were Charlie Martin and brothers Willie Sanders and Ezekiel Sanders. Shortly after arriving at their camp in Florida, Cochrane wrote of his four-man mess:

> Our mess is progressing very well. We have beef and crackers and sometimes cornbread for our diet and sometimes bacon and biscuits. We have one thing until we are tired of it and then have another thing.[130]

Several months later Cochrane described how they had even set up their own vegetable gardens.

> We have been living off of potatoes and meat for a good while. We sometimes have the same for bread on the table. Potatoes are very easily raised and I think if we had enough of them we could economize in meal. I would have a great many watermelons planted next year, turnips, peas and things of that sort.[131]

A museum exhibit entitled "Voices of Alabama," at the Alabama Department of Archives & History, lists some basic recipes that were commonly used in Alabama homes of the time and most certainly employed by the 2nd Alabama in their camps, although the end result was rendered worse by poor cooking in the field — the rations were almost always fried in skillets.

Fried Ham
Rinse off mold, if any. Slice off several pieces from the ham .... Put only a little grease in the skillet. Fry, browning good but not till tough. Make gravy by adding some coffee or water.[132]

Pone Bread
Take 2 cups of corn meal, salt according to taste. Work into a stiff dough with water. Make large pone with hands. Put in well-greased baker. Put lots of grease on top and sides. Bake ... until done.[133]

Corn Bread
1 quart of sour milk, 2 tablespoonsful of saleratus (baking soda), 4 ounces of butter, 3 tablespoons of flour, 3 eggs, & cornmeal enough to make a stiff batter.[134]

Hominy
Get corn, put in pot. Add about a teaspoon of lye to a gallon of corn. Put in water to cover corn. Then boil corn until tender and wash it until the eyes of the corn comes out. Boil again until tender.[135]

As the War progressed and scarcities increased, the soldiers would have to make do with government rations of corn meal and some sort of pork or salted beef in various stages of preservation.[136] One disgruntled Confederate wrote in 1864:

> I don't think the Confederacy treats her troops right. She feeds us on pickled beef — nasty, stinking blue stuff, a dog will hardly smell it. I get vexed at them flies and commence killing them, but I believe forty come to every one's funeral.[137]

Since there was no common kitchen, each mess-mate would receive a portion of the by-weekly issue of food designated for the entire company and the men had to be careful not to eat all of their rations at one setting, but to stretch them out for several days until

the next issue. "Our living is very rough," Major S.H. Giles, the quartermaster for the 11th Mississippi (part of Ferguson's Brigade) wrote from his cavalry camp at Morton, Mississippi, to his wife, on July 29, 1863, "beef & corn meal, with sifting, but I eat my rations & enjoy it as much as any person you ever saw."[138] However, two days later, Giles happily reported a vastly different experience to his wife. In a letter from the same camp, he wrote on July 31, 1863:

> We are now having our [mess-mates] cooking done at a house. There is a widow living close to our Camp & we furnish her the provisions for her family and our mess & eat with her. It looks almost like home to see us all sitting around the table with a woman at the head of it so you see we are living in clover. I have just bought some squashers & roasting ears & snaps. We will have roast beef, ham, stewed beef, and vegetables for dinner. Your light bread all spoiled again. Do not send any more cooked provisions. Tell Ben the plum brandy was fine & passed around like hot cakes. I tell you we enjoyed it. We drank the health of everybody at home.[139]

Coffee was the predominant topic of concern; it fueled the military. If available, soldiers would drink the caffeinated liquid morning, noon, and evening. The Union issued 3 pounds of the green beans per soldier per month, but in the South coffee quickly became a rare commodity and Confederates on the frontlines would eagerly barter with the enemy at every opportunity, trading tobacco for coffee. Others took to grinding up and boiling certain types of tree bark or even roasting horse feed just to get something hot and brown to gulp down.

During short excursions away from camp the cavalry mess would "cook rations" for a given number of days specified by the commander and stuff them into their haversacks. Corn shuck was used to wrap the food and to later serve as dish rags and "toi-

let paper." Since shorter cavalry missions were built for speed all unnecessary items such as frying pans and kettles were left behind. In those instances, the cavalryman might use his ramrod as a cooking utensil, on which he broiled his meat and corn pone over an open flame.

Riding along beside the 2nd Alabama in the Atlanta campaign in the summer of 1864, a Georgia cavalryman described to his sister the standard Confederate fare during these long periods of continuous fighting conducted on "half-rations."

> [W]hen I get up the first thing I do is to get my haversack and take out a pone of corn bread, split it open and take a piece of bacon and hold it over the fire by means of a stick until the grease runs out of it, then let it drip on the bread, by the time the meats gets done, the bread is pretty well greased over, I then put the bread on a stick and hold it over the blaze until it gets a little brown, my breakfast is then cooked. Dinner & supper are the same, except when I am marching [riding], when I have to eat the bacon raw, and the bread cold …. I am always hungry and eat all I draw [from the quartermaster] with the greatest relish.[140]

— Leisure Time —

Time not spent on the drill or caring for the animals would be occupied by a myriad of activities to include playing games of cards (cards were always handled tenderly as they were generally irreplaceable), chuck-a-luck, or chess; chewing or smoking tobacco; playing or listening to music; reading; and horse racing. Those that were literate would hungrily read whatever they could get their hands on — the Bible, newspapers, periodicals, letters, and popular novels of the day.

Some of the men kept detailed diaries and all wrote letters home, or had someone write for them. The letters they received in return were sacred treasures read over and over around evening campfires until the paper became dog eared and stained with dirt. Surprisingly, mail was plentiful, especially for the first three years of the War with the means of delivery through the Confederate mail system or by servants, civilians, or soldiers coming and going on special duty, furlough, transfers, or sick leave. One Rebel rated the conditions in which letters were penned.

> I write this letter in regular camp style .... I am by a motley crew of boisterous fellows who are either talking, laughing, singing, dancing, or quarreling; turning over my ink or striking my arm, making it impossible for me to bestow much care in my correspondence.[141]

Music was a very important supplement to confront the dullness of military life. Although cavalry regiments did not have a regular band, there was always those who carried with them the South's dominant folk instrument, the fiddle. Individual troopers who possessed one, such as Tom Mosley of Company E, would invariably break out the fiddle at the drop of the hat and gladly play tunes.

As one might suspect in a cavalry regiment, horse racing occupied a prime spot in leisure activity. However, because a horse could be injured at improvised race tracks the practice was frowned on by the government yet continued unabated anyway, with officers often heartily participating.

The 2nd Alabama troopers loved nothing better than to race their horses.[142] Just a few months before the War ended, an Inspector General (IG) report on the regiments in Ferguson's brigade (the 2nd Alabama included) observed that horse racing was a popular past time which tended to boost unit cohesiveness and morale.[143] The IG also found that the men took better care of their horses than themselves. Indeed, the most likely injury in racing was to the

rider, a phenomenon Ferguson recorded on a January 25, 1865, diary entry:

> Capt. Freeman Johnson of the 56th Ala., while running a horse race, was struck against a tree, by his mare bolting & so much injured that he died just as we left the dance, in the adjoining house.[144]

— On the Move —

Riding at full strength the regiment consisted of almost 1,000 men (by mid-War the size was lucky to be a third that number). Accompanied by hundreds of pack mules, scores of wagons, horse drawn artillery, and even a small herd of cattle, the predominate sound on the march would be the clang of equipment and the squeaking of leather saddles punctuated by the ever present chatter of human conversation, animal grunts, and the high-pitched whinny of the horses. Road conditions permitting, the command would move in columns of two or four abreast giving the regiment a snake like appearance as it traversed the landscape leaving behind the smell of lathered sweat and fresh animal excrement.

The roads were dirt and often in poor condition so that the horses shuffling along quickly filled the air with choking dust. During the summer when the penetrating rays of the sun blazed the hottest, uniforms and bronze faces were blanketed by dirt, covering even the eyebrows and beards so that from a distance it was impossible to tell the difference between Confederate gray or Union blue — all was a brownish hue.

On rainy days everything turned another kind of miserable with red or brown mud sticking to the horses and wagons like glue. Wet clothes and wet leather guaranteed painful body sores. Then there was the cold. While the horses generated their own body heat and pushed out steamy puffs at every step on a march, the cotton or wool uniforms of the men were no match for the bitter snow and ice of winter and some literally froze stiff in their saddles.

Typical Confederate Cavalryman in the Western Theater. Jeffrey Addicott Collection.[890]

To sustain the troopers on long marches the regiment was assigned a variety of mule-drawn wagons and/or pack mules (compared to horses, mules are stronger, sturdier, and can bear greater loads with less feed), collectively called "trains," which carried supplies to include ammunition, salt pork, salt beef, flour, corn, bacon, dried fruit, whisky, cooking utensils, bedding, blankets, tents, clothing, and other baggage. The canvas covered wagons or pack mules were divided into commissary or ammunition and would either precede the regiment to a pre-determined spot or trail along behind intending to catch up to the main body once it halted for the night.

Wagons were not used on shorter excursions. Instead, the command relied exclusively on pack mules who carried on their backs, by means of two X shaped wooden braces, large heavy canvas saddlebags covered by tarpaulins and tied down with strong ropes to keep the rain out. In addition, each trooper would carry with him a

three or four-day supply of cooked rations for himself and a supply of shelled hard yellow corn in sacks or saddle bags for his mount.

At every 50 minutes, the line officers would call a stop to allow for a ten-minute rest and at noon, the troop would halt for about an hour to allow the men to eat and relax before the afternoon march began. At evening, the men would set up small pup tents, eat and sleep, and move out in the morning.

One of the greatest challenges facing the cavalry — whether in large groups or small scouts — was to successfully ford the many rivers and streams encountered. In many cases, wooden bridges would be out due to flooding or burning and without the benefit of portable pontoons, crossing over a large body of water took ingenuity and guts. Ferguson recalled a typical cavalry crossing during Sherman's march in Georgia after the Federals had burned the bridge behind them.

> I found some rope with which I tied the raft to the middle pier of the bridge so that it could swing from shore to shore and had it pulled backwards and forwards by grapevines tied together. The men stood on the raft with their saddles and accouterments in their arms and knee deep in water. The wagons were crossed in the same manner. While this was being done a few of the horses were swum over, led by the dugout and a few other boats which had escaped the general destruction [by Sherman's forces]. These horses were led to the river bank, then the rest were driven in. As soon as they reached the bank they joined the horses there assembled. And so the brigade got over in a very short time.[145]

When absent from their base camp, the men would mostly sleep "under the stars" with their saddles serving as a pillow, or in small "dog" tents, 72 inches by 18 inches, which when buttoned

together and stretched out across a cut pole could accommodate two. Whenever possible the troopers slept on a bed of straw, or leaves and wrapped themselves in a blanket or gum-cloth (oil-cloth) next to a small cooking fire kept smoldering all night to ward off mosquitoes and provide warmth. It was also a common practice when the weather was inclement for two men, or even the entire mess, to sleep on gum blankets spread out on the ground with regular blankets covering their bodies topped off by another set of gum blankets to ward off rain or snow. Like Cochrane, the troopers soon grew accustomed to the exigencies of life in the open.

> I believe after a soldier gets used to camp life and also used to sleeping under the broad canopy of heaven, with the midnight breeze upon his brow, the dew upon his face, he is as healthy as man can be.[146]

Bright moments on the move occurred when the command passed near a town or village — the men were always on the lookout for paper, coffee, tobacco, and the ever present quest for food and strong drink. Desiring to support their heroes in arms, it was not uncommon for locals to stand along the roadside and hand up various comfort items as the men rode by. Cigars, chewing tobacco, fruits, and cakes were always favorites and occasionally some of the undisciplined would "fall out" of formation to better enjoy the goodies. One of the more humorous jingles sung in the Army of Tennessee that captured perfectly this undisciplined phenomenon was the popular, "Eating Goober Peas,"[147] recalling an officer's frustration with his men stopping along the roadside to eat peas instead of charging the enemy.

Another attraction of great temptation which saw many riders stray off was the sighting of wild honey hives. From the senior officer to the enlisted man, all scoured the canopy for beehives as the column moved through wooded areas and straggling would soon follow suit as groups kindled small fires to smoke the bees out and grab the honeycombs.

— Mothers, Wives, and Others —

Always a factor in motivating and sustaining the soldier's strong sense of duty was the support given to him by those left behind, especially the women. The women of the Confederacy understood their purpose and role. It was the soldier's duty to fight, it was their duty to support him and they willingly shouldered herculean responsibilities for the maintenance of home and hearth. A plaque on display at the Columbia, South Carolina State Museum's Confederate Section, quotes a wartime letter from Mrs. Judith McGuire to illustrate:

> Women must all work for our country ... while men are making a free-will offering of their life's blood on the alter [sic] of their country, women must not be idle. We must do what we can for the comfort of our brave men. We must sew for them, knit for them, nurse the sick, keep up the faint hearted, given them a word of encouragement ....[148]

Volumes can be written on the moral fiber and character of these women. Although better educated than most, Mrs. Manolete Pendleton exemplified the indomitable spirit of the Southern female. During the final months of the Army of Northern Virginia, when her husband General William Pendleton wrote that he was considering resigning from the army, his no nonsense spouse fired off an immediate dissent. She admonished him in no uncertain language.

> [D]ismiss ... all such thoughts from your mind. I am sure you are in your place and if you wish to benefit us, will remain in the important duties God has given you to do. Duty and honor were more important than any hardships they [the family] had to endure.[149]

This same woman had instilled the fundamental values of God and country into her son Major Sandie Pendleton, who was killed on a Virginia battlefield in 1864. A telling episode reflecting just how well she reared him occurred between young Sandie and a school bully. Mrs. Pendleton told the boy that he must not run away but strike the bully in return for blows received. When Sandie replied that the bully was big and hit hard, his mother warned him: "If he strikes you again, and you don't strike back, I will give you a good whipping."[150] Such was the fabric of Southern women. In general, they did not raise, nor did they reward, cowards or yellow-bellies. They impressed on their young a spirit of industry and integrity, without which no success in life can ever be fully satisfied.

During the War years, when all found themselves in charge of the households, farms, and businesses, females were required to do things that previous social conventions in the South sometimes dictated against. One taboo that quickly evaporated in this new normal was that respectable women should not travel alone without male companionship. The fact is that many women traveled great distances to visit loved ones and deliver whatever comforts from home they could haul with them, from socks to hams. Starved for attention and affection, the men immensely approved of the efforts wrought by these women and few condemned it as "impolite" conduct.

Then, as now, Southern society assumed that women were more pious than men and immune to the base desires baked into the DNA of all humans. Indeed, while the Rebel soldier certainly held Southern womanhood in high regard, the War presented him with things and situations that were not to be experienced back home. While their upbringing stressed those sustaining values set out in the Bible, most of the men were single and always on the lookout for excitement. Coupled with the fact that many of the camps were located near towns, the young soldiers were keen to take part in local events, where they met families and their eligible daughters.

In the vast majority of instances, such activities were exercised in the proscribed and proper manner of the day and courting might occur at church socials, organized dances, or "bees," where girls

knitted for soldiers while the soldiers entertained them. But there were times where untoward things occurred as well.

The magnitude of dishonorable conduct, i.e., illicit consensual sex, is difficult to gauge, but those familiar with the strong sense of propriety that existed 165 years ago know that the topic of male/female relations were seldom mentioned in direct terms. While a general survey of surviving writings would lead one to believe that soldiers never swore, gambled, got drunk, or had illicit sex,[151] the alert scholar guided by common sense can find a plethora of evidence to the contrary in the proceedings of court-martials and sometimes indirect evidence by reading "between the lines" in personal correspondence. For example, when the Confederate Army of Tennessee pulled out of Tullahoma, Tennessee, in the summer of 1863, one soldier from Indiana wrote home to his brother about a certain practice in that Southern town that few would ever mention to family.

> Jim, last night four of us broke into one of the Reb's storehouses. We had taken a bucket and filled it up with sugar from a barrel then went down the street and traded the sugar for skin [sex]. For god's sake, Jim, don't let Mother know of this.[152]

In fact, all of the major cities, to include Atlanta, Mobile, and Richmond, were home to gambling establishments and brothels. Local ordinances prohibiting prostitution were frequently violated and large numbers of prostitutes enjoyed a measure of autonomy and could be found frequenting "saloons, hotels, restaurants, bawdy houses," and walking in the evenings on certain well-known city streets.[153] Interestingly, "prostitutes, but not the men visiting them, were considered to be violating the laws."[154] On the other hand, given that the War demoralized and impoverished so many women, some females in grave or dire conditions were driven, when occasion presented itself, to do things for money that they would never have imagined themselves capable of.

All soldiers were anxious to get a furlough to go home to see wives, sweethearts, loved ones, and "eligible" females and while some troopers saw every woman as a beauty who deserved attention, others, on occasion, lamented the quality of the fairer sex that they encountered. One Confederate wrote about the appearance and morals of "Tory" women in northern Alabama in quite disparaging terms.

> The state of the morals is quite low as the soil, almost all the women are given to whoredom & the ugliest, sallow faced, shaggy headed, bare footed dirty wretches you ever saw.[155]

Still, the men would take advantage of any opportunity to socialize. Private Cochrane was no exception. "There are several young ladies not married here [Shelby Springs, Alabama]" he wrote to his father back in Tuscaloosa, "and as these kind are scarce in this part of the country, I intend to get introduced by one of the Duggars, as they are relations."[156]

Another Alabama cavalryman penned a short story about a fellow soldier's encounter with a girl who had arranged a rendezvous.

> He obtains a short leave, and comes flying in, his horse and heart in an equal gallop. "Can it be she?" he asks himself — "she never wrote she was coming!" He dismounts at the gate, hastily flings the rein over a post, double quicks it up the yard, and greets the door with a nervous "rat-tat-tat." The door opens ... and the next moment, with only the exclamations, "John!" "Mary!" her face is buried in the bosom of his woolen shirt.... Such meetings as these are what people around here have got into the habit of calling "weddings." The name isn't such a bad one, is it? Wouldn't mind having one or two such weddings myself.[157]

In the last known letter written by Cochrane, dated November 30, 1864, he spent far more ink describing to his sister his courting experiences than his battle experiences. Even though Cochrane had just come out of five bloody months of fighting Sherman's hordes and had been promoted to the rank of sergeant major of the 2nd Alabama Cavalry, young ladies dominated his thoughts. He wrote from camp in Greensboro, Georgia:

> I have spent the last three days very pleasantly. Lieut. Foster had a cousin named Jim Krown who had a pretty daughter who I visited and I went to church last night with a Miss Julia Hunter, who is a very pretty lady and I intend to give her a call tomorrow before I leave.[158]

— Christ in the Camp —

Since the South had always held to the Reformation's view of salvation by grace — by faith alone in the substitutionary work of Jesus Christ on the cross who was judged by God for all human sin — the Confederacy was primarily associated with the Protestant branch of Christianity, although not a few Confederates were Catholics, with some Jews filling the ranks as well.[159]

Grace was the touchstone for vast numbers of Southerners and Robert E. Lee, a man of impeccable moral fiber by any societal measure, reflected this belief in word and deed, humbly acknowledging that compared to the perfect essence of God he was in a state of total depravity and helplessness to save himself by human good deeds, rituals, or morality.[160] Unlike Lincoln, who left no written or verbal evidence that he had ever expressed a belief in Jesus Christ as savior, Lee unequivocally expressed his faith in Christ on numerous occasion:

> I can only say that I am a poor sinner, *trusting in Christ alone* for salvation [emphasis added]."[161]

Of course, those who accepted grace salvation still sinned and having left the farm or small town for the first time in his life (most had never traveled more than 20 miles from where they were born) the average Johnny Reb was far more apt to practice in public that which he had only remotely thought about doing in private back home. To moderation in most cases, but sometimes to excess, Confederate Christian soldiers cursed, got drunk, and "chased."

For certain, such conduct did not mean that the soldiers considered themselves nonreligious, only that many rejected, or just plain ignored, the more legalistic brands of certain denominations. In other words, many understood the central tenants of Biblical Christianity and considered themselves to be saved by grace, but would willingly engage in drunken brawls and other vices from time to time.[162]

On the other hand, while some of the men checked their "religious life-style" and beliefs at the door when they enlisted in the military, others keep faithfulness to their beliefs and quite a number advanced in their spiritual life as they learned the basic and advanced doctrines of Biblical theology taught to them by properly prepared camp preachers and chaplains.

From the first enthusiastic days of their muster to the filthy lice ridden trenches of Atlanta and Richmond, many of the men who fought on were firmly anchored by their faith in God's Divine providence.[163] Speaking before Virginia's Hollywood Memorial Association in 1909, Reverend H.D.C. MacLauchlan reminded the audience of certain fundamental truths that sustained the Southern soldier. He rhetorically asked:

> Without faith in both God and country "what could their half-fed, half-clothed, less than half-equipped forces have accomplished against the sleek and comfortable millions of the North?"[164]

The soldiers of the 2nd Alabama would have fully understood what Reverend MacLauchlan meant when he spoke of faith in God

and duty to country. If the self-evident categories of truths about the sacredness and protection of family were the building blocks of their conviction to fight, then the Bible provided the mortar.[165]

Unfortunately, not a few of the Christian churches throughout the South labored under the false impression that the Christian *modus vivendi* (way of life) post-salvation was directly gauged by how well one could keep a set of moral taboos. Many incorrectly defined the Christian life-style by measuring it against the morality provisions of the Mosaic law, i.e., do not steal, do not murder, do not commit adultery and then added in large doses of man-made legalistic traditions too boot — no swearing, no gambling, no dancing, no drinking, no smoking, etc. Thus, in many social circles of those times, a "good" Christian must not only be a law-abiding citizen, but he must also completely avoid the afore listed taboos. Some apostate pastors, blaspheming the doctrine of eternal security (the Bible teaches that salvation cannot be lost regardless of lifestyle choices or subsequent sins), preached blistering fire and brimstone sermons on all who violated their list of taboos or who engaged in overt immorality. They falsely implied, if not openly stated, the lie that a Christian involved in such lascivious activities could lose his salvation, or, in the alternative, was never *really* saved in the first instance.

Nevertheless, with regard to the establishment of religious services within their commands, officers were typically supportive. Interestingly, the Confederate Articles of War also encouraged the men to attend religious services as part of military life.

> It is earnestly recommended to all officers and soldiers diligently to attend divine service; and all officers who shall behave indecently or irreverently at any place of divine worship, shall, if commissioned officers, be brought before a general court-martial there to be publicly and severely reprimanded by the president.[166]

Lee himself wrote of the superseding obligations of Christianity as well as following basic human morality, reminding his army on its march into Pennsylvania that "the duties exacted of us by civilization and [by] Christianity are not less obligatory in the country of the enemy than in our own."[167] Thus, while Lee did not believe in "enforced religion," and never required his soldiers or, later, his students at Washington College in Lexington, Virginia, to attend any religious ceremonies, "he did everything in his power to influence them to do so."[168]

Furthermore, much to the credit of Southern culture, there was little mixing of the functions of church and State which meant that the common soldier was assured that he could practice his religion or non-religion as he saw fit. Colonel James Nisbet, who was promoted through the ranks from captain and saw extensive combat service in both the eastern and western theaters, pragmatically wrote: "During my four years of service, I do not recall meeting an avowed infidel."[169] Although Colonel Nisbet's view about the absence of infidels must be taken with a grain of salt, his general observation that "from the commander-in-chief to the private in the ranks there was a deep religious feeling in the Southern armies,"[170] was undoubtedly accurate.[171]

— Confederate Preachers —

The Confederate government appointed chaplains in the Army, providing them by law with a meager salary and the rations of a private. Legislators also anticipated that each regiment would procure its own chaplain and local denominations supported the effort by sending preachers into the camps whenever possible. Needless to say, especially in the first years of the war, many of the more self-righteous types found the rather blunt lifestyles and mannerisms of their constituents unbearable to their "righteous" souls. One officer in Ferguson's brigade bemoaned to his wife that he not only had to "inhale the sickening stench of bodies in every state of decomposition" on the battlefield but he also had to endure listening "to the obscenity & blasphemies that are being continually uttered all around."[172]

In fact, quite a number of the more legalistic preachers left the Southern Army in total dejection when confronted with the aforementioned sins,[173] lamenting that Christianity was wreaked by the numerous vices of camp life.[174] Indeed, when soldiers did opt into the ascetic brands of Christianity, they often discovered the rigors of the religious regime was more than they could bear. One Rebel sergeant, who had succumbed to the temptation of apple brandy during a particularly hot day, found himself being scolded by a fellow "brethren in the Lord." Wiping his lips with his sleeve, the sergeant straightened himself and replied, "I think as much of religion as any man. But there's such a thing as having too damn much of it."[175]

Fortunately, the average battlefield minister took a more pragmatic view of his job. The Reverend Moses B. Hoge, for instance, concerned himself less with passing judgment over the activities of the soldiers and more with providing Biblical information about the mechanics of salvation by grace and then confession of sin for "fellowship" with the Holy Spirit, per 1 John 1:9.[176] Standard themes for sermons included the necessity of salvation; the mechanics of salvation; the uncertainty of life; sin; hell; "the importance of Christian vigilance; the omnipotence of God; and the universality of divine mercy [unlimited atonement]."[177]

Like most all other regiments, Christian preaching in the 2nd Alabama Cavalry was very common and services were conducted by military chaplains, civilian preachers, or even members of the command that were recognized as being "learned in the Bible."[178] These, laymen parsons would also provide church services when no chaplain or preacher was available and while some remarked that "[t]he men were fond of hearing in camp any kind of address, and were easy prey to sharpers [who would fleece them of money],"[179] most of the Bible teachers seemed honest in their efforts.

For the purposes of giving the gospel and providing Bible doctrine, various Southern Bible societies provided copies of the New Testament, tracts, and songbooks to the soldiers. In turn, the men of the 2nd Alabama were always eager to attend local church

services when camped close to civilian communities — for the girls if not for the preaching! In March 1863, Private Hall wrote:

> We have preaching in camp this evening .... We have however services in the different churches in town, every Sunday; and the Methodist, every night.[180]

Chaplains were free to create their own time table for conducting religious activities, with many choosing to hold short prayer services in the morning and evening, followed by short addresses. Private Cochrane described how civilian preachers like a "Mr. Cushman" would visit the various camps to preach.

> I went yesterday to hear Mr. Cushman preach over at the 29th Ala. regiment [infantry stationed at Pollard, Alabama]. Mr. Cushman saw Captain Pegues [commander of Company D, 2nd Alabama Cavalry] and asked him to bring the Church people in his company.[181]

As the bitter reality of defeat loomed on the horizon, Southerners were tested in their religious convictions as few people ever are. To Christians like Lee, defeat did not mean that the South was wrong, it meant only that it was the will of God that the nation called the United States of America should remain united. In 1866, Reverend J. William Jones asked Lee about the outcome of the War and the rightness of the Southern bid for independence. As if chiseled in stone upon his mind, Lee thoughtfully answered:

> Yes! All that is very sad, and might be a cause of self-reproach, but that we are conscious that we have humbly tried to do our duty. We may therefore, with calm satisfaction, *trust in God and leave results to Him* [emphasis added]."[182]

Consequently, the War's outcome was always in God's perfect control of history, just as General Stackpole so aptly remarked about God's "overruling will"[183] in his excellent book concerning the pivotal battle of Gettysburg:

> The Almighty must have taken a direct hand in shaping the events which culminated in Gettysburg, either because He just couldn't trust the North to win the war by themselves or else on the premise that He had universal plans for later centuries which called for a united America and developments by 1863 had failed to conform to his long-range program.[184]

— Death in Service —

Given the paucity of surviving records, it is impossible to reconstruct an accurate picture of the number of 2nd Alabama troopers that perished while in service. One can only say that the regiment started out in 1862, at the full regulation size of just over 1,000 men and despite constant replacements, ended with probably one-fourth that number when it disbanded in May 1865.

Although the harshness and brutality of fighting occupied their attention, for those who paid the ultimate sacrifice it is certain that most of the deaths during the War were due to disease, with combat action a distant second, followed by exposure to the elements. In fact, probably only a quarter of all the deaths were attributable to the results of battle wounds.[185]

The men injured or killed in combat were most likely hit by a projectile known as the Minnie ball, a fat conical piece of lead that mushroomed when it hit bone or cartilage, causing tremendous damage. Gunshot victims usually didn't die upon being shot. Not right away. The mortally wounded man often lingered in horrible pain for quite some time emitting moans and other gurglings, accompanied by the smell of urine and excrement as his lifeblood

soaked the ground, not red, but dark, almost black. Without proper medical attention, the internal organs soon shut down and the blank stare of death quickly followed.

In any event, even if a soldier survived the initial shock of being shot and then "treated," the wounded man had many other adversities to overcome in the healing process to include the hazards of unsanitary conditions and infection. For those that did receive medical attention to a limb shot, the grisly medical procedure of amputation occurred with some regularity.

The challenges to health associated with combat took a heavy toll on the 2nd Alabama, but all quickly came to realize that the black hand of death was more likely to come from invisible diseases, particularly so for those that hailed from rural areas as opposed to city dwellers. Because the men from the small farming communities had never been exposed to the more common diseases of measles, mumps, scarlet fever, and smallpox, they had no natural immunity to protect them.

The chief cause of infectious disease spawned from the military camps themselves where poor sanitation, poor nutrition, and an extremely limited understanding of the cause and transmission of diseases spelled misery and death. In early July 1862, about a month after the regiment was formed, Private Cochrane wrote a rosy assessment to his cousin about the general health of his company as it comfortably camped at Bluff Springs, Florida.

> I heard before I left home that the cavalry service was healthier than any other. I now believe it. Our Company [D] as a whole keeps very good health and there is very little sickness comparatively in the regiment.[186]

Cochrane was right about the benefits of staying on the move as a plus in terms of minimizing the transmission of infectious diseases, but wrong in his expectation that cavalry life was a permanent

shield from sickness. Not to the degree of their compatriots in the infantry, the cavalryman also spent long periods of time in the close quarters of tent/cabin life. In addition, due to the very nature of its mobility and mission, cavalrymen logged many hours on the move enduring bad weather, colds, aches, stiffness, pains, hunger, and the curses of the insect and plant world. With his evening covering often nothing except the canopy of the heavens the men had to be resolute in their constant struggles with nature.

While annoyances emanating from the plagues of the plant kingdom included poison oak, sumac, poison ivy, stickers, and thorns it was the insects that tormented the most. Lice (called gray backs) infestation was rampant and all forms of living creatures — man and animal — were plagued by biting flies, mosquitoes, sand flies, red ants, chiggers, red bugs, ticks, fleas, and the seemingly incurable affliction of mites called the "Scotch fiddle" (scabies).[187] Still, as bad as these pests were, they seldom spelled death to the host unless they were transmitters of disease like the swarms of mosquitoes that carried malaria and yellow fever during the sweltering summer months.

All manner of illness and disease were also exacerbated by a lack of proper sanitation, poor hygiene, and unhealthy diets. Sometimes the water near a particular camp was so foul smelling that the horses refused to drink it.

In terms of mortality, pneumonia and dysentery were the top two killers. Typhoid fever was deadly as well, accounting for a full 17 percent of all military deaths. Caused by drinking polluted water (usually spoiled by human feces), by 1865, the "mortality rate of typhoid had reached 56 percent of all those who contracted it."[188] Accordingly, Cochrane's upbeat view about the health of the regiment in July 1862, was soon replaced by a grimmer reality of things as reflected in a letter sent home just a few months later, in late November 1862. Specifically, pneumonia seemed to haunt the 2nd Alabama like a shadowed specter, aggravated no doubt by the constant requirement to travel long distances in wet weather conditions.

I forgot to mention that Tom Blocker, Mr. Rufus Clements' old overseer, a member of our company, died on Sunday at the hospital at Greenville [Alabama] with pneumonia, making the seventh of our company [to die of pneumonia] since we left [Montgomery in June 1862].[189]

Another member of the regiment, Private Perry Andrews, Company A, wrote about the deadly toll caused by malaria while stationed in the Florida panhandle. In contrast to Cochrane's July letter about the healthy state of company D, Andrews's company was suffering greatly from disease as he related to his father, Mr. Warren Andrews, on June 28, 1862.

We are now encamped in a very pretty place [Bluff Springs, Florida], with good water, and I would have thought it to be a healthy locality; but it has not proven so, for we [Company A] have a great many sick, and a good number of deaths — about one or two pr. day.[190]

Company B of the regiment was also hit hard by typhoid fever and measles during the summer of 1862. Out of the 86 men in the company, eleven died and three were discharged on a surgeon's certificate — about one out of every six.[191]

The most common sickness which struck the men was diarrhea and dysentery, a disease of the digestive organs caused by drinking from polluted water sources along with the problems brought about by the constant diet of greasy corn meal and pork.[192] The corn meal often came with swarms of weevils or maggots mixed about and the pork varied as either fresh, mostly fresh, or heavily salted. In fact, dysentery could kill. By 1862, general diarrhea amongst the soldiers hit an incredible rate of 99.5 percent[193] and those diagnosed with "*severe* diarrheal illnesses reached a mortality rate of almost 60 percent."[194]

If gut-wrenching bouts of diarrhea did not result in death, it certainly made riding a horse intensely painful. Disgustingly, the evidences of this chronic problem of the bowels was literally everywhere. Forced to dismount and evacuate at the most inopportune times, the results contributed to a trail of filth wherever a column of riders passed. According to Confederate medical officer, Paul F. Eve:

> Chronic diarrheas was very prevalent and quite difficult of management. Indeed, so common was looseness of the bowels in the army, that few soldiers ever had a natural or molded evacuation. The camping grounds, privies everywhere, and too often the depots, streets, etc., of villages and towns presented disgusting evidences of this fact.[195]

— Doctors and Treatment —

Hospitals were viewed as places of death, and rightly so. Incredibly, about 50% of the wounded admitted to a Civil War hospital died there, compared to about 5% for World War II admittees. Private James A. Gould of Company B, 2nd Alabama, was one of the lucky ones, he was hospitalized for 41 days with malaria and recovered.

It was the time before antibiotics, blood transfusions, and the discoveries of Louis Pasteur and Joseph Lister. Even ideas about germs were not standardized so that the actual treatments for wounds and diseases varied widely.[196] Paradoxically, the deplorable state of medicine in America on the eve of the War is best summed up from a quip delivered by Oliver Wendell Holmes, Sr., in an 1860 address before the Massachusetts Medical Society.

> [I]f the knowledge of all our medications now known could be sunk to the bottom of the sea it would be better for mankind and the worse for the fishes.[197]

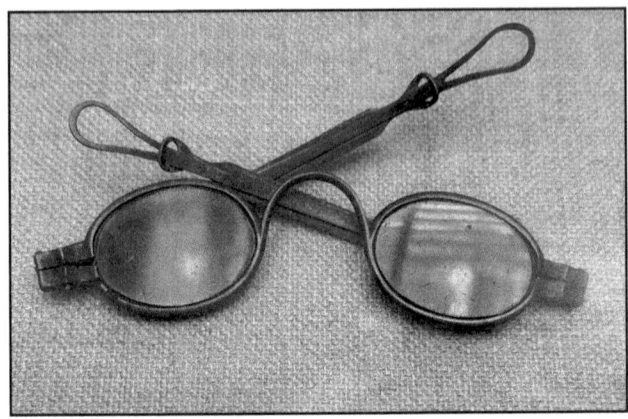

Medical Book and Eyeglasses. Dr. John Baldwin, Co. F, 2nd Alabama Cavalry. Deborah Addicott Collection & Jeffrey Addicott Collection.

With "no transfusions, IV fluids, epinephrine, tetanus vaccine, antibiotics, or even aspirin,"[198] the practice of medicine was more of an "art" than a science. For example, believing that wounds needed "pus" to heal properly, many physicians would transfer pus from one person's wound to a new patient's wound. This strange practice was called *suppuration* or simply "laudable pus."[199] Another bizarre practice, called "bleeding," entailed cutting the patient with small triangle-shaped instruments in order to remove "toxins" from the blood.

The doctors themselves were graduates from the handful of medical colleges where they were required to attend a certain number of lectures and conduct some practical exercises before being granted a degree. The longest academic regimen in any medical college was two years and since there were no standardized tests to ensure a minimum level of competency, anyone who could afford the tuition could obtain a medical license.[200]

By legislation passed in March 1861, each regiment was assigned one surgeon and one assistant surgeon.[201] A small staff of enlisted men were also assigned as orderlies. Per Army regulation, the surgeon was given the rank of major and the assistant surgeon the rank of

captain, but neither were authorized to exercise command authority. Clothed in an officer's uniform of gray cloth with black piping and a green sash, the surgeon and assistant surgeon were "responsible for the medical care of all soldiers in the [regiment], including treating wounds, injuries or diseases, as well as prescribing medications."[202] In addition, the surgeon was tasked with examining new recruits to determine fitness for duty and issuing medical discharge certificates to the disabled or seriously ill.

One of the assistant surgeons for the 2nd Alabama was Dr. John A. Baldwin. Dr. Baldwin, a licensed physician, graduated in a class of 57 students from the prestigious Atlanta Medical College (now Emory University) in Atlanta, Georgia, in 1859, and soon thereafter relocated from Atlanta to Alabama's Butler County where he began his medical practice in the Garland community. A tall, lanky man of twenty-six, with straight brown hair and a mercurial temperament, he enlisted as a "high" private in the regiment at the courthouse in Greenville, Alabama, on August 12, 1862, about three months after the regiment was officially mustered into service. After completing a basic cavalry training course at the conscript camp in Montgomery, on November 19, 1862, Baldwin was assigned to Company F, 2nd Alabama Cavalry, then stationed near Pollard, Alabama.[203] Because Baldwin enlisted after the regiment was formed, the approved slots for the regimental surgeon and assistant surgeon were already filled. However, as a trained physician he was in great demand[204] and when Baldwin reported for duty to Company F, he was immediately designated as an "Acting Assistant Surgeon" and placed on "extra duty," a position he held throughout the remainder of the War.

Even though the assistant surgeon slot was an officer's billet to be filled at the rank of captain, the War Department was able to avoid providing Dr. Baldwin the increased pay and officer rank (about $1,300 a year plus stipends) by appointing him as an *acting* assistant surgeon. This bureaucratic two-step of delaying promotions for medical doctors was not uncommon, particularly when it came to cavalry regiments.[205] In any event, Dr. John Baldwin fulfilled his patriotic duty and utilized his medical knowledge and experience to the best of his ability while on this extended "extra duty" tour

working both directly with the regiment and also at various hospitals in Mississippi, Alabama, and Georgia as ordered.[206]

Interestingly, as a reminder that in the time before antiseptics, those who cared for the wounded were exposing themselves to harms almost as dangerous as the battlefield. Baldwin himself was struck down by a severe case of dysentery in May 1864, while serving as a doctor at French's Division Hospital at Shelby Springs, Alabama.

Even though the corresponding medical admission card indicates that Dr. John Baldwin was at the 1st Mississippi C.S.A. Hospital at Jackson, Mississippi, that hospital had been burned to the ground by the Yankees in 1863, just after the fall of Vicksburg, causing the staff to relocate to a spacious hotel in Shelby Springs, and the old hospital cards stamped for the 1st Mississippi C.S.A. Hospital were used until they were depleted.[207] Luckily, Baldwin recovered in a month's time and on June 10, 1864, returned to his duties and was soon thereafter sent back to his regiment.[208] Sherman's movement into Georgia had begun and Baldwin's medical skills were sorely needed in the brutal months ahead.

A doctor's standard surgical kit contained a variety of cutting and probing instruments, the most menacing of which was the surgeon's saw blade used to amputate limbs, hence the term "sawbones." A practiced doctor could saw off a limb and bind up the stub in ten minutes!

Due to the lack of cloth string, boiled horsehair was the most common "thread" for wound closure, with cat gut and silk also used. Unbeknownst to the world of medicine at the time, wounded Southerners actually suffered far less from wound infection than their Northern counterparts who used cloth thread — the boiling made the animal hair flexible and also sterilized it of harmful germs.

Access to medical supplies was spotty at best, with chloroform manufactured as a general anesthesia from Confederate laboratories in limited quantities. Opium pills and laudanum were also available. The most common liquid "medicine" was whiskey mixed

French's Division Hospital at Shelby Springs, Alabama.

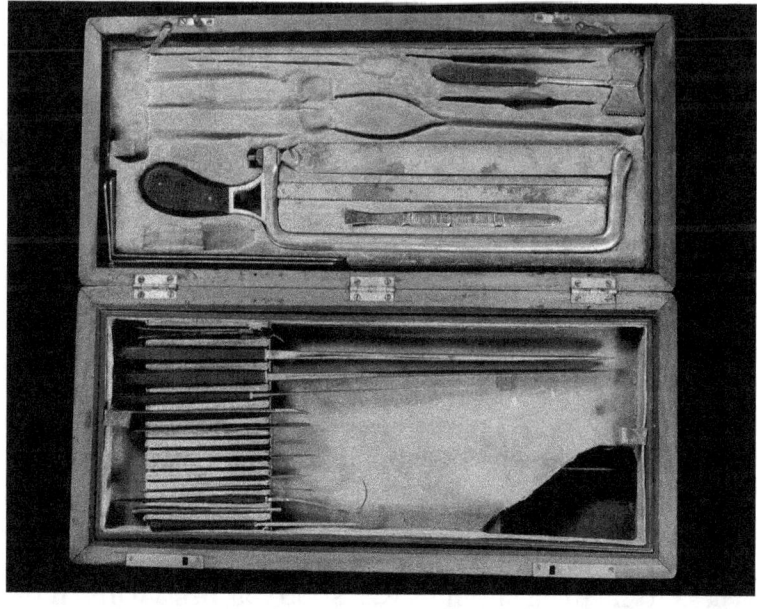

Surgical Kit Captured by the 2nd Alabama from the Divisional Medical Wagon of Union General Peter Joseph Osterhaus, October 1863, and Used During the War by Dr. Robert McCullough Hill, Surgeon, 2nd Alabama Cavalry. Photo Courtesy of the Alabama Department of Archives & History.

with quinine, which was used on a regular basis to treat malaria, infections, pneumonia, diarrhea, neuralgia, syphilis, and consumption (tuberculosis). The treatment may have filled the patient with a sense of temporary confidence for a favorable recovery, but not much else.

On one occasion, Private Cochrane noted that it was "a very good thing I got sick when I did for the surgeon had some medicine then but now he only has salts."[209] Cochrane went on to describe how he was treated for a bad fever by receiving "a blue mass pill that night and two doses of quinine the next morning."[210] Used to treat everything from toothache to constipation, the popular blue pill's main ingredient was elemental mercury (now known to be toxic) mixed with licorice root, rosewater, honey, sugar, and dried rose petals.

Perhaps the most widespread medical success was the prevention of smallpox by means of vaccinations, a practice used on soldiers since George Washington's Continental Army. In December 1862, Cochrane reassured his "Ma [that] she need not be uneasy about the smallpox for it is not near here and besides I have been vaccinated three times and am going to be again."[211]

Cavalrymen wounded in fighting were often far from medical help. Every effort was made to bring the injured by wagon or horse to a medical field station which could be a special tent or other covered structure such as a nearby barn, church, or house. For larger engagements, a solid red flag was run up to mark the place of treatment where the surgeon or assistant surgeon administered whatever initial aid could be given. In most cases, to alleviate pain and counteract shock, the patient first received a drink of hard liquor and/or morphine powder which was rubbed into the open wound. The next step was to stop the bleeding. Once that was accomplished, the surgeon would most often use his finger as a probe to locate the foreign object to determine if it could be removed. Then, after cleaning away any grass or dirt, the wound was packed with cotton lint and bandaged or, if necessary, a splint was applied. In other

cases, amputation occurred, usually within 24 hours. Three out of every four limb injuries resulted in amputation.

The most seriously injured were transported to a main hospital to "recover." For many, however, these places were the stuff of nightmares. Accompanied by pestiferous odors arising from gangrenous infections, blow flies swarmed around the patients laying their eggs in open wounds so that within hours large maggots were eating away the infected flesh. The maggots might actually help, but in the cases were stomach acids or bowel contents seeped into the trauma area the results was almost always fatal. Doctors would not even treat gut-shot wounds.[212]

One of the more poignant stories of a wounded cavalryman provides a fair picture of what it was like to "treated" at a Confederate hospital. Lieutenant Colonel James C. Bates of Ross' Texas brigade, was knocked off his horse by a Yankee Minnie ball to his face on May 15, 1864, during a skirmish in the Atlanta campaign. Bates somehow survived and wrote his mother from the Fair Ground Hospital in Atlanta on June 17, 1864.

> My dear Ma: I am just recovering from a very serious wound received about a month since .... I was wounded in the mouth by a Minnie ball. The ball entered my mouth & cutting my lips, but very little broken off. Four of the upper front teeth are knocked entirely out by the root, all my lower front teeth and also all my lower jaw bone on the left side. My jaw bone was pretty badly broken also, the ball came out some three inches behind my left ear inside of my neck.... The first days after I was wounded my sufferings were intense, after this time they were not so severe. On account of my tongue & mouth & throat being so swollen I was not able to get anything down my throat until the seventh day after I was wounded. The surgeon made dismal efforts to put a tube down

Private Edwin Hart Robinson, Co. H, 2nd Alabama Cavalry.

my throat but failed. I then took it myself & after an hour or so succeeded in getting it in my throat & had some water introduced into my stomach.[213]

As horrible as it was to be maimed for life, it is interesting to note that in the few extant writings from those wounded members of the 2nd Alabama Cavalry, there is always a sense of pride associated with the injury — it was a badge of honor. For instance, Private Edwin H. Robinson, Company H, wrote some years after the War in the *Confederate Veteran* magazine that he intended to apply for a pension offered by the State of Florida due to his many combat wounds. Having joined in 1862, "at the early age of sixteen ... a Soldier-boy with patriotic zeal," Robinson received what he quipped as an "unlimited furlough" at Kingston, Georgia, in April of 1864, by "some careless (?) Yank."[214] Robinson, then 61, boasted that he had "hobbled through life, engaged often in a desperate struggle against poverty, for an honorable maintenance for self, wife, and little ones."[215]

A recent law enacted in Florida gives all Confederates of sixty years a pension of one hundred to one hundred and fifty dollars a year. I am just within the age limit, am sixty-one, but have never asked for relief, though I stopped two blue whistlers [bullets fired by Federal troops] and left a leg in Georgia, and am so presumptuous as to deem myself worthy of a share of this benefaction, and expect to make application.[216]

— The Elements of Nature —

Nothing could erase the reality and hardship of wartime conditions, yet sometimes, surrounded by the splendor of the natural world the men might for a day or two forget. On the other hand, they all knew that the angel of death was not only lurking about in combat or disease, but also appeared in other ways. A horse that bolted, a gun that accidentally discharged, or the vicissitudes of mother nature herself. For instance, General Ferguson, the brigade commander of the 2nd Alabama was the victim of a wagon accident in early 1864, which knocked out his two front teeth.[217] He also recalled a special danger that many a cavalryman encountered riding through thickets and dense foliage — hornets. During the desperate fighting to retake the city of Decatur, Georgia, on July 22, 1864, Ferguson endured both gunshots and hornet stings at the same time.

> The resistance was stubborn, we were driving the enemy back slowly when I rode into a hornets nest, my horse dashed off, almost scraping me off through the thickets. My hat was knocked off and the hornets struck me on my head and neck. I was between two fires [the Yankees and the hornets] altogether in a very hot place. As soon as an opening was reached I threw myself from my horse, landing on my heels and jerked the horse down. The hornets had been

distanced and for a moment or two I did not know which way to go for I had not taken notes of direction in my little excursion. However, a glance at the sun and habits as a hunter enabled me to make the way back to my command. The first man I met had my hat in his hand.[218]

Another deadly hazard was the ever menacing effects of deadly thunderstorms that would pop up in the Southern skies with little warning. It was not uncommon for man and horse alike to be killed by lightning strikes and the savvy rider was always on the lookout for dark clouds as they piled up in the sky, paying special attention to any signs of white-hot bolts of lightning. Private Robinson of Company H described the tragic effects of one such freak storm that occurred in the summer of 1863, killing Lieutenant Nick W. Lovell (his remains were sent home to Tuscaloosa) who had taken refuge under a large stand of oak trees.

> A detachment of some one hundred and fifty of the 2d Alabama Cavalry had been on extended scout within the enemy's lines, then about Corinth [Mississippi]. We were returning to camp at Okolona [Mississippi] when overtaken by a severe thunderstorm. A party of us took refuge in an oak grove under a heavy-topped black-jack. In this group were Capt. Bill Allen, Captain (or Major) Carpenter, Captain McCreary, Captain Peguese [Pegues], and First Lieutenant Lovell. Lieutenant Lovell had just pulled down a limb of heavy foliage to screen his face from the rain when the crash came. Lightning struck the tree, the current supposedly following this limb. Lieutenant Lovell, a gallant young officer, was killed instantly, and the others were all severely shocked, Captains Allen and Peguese [sic] remaining unconscious for some time. All recovered without permanent injury except

Trampling Union Terror

> Captain Peguese [sic] who lost entirely the sight in one eye, and was off duty for some time. Seven of the horses in this squad were killed instantly .... All were fine horses, that of Captain Peguese [sic] being a beautiful and splendid charger, a present to him from the ladies of Tuscaloosa, Ala.[219]

Robinson went on to relate what another lightning bolt did to him and his comrades, who had bundled up in an open field.

> Only a few yards distance, sat in line, close order with knees touching, three men — J.J. Hodges ... old man Harp in the center, and I to the left. The bolt struck Mr. Harp's mount, a fine black mare. Hodges's [sic] horse sprang away to the right, running crazily for some distance. Both horse and rider were severely shocked. My horse fell also, but recovered at once uninjured, and faced the music as though he expected a charge [from the enemy cavalry].[220]

Private Cochrane wrote of his own lightning strike experience in July 1862.

> One of the worst accidents happened in Captain Stacy's company [Company K, Captain Stacy resigned in December 1862]. The lightning struck a large pine tree in his encampment and killed one man, nearly killing two more and hurt about a dozen more. It also knocked down 3 horses and one of them has not got up yet and may die from it.[221]

One thing was certain, the struggle just to survive was very real. As the War dragged on, the sufferings brought about by the cumulative effects of combat, mother nature, accidents, and disease

took a terrible toll on mind and body and a debilitating psychological condition diagnosed by modern medicine as post-traumatic stress disorder (PTSD) meant that even the stoutest of soldiers needed periods of rest and recuperation to maintain their ability to fight effectively.

Part II

Chapter One

Second Alabama Cavalry Regiment

> *[The] regiment was splendidly mounted and owing to the fact that each man was required to furnish their own horse, arms, and equipment, resulted in bringing together a more select body of men than would have been possible under other conditions.*[222] — *J.J. Pegeus*

THE 2ND ALABAMA CAVALRY Regiment was part of the second wave of soldiers mustered into Confederate service, a year after the Southern States declared their independence from the United States. The men who made up the regiment were not the super-ventilating volunteers of 1861, who eagerly signed up for one-year enlistments, a large number of them had previously served in other outfits. One veteran recalled:

> This regiment was composed, both in its officers and men, largely of the experienced and seasoned twelve month volunteers whose term of service and enlistment expired in the spring of 1862.[223]

Others who joined the 2nd Alabama had tried to enlist earlier on in the War only to discover that they were not needed, while some had simply held back until obligated by the 1862 conscription

law. For the latter, it was far better to now volunteer than to be drafted, since all Southern men wished to avoid the odium of being marshalled into service which was "regarded by many as a [negative] reflection on manly honor and patriotism, virtues keenly felt in that day."[224]

James A. Gould at the age of 33 years left his home, a wife, and three young sons behind, near Shelby, Alabama, as he voluntarily enlisted into Captain John Porter West's Company of Alabama cavalry in the spring of 1862. With Gould's two younger brothers, Thomas M. and Loflin Q. Gould, already serving, since 1861, and a third soon to serve (Michael S. Gould), James Gould was the only sibling to join the cavalry.

When Alabama Governor John Gill Shorter authorized the creation of the 2nd Alabama Cavalry in late January or early February 1862, ten full companies were independently organized from various counties in the eastern and central parts of the State. From March to April of 1862, the men said tearful good-byes to wives, children, mothers, and sweethearts and headed to a rendezvous at Montgomery, Alabama.[225] Then, on May 1, 1862, ten companies were consolidated into a full regiment and officially mustered into service as the 2nd Alabama Cavalry Regiment of the Provisional Confederate States of America.[226] Each trooper took an oath to serve for three years or the duration of the War and all proudly touted themselves as forces to be reckoned with.

The allocated slots in the 2nd Alabama were easy to fill as no branch of service was more appealing to recruits than the cavalry. Not only did the young men equate the job with stories of cavaliers and knights of old galloping about on high adventure, the aurora of gallantry and independence offered by cavalry life also played directly to a certain "devil may care" attitude of invincibility. Further, such duty avoided the curse of the infantryman who was obligated to slog about on foot.

Surviving photographs of Rebel cavalrymen taken early in the War often reflect cocky troopers clad in spruced up hats and polished boots, with braces of shiny pistols tucked in wide leather

belts. However, as the hardships multiplied subsequent images reveal that thousand-mile gaze born from the rigors of endless days of campaigning. In many ways, while the draw to the cavalry was almost irresistible, the grueling lifestyle could be far more debilitating than what the foot soldier ever experienced.

Allowed by law to elect their own regimental officers, a process that often saw the favorite, not the competent, taking leadership positions, the men elected Fountain W. Hunter, James Cunningham, and Matthew R. Marks as their new regimental colonel, lieutenant colonel, and major, respectively. The 2nd Alabama's first commander, Colonel Fountain Winston Hunter, was a man of some means and a veteran of the Mexican War (1846-1848). Sensing the growing tensions between North and South, he had organized a local company of Alabama volunteer militia at Selma, on October 24, 1860, and was quite naturally selected by the men as the militia's company commander. When the War started, Hunter's local militia company was quickly put into provisional Confederate service and designated as Company F, Third (3rd) Alabama Infantry Regiment, with Captain Hunter serving as their commander.

Apart from Hunter, Cunningham, and Marks, the other staff and field officers were Major James M. Bullock (adjutant) and Major Robert M. Hill (regimental surgeon).[227] The senior enlisted man was Sergeant Major Frank Boyakin. In chronological order, the officers that would eventually serve during the War as regimental commanders of the 2nd Alabama Cavalry were:

Colonel Fountain W. Hunter
(relieved by court-martial — Florida, 1862)

Lieutenant Leroy Napier
(temporary command — Florida, 1862)

Lieutenant Colonel James Cunningham
(relieved for incompetence — Mississippi, 1863)

Colonel Richard G. Earle
(killed in combat — Georgia, 1864)

Lieutenant Colonel John P. West
(resigned — Georgia, 1864)

Lieutenant Colonel Josiah J. Pegues
(temporary command — Georgia, 1864)

Colonel John N. Carpenter
(surrendered — Georgia, 1865)[228]

Considering the effects of disease, death, replacements, transfers, substitutes, resignations, captures, and desertions a composite roster of every person that ever served in the 2nd Alabama Cavalry Regiment shows a total of 1,942 names, which includes artillery and support personnel.[229] Of course, the true number is actually far higher when one adds the large number of black Southerners that served with the regiment in various capacities.

It is difficult to get an exact snapshot of the strength of the regiment at any given moment since the burn out rate was exceptionally high, particularly in the 1864-1865, period of service. To be sure, the only time the regiment maintained the regulatory 1,000 men was when it was first formed at Montgomery, in the spring of 1862, and sent on a year-long patrol duty in south Alabama and the Florida panhandle.[230]

From a practical matter the term "effective strength" was all that really mattered in terms of readiness. Effective strength referred to the number of troopers on hand that were ready to engage in combat — each man had to be able bodied, properly mounted, and equipped for battle. It is safe to say that at no time after the middle of 1863, when the regiment was sent to north Mississippi for active service, that the *effective* strength for active service was over 600, and by late 1864, to early 1865, it fell dramatically to probably hover around a range of 300.

The need for replacements of both men and animals was constant. For instance, an 1863 advertisement placed in the *Montgomery Daily Advertiser* sought replacements for Company K of the 2nd Alabama Cavalry and provides some insight on the rate of attrition attendant to a typical company in the regiment. When one considers that Company K was seeking new men during a "soft" period when the company was engaged in patrol duty in Florida, the number sought in the advertisement, which was "41," would indicate that over 1/3 of the men in the troop had already been lost or incapacitated in less than ten months' time! Most certainly, starting in the late spring of 1863, to the end of the War when the heavy campaigning occurred, the losses for any given company skyrocketed. Posted by Captain A.P. Wilson from Company K's winter cavalry camp in 1863, in the *Montgomery Daily Advertiser*:

Notice to Volunteers

Camp Lomax, Florida
February 20, 1863

Persons desirous of joining a desirable branch of military service (Cavalry), have an excellent opportunity of doing so by reporting to me at the above named camp. Being desirous of increasing the present number of my company (84) to 125 men, I will receive into my company as many able bodied men with good horses as required (41) to increase it to that number. They will receive the fifty dollars bounty, and all other immunities of volunteers.

Capt. Comd'ing Co. K, 2d Ala. Cav.[231]

Over the course of three years of active duty, the 2nd Alabama Cavalry Regiment was assigned to the following major commands:

Detachment of Observation, District of the Gulf, Department #2 (October — November 1862)

Eastern Division (General Cantey), Department of the Gulf (April — May 1863)

Ferguson's Brigade, General S.D. Lee's Cavalry Corps, Department of Mississippi and East Louisiana (August — December 1863)

Ferguson's Brigade, General Red Jackson's Division, General S.D. Lee's Cavalry Corps, Department of Alabama, Mississippi and East Louisiana (January 1864)

Ferguson's Brigade, General Red Jackson's Division, General Polk's Army of Mississippi (May — October 1864)

Ferguson's Brigade, General Iverson's / General Young's Division, General Joe Wheeler's Cavalry Corps, Department of South Carolina, Georgia and Florida (October 1864 — February 1865)

Ferguson's Brigade, General Young's Division, General Joe Wheeler's Cavalry Corps, General Wade Hampton's Cavalry Command (February — April 1865)

Ferguson's Brigade, Jefferson Davis' Escort (April — May 1865)[232]

A list of the initial company commanders at the regiment's inception (each of these line officers held the rank of captain) and the county where the troopers were drawn from shows the following:[233]

>Company A: Calhoun County, organized near Montevallo and mustered at Montgomery, Alabama, on March 21, 1862 — Captain Richard G. Earle (promoted to colonel and command of the regiment in 1863; killed in action at Kingston, Georgia, 1864). They were known as the "Tom Walker Dragoons" and later as the "Calhoun Guards."
>
>Company B: Shelby County — Captain John P. West (promoted to lieutenant colonel; resigned 1864). Organized near Montevallo, Alabama, in February and March 1862, the company was known as "Mary B. Powell Rangers."
>
>Company C: Greene County — Captain John N. Carpenter (promoted to lieutenant colonel; served as the last regimental commander). Known as the "Greene County Rangers."
>
>Company D: Tuscaloosa County — Captain Josiah James Pegues (promoted to lieutenant colonel and temporarily commanded the regiment). They called themselves the "Warrior Rangers." Pegues, aged 37, personally raised the company and the men came mostly from the vicinity of Sutton Road beyond Northport, Alabama.
>
>Company E: Butler County — Captain Richard W. Carter (promoted to major). This company was accepted into Confederate service at Bethel Church, Alabama.

Company F: Montgomery County — Captain William L. Allen (died in service of disease, Atlanta, Georgia, 1864). They called themselves the "Judge Bibb Rebels."

Company G: Coosa County — Captain William P. Ashley (wounded at Decatur, Georgia, 1864). They called themselves the "Knox Dragoons."

Company H: Monroe County — Captain James. H. McCreary (resigned). They were known as the "Governor Shorter Dragoons," named after the sitting governor of Alabama; also were called the "Ladies Dragoons."

Company I: Montgomery and Dallas Counties — Captain Felix Glackmeyer (resigned). This company was drawn primarily from the militia company raised by Captain Hunter. They called themselves the "Dallas Light Dragoons."

Company K: Montgomery County — Captain Thomas R. Stacey (resigned). They were called "Dillehay's Dragoons."

The 2nd Alabama established its first camp of instruction "on an open field just east of the capital building"[234] in Montgomery, named Camp Stone. Writing forty years after the War, Josiah J. Pegues, commanding officer of Company D, and later promoted to lieutenant colonel,[235] idyllically recalled a fine body of cavalry made up of select Southern men drawn from Alabama's "young planters and sons of planters" who were spirited horsemen of the highest order, "well accustomed to the saddle from boyhood."[236] Colonel Pegues related:

> [The] regiment was splendidly mounted and owing to the fact that each man was required to furnish their own horse, arms, and equipment, resulted in bringing together a more select body of men than would have been possible under other conditions.[237]

The new troopers were no longer civilian horsemen, they were cavalrymen. However, because the very nature and function of military life called for unquestioning obedience to lawful orders, these vigorous Alabamians would have to give up much of their *individual* independence in order to gain the independence of the new nation. Even though the men were already accomplished riders in their own right, they now had to learn the "Army" way of doing things. Thus, of immediate importance for the new regiment encamped on Montgomery's dusty grounds, was to master the drill. The men had to be taught the "language, the habit of obedience to orders, and the many skills needed to perform their duties and stay alive."[238] As previously noted, horse and the man memorized basic cavalry techniques so that on the proper bugle command the correct response was purely reflective.

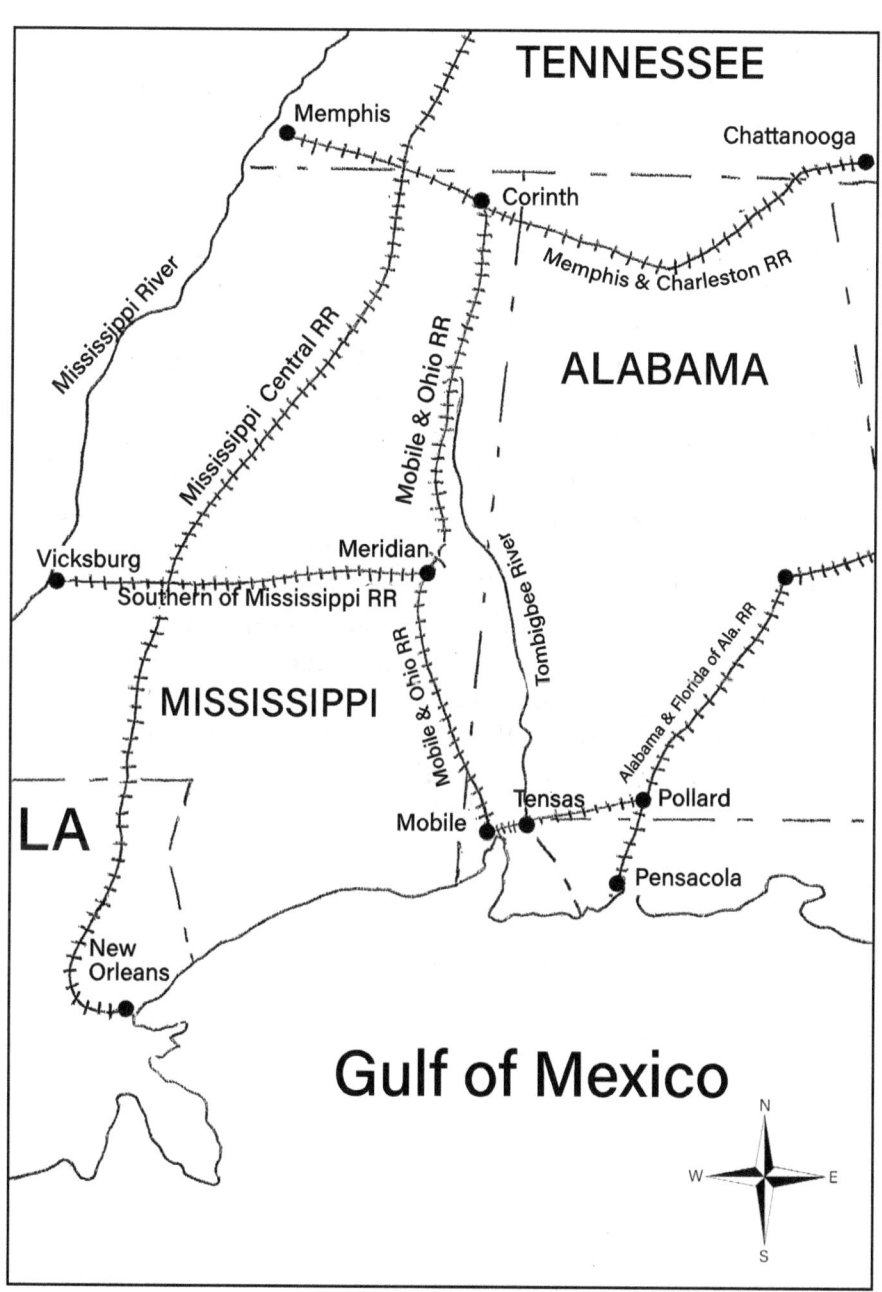

Straddling two railroads, Pollard was a key strong point for the Confederates. Pollard remained in Confederate hands until January of 1865.

Chapter Two

Patrolling the Florida/Alabama Line

"I don't like the service much, pretty much the same as it was in Florida [serving in the 2nd Alabama Cavalry Regiment], plenty duty & no fight."[239]
—Private Alex K. Hall

RAILROADS AND THE TELEGRAPH lines that ran along beside them were the equivalent of modern day interstate highways and the Internet. The South was desperately deficient in both arenas and all sides realized their importance — the Confederacy had to protect their railroads and the Union had to destroy or capture them. In tandem with the South's strategic seaports, the control of this critical infrastructure would largely determine the fate of the Confederacy's quest for independence.

With Grant's string of victories at forts Henry and Donelson in early 1862, and the death of General Albert Sidney Johnston at Shiloh in April 1862, all of Kentucky and Tennessee were abandoned to Federal control and the Rebel forces under P.G.T. Beauregard re-formed near the rail center of Corinth, Mississippi, which they soon thereafter left in favor of Tupelo, arriving at that place on June 2, 1862. By the end of June, Beauregard was out of command and Davis' close friend General Braxton Bragg replaced him, renaming the Army of the Mississippi to its new nomenclature, the Army of Tennessee.

As all these things were developing in the spring of 1862, the 2nd Alabama remained drilling at Camp Stone in Montgomery. The sense of enthusiasm was palatable as the men were very much aware of what was happening, particularly to their northwest at Tupelo. Rumors that the Confederates were concentrating for another huge battle caused most to believe that the 2nd Alabama would be called to do their part in the pending fight. But it was not to be. The 2nd Alabama Cavalry was sent due south, not north.

Reflecting the negative sentiment of the majority of the regiment over the new orders, Captain John P. West published a letter to *The Daily Selma Reporter*:

> To you and all others who may feel an interest of my welfare, and the welfare of the company that I command. It is a well-known fact with the company that my personal feelings, if left with me, would not have situated me in the State of Florida; I would have much preferred going to North Alabama, or Tennessee, to have endured what assistance I could in the great contest now going on, for the Independence of the Confederate States. But when I went into service, I knew that I, as a good officer and soldier, would have to be governed by my superior officers, hence I am here. The regiment to which I belong [2nd Alabama Cavalry] was ordered from Montgomery, and moved to Bluff Springs, Florida, in my absence, being on detached service from Montgomery to Shelby County, to buy guns to arm the company; and when I rejoined the company at Bluff Springs, on the 24th day of June, I was presented with a petition signed by fifty-men out of eighty, of the company that I command to go to North Alabama and report my command to General E. Kirby Smith, commanding a division in east Tennessee.[240]

— Pollard —

When Florida seceded in December 1860, one of the few Federal forts that was not turned over to the Confederates was Fort Pickens situated on the Gulf coast of Pensacola Bay just south of Pensacola, Florida, on the southern tip of Santa Rosa Island. Because Pensacola Bay was secured by the natural protection of barrier islands and boasted a water harbor depth of 20 to 50 feet, the largest ships of the day could easily sail right up to the shore and simply unload. The other three forts, Fort McRee, Fort Barrancas, and Fort San Carlos were given up by the Federals early on, but keeping Fort Pickens meant controlling the harbor port and also opened a window to capturing nearby Pensacola.

For almost a full year, nothing much was done to change the status quo on either side. Supported by gunships, the Union soldiers stayed in their island fortress content to expand the size and scope of the facility while the Confederates watched. Only in the aftermath of a massive two-day artillery duel in November 1861, which saw cannon fire from the ramparts of Fort Pickens and two Union ships nearly destroy Fort McRee, did the Confederate high command realize that an increasing flow of U.S. Navy warships and cargo supply vessels made it impracticable to drive the enemy out. In early 1862, the decision was made to evacuate the area altogether and pull back to a stronger point inland. Predictably, most of the civilian population had already deserted Pensacola leaving empty houses and streets high in weeds and bushes.[241]

The new center of gravity for the entire region was to be the freshly minted Confederate Military Post and Depot at Pollard, Alabama, heretofore a small town named after Charles T. Pollard, president of the Alabama & Florida Railroad. Situated at the crossroad of two rail-lines with its own railroad roundhouse, Pollard was a natural strategic pick.

As the only railroad heading north, the Alabama & Florida ran from Pensacola, straight up to Pollard and then on to Montgomery (the final connecting track was completed in May 1861),[242] a line

the locals jokingly called "the longest way round, the shortest way home."[243] The other railroad running through Pollard was the Mobile & Great Northern that went west to east, connecting to the vital port city of Mobile. This track ran from Mobile on east to Tensas Station (on the Tensas River in Florida), then into Pollard. The distance from Mobile to Tensas Station was 25 miles with another 47 miles from Tensas Station to Pollard.[244] The sole drawback to the Mobile & Great Western was that there was no rail bridge over the formidable Tensaw River which meant that all cargo and passengers had to be detrained and transported across to a waiting train. To that end, steamers operated daily and a fully loaded train on one side of the river could have its contents transported and loaded to a train on the other side "in about one and a half to three hours."[245]

Prior to the Confederate move to Pollard, the town of 200 to 300 people consisted of "[t]wo or three stores, mostly of frame construction," that "sold general merchandise and farm supplies."[246] Like most Southern towns, the post office was in one of the stores. When Confederates arrived in mass during the late spring of 1862, construction activity boomed resulting in hundreds of newly built wooden structures to include warehouses, hotels, hardware shops, sheds, stables, feed stores, hospitals, blacksmiths, administrative offices, and a spacious central tavern providing a much utilized "gathering place for townsfolk and visitors."[247] Situated just outside the city center, innumerable military tents in planned grids sprang up like weeds with the locals more than happy to rent out rooms to those who came to visit the troops or engage in business. In short order, long trains loaded with civilian passengers, troops, and military goods of all sorts arrived from Mobile twice a day. The trains "left Tensas Station at 10:00 a.m. and 4:00 p.m., and arrived at Pollard at 2:30 p.m. and 8:30 p.m., respectively."[248]

— Mobile —

Situated at the head of a large and sheltered bay fed by the Alabama and Tombigbee rivers, Mobile was called the Paris of the Confederacy and even as late as April 1865, a party could always

be found somewhere in the city.[249] Along with sister ports at Wilmington, Savannah, and Charleston, Mobile was a vital port of call for Confederate blockade-runners coming from the Caribbeans to deliver much needed munitions and other war materials to the Southern nation in exchange for cotton and tobacco. The foreign goods — primarily military equipment — were loaded onto trains and steamers for shipment all across the South, and when the city and port of New Orleans fell to a Federal naval assault in 1862, Mobile became the second leading destination for blockade-runners next to Wilmington.

The ring of Federal warships positioned outside of Mobile Bay since May 1861, did little to hinder the faster moving blockade-runners who would easily slip in and out of the bay. Protected by two heavily fortified Rebel forts set on either side of the entrance to Mobile Bay, Fort Gaines on the western tip and the larger star shaped Fort Morgan on the eastern tip, it would take a significant Union armada to break past. In fact, it was not until August 1864, that a huge Union Navy flotilla under Admiral David Farragut was able to blast through the forts and thereby put an end to foreign supplies entering the city.

However, in 1862, the greater fear was the possibility that a large enemy land force might be dropped by transport ships at Union held Fort Pickens and then simply march out following the railroad line to Pollard where they could then either head west to nearby Mobile or north to Montgomery. Indeed, the distance between Fort Pickens and Mobile was only 60 miles.

To address these concerns, Confederate Brigadier General John Horace Forney, commanding the Department of the Gulf in 1861-1862 (with headquarters in Mobile), decided to pull his forces out of Pensacola and concentrate a sizable infantry presence around Pollard. What Forney and his replacement, Major General Simon Bolivar Buckner also wanted was a good regiment of cavalry to serve as their eyes and ears for Federal activity all along the Gulf. Not only did the mobility of cavalry make them ideally suited to guard important points such as rivers, inlets, and water ways, but

they could quickly provide early warning of enemy movements. First, however, Pensacola had to be safely evacuated.

Accordingly, three companies of the 2nd Alabama, A, C, and F, were ordered to proceed to Obannonville, Florida, to be prepared to then join Colonel Sam Jones' 29th Alabama Infantry and assist with the evacuation of Pensacola, while the other companies of the regiment were sent to Bluff Springs, just a few miles below Pollard.[250] Barely had the three companies arrived to set up camp when they were directed to proceed to Pensacola with orders to: (1) provide a strong cavalry picket; (2) destroy the old Confederate camps and fortifications; and (3) perform a rear guard action while the remaining Confederates retreated out of the city. In this they were eminently successful. All military forces and government property got off in good order before the Alabama troopers incinerated the Navy Yard, boats, steamers, storehouses, and factories before departing. Afterwards, on the evening of May 9, the Federals cautiously ventured out of Fort Pickens and occupied the desolate city the next day.

Returning to Bluff Springs, the three detached companies joined the rest of the 2nd Alabama in their new assignment of providing reconnaissance in northwest Florida and south Alabama which included patrolling the three wooden bridges on the railroad between Pollard and Tensas Station.[251] Should these vital bridges suffer heavy damage by enemy raiding parties, the flow of war material and other civilian freight coming from Mobile could be badly disrupted. The railroad bridges were at "Burnt Corn Creek, the Escambia River [Spear's Bridge], and the Perdido River."[252]

Along with infantry troops, other elements of the 2nd Alabama also helped picket defensive positions all down the railroad stops from Pollard towards Pensacola, ranging in order (north to south) as follows: Milner's, Pine Barren, Cooper's Station, Shade's, Bayard's, and Gonzales. Also known as 15 Mile Station, Gonzales was the farthest Confederate held outpost in the Florida panhandle, about 15 miles from the Federal pickets at Pensacola.[253] The iron track and wooden beams of the rail-line from Gonzales Station to nearby

Oakfield Station and then on to Pensacola Station was by then nonexistent as the evacuating Confederates had torn up and carried off all of it. Eventually, all the track between Pollard and Pensacola was pulled up with the 2nd Alabama protecting the work crews.

For eleven months, from early May 1862 to early April 1863, the 2nd Alabama conducted wide ranging scouts all across the Gulf region. Although there were only a few skirmishes with roving enemy patrols, it was constantly impressed on the troopers that they must be vigilant as a huge force of Federals could appear at any time — the threat of larger action was always rumored and the trumpet-tongued cry of wolf concerning Union armies big enough to conquer the entire hemisphere was not uncommon.

To better perform their duties over such a large and open frontier, the regiment split into several different cavalry camps composed of various detachments or companies, with the main body of the regiment remaining at Camp Lomax at Bluff Springs. The other large cavalry camps were located in Baldwin County, Alabama, at Camp Hunter (named after its regimental commander Colonel Fountain Winston Hunter);[254] Camp Lee, just outside of Pollard; and Camp Tattnall (named in honor of Colonel John R.F. Tattnall, the departmental commander at Pollard) in Escambia County near Brewton, Alabama. Far roaming scouting parties were constantly sent out from these various camps in small squads consisting of between ten to thirty horseman.

While the cavalry duty settled into a rather monotonous routine, the Gulf Coast was not a bad duty assignment. In camp the soldiers were accorded "special privileges for visitors ... whereby a steady stream of wives, sweethearts, relatives and friends came and went with little restriction."[255] Private Cochrane admitted that the troopers had it pretty good.

> I am glad to hear that there was some gaiety at home [in Tuscaloosa] for when I was there [on furlough] there was so much sympathy for the "poor Soldier" that the home folks wanted to deprive themselves of

> pleasures because, they, the soldiers, were enduring such hardships so far away. I will assure the friends and acquaintances of Captain Pegues Co. D. 2nd. Ala. Cavalry that there is no need of depriving themselves of pleasure or of grieving themselves about us. We are enjoying ourselves, have plenty to eat, little to do, war houses to live in and nothing to care for. We only have to scout six days out of every eighteen.[256]

Furthermore, since the War had not yet touched this area of the South, the civilians were happy to see the gray troopers riding past their farmsteads and homes. The 2nd Alabama Cavalry represented tangible proof that the government was able to project the necessary force to shield them from the invaders and by largely remaining in their fortified stronghold at Pensacola, the Federals accommodated that perception. The other threat to civilians came from a small area of the Florida panhandle to the northeast of Pensacola which was known as a "common retreat of deserters from the army, Tories [Southerners loyal to the Union], and runaway blacks."[257] Having no desire to fight for either side, these outcasts preyed on the locals and avoided Confederate armed forces.

Of course, the grinning riders on these scouts were happy to accept the praise and any foodstuffs or hospitality offered by the locals with the smiles of the females always bringing out the best. In a December 1862 letter, Private Cochrane wrote from his camp at Brewton, Alabama:

> The last time I wrote a letter to you I was just going on a scout and now I have just come off of another. I had a very pleasant scout this time. I started last Monday so you see I have spent the week out. The day before Christmas I watered my horse with salt water down on the Escambia bay not many miles from Pensacola [Florida].[258]

Terrain in this region of the Deep South was heavily forested with longleaf pine trees. The climate was generally very mild in the late fall and winter, but turned intolerably hot and humid the rest of the year. Of particular note were the frequent spring and summer rains which came in heavy torrents, filling the gullies and soaking the earth, making the dirt roads huge mires of mud that greedily swallowed up shoes and wagon wheels alike.

The Gulf region was thinly populated with people who were strongly with the Confederates. It was not the place of grand plantations as in other parts of the South, nearly all the farms were small and without slaves, and the few families that had wealth were in the timber business. Corn, potatoes, tobacco, cotton, beef, and wool were farmed and raised for home use, but some money could be had by selling cattle, hogs, and sheep. A letter from a member of the 2nd Alabama describing camp life at Camp Hunter and the mission of the regiment was published in the *Mobile Evening Telegraph* on October 24, 1862.

> October 19, 1862. Since my last we have had quite balmy weather. The mornings are indeed brazing, while midday is exceedingly pleasant, being fanned by a gentle breeze from the gulf. We struck our tents at camp near Pollard on Wednesday last and pitched them here [Camp Hunter was located on the Mobile & Great Northern Railroad] on the evening of the same day. This is by far the best locality for a camp that we have ever had, being situated immediately on the railroad in an open field which is considerably elevated above the surrounding country. While the scenery is very fine, and the numerous small pines growing on its surface, which answer the purpose as pickets to stake our horses, the bright crystal stream which flows near the western side of the camp affords the copious supply of pure water for our horses. It is reported here and believed that the Yankee General...

has landed a considerable force at Pensacola. I have no doubt but that the Yankees intend concentrating a large force there and marching a column through west Florida to unite with the east which they have prepared to take Mobile.[259]

Although Rebel horse scouts ventured close to the Federal pickets at Pensacola, sometimes just to taunt them with the sight of a Confederate uniform, Cochrane often reassured his family of the limited danger related to his job.

We are 30 miles from Pensacola and there are a good many soldiers between us and the Yankees at Pensacola. Those below us [other camps of the 2nd Alabama Cavalry] scout to within 3 or 4 miles of Pensacola and we scout to within a few miles of our soldiers so you see we are not in danger for we can get intelligence of the enemy before they get to us.[260]

As stated, the Federals never launched a major military incursion out of Pensacola. Only an occasional Yankee raid would foray out in their small gun boats and transports from Pensacola into either Choctawhatchee Bay or Blackwater Bay (east of Pensacola) and then up the various tributaries where they disembarked to pillage the homes of defenseless civilians and disrupt the local economy. In fact, two significant Yankee incursions occurred, one in 1862, and the other in 1864, utterly destroying the main salt works in the area and causing great suffering to the inhabitants round about. The September 1864, raid destroyed 55 furnaces, 990 kettles and 200 buildings at the Ben Scour Saltworks.[261] While one could reasonably defend the destruction of the salt factories under the Lieber Code's definition of "military necessity," the vast majority of the Yankee raiding parties were about the business of plundering civilian homes and farms for the sole purpose of terrorizing and inflicting misery on families — all in violation of the law of war.

Sometimes the Confederate patrols were lucky enough to catch the thieves red handed. In a letter dated December 10, 1862, Cochrane describes one such episode where the Rebels ambushed an enemy raiding party.

> Lieut. [James M.] Foster [Company D] took a scout of about 30 men and went to Milton and hearing that the Yankees had landed below and were hauling goods and furniture from Arcadia, a little town two or three miles from Milton .... Lieut. Foster had the horses hitched a good way off and the men finding a log crossed over [the creek] and got between the Yankees who were at Arcadia and their boats. Lieut. Foster then made the men lay in ambush, waiting for the Yankees who were hauling furniture to return for another load .... [T]here came along three Yankees from Arcadia in the direction of their boats .... Lieut. Foster rose up and told them to surrender. One of them did and threw his gun from him. Another did like he was going to take his gun from his shoulder to shoot, while the third commenced to back [up] as if to run. I am told that about twenty [Rebel] guns went off at once .... The men then crossed the creek with the Yankee who surrendered with two Enfield rifles which they took. [The other two Yankees were mortally wounded and left behind as a warning].[262]

While the small-scale skirmishes seldom resulted in significant combat, the Alabamians did experience one full-sized regimental movement during their tour of duty that proved to be a source of much embarrassment. Private Cochrane recorded the regiment's reaction to its first "long roll," the bugle call to stand ready for combat. This occurred on the first Sunday of June 1862, just before the regiment broke up into their individual camps across the region.

[J]ust about the time preaching was to commence, the order was given to "saddle up," the Yankees were advancing, some said in 3 miles, others in 15 of us. This was our first alarm and a good many men had pale faces .... We soon formed into line. I mounted my horse which is lame .... After waiting until all the other companies [in the regiment] were ready we started and had to cross a river about a mile from here.[263]

The so-called trouble was actually 40 miles away at Milton, Florida. Colonel Hunter was not then present to command the regiment, so scouts led the next senior commander of the 2nd Alabama, Lieutenant Colonel James Cunningham, on the trek southeast towards the lumber town of Milton, on the Blackwater River, where a large Union force was reported to have landed.[264]

The pace of the march was set at a trot until a little before dark when the lead scouts were hailed down by a hatless man running out of a stand of thick timber causing the entire regiment to draw up. Even in the fading light the scouts immediately recognized him as one of their own. It was the popular and hard charging commander of Company F, Captain "Hell-Roaring" Bill Allen.

Before the War, William Lafayette Allen (1824-1864) was a tough as nails stage coach agent in Butler County, Alabama, where he was known far and wide as "the wildest man in the county," earning the nickname "Hell-Roaring" for his bare knuckled brawling and "outspoken and aggressive" nature.[265] Not only was Allen an imposing figure, he was handsomely debonair ... when he wasn't drunk. With broad shoulders and strong chiseled features an image of Captain Allen taken just before the War — cigar in mouth — perfectly captured a "devil may care" attitude emanating from laughing blue eyes.[266] At a time when no one ever smiled for the camera, Allen smirked!

His wife, Mary Shackelford, was said to be the only person on God's green earth who could stare him down. Although Bill and

Captain "Hell-Roaring" Bill Allen, Co. F, 2nd Alabama Cavalry and Mary Shackelford.

Mary were clearly polar opposites in temperament, she being described as "retiring, quiet, patient and even tempered,"[267] Mary was nevertheless the epitome of Southern womanhood. If not a great beauty, she possessed an indomitable will concealed by an exterior of grace and poise. For his part, Bill was clearly smitten, but it was Mary who chose him. Against her parents' wishes, Miss Shackelford shocked her aristocratic family and wed Bill Allen on November 30, 1854, just one day before she was promised to marry her betrothed and family favorite, a Mr. Bill Wall.

Once wed, all was soon forgiven and the Shackelford clan embraced the charismatic Bill Allen without reservation. In fact, when the War broke out, all four of the Shackelford brothers joined Captain Allen's Company F, 2nd Alabama Cavalry — Lieutenant Joseph Shackelford, Lieutenant Madison Shackelford, Private George Shackelford, and Private Francis Shackelford.

However, on this most unusual occasion, Captain Allen was found without hat or horse and in a state of mind that could only be described as "fit to be tied." Belting out a string of profanities that would make a mule skinner blush, the red-faced officer grumbled that he had barely escaped from a Union ambush the night before at Milton. Allen related that he was one of a group of 15 men, some from his own company, to include the 2nd Alabama's regimental commander, Colonel Hunter, that had gone to Milton for what one source called a "reconnoitering expedition, where they had spent the night."[268] Awakened by scores of Yankees spraying lead into the two-story house and outbuilding barns, it was a matter of "every man for himself," out the doors and windows and into the embrace of a thick black darkness.[269] Allen feared that Colonel Hunter might have been taken prisoner and did not know the fate of the others.

Armed with this intelligence, the mission now was to rescue Colonel Hunter and drive the Federals out of Milton. Private Cochrane obeyed the new orders to the men "to advance without rattling our sabers and to keep silence."[270] Marching several more miles in the darkness, forward scouts spotted a distance light flickering in the deep woods. Supposing it to be enemy scouts at rest, the regiment once again pulled up while a squadron dismounted and crept up on foot to better survey things. Shortly thereafter, one of the scouts returned to the regiment with a wide grin on his face. Instead of a Yankee camp they had found a thoroughly embarrassed Colonel Hunter warming himself by a small flame, minus his $1,000 horse and hat. Hunter was equally relieved to rejoin the command and at first light the next day he personally led the regiment into the town of Milton, but by then the Federals had long since departed, although other scouts came galloping back to report that a Union gunboat was spotted in Blackwater Bay. Once the regiment's supply wagons caught up to feed the command, the troopers proceeded about nine miles further south where they "found a small schooner which we burnt." Scouring the countryside for a few more days reveled no other signs of the enemy and Hunter led the 2nd Alabama back the 40 miles to base.

The local newspapers had a field day with the matter and the *Mobile Register & Advertiser* even suggested that Colonel Hunter and his entire regiment had been bested by a single Federal patrol.[271] While grossly inaccurate, the truth was only slightly less disturbing. The reality was that Colonel Hunter and his small entourage had gone to Milton to be treated by the influential "ladies of Milton" who had "prepared an entertainment for the gallant and unsuspicious Colonel of the Regiment,"[272] after which they were literally caught sleeping (or sleeping it off). Obviously, the group was not on a purely military mission and apparently the enemy had somehow gotten wind beforehand of the ladies' planned reception. Armed with this intelligence and hoping to bag a Confederate full colonel, the Federals acted with commendable spunk by sending out a gunboat full of soldiers to kill or capture him.

From their headquarters at Pensacola the distance was less than 30 miles up Blackwater Bay and into the mouth of the Blackwater River. Anticipating that the Rebels might be watching for a water-based assault at Milton's large wharf, the plan called for a land and water attack to converge on the prominent two-story house where the reception was to be held. Launching out around noon, the Federal gunboat docked near the small town of Bagdad, about two miles south of Milton. Part of the Union strike force disembarked and waited until well after midnight before forming up for action. After a final weapons, check the Union soldiers set out for Milton stealthily moving up the only connecting dirt road. Once the land force departed on foot, the gunboat waited about 30 minutes before slowly pushing out from Bagdad, carrying the other part of the strike force on board. Docking without lanterns was no easy feat but the vessel somehow was able to slip undetected to Milton's wharf and set anchor.

Luckily for the sleeping Confederates, a local sentinel was alerted by the sound of muffled voices and shadowy forms and shouted an alarm just moments before the flash and sound of small arms fire lit up the night. As a hail of bullets slammed into the primary two-story house and adjacent barns, the Rebels instantly realized their tenuous predicament and "everyone went for himself."[273] All

The Thompson House in Milton, Florida. Photo by Jeffrey Addicott.

but two of the cavalrymen were able to escape into the thick woods on foot, leaving behind at least eight horses, one of them Colonel Hunter's prized $1,000 bay. In his company muster roll, the notes which covered the period of April 3 to June 30, 1862, Captain Allen listed the names of four members of his command who were with him at Milton and the loss of valuable horses and equipment.

> Privates [EM.] Bonham, W.D. Courtney, J.F. Williams, and Jonas [illegible] were engaged in a fight with the enemy at Milton, Florida. All of the same came out whilst lost two (2) horses — four (4) saddles, and four (4) bridles.[274]

Even though the entire episode was exaggerated in the constant retelling, it did not sit well with many of the men in the 2nd Alabama and reinforced the general feeling that "Colonel [Hunter] don't seem to know much about his business."[275] Indeed, why was he in Milton and not with his command where he belonged? This question was also on the mind of Hunter's superiors in Mobile and, of course, Colonel Tattnall, the senior commander at Camp Pollard. Private Andrews wrote to his father:

> You no doubt heard of the surprise of Col. Hunter and Capt. Bill Allen by the Yankees at Milton. Though they all got back safe except two privates belonging to Capt. Glackmeyer's Co. [Company I] besides losing eight horses.[276]

The whole episode cast a pale over the regiment and to make matters even worse for the general *esprit de corps*, two companies of the 2nd Alabama Cavalry were soon thereafter detached and ordered to real combat duty in north Alabama, which meant that the remaining eight companies were now required to perform even more patrols in order to close up the gaps in a duty that was already of "the most demoralizing nature."[277] While their fellow

Confederates, to now include two of their own companies, were fighting real battles elsewhere, the bulk of the regiment was still meandering about expansive areas of empty geography. Coupled with the boredom of camp life, this lack of combat activity had a deleterious effect on the officers and men alike. After being transferred to an idle infantry command which also offered him no chances to fight the hated Yankees, Private Alex Hall summed up his time in Company I, 2nd Alabama Cavalry:

> I don't like the [infantry] service much, pretty much the same as it was in Florida [with the Second Alabama Cavalry], plenty [of] duty & no fight.[278]

J.J. Pegues also described the depression associated with the regiment's Gulf Coast tour of service:

> The service in which [the 2nd Alabama Cavalry] was engaged was of the most demoralizing nature and would eventually have required the finest body of troops that could have been gotten together. With no enemy in their immediate front and a long line of coast to watch and the enforced idleness of camp life, necessarily had its effect alike on officers and men.[279]

— Two Companies to Battle —

The two companies of the 2nd Alabama Cavalry sent north in July 1862, were Company A under Captain Richard Gordon Earle and Company K.[280] Along with other Rebel cavalry units also on "partisan ranger service," the Alabamians were tasked with scouting and confronting any movements of enemy forces in the area as Confederate General Braxton Bragg laid ambitious plans to drive the Federals out of Kentucky. The 2nd Alabama sister companies passed through Montgomery on July 9, 1862, and then

"to north Alabama via Selma by steamboats and railroad reaching the neighborhood of Decatur [Alabama]" on 23 July, where Earle's men spearheaded an attack that handedly brushed aside a force of "seventy-five Yankee cavalry."[281] Decatur had been a thriving town of about 800 before the Federals destroyed all but four structures in an April 1862 raid.

Directly assigned to Brigadier General Daniel Ruggles, a West Point graduate and "old Army" soldier who competently commanded a brigade of infantry in the Mexican War, the two companies of the 2nd Alabama saw plenty of brisk action clashing with Federal raiding parties all across north Alabama. In fact, right on the heels of his July 23 skirmish, Captain Earle's company scored a resounding victory over a superior body of Union troops at Trinity Station, about six miles west of Decatur, on July 25. Earle wrote:

> On July 25 at 4 p.m., surprised 200 of the enemy posted at Trinity Station [Alabama]. Killed thirty-one and wounded a large number. Two men and guide killed; thirteen wounded.[282]

The crusty, no nonsense Ruggles was thrilled with his aggressive Alabamians who gained a battlefield reputation that caused some to mistakenly conclude that these new additions were most certainly a part of the cavalry command of the great General Nathan Bedford Forrest himself.[283] Another battlefield success over a body of Yankee cavalry took place on August 7, 1862, when Captain Earle's hard riding Company A joined two other companies of Mississippi troopers in a bloody gun and saber bash near Russellville, about 60 miles west of Decatur. After an unusually vicious brawl that saw one Confederate officer shot dead off his horse, the Federals were ingloriously driven through the town and into the woods, admitting to only one officer and five privates killed and wounded, with an unknown number of blue cavalrymen missing in action. In reality, the enemy tally of dead and wounded was far greater. Captain Earle reported:

Brigadier General Daniel Ruggles.

In compliance with Captain commanding, surprised a train of wagons and escort, killed twenty and captured 125 prisoners, one wagon and team, eighty-six stands of arms. Lost one man killed and one wounded; two horses and equipage lost in action.[284]

While small in scope, the lopsided engagement caught the attention of Bragg and his headquarters issued a rare congratulatory dispatch dated August 21, 1862:

> A portion of our cavalry, consisting of the companies of Captains Earle [Company A, Second Alabama Cavalry], Lewis & Roddey, led by Captain Roddey has

made another brilliant dash upon a superior force of the enemy, resulting in their utter discomfort and the capture of 123 prisoners. The judgment and previous dispositions exhibited high military skill. The vigor and boldness of the attack is a striking example of the spirit that now animates our cavalry which is fast making them the terror of our invaders.[285]

Unfortunately, much to Earle's consternation, when General Bragg cautiously moved his army into Kentucky in the fall of 1862, the two companies of the 2nd Alabama were ordered back to their regiment which was still assigned to the Gulf. Passing through Selma they reposted to the regiment on October 14, 1862.

— Disaster in Command —

More than any other human endeavor, war requires strict physical and psychological preparation, certainly for the men, but especially for the officers that lead them. This is particularly true when it comes to facing the stresses of combat, but also applies when dealing with the dullness of inactivity which can present its own set of challenges. When boredom and frustration beset the undisciplined, particularly the idle of mind and body, even the smallest of tensions can become crisis events. It was in just such an environment that the officer leadership of the 2nd Alabama Cavalry fell apart at the seams. On the surface, the reason for the breakdown seems to have been a case of pure pettiness over a game of cards, though the root causes sprang from those insidious mental attitude sins of jealousy and arrogance. In fact, from the very start of their assignment to the Gulf, the men of the 2nd Alabama sensed that their field grade officer chain of command was quite worthless. The vast majority of the rank and file were patriotic and itching to fight, even if the senior leadership had far different ideas about what "patriotism" constituted. Private Andrews summed it up in a June 28, 1862, letter home.

[T]he fact of leaving my bosom companions and kind mother and loving sisters, in whose company I have passed some of the happiest moments of my life, then suddenly to be hurried away from their midst, and be brought to this lonely place [the main 2nd Alabama cavalry encampment at Bluff Springs, Florida], to be separated from them — and probably forever, and besides endure all the privations incident to camp-life has cast a gloom of sadness over my spirits, which no train of reasoning can cast aside. Yet when I remember Butler's [Union General Ben Butler who occupied New Orleans in early 1862] infamous proclamation [targeting Southern females], when I remember all the wrongs my beloved country have suffered at the hand of an indignant and licentious horde of vandal Yankee soldiery, I feel as if I would be proving miscreant to every sense of honor that should characterize a Man, if I would remain at home. But then when I look around and observe the inefficient commanders placed over us, who seek only their own aggrandizement and also observe the menial manner in which they treat the privates because they are clothed with a little brief authority [emphasis added].[286]

Apart from Andrews' pointed observation about the lack of command skills in the senior leadership, there is also the added matter of the so-called "code of honor" of the gentleman, which every Southerner keenly felt[287] (and still does) — what Andrews called that "sense of honor that should characterize a Man." While this ante-bellum code advocated self-restraint, virtue, and reason coupled with physical courage, it also recognized the importance of possessing impeccable manners, respect for hierarchy, and an obligation to protect one's good name as well as the reputation of family, particularly the female members. Indeed, to insult "his

wife, mother, or sister was to assault the man himself."[288] On the other hand, the mechanics of how one went about protecting one's *name* was where the code was often distorted. Exhibited in every way by the magnanimous Robert E. Lee, the true gentleman tended to disregard personal insults and embrace instead a higher moral imperative to do "a right thing in a right way" as the proper formula to exercise power over others and, more importantly, over oneself.[289] In this respect, Lee embodied the loftiest principles of Southern aristocracy, deeming it perfectly fit not only to give up himself for the public interest,[290] but to treat insults with forbearance. As one commentator on the Southern code of honor observed about Lee:

> As a means of contrasting the ideal model of gentility with the ordinary styles to which most Southerners were loyal, the familiar example of Robert E. Lee seems the most efficient. We shall not meet in these pages many others of his stature or moral bearing. Yet it is important to remember that such figures ... set a standard that affected Southern life far out of proportion in their number.[291]

While the arrogant place paramount emphasis on responding to *any* offense or perceived slight as a dire insult that demands immediate "satisfaction," this was a twisted distortion of the code. In this self-centered interpretation, seemingly harmless disputes can quickly escalate out of control. In sum, the Christian mandate to mentally "turn the other cheek" when personally insulted is *anathema* to the arrogant who are always hypersensitive about self and insensitive about others.

Charged with setting examples to those under their authority, officers might pay lip service to the honor code, but individual passions, arrogance, and self-interest would sometimes get the better of them. As with all armies throughout history, the officers in Southern regiments were not immune to jealousies and rivalries which often seemed to accelerate in direct proportion to one's climb

up the ladder of rank and while such is the common fare of all mankind, the vociferous impact of deep-seated and unrestrained arrogance always spells disaster to military efficiency.

On its face, the leadership crisis for the 2nd Alabama Cavalry started with the arrest and subsequent court-martial of two of its senior leaders — the regimental commander, Colonel Fountain Winston Hunter, and Major Matthew R. Marks. The arrest of Hunter, ordered by his superior Colonel John R.F. Tattnall, Commander, Detachment of Observation, District of the Gulf, took place in mid-November 1862, only a few months after the cavalry regiment had settled into their various winter camps on the Florida/Alabama line.

With Colonel Hunter's judgment skills already badly tainted by the earlier debacle at Milton, Private Cochrane correctly observed on November 25, that the initial arrest of Hunter involved an earlier dispute with Tattnall about command assignments. Instead of apologizing to Tattnall, Colonel Hunter penned "an insulting letter" to him on November 17, 1862, for which Tattnall had Hunter arrested and brought back to Pollard to await formal charges for disrespect to a superior officer. Apparently, Major Marks was also caught up in the matter.

> Col. Hunter is under arrest and Major Marks has not got out of trouble yet. A few weeks ago Col. Hunter allowed the Lieut. Colonel [Cunningham] to come over here [the camp of Company D at Brewton, Alabama] and take command of this post over Captain Pegues. Col. Tatnall [sic] heard of it and sent a courier over there in the night ordering Lieut. Colonel Cunningham back to his regiment immediately and probably said something to Col. Hunter for sending him over here. Colonel Hunter then wrote an insulting letter to Colonel Tatnall [sic] (who you know is acting General) for which Colonel Tatnall [sic] had him put under arrest. You see now

Colonel Fountain Winston Hunter.
Photo Courtesy Alabama Department of Archives & History.

what officers we have in our regiment. Some of them are almost always in a fuss.²⁹²

While Hunter was awaiting disposition of the allegations at a court-martial set for December 9, he was allowed freedom of movement at Pollard and on the night of December 2-3, found himself engaged in an all-night poker game with Major Marks and others. At the conclusion of the gaming, an altercation erupted over the settlement of losses, resulting in Colonel Hunter striking Marks and the Major then drawing his pistol and shooting Hunter in the arm.²⁹³

Given that drunkenness was a constant bane of the Army, what one observer politely called "a personal difficulty between he

[Hunter] and Major Marks"[294] was undoubtedly fueled by alcohol. Not surprisingly, the salacious incident caught the attention of the papers to include the *Montgomery Weekly Mail*.

> Rencounter Near Pollard,
>
> We regret to hear of a difficulty which occurred between two officers of the second Alabama cavalry regiment, about a week since, near Pollard, on the Alabama and Florida rail road. Our informant states that Major Marks shot Colonel Hunter in the arm, inflicting a flesh wound, but from which he will soon recover. Further particulars were not related to us.[295]

Commanding a regiment was a deeply challenging duty and mandated the highest levels of integrity and honor. In each of these respects, Colonel Hunter had failed. He was tried by general court-martial on December 9, 1862, and one of the three charges leveled against him was a violation of Article 6 of the Confederate States Articles of War, for his earlier conduct towards Colonel Tattnall.

> Art. 6. Any officer or soldier who shall behave himself with contempt or disrespect toward his commanding officer, shall be punished, according to the nature of his offence, by the judgment of a court-martial.[296]

In addition to being charged with Article 6, Hunter was also charged with Article 24 (making reproachful or provoking speeches and gestures) and Article 83 (conduct unbecoming an officer). Major Marks was cited for two violations of military law: Article 24 and Article 99 (all crimes not capital to the prejudice of good order and military discipline).

Both officers were found guilty of all charges and sentenced to be discharged from the army.[297] Mercifully, for all involved, they were sent home pending a formal approval of the proceedings by Richmond, which occurred on April 4, 1863,[298] when both

were formally "allowed to tender their resignations" and were immediately "dismissed from the Service of the Confederate States."[299]

Needless to observe, the entire episode caused much agitation in the regiment, but it was only the beginning of an even greater set of disciplinary problems. While Hunter was awaiting his court-martial, the company commanders in the 2nd Alabama speculated about who would be chosen to take command of the regiment, speculating that Lt. Colonel Cunningham, who would be the normal candidate, had fallen into disfavor for the job due to his close personal association with Hunter. Strangely enough, however, someone not even assigned to the regiment was also interested — the senior drill officer at Camp Pollard, Lieutenant Leroy Napier.

Prior to the War, Napier was an officer in the regular U.S. Army and had been brevetted to the rank of Major, which meant that he was not officially confirmed by Richmond to the field grade rank, only temporarily assigned to it. Angling for a way to advance his career, Napier somehow got himself appointed by Colonel Tattnall as the new "interim" commander of the regiment.

Napier's ascension to the command slot was met with wild protests from the company commanders of the 2nd Alabama who were all captains and therefore senior in rank to Lieutenant Napier. Captain Allen, never shy about his opinions, was the loudest critic and vowed to ignore any orders from Napier. Even Captain Richard Earle lodged a personal objection and refused compliance. Armed with his appointment papers, Napier responded by placing the three most outspoken protestors, Allen, Earle, and Carpenter (Company C), under arrest for violating Article 6 of the Articles of War and confined them at Fort Morgan, on Mobile Bay, to await military trial. Thankfully, Colonel Tattnall quickly realized the firestorm of his own making and rectified the matter by reliving Napier and appointing Lt. Colonel James Cunningham as the new regimental commander. Allen and Carpenter were soon thereafter acquitted at court-martial and reinstated to their positions in the regiment.

Earle was not put on trial. Instead, Captain Earle was ordered to go home and await his fate which would be determined by the War Department in Richmond. A subsequent article in Montgomery's *The Weekly Advertiser* provided the public with an overview.

> The commissioned officers [the Captains] protested, and Captain's Earle [commanding Company A], Allen [commanding Company F], and Carpenter [commanding Company C], were subsequently put under arrest and kept at Fort Morgan [at Mobile Bay, Alabama] for several months [it was several weeks]. By the intervention of friends they eventually obtained a hearing before a court martial at Mobile, and all were immediately acquitted and reinstated except Captain Earle, who was allowed to return to his home in Calhoun [Calhoun County, Alabama] until the decision in his case could be sent to Richmond.[300]

Due in part to his former high rank in the Mexican War and the Alabama State militia, Captain Earle's case was treated differently than the others. Although possessing no formal military training, he learned well the business of combat from hard service in the Mexican War as a Lieutenant Colonel in the First Alabama Volunteer Regiment,[301] and in 1858, Earle was promoted to the rank of Major General of the Alabama State militia. Coupled with a strong penchant for duty, Earle was the epitome of the Southern gentleman. He was fearless, gallant, and competent.

Indeed, anyone who met Richard Earle once never forgot him. Born in South Carolina in 1815, to a prominent family, Earle was tall, thin, and well-proportioned in frame. Many remarked that the full head of hair which he wore long and combed straight back served to accentuate his smoldering, hawk-like eyes and well-set angular nose. According to Union Lieutenant Colonel Charles Wills, who saw Colonel Earle's lifeless body just after he was killed in combat in May 1864, he was "a noble looking man; looks 50 years old,

Left: Colonel Richard Earle, Commander, 2nd Alabama Cavalry, circa 1858. Right: Photo of Mrs. Earle Found in Colonel Earle's Uniform Pocket at his Death in May 1864, Kingston, Georgia. Photo Courtesy Alabama Department of Archives & History.

and has a fine form and features."[302] The only known photograph of Earle was taken circa 1860, and depicts a stern demeanor in which intellect, great force, and the pride of thought are apparent. But there was more. Something in his bearing suggested a firm allegiance to the most sacred of all the manly traits — duty. Having proven himself an officer of excellence during detached service in north Alabama, Earle had easily won the respect and admiration of both subordinates and superiors alike.

Before he was a man, however, Earle was a boy. Like many boys of the South, he was raised in a strong Bible believing Christian home that yielded finely honed manners and rigid ethics. Though raised and educated in South Carolina, where he excelled in the study of law, the ambitious 21-year-old Earle moved west in 1836, and settled in the thriving city of Jacksonville, in Alabama's Calhoun County, where he wholeheartedly dedicated himself to the practice of commercial law. By the mid-1850's, not only had Earle earned a

sterling reputation in the region, he had amassed a small fortune from brokering land deals and other import/export business activities that often took him to Mobile, Atlanta, Savannah, and New Orleans. Although his work-related associations brought him into contact with numerous eligible females, Earle nevertheless remained a bachelor for many years before finally setting his sights on a strikingly beautiful widow in Jacksonville, who already had a young daughter by the name of Sarah E. Williams. Earle proved loving and chivalric in the best Southern tradition and although the happy marriage never produced any children, he cherished Sarah as his own and remained a devoted husband and father.

Once released from confinement over the Napier matter, Captain Earle left Fort Morgan and went home to Jacksonville as ordered, facing a future that promised nothing. It was unsettling.

He was not an old man, yet he was not a young man either. At 47, the hope of his supporters was that this gray-haired hero would not only be fully exonerated but that he would be elevated in rank and take command of the 2nd Alabama Cavalry. After all, it was common knowledge that the sole reason Earle had not been commissioned as a field grade officer at the start of the War was due to political infighting between President Davis and the Alabamian Confederate Secretary of War, Leroy Pope Walker. Walker, a longtime and close personal friend of Earle, had early on forcefully urged Davis to promote Earle to the regular rank of full colonel.[303] He was not alone. In fact, a March 1861 letter signed by 35 prominent members of Calhoun County also called on Davis to promote then General Earle (Alabama State militia rank) to colonel in the nascent Confederate military and give him command of an Alabama regiment. The letter candidly recognized that Earle was not a graduate of West Point like Jeff Davis, but stated in part: "He has not what may be termed a military education, but possessing a native talent and genius to command and considerable military skill."[304]

Unfortunately, Walker was not on Jeff Davis' good side and Davis succumbed to short-sightedness in opposing anything Walker suggested, in this case, refusing to promote Earle regardless

of the obvious indicators of great potential. The friction between the two culminated with Tom Walker himself being replaced as Secretary of War.

When Earle was denied a colonelship he did not react to the news with bitterness or self-pity. Quite the contrary. He rolled up his sleeves and spent the remainder of the year using his own funds to raise a "horse company and personally outfitting the unit."[305] When Governor Shorter authorized the creation of the 2nd Alabama Cavalry Regiment, Earle was elected as the company commander of Company A and his aptly named "'Tom Walker dragoons' paraded 109 men strong in Jacksonville on March 8, 1862,"[306] with Captain Earle proudly riding at the head of the troop.

Now, as Earle sat idle at home in Jacksonville pondering his future, things and events were being set in motion that would not only bring him back to his old regiment, but see him as their greatest chieftain. In the interim, the regiment had to endure the ridiculous Lieutenant Colonel Cunningham.

From Company I's cavalry camp in Baldwin County, Alabama, Private Alex K. Hall expressed the embarrassment of the senior officer meltdown to his mother noting that the new replacement regimental commander, Cunningham, was also not well respected. On December 8, 1862, Hall wrote:

> Colonel Hunter has been under arrest two or three weeks, which leaves Lieutenant Colonel Cunningham in command, he has come down on us pretty tight. I am on guard duty every other night besides other duties .... The mail is about ready to go so I will close. Give my love to all, I hope Charley is better.[307]

For the next several months, as the men performed their patrol duties in the coastal region they became increasingly dissatisfied with both their mundane mission and mundane commander. News of the spectacular December 1862 Confederate cavalry raid, which

destroyed the Federal supply depot at Holly Springs, Mississippi, and forced General U.S. Grant to pull his forces away from Vicksburg only served to amplify their discontent. Duty was light, yet with no prospect of meeting the hated Yankees in combat only quarrels and strife passed for the order of the day. Now reinstated to his previous position, Captain Allen recorded two court-martials during December 1862, in his Company F:

> We have had one scout in November, 30 miles and on Dec. 5th for the same distance [30 miles], have lost 4 horses within the last months for want of sufficient feed. [J.A.] Sharp and E.M. Bonham [Bonham was the Company F blacksmith], privates of the company, tried by court martial. Sharp acquitted and Bonham sentenced to 30 days hard labor without extra pay.[308]

The dullness would soon end. With the coming of spring 1863, great pressures were again building to the north at Vicksburg, pressures that would finally catapult the full regiment into combat.

Chapter Three

SHAM FIGHTING IN NORTHEAST MISSISSIPPI

"All the 2d [Alabama Cavalry] needed was an officer to lead them, or rather go with them into the fight, and not to lead them up to within four or five miles of the enemy and halt, wait until the enemy got a safe distance and then commence a pursuit, as has been done on some former occasions [the fights at Palo Alto and Kings Creek]."[309]   — *G.H.A. Letter*

WITH THE ARRIVAL OF THE SPRING of 1863, Grant had licked his wounds over the Holly Springs debacle and was once again pushing out a huge land force towards the prized Confederate base at Vicksburg. Deeply concerned about what the warm weather would bring in terms of new Federal attacks, the Rebel War Department redoubled efforts to reinforce Lieutenant General John C. Pemberton, Commander, Department of Mississippi and East Louisiana. Pemberton controlled scattered Confederate forces in Mississippi numbering no more than 50,000, to include a permanent garrison of 24,000 men hunkered down at Vicksburg. More troops would be needed to both hold Vicksburg and keep Grant's well-equipped 100,000 plus infantry at bay. As part of the effort to consolidate all available assets, Richmond wired Major General Buckner in Mobile to send a full regiment of cavalry to north Mississippi at once.

Major General S.B. Buckner, Commanding [Department of the Gulf], at Mobile

Richmond, May 1, 1863

If there is a cavalry regiment at Pollard, Ala. [the Second Alabama Cavalry], send it at once to Mississippi, to report to General Pemberton. Its place will be supplied by troops raised by Colonel Clanton, who has been instructed to that effect. If there is no such at or near Pollard, then send some other cavalry regiment of your command immediately to Mississippi.[310]

S. Cooper,
Adjutant and Inspector General

The next day, May 2, 1863, General Buckner responded by telegraph to the War Department that he had already sent the 2nd Alabama Cavalry into north Mississippi per an earlier request in late March from General Pemberton. On March 28, 1863, the 2nd Alabama had been ordered to report to the Department of Mississippi and East Louisiana, to be placed under Brigadier General Daniel Ruggles' independent command[311] then headquartered at Columbus, Mississippi. At the time, Ruggles was responsible for the defense of northeastern Mississippi and most of his dispersed command of about 2,500 consisted of a grab-bag of assorted cavalry regiments with some infantry.[312] In responding to Richmond, Buckner also voiced concern about his own dwindling forces:

> I sent nearly a thousand cavalry [the Second Alabama Calvary Regiment] from Pollard to General Pemberton several weeks ago ... only three small companies [of cavalry] remain to guard the coast towards Pascagoula [Florida].[313]

In fact, on April 4, 1863, when the 2nd Alabama departed Florida, the entire Confederate Eastern Division, Department of the Gulf, was left with only "756 Infantry, 132 Artillery and 320 Cavalry."[314] For their part, however, the 2nd Alabama was more than pleased to get away and the column made a respectable 45 miles in two days, reaching Mount Pleasant, Alabama, late on April 5, where they were greeted by enthusiastic crowds waving small Southern flags and cheering until hoarse.

Given that the regiment consisted of about 950 men, the individual companies were split up to wait their turn to ride boats up the Tombigbee River to Columbus, a 500-mile journey north. To be sure, with all their gear packed aboard privately owned steamboats contracted out by the government, the men, horses, and baggage made excellent time, even if the conditions onboard were miserably hot and overcrowded. Still, everywhere they went on the journey — either by land or water — the men were treated like heroes. While Company D was camped at Choctaw Bluff, Alabama, on 7 April, waiting for their turn on one of the transports, Private Cochrane described the tumultuous reception the Alabamians received to include townspeople pressing all sorts of delicacies into the troopers' hands. Cochrane was greatly impressed by their generosity and patriotism.

> [W]e will have to wait for a boat until tonight or tomorrow morning to take us to Columbus as the other boats have been filled with other portions of our regiment and sent on .... An old lady waved her handkerchief at us and we cheered her and she said, "God bless you all." She gave us a bundle of fodder and a cigar apiece .... Another man gave us a cigar around, not to speak of the numerous handkerchiefs waved by the young ladies. You see we are leaving Florida's world of pines where people can hardly make a living .... The order has been given to saddle up so I must close.[315]

After disembarking at Columbus, the individual companies rode the 30 miles north to the rendezvous point of Cotton Gin Port, Mississippi. Situated on the east bank of the Tombigbee River, the village was a long established Indian trading post which now served as a Confederate supply depot and gathering spot. As the troopers waited for the arrival of their fellows, Private Robert Wardroper of B Company, described the campsite as "very disagreeable being flat and other forces being encamped there before."[316] Furthermore, movement in the camp was greatly restricted due to the number of whiskey distilleries round about. Wardroper noted:

> We have stricter rules today than ever before, nobody passing outside the lines without a pass. Whiskey, I think is the cause as there are several stills about. There is one government one in sight but they neither sell nor give.[317]

Pegues recalled that about the "first of April [it was actually closer to mid-April 1863]" most of the companies of the "2nd Alabama Cavalry met at the "Cotton Gin Port above Aberdeen [Mississippi]."[318] In just over a week, with the help of steamboats, at least eight of the companies had traveled out of south Alabama and Florida and into northeast Mississippi. Company G was the last to arrive and would not join the regiment until April 22.

General Ruggles was anxious to personally review his new regiment. After all, he had been much impressed with the excellent work done in the previous year by the two detached companies. Much to his chagrin, however, Ruggles was shocked by the poor condition of his new troopers. The officers and men were in want of proper uniforms, the horses in bad shape, saddle/equipment repair sorely needed throughout, and the bulk of the "Second Alabama [were] in an unarmed and demoralized state."[319] Neither was Ruggles impressed with the pusillanimous looking regimental commander, Cunningham.

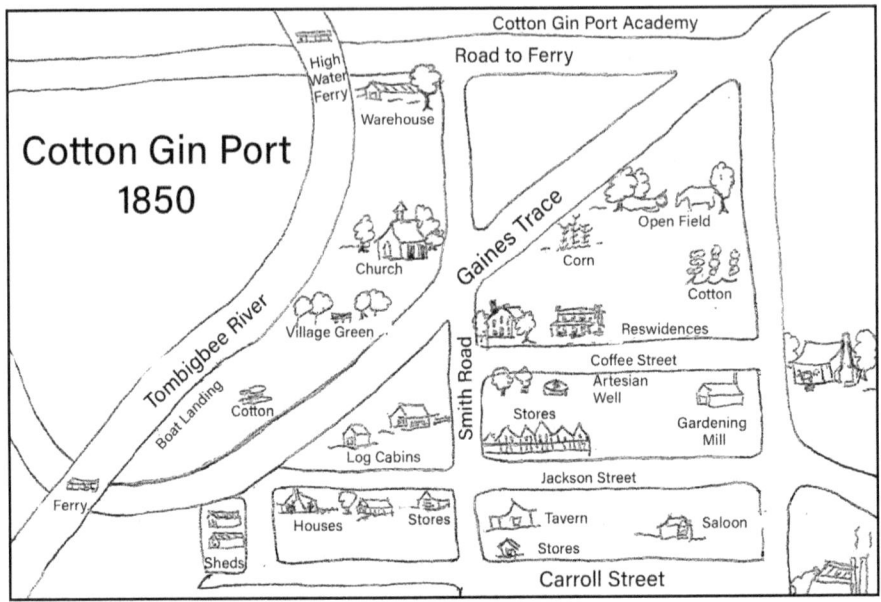

Cotton Gin Port, Mississippi.

Nevertheless, the weathered general moved quickly to rectify the most immediate problem and ordered his ordnance officer to arm the Alabamians with efficient weapons. It was here at Cotton Gin Port, or nearby Camargo a few miles to the northwest, where the regiment settled at Camp Johnston, that many of the troopers received for the first time serviceable arms and accoutrements. The Confederate ordnance department supplied about half the regiment with the best cavalry weapons of the day (for Rebel cavalry). Four companies of the 2nd Alabama Cavalry were issued brand new six-shooter Navy Colt revolvers along with top of the line London manufactured British Enfield muzzle-loading carbines. The cavalry carbines had been brought in by blockade runners through Mobile and stamped on the wooden stock with the distinctive "*JS* over Anchor" mark. Others received the infantry's standard weapon, the .57 caliber rifle. Captain Pegues recalled that his and three other companies happily discarded their old worn-out shotguns and smooth bore long-guns for the state-of-the-art weapons.

> [We] were armed with English carbines [Enfield] of the best type then made and navy [Colt revolver] pistols, and the balance of the regiment were given long range rifles [Enfield or Springfield .57 caliber].[320]

Pegues observed that a good portion of the regiment was now "well equipped with effective weapons" for cavalry combat duty to include a conflagration of "carbines, sabers, and pistols."[321] With great armies maneuvering for position along the Mississippi River, those lucky enough to be issued the new instruments of war were boosted in spirits, while the rest anticipated similar blessings.

Again, the situation for the Confederacy at this point in the War was tight but still hopeful. With the fall of both Memphis and Corinth, not only was Tennessee overrun, but large portions of northern Mississippi became untenable to hold and had to be abandoned, making the low-hanging fruit of Vicksburg — the Gibraltar of the South — even more vulnerable. Tenacious as a bulldog, for months Grant had been probing and pressing his massive army towards Vicksburg without success. Grant now shifted his blue juggernaut to the western side of the Mississippi River, intending to re-cross at some point below Vicksburg and then launch a full-scale attack from the south. More than ever, effective Rebel cavalry was needed to scout out the enemy's movements and to confront the raiding parties coming down into Mississippi from Union bases along the Tennessee border.

Indeed, in order to stir confusion within the Confederate command system as to his true intention and also further demoralize the civilian population in the area, Grant ordered increased cavalry terror raids into northern Mississippi and Alabama, starting in the spring of 1863. As General Ruggles noted:

> [T]he enemy's disclosed new signs of life along the northern Mississippi border [with Tennessee], and made constantly recurring incursions within the then Confederate lines, with the apparent intent of

impeding the concentration of Confederate troops in any attempt to relieve Vicksburg.[322]

With the question of Cunningham's unproven leadership capabilities a huge factor, the 2nd Alabama entered into a new phase of their regimental history. They were now smack dab in the seat of conflict and would soon be tested in fiery crucibles of deadly combat. As in the Gulf Coast tour of duty, the 2nd Alabama was assigned a long stretch of geography between the two sprawling armies, just above the rich grain farms that were absolutely vital in keeping the animals and soldiers of the western Confederacy in service. Along with Alabama and Georgia, central Mississippi was the food basket of the Confederacy.

The primary difference in duty was that instead of encountering a handful of marauding Federals that might venture out from Pensacola, they now faced off against thousands of heavily armed Union cavalry just to their north, poised like rattlesnakes to strike out at any time from their well-fortified dens. The only other regular Confederate cavalry regiment to assist them was the hard fighting 2nd Tennessee under the leadership of a brilliant young officer by the name of Clark R. Barteau. While Pegues recalled in exaggerated terms the new task General Ruggles assigned to the 2nd Alabama, which he claimed ran almost across the entire State of Mississippi, when it was only half that distance, the assigned mission was still quite daunting. Pegues recalled:

> The service that it was now called upon to do was such that would have tested the courage and endurance of veteran troops. For several months this regiment and only one other, the 2nd Tennessee Cavalry Regiment, under Col. [Clark R.] Barteau, had nearly one hundred miles of front to guard extending from Iuka and Corinth [Mississippi] on the east, and nearly to Memphis on the west, from which raiding parties of the enemy were constantly on the move at

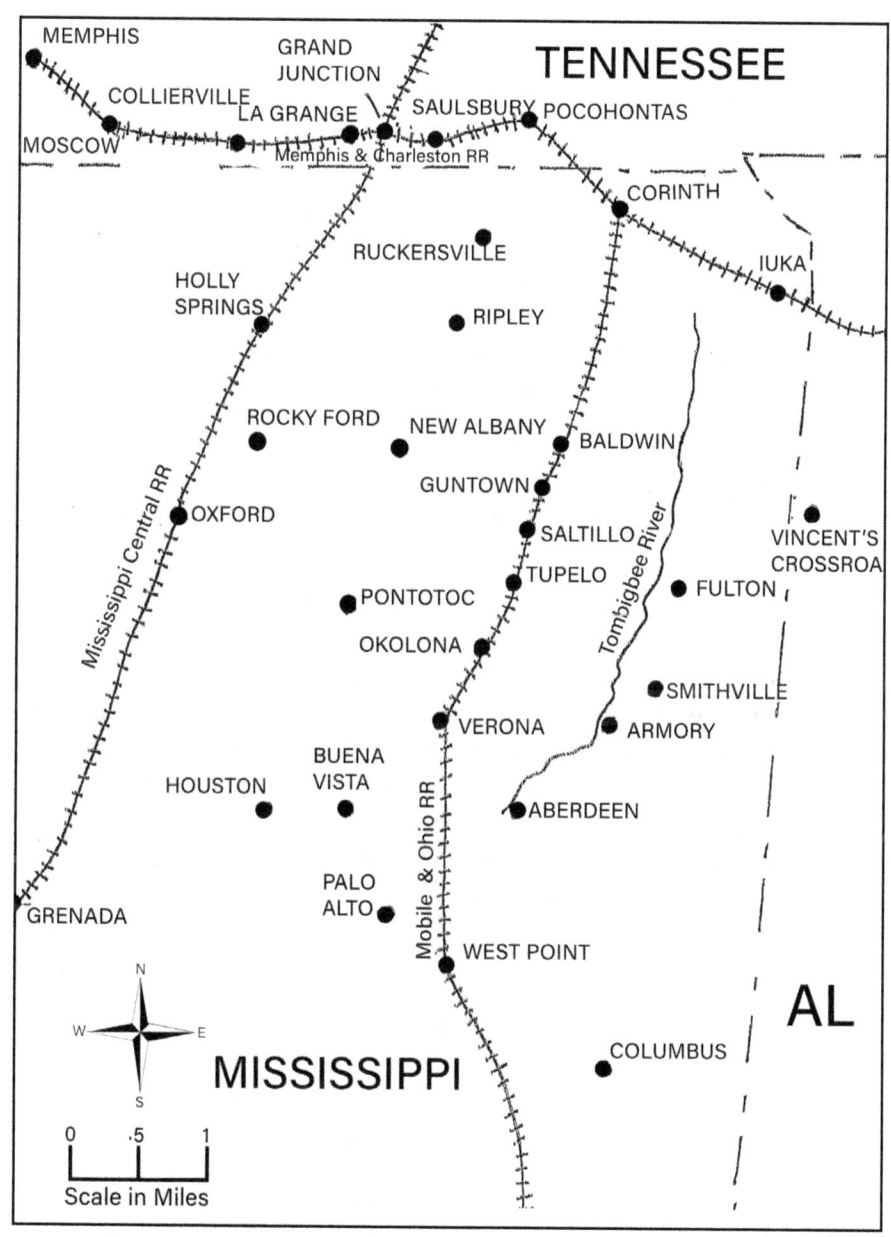

2nd Alabama Cavalry in Northeastern Mississippi.

all times far superior to our own troops in men, and munitions of war with infantry support.[323]

In reality, General Ruggles' cavalry was simply too small to project a stable shield against Federal raids. Consequently, the Alabama and Tennessee troopers concentrated on protecting an area just past the town of Pontotoc and then across to Verona, Fulton, Smithville and the Alabama line. Besides the State cavalry militia regiments which were not under his command, the only other cavalry that Ruggles could call on was an undersized force led by Brigadier General James Chalmers whose own mission was to watch the Union Army of the Tennessee ambulating about the western parts of northern Mississippi. As early as June 1862, Ruggles wrote from Pontotoc:

> [M]y [cavalry] force is too small to enable me to occupy permanently any line of defense in advance of Pontotoc, Verona, Fulton, and Smithville, although my detachment [cavalry] scouts much higher up [towards Tennessee].[324]

In addition to a lack of cavalry, General Ruggles also had very little in terms of effective infantry to employ. Almost all of the best Confederate ground troops had been stripped from him and sent to defend Vicksburg. Ruggles accurately reported the predicament and the challenges:

> The interests involved in the protection of this district [northern Mississippi] have been and still are so great, comprising the great grain growing region, the several important towns, and the main railroad communications by which supplies are forwarded to the armies, that my means are quite inadequate.[325]

After the pattern of the Gulf assignment, the 2nd Alabama was split into several outpost camps from which small scouting patrols would fan out far to the east, west, and north. Unlike the Gulf terrain which was piney and flat, the landscape in north Mississippi was very hilly and densely forested, with countless gullies, creeks, and streams that regularly overflowed into impenetrable marshes. The few roads that then existed were hardly more than narrow Indian trails, extremely difficult to navigate let alone see through due to the abundance of trees. Long-range views of the surrounding countryside were almost non-existent.

Nevertheless, even with the new challenges in Mississippi, the men of the 2nd Alabama had no sense of defeatism, they were too preoccupied with how well they would perform in combat to mull over the past. Now that they were united and on the path to being properly armed, there was a shared hope that redemption awaited. The predominate question: Would they be successful as a fighting unit? Or more specifically, did Lieutenant Colonel Cunningham possess the skills necessary to lead them to victory on the battlefield?

As it turned out, fitness and competency issues were not just an issue for the 2nd Alabama. The disjointed Confederate forces then operating in northern Mississippi were in a state of total disarray. While General Ruggles had some stalwart cavalry such as the Barteau's phenomenal 2nd Tennessee, there were also significant numbers of ill-disciplined and poorly armed bodies of Mississippi State militia cavalry under the control of General J.S. Gholson, who answered to Mississippi Governor John Pettus and not General Ruggles. These militia regiments were generally composed of "left overs" — old men and young boys — but they also attracted the less patriotic class of men who had little desire to join the Confederate regular army. In many instances, the militia officers were a collection of peacocks who clung to their ceremonial posts and seldom sought out the enemy for battle. As a result, at any given time, more than half of the militia listed on various rosters were more likely to be found malingering at home. In sum, coupled with a lack of proper coordination and communication between the State government

and the Confederate high command, effective joint operations between Ruggles and Golson proved almost impossible to achieve.

— Grierson's Raid —

Before the 2nd Alabama Cavalry could fan out to set up their assigned defensive camps stretching across north Mississippi from "Pontotoc, Verona, Fulton, and Smithville,"[326] the regiment was drawn into what would soon be an all too familiar pattern of inefficiency under Cunningham's leadership. On the early morning hours of April 17, 1863, Union Colonel Benjamin H. Grierson led a full brigade of Federal cavalry, consisting of the 6th Illinois, 7th Illinois, and 2nd Iowa, on a vigorous horse raid aimed straight at "what should have been the strong points of Confederate cavalry."[327] The raid started out from La Grange, Tennessee, with 1,700 seasoned veterans and a battery of artillery, pushing into Mississippi. Riding in columns of two and extending out two miles in length, Grierson's orders were to destroy the important Confederate train depot at Newton, Mississippi, and to do as much damage as possible to the military infrastructure before returning to Tennessee.[328] As things turned out, circumstances on the ground saw Grierson shove his way right on through the entire State successfully dodging every Confederate force sent to intercept him and ending up two weeks later, on May 2, 1863, with a boisterous victory parade in the streets of Union held Baton Rouge, Louisiana. All told, the Federal horsemen covered a distance of about 500 miles in sixteen days. In addition to destroying almost 50 miles of railroad track along the way, the Yankees captured and paroled 500 prisoners and stole 1,000 mules and horses from civilian farms (no pay was offered the owners).

Because Grierson's force was initially shielded by two other smaller Union raids aimed at distracting Colonel Chalmers cavalry, the blue-coats were able to slip across the Tennessee border undetected and then ride all the way to Ripley before being spotted by scouts from Colonel J.F. Smith's regiment of Mississippi State militia on April 19. Smith sent word of the incursion to Confederate forces to the immediate south to include Barteau's 2nd Tennessee

and Cunningham's 2nd Alabama. True to character, Barteau quickly pulled his regiment together at Verona and rapidly moved out to make contact with the enemy raiders. On the other hand, similarly alerted to the Yankee threat, Cunningham struggled to get his already taxed men prepared for action at their Prairie Mount camp, located about 15 miles south of Verona and 7 miles west of Okolona. With the 2nd Alabama Cavalry new to the area and unfamiliar with the territory, Barteau allotted that they would probably be slower to organize and would catch up later. Barteau also sent word to alert various groups of State militia to join him, speeding other riders to General Ruggles at Columbus and General Gholson just to the north of that city.

Born and raised in Ohio, Clark Barteau moved to Tennessee only six years before the War and began a new life as a newspaperman and teacher. When war came, he threw in with the South. Whatever the chronicled circumstances of his background, there was no such thing as "quit" in this adopted Southerner's vocabulary, he was determined to rush straight at the Federal cavalrymen and do everything in his power to smash them up.

Bolstered by the 12th Mississippi Cavalry Battalion (Inge's Battalion), Barteau counted over 600 regular cavalrymen which were later joined by another 800 Mississippi mounted militia made up of the 16th Battalion Mississippi State Cavalry (Ham's Battalion), Smith's Mississippi State Cavalry Regiment, and Captain Weatherall's State Calvary Regiment. Other cavalry regiments, such as the 18th Mississippi State Cavalry Regiment, also went on full alert. In short, a Rebel hornet's nest was stirred up.

Where were the Federals headed? Guessing that the enemy was aiming to destroy track somewhere on the Gulf & Ohio Railroad (also known as the Mobile & Ohio Railroad), the hard-riding Barteau pushed his men all night through pounding rainstorms to cut the Federals off, only to be disappointed to find no trace of them. Obliged to give his men a rest, Barteau then turned back to the southwest fanning out his best scouts for the whereabouts of the enemy.

Sham Fighting in Northeast Mississippi

Members of Colonel Clark R. Barteau's 2nd Tennessee Cavalry Regiment.

Although Barteau's rush to the railroad was perfectly logical, Grierson had struck a beeline straight through Pontotoc County riding deeper south, more or less on a path parallel to the Gulf & Ohio off to his east. Hindered in part by two days of torrential downpours which had turned the roads into quagmires of mud, it would take a full day of grueling effort before Barteau's scouts finally located the Union cavalry and returned with the prized intelligence.

On the very dark night of April 20, Barteau somehow managed to get his regiment of exhausted men and horses within striking distance of the Union column, about 13 miles away, and despite being outnumbered three to one, he was determined to pitch into the enemy on the morning of the next day. Of course, the Rebel commander contemplated that he only needed to slow the enemy riders down so that other Confederates, like the 2nd Alabama and additional Mississippi militia, could converge and assist in the fight. Barteau camped about a mile north of Houston ready to resume the pursuit at first light, while the equally tired Federals bedded down 12 miles south of Houston where they greedily looted the foodstuffs at a local plantation. April 21, offered to be an interesting day.

Grierson was a slippery foe. Realizing from his own sharped-eyed patrols that his rear was dangerously close to being attacked,

the Union commander had already decided upon a series of skillful maneuvers to elude his pursuers. Earlier on the previous day he had sent a group of 175 sick and disabled men back north on the same road just traveled to give the impression that the entire expedition was ending the raid and heading back to Tennessee. This dirt spattered group successfully headed up the trail before veering off to La Grange and ultimate safety. Then, to further deceive the Rebels the Union commander split off a full third of his remaining command on the early morning hours of April 21, and directed them off to the east towards the supply depot at Columbus, while the main body continued south. Intending to go further into Mississippi, he wanted this 500-man diversionary force to also destroy precious Southern railroad track on their way back to Tennessee.

Grierson chose Colonel Edward Hatch, a savvy and courageous officer, for the dangerous mission. On the plus side of the risk was the fact that Hatch's 2nd Iowa was the largest of the regiments and the only one armed exclusively with the dreaded Colt revolving rifle, ensuring a spectacularly heavier rate of firepower than his Rebel counterparts. Hatch was also given one of the very excellent four Woodruff horse drawn artillery pieces to take with him.

On the negative side of the ploy, Hatch knew that if Grierson's plan worked as intended that he would be placed in a very tight spot. Not only would swarms of Rebels be targeting his command, but intelligence reported that the 2nd Alabama Cavalry had already positioned itself near Okolona and would most likely be heading to cut him off from reaching the target of the Gulf & Ohio depot at West Point. In short, Hatch could very well be surrounded and cut to pieces. He noted:

> In my front, between me and West Point, was an Alabama Regiment recently from Pensacola with Artillery.[329]

Just before dawn on April 21, 1863, about the same time that Barteau's sergeants were urging his sleep deprived troopers to

get moving, Grierson's men rolled up their gear, saddled up, and trampled south under low-hanging gray clouds, another rainy day. Hatch simultaneously moved out on the Columbus Road, but he also dispatched a smaller contingent of his 2nd Iowa to take the Woodruff gun and trail along behind Grierson's force until it reached Clear Springs, where they would about face and traverse on the same road backtracking in columns of four to then head southeast to join Hatch, all the while turning the wheeled artillery piece in various directions to help mask Grierson's path.

The hope was that the pursuing Rebels would simply follow the artillery and the 2nd Iowa down the Columbus Road to the southeast and not venture further southwest to pick up the tracks of the Federal main body. In addition, Grierson well understood that the huge cloud of dust that normally hovered above a moving cavalry column was absent due to the rain, giving him a huge advantage. When the smaller diversionary force with their single gun reached Hatch's waiting regiment, all that remained was to see whether or not the pursuing Rebels had taken the bait. Would they follow Hatch or Grierson?

With the rain-soaked ground to their benefit the diversion worked beyond all expectations. Barteau's scouts found the heavily marked Yankee trail and incorrectly reported that the entire Union body was marching on the Columbus road most likely aiming to strike West Point. Since Barteau still held to the belief that the raiders were after the railroad, he incorrectly credited the reports and wasted no time following the decoy, totally unaware that Grierson was moving completely unmolested due south.

Just after noon, about eight miles east from the turn off point, a strong contingent of Barteau's forward guard overtook Hatch's command as it rested at the Calvert plantation near the small village of Palo Alto, Mississippi, about ten miles from West Point. Instead of reporting back to Barteau for orders, the Rebels slammed straight into the Yankees firing a series of volleys and nearly succeeding in cutting off an entire company. Barteau was not far behind.

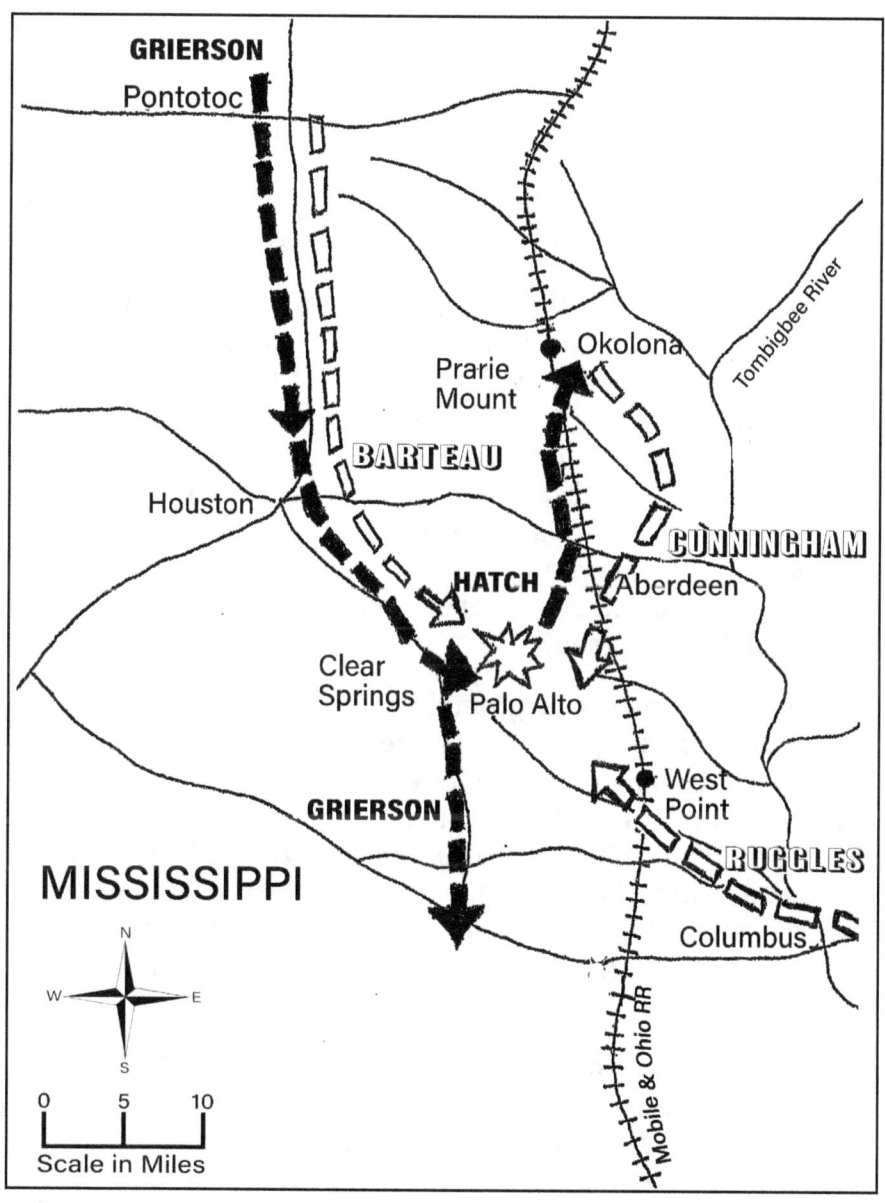

Hatch and Barteau Line of March.

When the gunfire started, the majority of the Union horses were grazing off in a large open field as their riders ate dinner, but there was no stampede or panic. The Federals methodically grabbed their stacked repeaters and fell back on foot about a mile or so to the small village of Palo Alto, where Hatch quickly spread them out alongside the main road, taking up strong defensive positions at the far end of the village in a tree line. It was just in time. Within minutes, Barteau's yelling Rebels came tearing down the road, only to wisely draw up at first contact with the enemy's deadly carbines. No stranger to combat, Barteau dismounted his gaunt, thin-lipped men and took up his own firing positions. After so much time in the saddle, the sharp hollow places in their bellies gnawed, but all that was now forgotten, they finally had the enemy at bay.[330]

Relying on earlier assurances from couriers that Cunningham's 2nd Alabama and more Mississippi militia were close at hand, Barteau's plan was to keep what he presumed to be at least a large chunk of the Federal force fixed in place until reinforcements came up. He ordered the bulk of the arriving militia, under Smith and Ham, to dismount and fed them into firing lines which anchored around the village church and some other minor structures scattered about. The Rebel commander then stealthily circled most of his 2nd Tennessee around to the front of the Federals, about a mile from Palo Alto, where they dismounted and formed a strong semi-circle across the central road leading to West Point. In this manner, the Confederates had the Federals pinned up — front and rear — so that with the anticipated arrival of Cunningham's 2nd Alabama from the west, the combined forces could either launch a strong attack or simply prohibit the bluecoats from advancing or retreating. But where was Cunningham?

For two long hours things remained static as the two sides exchanged sporadic gunfire, although at one point, some of the Mississippi militia decided to edge forward to taunt the Federals and were met with a storm of lead sending them scrambling back to their original spots for cover. Sergeant Lyman Pierce of the 2nd Iowa wrote:

> Our boys kept the cover of the trees until they [the Rebels] were in short range, when they opened upon them such a fire from their trusty revolving rifles, that they were not only repulsed but stampeded.[331]

While the Yankees were easily able to keep the sweat-covered militia in place with their Colt's, things were not all rosy. Not only was Hatch deep behind Rebel lines with no chance of reinforcements, but his men did not have an unlimited supply of cartridges; each trooper carried only 40 bullets, with additional rounds in wooden ammunition chests strapped on the pack mules. As bullets flew back and forth in a blistering sun which turned everything miserably hot, Hatch knew he was surrounded and that every minute he remained static courted disaster.

Hatch's escape plan was simple. In order to split the Confederates and clear an exit path, a single assault would be made against the force to his rear which he calculated was smaller than the force aligned to his front towards West Point. Before ordering the charge, however, he had the Woodruff gun wheeled up close to the militia and instructed the cannoneers to barrage them with canister rounds. With each blast sending out 169 lead balls (.69 caliber) the effect was perfectly terrific on the skittish militia and thoughts of resistance turned as faded as their uniforms. In the interim, the Federals facing Barteau continued to fire away in order to keep them at bay. After what seemed an eternity to the dismounted Yankees waiting to make the assault on the militia, Hatch halted the artillery and charged his men forward on foot, guns blazing.

It worked. Much to Hatch's delight, the inexperienced Mississippi home guard that had earlier been bold enough to creep forward and mock the enemy, now retreated with great confusion and little fight. Once the Rebels were flushed out and scattered off about three miles distant, Union horse holders wasted no time getting everyone mounted and the whole lot happily galloped off so that by the time Barteau could remount his own men and come up through Palo Alto, the entire Federal regiment

was long gone. A greatly disgusted Barteau rallied what he could of the militia, and the chase was on once again. Barteau was still hoping for tangible support from the 2nd Alabama. Again, where was Cunningham?

Cunningham had left Prairie Mount with half his command, only taking those that had been properly equipped with new carbines and pistols and leaving the poorly armed men behind. Arriving with 450 troopers at Okolona, about ten miles east of Palo Alto, Cunningham definitely heard the Union artillery booms starting about noon, yet made absolutely no effort to speed his men to the sound of the guns, thereby missing the entire action at Palo Alto.[332]

Meanwhile, with the escaping Federal cavalry now heading at a moderate pace north towards Buena Vista, they encountered only sporadic skirmishing at the rear of their column, successfully crossing the Houlka River. The Federal commander wrote in his after-action report:

> In the [initial] attack made by the enemy, a company in the rear was cut off and nearly all taken. The enemy then closed in on my flanks [Barteau], and advanced in two lines on my rear [Mississippi militia].... Changing my front to rear, I waited until the enemy were close upon me, and opened with my rifles and one 2-pounder from the front and with carbines on the flanks, breaking his lines and driving him back, pushing the enemy about 3 miles, capturing arms and horses.... From that time until dark it was constant skirmish, the enemy having taken me for the main column.... I moved slowly northward, fighting by the rear, crossing the Houlka River, and drawing their forces immediately in my rear.[333]

Darkness did not stop Barteau. Ever believing that the Yankees would veer back around towards the Gulf & Ohio somewhere below

Okolona, Barteau once again maneuvered his exhausted troopers in the dark to be able to block them. Unfortunately for Barteau, on the morning of April 22, when the Rebels rolled out of their blankets before the break of dawn to prepare for battle, the Federals were not at all where logic would dictate that they should be. Instead of circling back and heading due east, which was the shortest route to the railroad, a local guide had led Hatch's command due north along old farm trails and then through a large swamp before turning east and emerging at the railroad town of Okolona that late afternoon, stealing a few hours of rest along the way. Finding the place largely void of Confederate troops, Hatch's men spent a couple of hours tearing up rail and stealing wagons, horses, and mules, before torching all the empty military barracks, which were designed to hold several thousand men, along with burning down the "hospitals and female institute,"[334] before heading once again into the protective arms of the deep swamps back to the west on their journey to Tennessee.

Hatch was right to keep moving by the backroads. It would have been suicide for the Union horsemen to travel north by means of the faster roads which ran parallel to the rail-line. Paradoxically, the feckless Cunningham and the 2nd Alabama had just passed down from Okolona the day before on their way to finally join Barteau's frustrated command. Indeed, when Cunningham at last appeared to join in the action, his immediate demand that Barteau turn over full command of the now combined force to him (being the senior officer in rank) only aggravated the scene. A furious Barteau tartly declined.

By now the Rebels realized that they were chasing only a single Federal regiment, others would have to deal with Grierson who had obviously slipped past many days ago. Still, Barteau was hopeful that with the added men of the 2nd Alabama that they might yet be able to chase down and destroy Hatch before he crossed into Tennessee and safety. The Confederates would have to move briskly and in unison to do so.

After crossing Chuckatouche Creek, Barteau and a petulant Cunningham followed after the Yankees on the Pontotoc road all day of April 23, the boiling dust kicked up by the many stolen horses, mules, and wagons easily marking the enemy's progress. Guided along by "conscripted" slaves, the slower moving Federals were encumbered by their stolen goods and only barely kept ahead by thoroughly burning each of the wooden bridges they crossed so that the pursuing Confederates were obliged to spend precious time getting over the water, often swimming their horses in small groups led by a trooper in a skiff holding the bridle of a lead animal, while the other men splashed along. Although the Rebels were closing the distance, they had yet to scoop up more than a handful of stragglers and some broken down mounts and wagons.

Incredibly, after only one day of pursuit, the tepid Cunningham unilaterally determined that his men would no longer continue due to fatigue and lack of rations. At Bramlett's, 3 miles from Edwards Mills, he informed Barteau and the militia commanders that the 2nd Alabama was breaking off to return to their camps at Prairie Mount. Barteau wrote:

> But before marching from Bramlett's, Lieutenant-Colonel Cunningham informed us that his command was exhausted and without rations; that he could not continue the pursuit. This materially reduced our strength, for many of our men had to be left on account of horses broken down by such continuous marching.[335]

With Cunningham peeling off, Hatch was now assured a successful conclusion to his mission. After pushing another 35 miles over rough terrain made colorful only by spring flowers, the Federals arrived in the vicinity of Birmingham, Mississippi, on April 24 (just west of Saltillo) with Barteau only a mile behind. To escape, Hatch would have to get his wagons, stolen livestock, and people over Camp Creek by its single bridge. Hatch wisely deployed half his command for battle with stern orders to keep the Rebels back

and sent the remainder of his force on ahead with the cumbersome wagons, "31 prisoners and 200 escaped slaves who were helping to drive the 600 captured [stolen] horses and mules."[336] While the unsightly caravan moved as fast as possible along the main road which ran into the town and then across the wooden bridge, the rear Union guard held off the dismounted Confederates for two hours before themselves crossing and then setting the bridge afire, allowing all to retire in fairly good order. The remaining Rebels were fully played out and Barteau returned south to camp at Verona.

Hatch reached La Grange, Tennessee without further incident. His losses were put at "sixteen killed" with six large wagons full of Union wounded carried off.[337] Another source put Hatch's dead at "thirty of his men and ... fifty prisoners."[338] Whatever the true count, Hatch had proved himself a right formidable opponent.

The 2nd Alabama could take little comfort in the story-line that they had helped "chase" Grierson's decoy Federal regiment back into Tennessee. While it was true that Hatch had failed in his mission to destroy Confederate rail, Cunningham had performed shamefully throughout. Proper coordination with the aggressive Barteau should have resulted in the Yankees being enveloped and destroyed. Not only had the 2nd Alabama's commander demonstrated zero interest in getting at the enemy at Palo Alto, Cunningham had purposefully dragged his feet in the subsequent joint pursuit, dropping out after only a single day! Although one post-war account incorrectly claims that the 2nd Alabama lost 70 men killed and wounded during the Grierson raid,[339] this is grossly inaccurate. Their only losses were broken-down horses and *esprit de corps*. Barteau correctly summed up Cunningham's worthless efforts as follows:

> The reinforcement [2nd Alabama] was too late to be of any service. In fact, the tardiness of his [Cunningham's] movements allowed the enemy to reach Okolona; for had he joined me before reaching Palo Alto, we should have routed and scattered the enemy.[340]

To note that the Grierson/Hatch expedition produced no real military gains — Grant's movement to the south of Vicksburg would have occurred regardless of Grierson's raid — it caught the imagination of the Union press who were desperate for good news and Grierson's feat was heralded as the most fantastic accomplishment of any cavalry raid of the War. With his picture splashed across the June 6, 1863, cover of *Harper's Weekly*, Grierson's new found celebrityship saw him quickly promoted to brevet Brigadier General. In point of fact, Grierson's greatest value to the Union was as a propaganda boon, the raid had certainly proved a great embarrassment to the Confederate cavalry. Still, a silver lining for Richmond was the realization that organizational changes were sorely needed. At a minimum: (1) the Mississippi militia cavalry needed to be incorporated directly into regular Confederate cavalry service; and (2) all existing cavalry forces in the area had to be reorganized and placed under the command of a single cavalry brigade commander of general officer rank.

From the Union perspective, Grierson's success emboldened General Grant and later General Sherman to direct greater numbers of slash and burn cavalry terror raids into northern Mississippi and Alabama. The added kicker, however, was that the new forays would focus not on military targets but on a larger and more heinous objective — breaking the spirit and morale of the civilian population. While Yankee raids were euphemistically still called "scouts," the real purpose was to brutalize civilians and strip the Confederate countryside of food and the livestock needed to cultivate the fields. With the Southern men away at war, his women and children were unable to resist and fear gripped the land, for no one knew which home, farm, village, or town would be next for the scorched-earth depredations.

In fact, if there had been any doubt about the need for the Confederate high command to reorganize their cavalry to blunt such Union terror attacks, the subsequent events of May 4-5, 1863, sealed the case, while simultaneously putting an end to the 2nd Alabama Calvary's cowardly James Cunningham.

— Kings Creek Fight —

On May 4, 1863, just two short days after the Grierson affair concluded, yet another Yankee cavalry raid was launched. This time from the Union stronghold of Corinth, Mississippi, heading towards Tupelo. Led by Colonel Florence Cornyn, this movement consisted of mounted infantry, regular cavalry, and three light mountain howitzers. Numbering almost 1,400 men made up of the 9th Illinois, 10th Missouri, and 7th Kansas, each of them carried two pistols and many were armed with the Colt revolving rifle. Their mission was to terrorize but also to provide a screen to a previous Union raid under Colonel Abel Streight. Streight had left Mississippi on April 26, 1863, but ran into the "buzz saw" of Nathan Bedford Forrest where he was decisively defeated and on May 3, surrendered his entire command of 1,700 near Rome, Georgia. All this was unbeknownst to Cornyn as he set out to cover the imagined successful return of his fellow colonel.

Spotting the columns of dust, Rebel scouts located Cornyn at Baldwyn, about 15 miles north of Tupelo. On May 5, elements of Colonel W.M. Inge's 12th Mississippi Cavalry Battalion found the Yankees at Guntown where they exchanged small arms fire, took some prisoners, and prudently retreated. Major General Gholson, commanding the Mississippi State militia cavalry, frantically called for all available Confederate horse regiments in the area to rendezvous with his large home guard command near Tupelo, and under orders from General Ruggles, Barteau and Cunningham rounded up their respective regiments and grouped together at Verona, about 4 miles south of Tupelo to do so.

The Confederate forces moving to support General Gholson consisted of Barteau's regiment, Colonel W.M. Inge's 12th Mississippi Cavalry, the 13th Alabama Battalion under Major W.A. Hewlett, and the 2nd Alabama. Since Cunningham was the senior ranking officer of the three active Confederate regiments, he imperiously asserted sole command over the entire task force as proscribed by Article 62 of the Articles of War.[341]

Learning that Gholson had shifted to Chesterville, about two miles west of Tupelo, Cunningham directed the regiments out from Verona, not to seek out the enemy to engage them, but only to link up with Gholson. In order to take the primary road from Tupelo to Chesterville, Cunningham led the task force forward into the "thick woods and swamp south of Tupelo"[342] in order of movement as follows: Cunningham, leading the 2nd Alabama, then Hewlett, then Barteau, with Inge bringing up the rear.

After getting the entire body over Kings Creek, Cunningham soon entered into an area of even thicker timber sprawled out over extremely marshy ground. Meanwhile, just on the outskirts of the southern limit of Tupelo, a portion of Inge's command again bumped into Cornyn's force and engaged in a brisk skirmish just as the Federals were crossing a bridge over Town Creek. Badly outnumbered, the Rebel horsemen fell back and Cornyn shifted his command for about a mile before setting up a formidable line to either attack or defend as circumstances might require. Amazingly, this contact with the enemy by Inge's men caused no increased suspicion from the dull-witted Cunningham that he might have to engage in a fight. Instead of immediately sending out scouts to ascertain the exact strength and disposition of the Union cavalry, Cunningham blissfully continued straight ahead right into the waiting arms of Cornyn's now well positioned forces. According to his official after-action report he admitted as much but in the typical fashion of the arrogant, blamed it all on "others" who had not warned him about the presence of enemy forces in the area. Cunningham wrote:

> I had been ordered to Tupelo without any warning that there was any probability of being intercepted on my way thither. I must state that my coming upon the enemy was quite unexpected.[343]

What happened next might not be described as a *complete* ambush but the end result was tantamount to one. Fixated only on reaching friendly forces, when Cunningham himself made contact

with outlaying Federals pickets to his front, he half-heartedly drew up his regiment just as both flanks of the 2nd Alabama were hit by a severe storm of lead spewed out by hundreds of dismounted Union troopers accompanied by deep-throated blasts from three mountain howitzers strategically positioned atop a rolling semi-circle shaped ridge just north of Kings Creek.[344] Partially hidden by heavy clouds of smoke, the Federals *were* in a mood to attack and made quick efforts to get in behind the halted Alabamians. A bewildered Cunningham chronicled the situation and his own predictable response — to run away as fast as possible.

> [T]he enemy opened upon me a cross fire of artillery and musketry. I then discovered that I was ambuscaded on the right and left, and I determined to extricate my command as soon as practicable.[345]

Instead of falling back, reorganizing, and giving fight, Cunningham's only thoughts were to skedaddle. He yelled at his bugler to signal a "countermarch from the left,"[346] a move which left two companies of the 2nd Alabama, B and I, — that had prudently dismounted and taken up firing positions — cut off while the bulk of the regiment raced through the Union gauntlet towards Chesterville.

Inexplicably, not only had Cunningham failed to give notice of his cowardly maneuver to the other regimental commanders in his wake, but he had abandoned his own two companies on the field of battle. Cunningham disingenuously wrote:

> I ordered a countermarch from the left, but as Companies "B" and "I" had faced to the rear and left to check the enemy, who were closing in upon my rear, they did not receive my orders and were left on the field. I passed on with the rest of my command [the 2nd Alabama] out through the west edge of Tupelo and took the road to Chesterville, where I learned General Gholson was at the time.[347]

As soon as Cunningham and his understrength regiment got free and recrossed Kings Creek to the west, the Yankees quickly reoriented their field of fire to address the remaining Confederate regiments, making it far too dangerous for anyone to follow Cunningham's cavalrymen out in the same direction. Hewlett, being next in line of march, was now the primary focus of the Union fire and recalled the tight spot his men faced as his command was assaulted at extremely close range.

> On reaching a ridge about one hundred yards from the creek I first received the fire from the enemy's left wing, at a distance of from twenty-five to forty yards. I returned the fire and dismounted my right wing. Several of the horses of my left becoming unmanageable, they faltered.[348]

Sensing Hewlett's tenuous position, one of the Federal lines sprang out of hiding and launched a vigorous foot assault, pouring a galling fire into the still mounted Confederates. As the Federals pressed steadily forward firing their repeaters, Rebel saddles were emptied and dozens of horses were killed and wounded. The confusion was so intense that only two companies in Hewlett's regiment were able to effectively respond to hurried calls to dismount and form firing lines. The men in blue were intent on crushing Hewlett and when fully supported by redirected booms from the well serviced mountain howitzers, this new Union attack portended to be more terrific than the first.

Fortunately for Hewlett, the ever-imaginative Barteau was close at hand. A man of great personal courage, Barteau was not about to abandon his fellow Rebels or the field without one hell of a fight. Not then under attack himself, Barteau rushed his men toward the sound of gunfire and in so doing managed to swoop down upon the unsuspecting Federal line then closing in on Hewlett's right. Led by their chieftain, the Tennesseans let out such chilling yells and well-placed shots that the Yankees quickly broke off their assault and

scrambled back on their initial positions. Major Hewlett recorded the much welcomed rescue operation and what happened next.

> At this time Lieutenant Colonel Barteau came to my assistance on the right, poured a volley into the enemy, driving them back.... The firing then commenced from their [the Federals] whole line, with three pieces of artillery, two making a cross fire from each wing and one from the center. It is said by those at a distance that they fired forty rounds from each gun.[349]

With the immediate danger to Hewlett blunted, Barteau dismounted his men and picked out uneven firing positions alongside Hewlett. The situation was still tenuous given that Federal artillery and musketry remained at full work all across the Rebel front forcing the troopers to huddle behind whatever cover could be had amongst the trees and underbrush where they returned fire, reloaded, and fired again. The Confederates would not be dislodged and scattered if Barteau had his way. "I at once ordered the Second Tennessee into line and to dismount," Barteau recorded, "which was executed promptly and in good order, and the horse sent to the rear out of the reach of the enemy's fire. By keeping the men close to the ground and behind trees, taking deliberate aim at the enemy,"[350] the Confederates held their ground. Incredibly, Barteau stayed mounted throughout the fighting, spurring his steed here and there encouraging the men to hold firm.

As the firefight continued unabated, Barteau's personal escort spotted a new threat. Large numbers of dismounted Federals were maneuvering around to the left intent on enveloping the bogged down Confederates. To protect the flank and rear from this developing menace, Barteau hesitated not a second, asking Hewlett to remount the bulk of his command and then circle back across Kings Creek to get behind the Yankees so that instead of being outflanked, they would outflank the Federals! Under the wild

uproar of explosions and general chaos all across the field, it was a risky maneuver and failure meant drastic consequences. But luck favored the Rebels. Hewlett's mounted troopers moved rapidly and within a short time the Union troopers were themselves enfiladed and receiving blistering fire so that *they* were now in danger of being swept away. Union bugles sounded the retreat and the blue-clad troopers fell back on their comrades.

The hard-fought battle which had gone on for the better part of two hours was now about over. As the sun dipped ever lower into the western sky, Colonel Cornyn imagined that he had already played the game far too long, deeming it inconceivable that large bodies of fresh Confederate cavalry would not soon arrive on the scene. Despite his best efforts to get at the stranded Rebels pinned down around Kings Creek, the tenacious Barteau had blunted him at every turn so at this late hour the Union commander elected to break contact and retire. Only a few Rebel scouts followed cautiously behind. Drenched in sweat, Cunningham's lost companies B and I were now able to extricate themselves from the battlefield where they had also been holding firm.

Cornyn could not have known it at the time but he had greatly overestimated any danger to his command. Neither Cunningham nor the Gholson's Mississippi militia had entertained for a moment any notion of joining the battle. When Barteau sent fast riding couriers with dispatches to Gholson during the fighting to request reinforcements, the militia general flatly denied them and instead advised Barteau and Hewlett to retreat.

As it was, the Yankees had ample time to collect their wounded and dead, comfortably saddle up, and then head totally unmolested back to Corinth. In fact, only when it was absolutely certain that the Federals were moving away, did General Gholson send out a small reconnaissance party to sheepishly see the raiders out of his geographic area of responsibility.

Union forces reported 23 total casualties while the Confederates lost 20 killed, with 40 wounded and 81 taken prisoner — many of the losses emanating from companies B and I of the 2nd Alabama.

According to W. Brewer's historical sketch, the 2nd Alabama Cavalry accounted for 8 of the dead and an unknown number of the wounded and prisoners at the Kings Creek fight.[351]

Once again, with the exception of Company B and I that acted with great valor, the majority of the Alabamians had no part in the affair, thanks to Cunningham's abysmal performance. In his after-action report, Lieutenant Colonel Barteau expressed open disgust. Barteau anticipated that having successfully run the gauntlet of the Federal ambush that Cunningham would have immediately circled around to the north to hit the Yankees a heavy blow from behind. That's what Barteau or any leader worth their salt would have done. Unfortunately, Cunningham was not only an incompetent leader, he was a coward to boot. Even though he was no more than two miles away at Chesterville and could clearly hear the fight raging, Cunningham never returned to assist, leaving his comrades in gray to their fates to include the two stalwart companies of his own regiment! It was difficult for Barteau to hide his angst. He wrote:

> It may be well to state that, after running the gauntlet of the enemy's fire and getting in his rear, Lieutenant Colonel Cunningham continued his march to Chesterville or vicinity, where, finding General Gholson, he returned by a circuitous route to Verona at 9 p.m. Had he fought the enemy vigorously in his rear, or rejoined the troops that were left in the ambuscade, the result might have been more favorable for us.[352]

Barteau's words did not fall on deaf ears. A sober-minded assessment of Cunningham's deficient performance during the Grierson raid and now his absolute disgraceful conduct at Kings Creek warranted meaningful action and he was relieved of command of the 2nd Alabama Cavalry Regiment by General Ruggles, "due to incompetence."[353] Cunningham quickly resigned his commission and Captain John P. West was put in temporary command[354] (shortly thereafter promoted to Lieutenant Colonel). On the other

hand, in recognition of his superb leadership skills, Barteau was promoted to full colonel.[355]

Just as they had regarded Colonel Hunter with disdain, the rank and file of the 2nd Alabama shed no tears for the now disgraced Cunningham. They were fighters true and brave yet their two previous commanders Hunter and Cunningham were not. Reflecting the words of Alexander the Great — "I am not afraid of an *army* of *lions led* by a *sheep*" — Private Hunter of the 2nd Alabama summed up Cunningham's leadership deficiencies perfectly when he sarcastically observed:

> All the 2d [Alabama Cavalry] needed was an officer to lead them, or rather go with them into the fight, and not to lead them up to within four or five miles of the enemy and halt, wait until the enemy got a safe distance and then commence a pursuit, as has been done on some former occasions [Palo Alto and Kings Creek].[356]

Chapter Four

Glory at Last

"The 2nd Alabama cavalry were the best fighting troops I ever saw."[357] —*General Daniel Ruggles*

IN THE WAKE OF CUNNINGHAM'S relief for incompetence, the Confederate War Department in Richmond moved quickly to exonerate Captain Richard Earle of all criminal charges and sent a telegraph to Jacksonville, not only ordering him to report to his former command, but placing him in charge of the regiment. An energized Earle packed up his gear, gave heartfelt goodbyes to wife and daughter, and headed to Okolona to report for duty. It was late May 1863, and things were about to change for the 2nd Alabama.

On his hurried trip north, Earle's story of arrest and subsequent exoneration was picked up by Montgomery's *The Weekly Advertiser* which sympathetically wrote:

> Cpt. R.G. Earle of the 2nd Alabama Cavalry passed through this city yesterday, on his way to his command in Mississippi.... We understand that Col. Cunningham, who has been commanding this regiment ... has resigned. Under this state of things we presume either Col. Hunter will be reinstated or Capt. Earle will take command as ranking officer.[358]

As the admirers of Earle had hoped for all along, on May 27, 1863, he was brevet promoted to the rank of colonel and given command of the 2nd Alabama Cavalry. On February 16, 1864, the Confederate Congress formally confirmed the promotion and in a mark of respect for his inspiring leadership and battlefield successes in the ensuing months, the commander of the Army of Tennessee, "General Joseph Johnston, personally delivered the official commission to Colonel Earle."[359]

Knowing Earle from the time he had spent in 1862, on detached duty, General Ruggles was overjoyed to greet the returning *Colonel* Earle. Always commanding from the front, like a medieval knight inspiring his soldiers to fight, Earle's combat prowess, high military fitness, and gallant soul had left a strong impression and now fueled even higher expectations. Of course, the troopers were also itching to prove their mettle under Earle's leadership, for too long they had been held back from battle. The fulfillment of all those desires would soon transpire and none would be disappointed.

Along with new leadership in the 2nd Alabama, came a general reorganization of the core structure of all cavalry units in Mississippi. The confusion in command between State and Confederate cavalry units had proven disastrous in confronting repeated Yankee raids into his State, so much so that Mississippi Governor John Pettus was finally persuaded to deliver large sections of his militia cavalry over to regular Confederate service. On June 4, 1863, the governor ordered Colonel J.F. Smith's Mississippi State Cavalry Regiment and Major T.W. Harris' State Cavalry Battalion turned over to General Ruggles. Ever the astute manager, Ruggles sent his inspector general to conduct a thorough inspection of the two bodies of Mississippi troopers preparatory to their formal reception into his command. Sadly, however, upon receiving the governor's order to consolidate, the Mississippi militia vanished like a puff of smoke. Informed of the abrupt "disappearance" of the militia at his Okolona headquarters, Ruggles reported the disappointing news to General Joseph E. Johnston:

Only thirty-five of Harris' battalion could be assembled, and Smith's entire regiment, which had been stationed near New Albany, disbanded on the 9th and 10th [June 1863] before any inspection could be made.[360]

Ruggles took the disappointing developments in stride and desiring to reassure the nervous locals, he decided to personally conduct a show of force movement across the now abandoned territory around New Albany, where Smith's militia had formally been stationed. Unfortunately, when General Ruggles arrived at Pontotoc on the evening of June 13, 1863, he learned from scouts that Yankee cavalry had already beat him to New Albany and ruthlessly fired the business district, church, and many private dwellings. Enraged by the senseless depredations against civilians, Ruggles briefly rested his men and pushed them out at midnight, traveling as fast as practicable in the pitch black the 20 miles north to New Albany, reaching the town at about nine in the morning of June 14.

He was too late. The Yankees had gone, having stolen or burned everything of value, military or civilian.

The raiders belonged to the Ninth (9th) Illinois Volunteer Infantry (mounted). Separating from a larger Federal group of raiders camped at Pocahontas, Tennessee,[361] the 9th Illinois had launched their own incursion into northern Mississippi to seize food and burn homes. Their commander was Lieutenant Colonel Jesse J. Phillips and he led about 300 mounted men with two pieces of light artillery.[362] His mission also included specific orders to completely destroy the civilian town of New Albany. Along with this group of terrorists in blue rode the regimental chaplain, Marion Morrison, who chronicled the three-day raid.

On the morning of June 13, 1863, Phillips entered the town of Ripley and took possession without opposition. While the town was looted and a sizable group of black Southerners were impressed into labor, the place was not torched. According to Chaplain Morrison:

> The town was searched, but nothing of a contraband nature [was found], except a number of negroes, who were confiscated for the Government [emphasis added]."³⁶³

The next town hit that day was nearby Orizabo, which also offered no resistance. Unlike Ripley, however, Orizabo was completely burned to the ground under the absurd excuse that it "was a place of rendezvous"³⁶⁴ for the Rebels. Of course, under such distorted criterion for inflicting raw criminal violence, every Southern town would be subject to destruction, which was exactly what was taking place. In this light, the reason Orizabo was destroyed and Ripley spared was not because of any law of war or humanitarian concerns, but rather because Ripley was only a half-day's ride to New Albany and the arsonists would be returning through Ripley to rest up the night on their way back to friendly lines. They would burn it then.

Making sure that sufficient flankers were sent out to report on any lurking Confederate cavalry, the terrorists then moved with their loot to the south towards New Albany as fast as the heavily loaded wagons could travel. While enroute, Morrison dryly recorded that the Yankees stopped a large family on the road and robbed them of all their property because in roughly searching the group's personal possessions they found a letter tucked inside an elderly woman's carpet-sack with a single Confederate postage stamp affixed to the outside. Naturally, the Yankees would have stolen the wagons and horses anyway — finding a Confederate stamp served as their so-called justification for highway robbery.

> While stopping to feed, about four miles south of Ripley, a family moving to Ripley came along. Their wagons and carriage were searched, and a Rebel mail was found in the old lady's carpet-sack. Their horses and mules were all confiscated, except one old team of mules which they were allowed to keep.³⁶⁵

By late afternoon of June 13, the Union horsemen entered New Albany which they promptly pillaged and then utterly burned. Chaplain Morrison gleefully described the war crimes, justifying them with the perverted notion that since all Confederates were illegal guerrillas and should not be covered by the civilized rules of warfare, the Secesh civilians were equally guilty by "aiding" them and were thus fair game for robbery, arson, and pillage. Nevertheless, the goodly Chaplain was careful in his history of the regiment not to mention the horrible details of the wanton destruction of private homes, churches, or hospitals other than to dryly record, as in the case of his observations about New Albany, that the town was "entirely destroyed." In point of fact, the Union troopers had forced their way into every private dwelling rifling for valuables and stripping away what they could carry, then smashing all the windows, porcelain, and mirrors before applying the torch. Domestic animals which were not taken were slaughtered and left to rot. He wrote:

> The Regiment then proceeded to New Albany, reaching that place about 4 P.M. Finding the town nearly deserted by citizens, and used as a general Headquarters for guerrillas [Confederate cavalry forces], and a supplying point for them, it [New Albany] was entirely destroyed, after any stores of value [civilian and military property] that could be carried away were taken [stolen].[366]

After sacking and reducing the town to ashes, Colonel Phillips moved his command out of the smoldering mess and camped for the night about three miles north of New Albany, intending to head back north the next morning to reach Ripley by late afternoon. Fortuitously for Phillips, at 2 a.m. on the dark morning of June 14, he became spooked by intelligence reports that Confederate cavalry (Ruggles) was heading in his direction and wisely packed up for a rapid movement back to Pocahontas. The Yankees traveled at breakneck speed going right through Ripley, not even stopping

long enough to raze the town, reaching Pocahontas at eight in the evening. Having traveled well over 100 miles on the raid, they brought in "25 Rebel soldiers, 50 contrabands [black Southerners], and 100 head of horses and mules"[367] stolen from civilians.

Phillips had escaped Ruggles just in the nick of time, but his raiding activities were far from over. Three days later, the Yankee commander was ordered out on another raid and given command of an even larger body of Federal cavalry consisting of parts of four regiments — the 9th Illinois, 10th Illinois, 11th Missouri (some sources claim it was the 18th Missouri), and 5th Ohio. In addition, two full companies of Tories and several pieces of light artillery were assigned, making this destructive body of about 1,000 a force to be reckoned with as it headed south on the main road straight towards burned out New Albany. This time Phillips was ordered to strike the strategic Mobile & Ohio and do as much damage to the locals along the route as possible. On June 18, a small detachment of Confederates under Captain Thomas Puryear, of Barteau's 2nd Tennessee Cavalry, brought fresh news to General Ruggles about this new group of vandals which was first sighted near Ripley moving swiftly on its way to New Albany.

Puryear's information was accurate. Colonel Phillips had moved out from Pocahontas on the rainy evening of June 17, with six days cooked rations and lots of empty wagons. Little did he know, what Phillips thought to be another quick looting and arson adventure would turn out far different this time. A harbinger of troubling things to come for the Yankees occurred on the morning of June 19, when Captain Puryear's rear guard of only 20 gray troopers put up a furious skirmish with elements of the enemy on the outskirts of New Albany. This determined handful of Rebels significantly slowed the Union column and it was nearly three hours before the Federals were able to elbow them aside and enter the place.

Meanwhile, having been altered to the danger the day before, General Ruggles moved his main body with four pieces of horse artillery from Guntown and headed due west, anticipating that the Federals would probably move towards the railroad. Hoping

to perhaps catch them in a pincer, Ruggles held a council of war with his chief commanders (Barteau's regiment was absent) and the decision was made for Colonel Earle to take the 2nd Alabama straight to New Albany to seek out the enemy and hopefully pin them down in a blocking movement, then, depending on how things developed, Ruggles would bring up the artillery and the rest of the force so together they would strike hard at an opportune moment.

Sundown of June 19, found the Federals bivouacked three miles south of New Albany on the road to Pontotoc. In a stroke of good luck, Earle's far-ranging scouts located the Yankees at their evening camps and when so advised, Colonel Earle rode most of the night in order to get to nearby Pontotoc to be ready to head up the road to New Albany at daybreak. In turn, Colonel Barteau's Tennesseans caught up with Earle's night march and happily fell in with the column. A relay of scurrying couriers kept General Ruggles informed of developments and in tandem with the fast moving 2nd Alabama and 2nd Tennessee, Ruggles rushed the remainder of his command northwest to get at the rear of the enemy so as to catch the entire batch in a neat little trap. The Rebels planned to strike simultaneously at first light — Earle and Barteau coming up from the south and Ruggles pushing down from the north. Things were shaping up well.

Unfortunately for the Confederates, Colonel Phillips proved to be a slippery foe. Whether alerted to the dangerous developments by friendly locals or through the perceptive abilities of his own scouts, the wily Union commander once again sidestepped away. Employing an old ruse, while it was still dark he left his sick and disabled in place with orders to keep the campfires burning bright and then stealthily took his troopers off the main road angling them to the west. The Federals gingerly picked their way through the darkness and on into the dawning of a new day before halting to get a few hours shut eye. Phillips chose his camp site in one of the many muddy cane-brake swamps of the "Atchchubby-paliah" (also called the Octohatchie Swamp or Etta Swamp) adjacent to Mud Creek (also known as Lappylubbee Creek),[368] off the Little Tallahatchie River, about 15 miles due west of New Albany. The town of Rocky

Ford sat not far off with its single bridge over the river. It was a perfect hiding place, or so Phillips thought. After posting a strong picket line just inside the entangling undergrowth, the Federals rested while Phillips assessed his next move.

Meanwhile, some hours before the crack of dawn on June 20, after pushing his regiment hard to get in position for the anticipated morning assault, Earle was informed that the enemy had once more shifted in the night towards the vicinity of Rocky Ford. The ambush had been sprung and the unwelcomed news meant more pursuit for his already winded men. Earle and Barteau had no choice and called a much-needed respite to give men and animals a short breather. Aching and dizzy, the bone-weary troopers dismounted, untied leather girths, and slid saddle blankets and saddles off the matted, wet backs of their mounts. No camp fires were allowed and after wolfing down cold rations, most were soon stretched out on the warm ground, which after so much riding seemed as soft as goose feathers. Although the horses were unsaddled, they stayed hobbled close by as the men fell fast asleep perfectly indifferent to what tomorrow might bring.

Colonel Earle himself got little rest. He knew that the quarry was still close and sent additional couriers to Ruggles to guide him along the new path that now led further to the west, suggesting in a scribbled note that a forceful thrust by his and Barteau's men could hold the larger Federal body in place until Ruggles arrived with the artillery and reinforcements.

The sun was barely up on the morning of June 20, when Alabama and Tennessee sergeants began kicking at booted feet and brawling orders for the men to saddle up. The troopers did their toilets and gobbled down cakes of cornbread and salty pork while the horses hungrily consumed the remaining corn from the saddlebags. Once more, the trek resumed with hundreds of hoofs spattering red mud high in the air.

By early morning it appeared that Colonel Earle's dogged persistence had finally paid off. Like fingers on a gigantic hand, forward elements made contact with a body of the 5th Ohio Cavalry,

which Phillips had prudently sent out that morning to serve as a screening guard while his command made preparations to pack up and move out. Both sides of the meeting engagement were mounted and a short but violent pistol battle at point blank range ensued emptying several saddles. Barteau's forward squadron consisted of Lieutenant French and 13 members of his command and French well recalled his face-to-face encounter with one of the Union officers.

> For my part, I [fought] … a very cool-headed officer, for nearly every shot that he fired at me took effect. [T]he first [ball] that I felt burnt my neck, the next passed through my pistol scabbard on my right side and another took effect in my right arm, passing through and shivering the ulna; this last shot he fired after he was wounded by me. I shot at him five times. My first shot was too low, striking his horse and causing him [the horse] to drop. The officer lit on his feet and continued to fire, until one of my shots took effect in his thigh; he then fell, but raising up again, he fired again, with the result above mentioned — breaking my arm which dropped at my side powerless.[369]

Hearing the commotion of the not too distance lively gun fight, Colonel Phillips barked off orders to prepare for battle and aligned his dismounted men in a strong defensive posture with skirmishers hustled out to the front. Earle and Barteau likewise deployed their forces, sending a robust body of skirmishers picking their way forward with orders to open fire at anything they encountered.

It was not long in coming. One, two, three, in quick succession, and then like a thunderstorm, a swarm of bullets flew between the two opposing skirmish lines. The Rebel probe had hit pay dirt.

As if by design, General Ruggles suddenly rode up to join Earle and Barteau, leading Colonel William Boyles' 1st Alabama Cavalry

(recently formed by combining the 1st and 13th Battalions) along with four pieces of light artillery under Captain Owen and Lieutenant Holt. Encouraged by Earle's earlier penciled note, Ruggles had also force marched his men straight through the June night. At long last the stage was shaping up for a full-scale battle and Ruggles wasted no time in deciding what to do.

The plan to dislodge the enemy was simple and daring. In his after-action report, General Ruggles correctly observed that the conditions were greatly in favor of the Federal defenders since there was no way to flank them due to the thick terrain features on either side of the battlefield. The only option was to charge straight ahead. Ruggles noted:

> It only remained to accept battle in the midst of an extensive, dense cane-brake and impenetrable thicket, covering both banks of a deep, muddy stream, on the enemy's own terms.[370]

In fact, the disjointed "open" ground over which the fight would take place, consisted of nasty wetlands populated by head-high stalky cane-breaks, about a mile deep, thickly spread out on either side of a muddy creek meandering more or less parallel through the middle, with nothing to distinguish the ugly and snake infested landscape except for three widely spaced thickets of scrawny trees popping their heads above the tall vegetation.

The Federals had taken up fairly good firing positions tramping down large swaths of the grasses and anchoring themselves along two out of the three aforementioned belts of thickets. The only hazard was that if they were obliged to fall back, there would be no easy way to exit — a swampy landscape loomed behind the cane-breaks with only a single winding road cutting through to the bridge leading into the town of Rocky Ford.

The 2nd Alabama Cavalry was finally facing its first full scale head-to-head engagement and as an added bonus, they were squared

off against a particularly despicable group of Yankee looters who demonstrated no moral reservations whatsoever about viciously abusing civilians. Correctly guessing that the enemy was not really anxious for a prolonged fight so deep behind Rebel lines, Ruggles made the necessary dispositions for a slamming frontal assault. Supported by robust fire from the four pieces of field artillery, the three dismounted Confederate regiments would head straight together into the four dismounted Federal regiments for a general slug fest. Besides counting on the sheer audacity of the move and the height of the thick reeds to conceal his true numbers, Ruggles' hope for success most certainly hinged on the aggressive spirit of the regimental and company commanders who were expected to exploit any weaknesses that might occur once things kicked off.

Barteau could be counted on to press the attack. In turn, unlike the extraordinarily inept Cunningham, the gray-haired Earle was also a tested man of action and given the recent stain on his honor that the threat of a court-martial had brought, the iron-spirited warrior was absolutely primed for combat. More importantly, Earle's confident command presence resonated well with his company commanders who were finally given an opportunity to exhibit their own battlefield prowess. In contrast to Cunningham, Earle's defining characteristic that he brought to the battlefield was aggressiveness and he inspired his subordinate officers to use any and every means at their disposal to achieve a victory.

As the horses and horse holders were sent to the rear, the company commanders remained mounted in front of their respective companies directing the Alabamians by troop to form up in two long battle lines. All realized the limitations and deadly risks of attacking well defended positions, but were much gratified to hear deafening booms overhead from skillfully positioned Confederate artillery pounding away at the enemy. Indeed, the artillery gunners found their mark with spectacular effect causing great distress along the blue line, with one well-placed shot bringing "down five horses and four men."[371] Conversely, the Federal artillery had also unlimbered but were unable to properly sight their targets doing little real damage.

In what seemed like the blink of an eye, the bugles sounded the advance and the move across the ground began in a slow methodical roll, with energy reserved for the final push. The Rebel cannons continued to lob shells for a time before falling silent to avoid the untoward effects of friendly fire. The only thing now accompanying the stalwart Rebels through the wet mire were thousands of swirling mosquitoes and bugs. Reminded over and over by their line officers, the men were ordered to hold their fire as they advanced, leaving only the forward skirmishers to shoot at will with Union bullets returning the favor. At this early juncture of the contest, which was truly Indian-style, the Confederates were content to methodically trudge along through the cane-brakes with most of the Federal bullets missing flesh.

Mounted in front of the gray and snuff-colored uniforms in this unpleasant Mississippi marsh were the courageous company commanders of the 2nd Alabama. Brandishing drawn sabers and ignoring the zip zap of Union Minnie balls, the officers *led* their men across and around various hazards to include large puddles, watery logs, and stumps, doggedly keeping their companies together with words of encouragement and the occasional invective! "Remember Your Families." "The Cowards Won't Fight."

Captains John Carpenter of Company C and "Hell-Roaring" Bill Allen of Company F, were particularly conspicuous in hurrying their men forward so that C and F soon bulged an already jagged line causing the two-tiered formation to badly curve even further. Of course, Colonel Earle's stalwart form was everywhere, watching everything. As the Confederates closed the distance, the ground became slightly less tangled allowing the impetuous Captain Allen to pick up the pace and skillfully maneuver Company F even further ahead of all the others.

Allen seemed that day to be the hero. More sensing than knowing that the time was ripe for a final charge to victory, the instinctively courageous leader clinched down hard on the ever-present cigar and spurred "his gray charger far in advance"[372] of his own company in order to personally determine enemy dispositions. At a mere

hundred yards out Allen thrust his legs straight in the stirrups and abruptly pulled his mount to a halt. Absolutely indifferent to the incoming rounds singing all around, he observed significant groups of Yankees shifting about, some on foot and some on horse. Understanding that fluidity was not a positive sign for soldiers preparing to receive an attack, this told the blue-eyed commander all that he needed to know. The time had come to surge his men forward and smash head-on into the enemy, what the old school British military affectionately termed the "forlorn hope," and he wasn't waiting for formal orders from Colonel Earle.

"Hell-Roaring" Bill Allen whirled his war horse about and sped pell-mell through the grasses back to his astonished men. Accustomed to that well-known booming voice, the urgency of the waving motions from Allen's glittering saber left no doubt about his desire for swift action. "Company F, Form Up!" "Double Line!" "Prepare to Charge!" With rifles and pistols already primed and cocked the junior officers and men readily obeyed.

One mark of great leadership is the ability to turn on a dime when plans go sideways or, in this case, opportunity emerges. Colonel Earle also observed Allen's unmistakable gestures and instead of viewing such boldness as a threat to a successful general assault, Earle seized the moment and immediately ordered bugle calls directing all to follow Allen's boys into the fray. Boldness had met opportunity.

Positioned now at the head of his energized men, Hell-Roaring Bill Allen theatrically eye-leveled the tip of his blade and pointed it directly at the Yankees. Turning around in the saddle, he bellowed: "Charge Them Boys, Kill the Damn Thieves!"[373] Hearing the word *thieves* sent an electrifying adrenaline rush into their beings. After all that's exactly what these Yankees were, thieves and arsonists who terrorized women and children. Scottish tempers exploded and all knew Yankee blood would mark this day.

As if hit by lightning, the sounds of the men, which had up to then consisted primarily of low grunts and curses as they groped through the grassy terrain, was now far different. Hundreds of voices

mingled together in an ear shattering crescendo which one Union soldier said "the devil ought to copyright"[374] — the exhilarating and unmistakable yelping screech universally known as the "Rebel Yell."

It was on. Earle's screaming Alabamians bounded across the final yards of slashing reeds and soon thereafter their revolvers began popping off with loud bangs and black smoke. Throwing all caution aside, the Rebels literally crashed in amongst the Federals, dealing them dark death in close quarter combat. 2nd Alabama trooper Private Hunter was in the thick of it — "[o]ur boys went into the fight like tigers; yelling and whooping; all fought bravely."[375]

The men in blue were certainly not outmatched in numbers, but clearly outmatched in spirit. Even so, at first many held their ground and fought stubbornly, a few hand-to-hand, but the savagery was with the attackers and the Yankees soon had enough and crumbled in disorder. Ignoring pleas from their officers to stand firm, whole clusters of blue-bellies fled rearward for the cover and concealment offered by the pristine taller reeds behind them. Others ran directly for the horses, accelerating their escape by ditching arms and equipment.

The beautiful sight of so many Federals fleeing in wild panic further electrified the men of the 2nd Alabama who gave out excited shouts of triumph. Barteau and Boyles also followed suit, with their men punching out large holes to their own respective fronts, raking the enemy with blistering barrages of lead.

It was now contagious and most of the dumb-struck Federals that had not surrendered were now gunless and hatless, running into the cane-breaks behind them. Directed by shouting mounted officers, successive squadrons swept in to flush the enemy out of their hiding places. Union Chaplain Morrison wrote:

> Men could not see each other more than a few feet. Our men could hear every command given by the Rebel officers, but could not see the enemy.[376]

The shameful rout was certainly helped by the fact that Colonel Phillips had decided even before the fight had begun to retreat and make a run to the west across Mud Creek.[377] Thus, instead of preparing to meet the attackers with all he had the Union commander had shown no stomach for a real fight and his men knew it, having witnessed with their own eyes the supply wagons hurried out toward Rocky Ford preparatory to the battle. Furthermore, Phillips certainly did not count on the grit of so many energized Rebels baying at his heels, leaving insufficient time to properly organize a decent rear-guard defense.

Trooper W.G. Hunter of Company A, a brother of Colonel Winston Hunter, proudly documented the participation of the 2nd Alabama in the rolling attacks that relentlessly pressed the enemy back towards Mud Creek. The Rebels only halted to reload before charging forth anew to pour horrendous convergent fires into any Federals they encountered. Hunter bragged:

> We had been pursuing them near twenty-four hours, and would not have caught them probably, had not the cowardly dogs thought themselves secure in the almost impenetrable swamp in which they took refuge. It would have delighted you to see the gallant 2d make charge after charge, killing and driving the enemy from the brushwood and cane, in which they concealed themselves."[378]

Ruggles likewise beamed in his after-action report that all three "regiments of cavalry vied with each other in pressing the enemy home,"[379] with the fighting so up close and personal that the ground was literally painted red with blood. In addition, because the tall reeds concealed all but their upper extremities many Yankees suffered horrific head wounds spraying the surrounding vegetation with mists of brain matter. But no quarter was given. Shouting and shooting, gore splattered horsemen flushed out both small and large pockets of the enemy, each encounter sending panicked

Federals reeling further and further back. Hunter killed two of the Yankees himself and other eyewitnesses described how "[O]ur men would get their clothes and shoes or boots bloody in going through the woods [after them]."[380]

In just over an hour Ruggles' men had completely vanquished their opponents. The only favorable development for Colonel Phillips was that most of the Rebels were still on foot allowing a significant portion of his bewildered men to scramble to their animals and ride pell-mell across Mud Creek to then make their way to the Little Tallahatchie River leading to an exit at Rocky Ford. Sergeant Hancock of Barteau's command keenly felt the disappointment that the enemy was not annihilated. "Having to halt here to assist the artillery in crossing the creek [Mud Creek]," he wrote, "and to wait for our horses to be brought across, it gave the Federals the start on us."[381]

Still, for the next two hours or so, Phillips was not left the option of enjoying an unmolested retreat. Earle made sure that the 2nd Alabama's horse holders were first to bring up waiting mounts and he personally led his regiment in a prolonged chase riding down the enemy and scooping up large quantities of prisoners and abandoned gear. Fortunately for the men in blue, after about ten miles of this, Earle received hurried orders to break off and return to assist in blunting what was thought to be a new Union raiding party approaching from the west.

General Ruggles had received word at 1:30 p.m., while on the Cane Break battlefield, that another force of Federal cavalry numbering 3,000 was spotted moving against Brigadier General James Chalmers' cavalry command. The subject dispatch from one of Chalmers' couriers was dated June 19, so Ruggles could ill afford to continue to pursue Phillips should he now receive a second dispatch asking him to help meet this new and greater threat. As it turned out, Ruggles was not needed. The heralded Union foray was much smaller than reported and Chalmers was able to thwart one of the Federal columns on his own sending the entire body back to its camp near Corinth.

The Cane Break fight, also called the battle at Mud Creek, had lasted three hours costing the Union well over 100 troopers in killed, wounded, or captured. The company commander of the 2nd Alabama's A troop recorded that the enemy was routed "completely, killing and wounding about 100."[382] With no mention of the wounded, another source estimates the Federal loss in dead and captured at 75 and two pieces of abandoned artillery.[383]

> We soon drove them across Mud Creek, killing and capturing in all about seventy-five men. Destroying the bridge and deserting two guns, they [the Federals] hastily retreated. Our loss was light; few killed and wounded.[384]

According to Private Hunter, the 2nd Alabama bore the heaviest of the fighting, having led the main charge, and was rewarded with a gruesome harvest of the enemy's silent stare of death.

> [The Second Alabama Cavalry Regiment] killed over fifty of the vandals, had buried thirty nine and still burying them; don't know how many were wounded, as the Yanks carried them to the rear as fast as they fell.[385]

A couple of weeks after the fight, while accompanying some Confederate officers sent to parley at the Union held city of Corinth, Private Cochrane gleaned additional information about the battle. While the officers were conducting their business, some of the Federals who had been in the Mud Creek fight ventured out to the Rebel campsite to exchange coffee for tobacco and otherwise eyeball things. It was then that Cochrane learned new details.

> These Yankees said they had six hundred and ten men at the Mud Creek fight and if we had followed them on to Rockyford [sic] where they had to cross

we would have got every cannon, wagon, and horse they had.[386]

General Ruggles put the loss on the Confederate side as "two killed and seventeen wounded in this day's fight."[387] A review of the surviving company papers of the 2nd Alabama indicates that at least ten of the men were severely wounded (one subsequently died),[388] which accounts for over half of the total casualties and confirms the leading role which the 2nd Alabama played in the fight. Captain Allen recorded that "Private E.J. Lewis [Company F] was wounded in the leg which has since been amputated."[389] After noting the death of a prominent officer in Company G of the 2nd Alabama (Lt. Gaddis was hit in the thigh by a Minnie ball), Hunter spoke of a disfiguring face wound to an officer in his own company.

> [The Second Alabama] had eight or ten wounded. Lieut. Gaddis of Co. G, 2d Reg. of Ala. cavalry was mortally wounded and has since died from the effects of the wound. Lieut. Daniel Boyle of Co. I, same regiment, was wounded in the nose, a buckshot passing through it.[390]

The Yankees also left behind several well stocked wagons loaded with commissary goods consisting of "bacon, crackers, corn, oats, etc.,"[391] which thrilled the always-hungry Rebels to no end. Private Hunter reported:

> We captured seven wagons loaded with commissary stores, one piece of artillery and one caisson .... Our boys got some good eating, as they got sardines, crackers, sugar, coffee, etc.[392]

Union chaplain Morrison admitted tongue-in-cheek that the Federals "fell back rapidly"[393] and had to leave one of the artillery caissons stuck in the mud and "destroyed the five baggage wagons

that were behind it, to prevent their falling into the hands of the enemy."[394] Nevertheless, the rest of his recollection of the battle to include the number of Confederates and the casualties sustained were self-serving nonsense. The chaplain wrote:

> While we were preparing a crossing of Mud Creek, the enemy, 8,000 strong, under Gen. Ruggles, made a furious attack upon the rear guard, but were gallantly met and checked by the 5th Ohio Cavalry, held the enemy in check for two and a-half hours .... Our loss in this engagement, was 5 killed and 18 wounded. The loss of the enemy ... was not less than 200 in killed, wounded and missing.[395]

Sergeant Hancock of the 2nd Tennessee penciled in his daily diary that the match up was actually very lopsided in favor of the Federals — there were between 500 and 800 Union and between "three and four hundred [Confederates] engaged."[396] Considering again the number of horse holders set at the rear, Hancock's assessment of 300 to 400 Rebel fighters is certainly correct.

Private Hunter's Company A of the 2nd Alabama took five Federals as captives, three of whom were wounded, two mortally. Hunter noted with particular pride the observation of one Yankee prisoner about the coolness and battle courage of the 2nd Alabama.

> But the Yanks that we captured wanted to know if the 2nd Ala. cavalry were not old and tried troops, as they said "the 2d went rushing into the fight like they were used to it," and when told that it was the first fight they had ever been in as a regiment they seemed to be surprised.[397]

Without question, the battle of Mud Creek was a brilliant thrashing of a superior enemy force and a much-needed confidence

builder for the 2nd Alabama. All along the men had been eager to fight for their country and to protect the homeland from Union terror attacks. Reversing his earlier negative assessment from just two months ago when the regiment first arrived in northern Mississippi under Cunningham, General Ruggles was fully impressed, remarking with high praise that the "2nd Alabama cavalry were the *best fighting troops* he ever saw [emphasis added]."[398] From that time until the very end of the War, the 2nd Alabama Cavalry would live up to that reputation. They were hard fighting and patriotic men, the best of the best. The general wrote in his report:

> In this crisis I relied with entire confidence on that undaunted bravery of those chivalric sons of the South, which, when skillfully directed, no enemy could resist.[399]

For as much as Lieutenant Colonel Cunningham had brought shame to the regiment, Colonel Earle's staunch and courageous leadership brought it glory. Earle proved himself the ideal cavalry commander — he never asked his men to go where he would not lead them, and for this they loved him. Like the rising of a new day after a long dark night, the regiment was justifiably filled with a fierce pride in itself and their new hard hitting leader. In a private letter that was reproduced by the local newspaper in Pontotoc, a prominent member of the 2nd Alabama summed up the spirit of the regiment, now that the "one party," Cunningham, was finally gone.

> The 2d Alabama has now a merited distinction, and it is to be hoped, will have a respite from the calumny and slander so long heaped upon it .... The regiment is in high favor with the General commanding [Ruggles], and the citizens in Northeast Mississippi, and has reason to be proud of the occasion which afforded the opportunity for wiping out the stain

brought upon it soon after it came to Mississippi, by an act for which only one party is responsible [Cunningham's cowardly actions at Palo Alto and Kings Creek].[400]

For their part, the 2nd Alabama returned to the vicinity of Pontotoc to reconstitute and after a two-day rest and resupply, the companies dispersed back to their various outpost camps allowing them to obtain ample forage for the horses. For a couple of weeks there was an eerie stillness in northeastern Mississippi, as all attention focused on Vicksburg. The hope was that General Joseph E. Johnston would come to the relief of the besieged city, but regardless of the outcome the general spirit of resistance was very strong for the Alabamians. Come what may, they were eager to fight. Private Hunter wrote:

> It was reported here this morning [June 22, 1863] that the Yanks had been reinforced and were advancing towards Pontotoc. Let them come, they will receive a warm reception. The health of the 2d Ala. is very good. Corn crops are splendid in this State.[401]

Chapter Five

IN FERGUSON'S BRIGADE

"Gen Ferguson is very gallant & we like him very much, since writing the above we were ordered to charge the Yanks."[402]   —*Major S.H. Giles*

ON JULY 4, 1863, Vicksburg surrendered to Grant and over 35,000 Confederates were taken prisoner. Northerners were delighted and as they had done after his victory at Fort Donelson in 1862, Grant was swamped with cigars. Never a man to refuse a gift, he soon thereafter tried to smoke them all.

Although the Mississippi River was now in Union control, the Confederates still held onto much of the land territory in Mississippi. Whatever the Yankee high command had in mind as their next step, it was certain that Union terror raids into the rich grain producing areas of northeast Mississippi would be stepped up and defending the area with disjointed regiments subject to conflicting orders was no longer practicable, if it had ever been. The past several months had made it abundantly clear that the Southern cavalry required drastic attention, particularly given the poor performance of the Mississippi State militia which were increasingly seen as havens for skulkers who often dispersed at the first hint of combat.

With the approval of Davis' War Department, General Johnston reorganized the cavalry in the western theater from top to bottom.

In July 1863, the various cavalry regiments operating in the area, to include the 2nd Alabama Cavalry, were assigned to permanent brigades. The 2nd Alabama was posted to the newly formed "Ferguson's Brigade," under the command of Brigadier General Samuel Wragg Ferguson, a twenty-eight-year-old South Carolinian. Though later placed under Brigadier General William Hicks "Red" Jackson's Division, Ferguson's Brigade served for quite some time as an independent brigade and reported only to the regional corps cavalry commander, Major General Stephen D. Lee, also a South Carolinian. S.D. Lee took this position in late July 1863, after his prisoner exchange from Vicksburg, where he had served as the commander of an infantry brigade.

Born in 1834, in Charleston, South Carolina, Ferguson was the son of a wealthy planter-politician and every bit the Southern aristocrat. He inherited a large rice plantation on the Cooper River just outside of Charleston, called Dockon and according to his wife Kate, whom he married in late 1862, their mansion was "situated at the head of a beautiful avenue of live oaks."[403] He graduated from the United States military academy at West Point in 1857, and served in the U.S. Army in Utah during the Mormon War of 1857-58. Ferguson resigned his officer's commission in March 1861, and entered the provisional army of the Confederacy where he performed with great distinction at First Manassas and then in several bloody battles along the Mississippi as the lieutenant colonel of the 28th Mississippi Cavalry Regiment. Promoted to full colonel in early 1863, Ferguson continued to demonstrate exceptional abilities along the Mississippi Delta.

Ironically, Ferguson was present at both of the key events of the War, marking the very beginning and the very end. As aide-de-camp to General Pierre G.T. Beauregard, then Lieutenant Ferguson was the officer in charge of the contingent that accepted the surrender of Fort Sumter from the Union commander, Major Anderson, and it was he who supervised the raising of the Confederate national flag over the brick fortress.[404] Ferguson was also one of the last Confederate generals in the eastern theater to surrender, after his

*Brigadier General
Samuel Wragg Ferguson.*

cavalry brigade helped escort the fleeing President Jefferson Davis and his small party of government officials into Georgia.

Ferguson was a firm disciplinarian and looked the part. Fair of skin, he kept his hair well-trimmed but sported an unusually long black beard that served to offset a kinder set of eyes. A neat dresser, he wore a splendidly tailored gray uniform with pant legs securely tucked into well-polished riding boots.

Being a fellow West Pointer, Jefferson Davis was marginally acquainted with Ferguson, at least well enough to exchange the occasional personal correspondence. In a letter to Davis dated July 12, 1863, Ferguson showed much humility for his elevation in rank and expressed an earnest desire to secure "about three thousand men" for his brigade depending on whether or not he could also take hold "of the companies of State troops already formed" such as Lowry's Mississippi State Cavalry Regiment and Major Ham's Mississippi State Cavalry Battalion.[405] In reality,

however, Ferguson was not able to secure these additions and his small command consisted of three rock solid regiments, one battalion, and a fine artillery battery, all very familiar to each other as General S.D. Lee stated:

> Earle's, 2nd Alabama Cavalry Regiment; Barteau's, 2nd Tennessee Cavalry Regiment; Boyles', 56th Alabama Cavalry Regiment and Inge's, 12th Mississippi Partisan Rangers Cavalry Battalion. Ferguson also had one artillery battery of six pounders, Owens' Arkansas Artillery Battery, commanded by Captain James A. Owens.[406]

On July 23, 1863, even before obtaining the formal date of rank to Brigadier General, Ferguson set about organizing the new brigade of horse soldiers from his headquarters at Pontotoc, which he soon shifted over to newly rebuilt Okolona. Relying on Ruggles' advise that the 2nd Alabama were his best fighters, Ferguson wisely pulled his personal escort from Colonel Earle's regiment.[407]

S.D. Lee had confidence in his fellow South Carolinian and thought that Ferguson's 1,500 (effective number) veteran troopers were strong and able, although irregularly equipped. In August 1863, he reported the following conditions for the new brigade:

> General Ferguson's cavalry command occupies the line from Rocky Ford to the Alabama line, and consists of the Second and Fifty-sixth Alabama regiments, Second Tennessee Cavalry, and Twelfth Mississippi Partisan Rangers, numbering about 1,500. I was able to see but one regiment, the Second Alabama, which presented a fine appearance. From the general's statement [General Ferguson], in which I have perfect confidence, his command may be considered reliable, though very indifferent

Lieutenant General Stephen Dill Lee.   *Brigadier General William Hicks "Red" Jackson.*

armed and equipped. His supply of ammunition is quite limited, and the Twelfth Mississippi is mostly without accouterments.[408]

In the same report, S.D. Lee provided an outline of the disposition of all his cavalry forces in northern Mississippi which showed Brigadier General Chalmers's Brigade (in General "Red" Jackson's Division) covering the area from Rocky Ford to the west and Ferguson's Brigade covering east from Rocky Ford straight across to the Alabama State line. All these forces were focused towards the Union strongholds to their north, with Ferguson particularly charged with protecting the vital north-south Ohio & Mobile. The rest of Red Jackson's Division, which consisted of two other brigades and a very excellent battalion under the intrepid Colonel Sul Ross, occupied a line in the middle of Mississippi, from Raymond to Lexington.

For the 2nd Alabama Cavalry, acting as part of a brigade meant larger and more bloody combat operations. On the other hand,

it also meant that the overall scheme of activity for the regiment was more predictable. With the men pledging total confidence in Colonel Earle — they would stand by him under any conditions no matter who was in charge of the brigade — all were anxious to learn the ropes of operating as a unified brigade. As it turned out, the familiarization training would be learned on the fly.

The Union horse raids resumed on August 13, 1863. Coming out from their dens at La Grange, Tennessee, the Yankees tested the post-Vicksburg waters with a relatively small force consisting of elements from the 2nd Iowa, 3rd Michigan, and 11th Illinois. Numbering probably just over 500 raiders, the troopers were led by Major Datus E. Coon and they carried no cannon or heavy wagons to slow them down. Per usual, they were on a terror and pillage mission with added instructions to disrupt the rich autumn corn harvest.

Coon's immediate destination was Grenada, but he would first have to penetrate the line patrolled by Chalmers to the west and Ferguson to the east. Armed with good intelligence from a network of Tories, the raiders slipped through unopposed right between the two Rebel commands, just 20 miles east of Oxford. It was not until August 17, at Coffeeville, that the Federals were finally picked up by some of Chalmers' butternut pickets who skirmished with the enemy for the next 15 miles all the way into Grenada. With nothing to stop them, however, the Yankees leisurely sacked the town and put public and private property to the torch, enjoying the sight of terrified civilians scattering into the woods.

By the time Ferguson pulled together his brigade for a pursuit, the Federals were well on their way back to La Grange. Although the new brigadier general had failed his first test of command, he showed no inclination of admitting it, as evidenced by a grossly misplaced communique to General Ruggles. The Yankees, who numbered only 500, had already left Grenada on August 18, when Ferguson sent his telegram on August 20, two days later.

> I move tonight to Houston with between 1,200 and 1,500 cavalry. Will unite with Chalmers tomorrow. Enemy 2,500 strong at Grenada.[409]

In all fairness to Ferguson, hit and run cavalry raids were always a plague for both sides during the War, with the Confederate cavalry under the likes of Forrest, Stuart, Van Dorn, Mosby, Morgan, and Wheeler masters at raiding behind the lines. Given the realities of transmitting accurate and timely information, as long as the riders kept on the move and focused on limited objectives they were almost impossible to stop. The primary distinction between the Unionists and the Confederates rested in the fact that the Rebel raiders struck only lawful military targets while the Yankees almost always included civilians and their private property as primary objectives.

In addition, with the Rebel cavalry stretched so thin, there were many open spots throughout the vast areas of geography that the enemy could penetrate. Furthermore, as previously noted, each trooper was required to furnish his own horse, so that finding suitable replacement mounts to perform the longer patrols greatly aggravated the situation regarding the number of effectives on hand for active duty. In some cases, to avoid assignment to the regiment's "slow train," the cavalrymen would be forced to buy mules, a particularly worrisome development. Private Cochrane acknowledged the perennial problem, writing from Pontotoc, Mississippi, in November 1863:

> A good many [of the 2nd Alabama] have gone home [into Alabama] after horses, among them W. Sanders who sent me word by Claiborne that he would bring anything I wish.[410]

— Trading with the Enemy —

With the fall of Vicksburg, the Union sought to gobble up additional chunks of land that had once belonged to the Confederacy. When these new areas were secured, the Federal policy was to divide the captured territory into military districts and place them under military law. However, as the Federals discovered in "occupied" Tennessee, much of the Union controlled territory was still strongly pro-Confederate, particularly in the countryside. The only reprieve for the civilian population was that the majority of the Union troops were not used to garrison the small towns and villages, but were instead allocated to small fortified forts and blockhouses all along the railroads at strategic spots to guard bridges, cross roads, water tanks, and culverts. Thus, while the Union controlled Tennessee, upper north Mississippi, and upper north Alabama, they generally confined their soldiers to protecting the railroads. Apart from the major cities which were occupied, the women and children living within these outlying areas were more or less ignored and left to fend for themselves. From the Union's view, keeping these country people in grinding poverty ensured that they would be passive.

Sadly, it was in the areas that immediately bordered the occupied lands that Southern civilians suffered the most. Far enough away from the enemy to be in Confederate territory, but close enough to be the subject of constant Federal terror raids, these poor people were placed in the harshest conditions conceivable and had great difficulty in just living. Many fled, others had nowhere to go, and all endured the grueling conditions as best they could. Writing from New Albany, a September 1863, letter from a trooper in Ferguson's command noted the conditions in the affected areas.

> Here the country presents, as ours [in Greenville, Mississippi], a dreary uninviting spectacle. Fields grown up, houses deserted, churches pillaged & the people plundered generally.[411]

For thousands of women, the only option to maintain a bare subsistence to feed their children was to trade what little cotton they could farm to the enemy for the necessaries of life. In other cases, they would purchase a bale or two of cotton with Confederate currency or other means and then sell the bales behind the lines to willing Union buyers. Above all things, these Southerners had great difficulty obtaining salt, a commodity absolutely essential for the curing and preserving of meat. Everyone in Ferguson's brigade understood the hardships on the loyal country folk and were extremely sympathetic.

> The people in the Northern portion of the State [Mississippi] who have been repeatedly despoiled by the Yankees and insulted by the insolent foe, notwithstanding the fact that they have repeatedly traded with the enemy, are in the main as true as steel to our cause.[412]

Unfortunately, the Confederate high command saw this practice as a threat to the war effort and in addition to picketing the long lines watching for new Federal movements, Ferguson and the other cavalry commands were ordered to enforce the government's policy of stopping civilians from trading cotton and other commodities with the enemy. No dispensations were allowed.

Considering the hopelessness and desperation of these otherwise good Southerners, Generals Chalmers and Ferguson openly expressed great reluctance to carry out orders from Joe Johnston and S.D. Lee to confiscate "all wagons and mules [from civilians caught] while transporting cotton toward the enemy's lines, and to seize all goods coming from the enemy and sell them at auction."[413] Chalmers wrote of one heartbreaking incident:

> A scene that I lately witnessed can best illustrate the point: a poor woman, whose husband was in the [Confederate] army, with seven small children to

support, and an old gray-haired father seventy-five years of age, had struggled for means sufficient to buy one bale of cotton, took it to DeSoto County [then in Union hands] and purchased salt and a few articles for family use. They were caught at Tallahatchie on their return, and, notwithstanding the most piteous and heart-broken grief, her goods and little truck cart with two oxen were ordered to be confiscated. Not a man present could restrain his emotion, and a generous officer present [probably General Chalmers himself] furnished her money to leave on.[414]

Ferguson also hated the order and in his memoirs related a similar story and how, in that particular case, he cleverly got around the odious policy.

At one time when camped at New Albany, I received an order from Gen Johnston, who was desirous to stop the trade with Memphis [then occupied by Federal forces] by means of cotton carried in wagons, to take active measures to suppress this trade, and to send out and capture all such wagons, both going in and coming out, confiscate the teams and goods and have them sold at auction [the money went to the quartermaster]. Some days afterwards I noticed that something of interest was attracting attention; looking out, I saw a party [cavalry detachment] sent in compliance with that order, coming into camp with quite a train of little one horse vehicles, all driven by women. ... There were tears and entreaties to melt one's heart; I would gladly have let them all go and take their plunder with them, but my orders were imperative. The next morning the Quarter Master had the auction [local civilians were allowed to bid]. When a wagon and team was

put up, the owner [woman] would make some low bid and would get the property without opposition; once or twice some outsider would attempt to run the property up, the men would cry "shame, let the woman have her team" and she would get it.... When it came to selling her goods [things she bought with the cotton] the case was different and the bidding was lively.... The article most eagerly purchased was snuff, which I learned could effect more in a trade than cash. The ingenuity of these people in getting their cotton into Memphis was wonderful. They would go by unused roads, or where there was no road at all, cross a considerable stream where there was neither ford nor bridge, by swimming the animals, floating the cotton bales, and taking the wagon piecemeal in dugouts, which perhaps could not carry more than one wheel at a trip.[415]

— Working on the Railroad —

On September 21, 1863, the 2nd Alabama Cavalry received electrifying news of General Braxton Bragg's unexpected victory at Chickamauga Station, Georgia, over Major General William Rosecrans' Union Army of the Cumberland. A bloody two-day battle forced Rosecrans to ingloriously retreat, lucky to escape with the remnants of his army back into the city of Chattanooga. In large part the victory was made possible by the timely arrival of Lieutenant General James Longstreet's veterans (11,000 infantry) dispatched by rail from Lee's army in Virginia. Predictably, the dull-witted Bragg failed to follow up on his first and *only* victory.

The reports were all the more impressive considering how Rosecrans had brilliantly outmaneuvered Bragg from Middle Tennessee just four months previous, forcing the clueless Confederate general all the way back past Chattanooga. It was here that Bragg turned and struck, but instead of immediately pursuing the badly

demoralized Federals, he reflexively went on the defense, content to lay a half-hearted siege to the city by posting his 40,000 men in a six-mile semicircle stretching along Missionary Ridge to Lookout Mountain. Sending only small elements of cavalry to disrupt enemy supply lines, Bragg basically sat on his hands waiting for the Federals to gain reinforcements and once again take the initiative.

Dumbfounded by Bragg's recalcitrance, his subordinate generals were in a foul mood bordering on open revolt and publicly urged President Davis to relieve him from command (except for General Wheeler). Inexplicably, Davis' response was to relieve two of Bragg's complaining generals instead and dispatch Longstreet's corps off to conduct an imminently useless raid in wintertime Tennessee![416]

Of course, all was not peaches and cream on the Union side of things. For a time, the Federals were in a tight spot trapped inside Chattanooga. Since Bragg had already cut the Nashville & Chattanooga, the closest Union controlled rail was the far-off Memphis & Charleston and until things stabilized or turned in their favor, the Federals were reduced to hauling supplies by wagons almost 70 miles over rugged mountains to get in just enough to survive. Forced to go on half rations, thousands of horses and mules would soon die of starvation or be eaten.

From his headquarters in Memphis, Ulysses Grant, who had assumed command of all Federal troops in the West, focused all his attention on getting reinforcements and provisions to the besieged city. Soon, a whole Union corps was heading from Memphis along the Union held portion of the Memphis & Charleston coming for the relief of Chattanooga.

Another short-lived silver lining caused by the victory at Chickamauga, was an opportunity for the Rebels to tear apart and otherwise smash Federal held rail-lines. On October 2, 1863, General Johnston arrived in New Albany to orchestrate an ambitious strike against the Union rail to the north. While there, Ferguson's brigade was paraded out and reviewed by Johnston, to the great amusement of the men who had never been inspected by a lieutenant general.

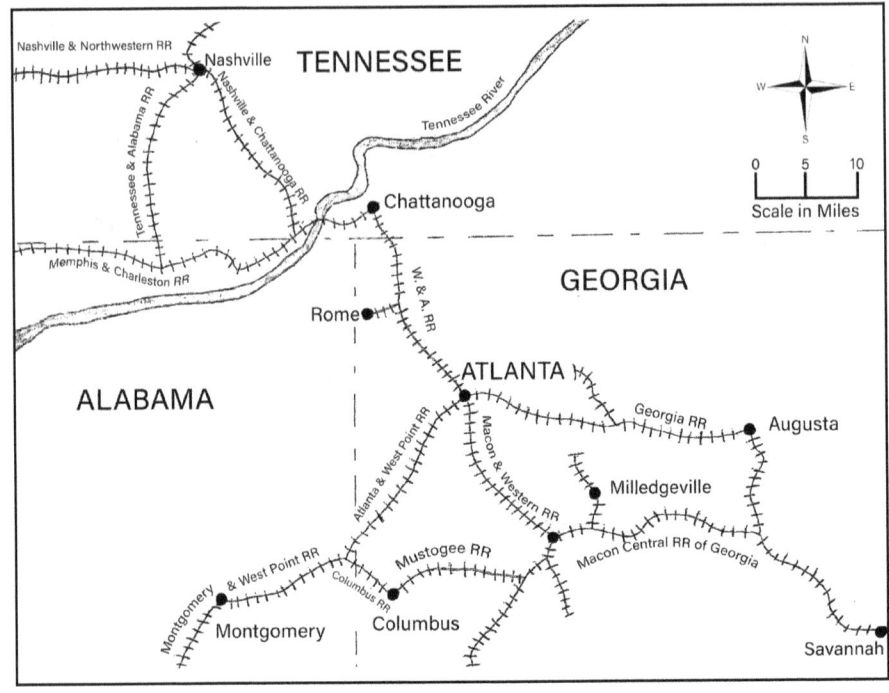

Key Rail-Lines.

The Union controlled Memphis & Charleston hugged the Tennessee/Mississippi border and then ran on across northern Alabama where it linked to the Nashville & Chattanooga. To disrupt this vital lifeline, Johnston's plan was to send two sizable cavalry groups under the overall command of S.D. Lee on a two-week raid to tear up track in Tennessee and Alabama and otherwise slow enemy movements heading to relieve Chattanooga. The first group of about 2,000 Confederate riders consisted of two brigades, one under Chalmers and the other under Colonel Robert V. Richardson (the 12th Mississippi from Ferguson's Brigade was detached and assigned to Richardson). The second group, led personally by General S.D. Lee, also consisted of two brigades, that of Ferguson's and the newly promoted Brigadier General Sul Ross.

Chalmers and Richardson would move up from northern Mississippi to strike the Memphis & Charleston in western Tennessee

at Collierville and S.D. Lee would march into northern Alabama to do damage to the railroad and then link up with General Joseph E. Wheeler's cavalry from the Army of Tennessee where, depending on circumstances on the ground, possibly combine forces and push into east Tennessee. Again, the overall objective for the two cavalry "battle groups" was focused on doing as much damage as possible to Union resupply efforts.

Both battle groups had only limited success in their respective assignments, with the Chalmers and Richardson team accomplishing the least. Not only were Chalmers and Richardson unable to get out of northern Mississippi, they weren't even able to unite their two brigades. Each ran into separate Union blocking forces totaling about 4,000 cavalry and 2,000 infantry. After some heavy fighting over a ten-day period, the gray-clad riders decided to return to their original positions, never reaching the Memphis & Chattanooga.

S.D. Lee had similar problems but was nevertheless able to achieve the larger part of his objectives. On October 6, Lee's troopers moved out of Pontotoc and arrived four days later near Florence, Alabama. Although S.D. Lee soon thereafter reached the railroad in north Alabama and did significant damage tearing up tracks, none of his cavalry brigades connected with General Wheeler's much larger force for further raids into Tennessee.

In the initial movement out of Mississippi and into Alabama, Ferguson's brigade split up into their respective regiments to increase forage possibilities for the horses, but as the Alabama cavalrymen entered "sweet home Alabama" they were unceremoniously greeted by heavy cold rains which lasted for four long and miserable days and nights. By October 20, the 2nd Alabama left a comfortable bivouac near Hennington's Spring and moved 23 miles to about three miles west of Tuscumbia where they joined the entire brigade and rested up for the work to come. The next day, Ferguson's full brigade rode the 12 miles west along the Memphis & Charleston connecting with Ross' Texas brigade to begin the hard yet enjoyable job of destroying and tangling miles of rail and telegraph wires.

To protect themselves from surprise attacks by enemy cavalry, one brigade of dismounted men would tear up track while the other provided a shield from any Federals that might materialize. Then, after a day or two, the brigades would switch roles. While on the later duty — guarding Ross' brigade as it tore up track — advanced 2nd Alabama patrols discovered a contingent of perhaps fifteen thousand Federal soldiers under General William T. Sherman marching alongside the tracks, heading to the relief of Chattanooga. After a delaying engagement fought in the rain with lead enemy elements, Ferguson prudently fell back to the east bank of Cane Creek. Even though the advancing enemy was slowed, being obliged to fix the broken tracks along their path of march, time was running out for the Confederate raiders. Nevertheless, for the next couple of days, Cane Creek would serve as a primary bivouac as the Rebels tore apart long stretches of the Memphis & Charleston. Ferguson recalled that his and Ross' men worked feverously with great enthusiasm "heating the rails in the middle, and twisting them around telegraph poles."[417] With a flair for dry humor, Sergeant Hancock described how the men "worked on the railroad" to *fix it.* Hancock recorded in his diary:

> Friday 23rd [October 1863]. Ferguson's Brigade, with two pieces of artillery, went out [from Cane Creek] to relieve Ross' Brigade. [S.D.] Lee still kept part of his division "fixing" the railroad in advance of Sherman [Sherman was the overall commander of the advancing Federal forces]. I guess that when he (Sherman) examined it he thought that someone had been fixing it.[418]

> Friday 25th [October 1863]. All quiet in front again .... It seems Sherman is moving very slowly .... Though perhaps, Lee is not fixing the railroad to suit him, and, therefore, he has to stop and refix it in some places.

Of course, given the increasing numbers of Federals pouring into the area and without Wheeler's men to bolster his numbers, S.D. Lee could stay in the Tennessee River Valley for only so long. In addition, food and forage was low and with winter fast approaching the troopers looked forward to the luxury of warm huts and stoves instead of the shiver and chill brought on by cold blowing rains against used up tents, oil-clothes, and thread-bare clothing. S.D. Lee began sending urgent wires to General Bragg seeking permission to withdraw his cavalry back to Mississippi.

— Whipping the Tory 1st Alabama Cavalry —

If certain strategic gains were a disappointment for S.D. Lee — not joining up with Wheeler and moving into Tennessee to wreak havoc — at least there was a gratifying bright spot at the tactical level for the 2nd Alabama. On October 25, 1863, while Ferguson and his command were busy prying up rails just north of Cane Creek at Barton Station, exciting news arrived in the late afternoon. A large raiding party consisting of the hated Union Tory cavalry had been reported about 50 miles south of Russellville, Alabama, in Walker County, where the city of Jasper served as the county seat.[419]

Confederates referred to all white Southern Unionists as Tories, harkening back to the derogatory term used for those Americans who remained loyal to the British Crown in the War for Independence. Most of the Tories in Alabama came from the mountainous region of the State where Union sympathizers abounded. In addition, those Tories who actually joined the Union military were viewed as worse than bushwhackers, and for good reason, they were notorious for their cruelty towards fellow Southerners. The looting and burning of homes were often accompanied by other unspeakable criminal acts against defenseless women. An Alabama historical source, published in 1900, noted the following:

> Forming themselves [Tories] into bands with such names as "Destroying Angels" or "Prowling Brigades" they would sweep down from the piney-woods [north

Alabama] to raid their more fortunate neighbors in the valleys. They burned cotton, cotton-gins, jails, courthouses and records, and houses, "confiscating" food and other property as they went. By their depredations thousands of Confederate sympathizers were driven from their homes — some to be stripped and shipped by the marauding guerillas and not a few to be murdered and raped. Even to the Union conquerors, the Tories were sometimes as vicious as copperheads [poisonous snakes].[420]

S.D. Lee wished to hit this Tory raid a heavy blow and ordered General Ferguson to take two regiments from his brigade and destroy them. The mission was daunting and the only intelligence Ferguson had to work with was that the Tories were thought to be returning back to Union occupied Iuka on the Mississippi border with Tennessee. While Yankee cavalry raids were nothing new to the 2nd Alabama, this particular group of miscreants held a special interest as they made up the much-despised 1st Alabama "Union" Cavalry Regiment, recruited from scattered pockets of Unionists who resided in the northern counties of Alabama, primarily from Marion, Winston, and Fayette and were led by the notorious Colonel George E. Spencer, well known for his outrages. Ferguson explained his orders.

> One afternoon while busy destroying the railroad track I received orders to repair at once to camp with two regiments, get them ready to start as soon as three day's rations could be cooked, and proceed, with a guide to be furnished me, across the mountains, and intercept a regiment of native Alabamians that had been enlisted in the service of the U.S. and were celebrating [pillaging] at a point designated.[421]

*Colonel George Spencer, Commander,
1st Alabama (Union) Cavalry Regiment.*

With no time to waste, the cavalry chief called upon Colonel Earle to round up all available effectives from his 2nd Alabama, stressing that he desired only the strongest and best for a mission which he anticipated would require grueling hours in the saddle. Likewise, the 2nd Tennessee's second in command, Lieutenant Colonel George H. Morton (Colonel Barteau was unavailable), was ordered to mount up all the Tennesseans he could muster. Bolstered by Mooreland's battalion of sharp shooters (from General Phillip Roddey's brigade), the hastily organized strike force provided Ferguson an effective command of perhaps 500 good men and mounts, but no horse artillery. After preparing three day's rations and stuffing extra ammunition into saddlebags, each man braced a knee against his horse's ribs, tightened the saddle girth, and mounted up. The Confederates started out just as the sun went down, Ferguson refused to waste precious hours waiting for dawn, though the general had no concerns about anyone lagging during the march as all were eager to give these traitors a large dose of Southern justice.

To be sure, it was a long shot that they would find, let alone intercept, the Tories. To increase the odds, Ferguson proposed to head due west across Alabama and into Mississippi intending to then take the primary road south to Fulton with the idea of snaring the returning northbound enemy somewhere along the way. He sent his best riders out ahead with orders to range far and wide to make contact.

Throughout the night, the command snaked its way slowly west across rocky landscape guided along by numerous lanterns attached to long poles bobbing up and down past the horses heads to illuminate the path. In the darkness, the steady tramp of hoof beats lulled many to brief moments of sleep in the saddle, an occupational hazard that often resulted in embarrassing bruises. After a grueling 35 miles, dawn was just beginning to chase the shadows away when the exhausted command halted for a short rest near the junction of Cedar Creek and Bear Creek. At this point the weather shifted against them and the river crossing took place in a cold brisk rain that seemingly came out of nowhere, causing almost two hours to pass before all were safe and accounted for on the other side and able to move south on the Iuka-Fulton road in the direction of Fulton. Thankfully, the rain stopped and a moderate wind sprang up to help dry things out.

Ferguson guessed correctly. The Federals were still in Alabama slowly heading north out of the Bull Mountain region intending to cut over to the west at Vincents Crossroads to then get on the Eastport-Iuka-Fulton road in Mississippi which would take them straight north to Iuka. In their unsatiable quest for plunder, the Tories were in their normal operational pattern which had them spread out to make full use of various rough trails where local guides directed small squadrons to outlying homes where the "soldiers" could steal, rob, and burn.

Determined to increase his odds to catch them, Ferguson audaciously ordered a separate column consisting of two companies under Captain Richard W. Carter, who commanded Company E, to move due west towards Bay Springs. Should the Tories somehow

slip past Ferguson's grip, Carter would serve as both a ready reserve and/or a blocking force. Private Cochrane, explained the situation.

> General Ferguson sent a Captain named [Richard] Carter [Company E] with two companies to a certain place and the Yankees did not come there and the Captain staid [sic] there waiting for orders. He is the strictest man in doing his duty in the regiment and he will fight well if he has an opportunity.[422]

Along with Captain Carter's command rode twenty-one year old Private Thomas M. Mosley. Mosley was a typical member of the 2nd Alabama possessing a wiry yet muscular five-foot ten-inch frame which sat comfortably in the saddle. With a black slouch hat pulled low over his brown wavy hair, Mosley had already seen much hard riding and fighting — he proudly sported a Yankee bullet hole in his hat — and he would soon see more.

Given that the 1st Alabama Union was at full complement and superior in number to Ferguson's force, splitting his command even by one company was a risky decision that could easily backfire. Nevertheless, Ferguson had full confidence in his men and in himself. His sole desire was to press the enemy into an all-out fight.

> I turned toward Fulton, and after reaching the intersection of this road [Eastport-Iuka-Fulton road in Mississippi] with that to Bay Springs, I sent one squadron [two companies] in the latter direction for the purpose of holding the enemy in check, should they move toward that point, and preventing their escape. With the remainder of my force I moved toward the Bull Mountain country [via Vincents Crossroads].[423]

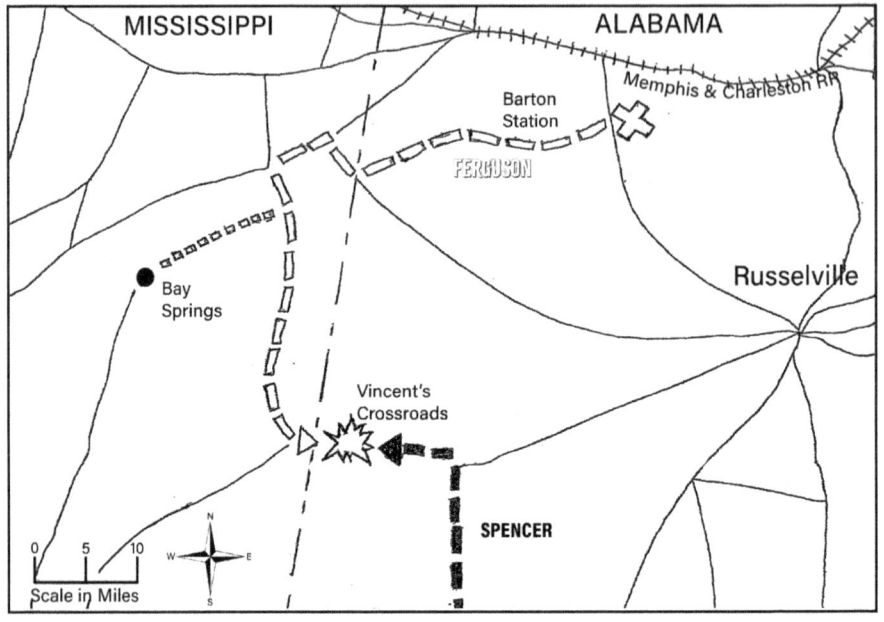

Ferguson and Spencer Movements.

As it turned out, Ferguson's gamble in splitting his command was unnecessary. After trotting on for barely three more miles south down the main road, one of his mud splattered scouts came galloping back to report that Tory looters had been located up ahead, just barely in Alabama and most likely aiming due west towards Mississippi via Vincents Crossroads (located near the modern town of Red Bay, Alabama) just on the Alabama/Mississippi border,[424] most certainly intending to take the same road north to Iuka that Ferguson was then traversing down. Elated with the news, Ferguson immediately sent fast moving couriers to recall Captain Carter and stepped up the pace of march while simultaneously sending out Captain Pegues' Company D to fan ahead of the main column and gather additional intelligence to confirm or deny the existence of larger bodies of Tories and their direction of travel. Private Cochrane, who rode out with Captain Pegues, explained the situation as they sought out the enemy.

> Gen. Ferguson sent Captain Pegues' squadron on a different road to find where the enemy was. The people [local civilians in the area] are such Tories they would not tell us a thing. We were in two hours ride from the Yankees when our company started but we did not know it.[425]

Just after noon, Ferguson reached the junction that led east to Vincents Crossroads and unhesitatingly turned his troopers straight towards the Alabama line. By 1:30, the Confederates hit paydirt. Scattered shots to the front told the Rebel commander that his personal escort guard had made contact and Ferguson could see the military situation clearly enough. Like a hungry wolf, Ferguson wished he had never divided his men, yet his prayer now was that the enemy would stand and put up a fight.

The Union commander must have heard Ferguson's whispered request, for that is exactly what happened. Instead of avoiding a general engagement, Colonel Spencer ordered his men to dismount, spread out on either side of the main road, and take up standard battle formations with skirmishers to the advance. Certainly, the last thing that Spencer should have done was to seek battle with unknown Confederate forces, but the Union commander was hoping for a measure of redemption to make up for his otherwise lackluster performance thus far. Having failed to reach the raid's initial objective of Jasper, even though he got to within ten miles of the place, Spencer saw an opportunity to at least gain some bragging rights about "besting the enemy" in a fight.

Assuming that his heavily armed men would certainly emerge on top of any skirmish, the egotistical Spencer proposed to make just enough of a demonstration to justify a glowing after-action report painting a "glorious battle victory over superior Rebel forces." Brushing aside exaggerated reports from locals that thousands of Rebels were in the area, he presumptuously assumed that he was facing either a small probing force or perhaps local militia. His tunnel vision would prove to be disastrous. Few of the Tories

imagined that they were in for the fight of their lives and this time it would not be against women and children which was all that they had "conquered" since leaving Iuka.

Indeed, with Colonel Spencer at the head of the regiment, the Unionists left Iuka on October 19, 1863, and took the Eastport-Iuka-Fulton road to the junction leading to Vincents Crossroads where they then turned east and entered Alabama uncontested. The raiders numbered between 700-800 heavily armed men with two pieces of light artillery and the usual compliment of supply wagons and support personnel. The mountain howitzers, which were extremely maneuverable over rough terrain and very deadly at close range, were each drawn by a single horse.

The Union regiment may have touted itself as a professional military force but pure and simple this "scout" was primarily designed to pillage. Relying heavily on local Union sympathizers to direct them to the best homes and farms to plunder, the guides also used the raids as opportunities to even old scores, helping themselves to the goods of their neighbors.

A wartime diary kept by Sergeant Major Francis Wayland Dunn, the senior enlisted non-commissioned officer, euphemistically recorded some of the outrages committed against civilians as the Tory cavalry marauded across portions of Alabama, recording Colonel Spencer's gleeful boast to innocent civilians that the Unionists "were the children of Israel bringing the plague on them."[426] When one realizes that Dunn's accounts of pillaging and plundering reflect only what was accomplished by soldiers in his immediate group, it is little wonder that the people were gripped by stark terror when they saw gangs of blue riders approaching their homes and farms. Of course, Dunn was careful not to fully implicate himself by recording the most heinous acts, yet he nevertheless openly confirmed that they were intent on "cleansing" the countryside which included gathering Southern blacks and putting them to forced labor. In fact, viewed as a valuable commodity, thousands upon thousands of Southern blacks were used to work as common laborers in Federal military encampments without compensation, except for the food

they were given.⁴²⁷ Untold numbers perished from malnourishment and abuse. Sergeant Major Dunn recorded the following:

> October 19: Left camp [Iuka, Mississippi] about 10 .... [After camping for the night] got [stole] some dried beef and chickens. The woman was going to knock Steve [another Yankee trooper] over with a club but he got [stole] the chicken. Camped there at night and had another time taking [stealing] things [private property].
>
> October 20: Went as far as Vinsons (Vincents) Crossroads today. Wagons all the time behind .... Stopped to feed [steal] at Daniels [a private farm]. He had robbed some of our men [Union sympathizers in north Alabama] and Colonel [Spencer] gave them permission to burn his house. Everything was destroyed. It looked rough enough.
>
> October 21: Country getting worse and worse. Went through a piece of woods about 20 miles with only one or two houses [to plunder] .... tonight had [stole] a sheep [for dinner]. We live pretty well [robbing and pillaging private property].
>
> October 22: Tonight got to Charley Knights [a private farm], stony and rough country as I ever saw. A detachment was sent out and burned Allen's factory [a private business of some sort], about $120,000 worth of goods .... At noon some of Company L went in advance to Underwood's [a private farm]. Got [stole] several horses and brandy, negroes and apples. When we started again I secured [stole] a horse at the same place. Took [stole] two wagons for [our] government in the afternoon.

October 23: Rained today. Burned the [civilian] wagons and packed as much stuff [stolen goods] as we could on the mules .... Intended to get to Jasper [Alabama] but only got within ten miles of the place. Stopped at Lovell's [a civilian farm] .... Here I got [stole] a fine mare and led her back to the column. Also got [stole] a coffee pot, a thing we have hard work to get [the owner resisted the robbery]. Slept in a corn crib.

October 24: Turned back in the morning [heading back to Vincents Crossroads to then cross into Mississippi], a disappointment to most of the men [they wanted to steal more booty]. Raining as usual .... At Underwood's [a civilian farm] I filled a bag [stole] with apples and chickens and got [stole] corn for feed. Went two miles further and there camped for the night. Had a good supper, [stolen] apple sauce.

October 25: Started about four o'clock. Guide [local civilian Tory] took us right through the woods. Stopped near Bull Mountain at Wallace [a civilian farm]. Caught [stole] a chicken also Steve [stole a chicken]. Eat with Colonel and staff. All of us slept under the shed. Sung and talked late into the night. Some of the men went two miles ahead to a house, Worthington's [a private farm] and played smash [wantonly destroyed private and personal property inside the dwelling] generally.

October 26: Started about six in the morning. Heard that there were plenty of Rebels, 5,000 of them ahead of us at Vinsons [Vincents Crossroads] .... At the crossroads did not find any tracks and thought the thing a hoax. Four or five miles from there we found

a squad of six [Confederate cavalry] out in the field. They all run. Fed [stole private fodder and corn] our horses at Patterson's [a civilian farm]. His wife is a rough woman [she probably cursed them as thieves]. [Colonel] Spencer told her we were the children of Israel bringing the plague on them [Southern civilians]. Colonel left me to guard the cotton [a large store of cotton bales]. Barker came down to burn it.[428]

As further recorded in the entry of October 26, after overseeing the burning of the cotton stores near Vincents Crossroads, the Tory sergeant major heard gunfire and headed to rejoin the main body, catching up with the command just after Spencer had deployed them for battle. "We went about two miles. I had not got to the front when several shots were fired," he wrote in his diary, "I pushed ahead and found the two guns [artillery tubes] on a little rise of ground and the gunners loading."[429]

Again, while fairly confident that the Rebels were few in number Colonel Spencer was taking no chances. Since the primary road ran east to west and the Rebels were approaching from the west, he quickly placed to his front a strong line of skirmishers along a skirt of woods straddling the road. Behind the skirmishers, the Union commander anchored companies B, F, and G to the left of the road and A, E, and H to the right. The two mountain howitzers sat just off the road itself, on a slight rise, easily able to fire in any direction. The horse holders were placed several hundred yards back of the front-line deployment.

Another quarter mile behind the first defensive line, was another large open corn field and empty pasture. This served as an ideal location for a second defensive line and it was here that companies L and D took the right of the road with I and K on the left, next to a small wood-framed house. All these troopers were similarly dismounted with their own horse holders safely tucked away behind them. Finally, Colonel Spencer stayed at the rear of everything with Company C, which was his ready reserve force.

Dunn recorded in his diary a description of the ground and how the Federals settled into this two-tiered defensive position about a mile or so west of Vincents Crossroads.[430] Dunn's observations, which meshed well with Ferguson's after-action report, provided the following about the Tory second line of defense:

> On the right was a narrow field 30 or 40 rods wide [a rod is 16.5 feet] for almost half a mile, only broken by a strip of underbrush about 20 rods through. Company L and D were put into the open field on the right, at first facing to the east and then L faced to the north. I and K were in a similar position on the west of the road. C was rear guard. Pack mules and refuges were also to the rear ....[431]

In a report sent to General S.D. Lee five days later, Ferguson recorded how the front of the battlefield initially appeared:

> The enemy were formed in thick woods across the road, with an open field in front, through which, swept as it was by two pieces of light artillery planted in the road, I had to advance to the attack.[432]

In short, the Unionists were firmly established across good defensive ground with an open field to their front and enjoyed the support of two maneuverable field cannons — the worst possible scenario for attackers. In fact, by the time Ferguson's scouts reported back as to the Tory dispositions, the Federal artillery had already opened up with roaring booms of solid shot, hoping to flush out and determine the number of Confederates concealed in and beyond the woods.[433]

Undaunted by the shelling, Ferguson used the natural cover offered by a terrain described as "thickly wooded with black oak"[434] to deploy his dismounted cavalrymen in an elongated, yet indented on the ends, double line, aligned so that once the men

charged out of their positions they might overlap the more compact enemy formations. The smaller in number 2nd Tennessee was bolstered with two companies of the 2nd Alabama and placed on the Confederate left, while Earle and the rest of his 2nd Alabama troopers took up positions on the other side of the road, constituting the Confederate right. In a stroke of great luck, given the uneven nature of the wood line, not only was Lieutenant Colonel Morton's wing significantly closer to the enemy to his front, but the alignment quite naturally promised an oblique strike once he came out of the woods, perfectly accomplishing Ferguson's desire of getting at the Tory flank. At the middle of the assault formation grouped on the main road, Ferguson kept back companies D and I of the 2nd Alabama as his own ready reserve. Finally, Ferguson assigned Mooreland's small battalion the difficult task of circling far around the entire battlefield in order to get completely behind the Tory position and hopefully harass or even attack them from the rear.[435]

Once things were set to his satisfaction, Ferguson brought his two regimental commanders together and thoroughly briefed them on his vision of the pending attack. At the proper bugle signal, both Earle and Morton would move their men forward and when out of the woods on open ground, advance them at the quick pace on their respective sides of the road. Not only did these two colonels represent the best in his brigade, Ferguson knew that the troopers showed Earle and Morton the respect that their skill and success on the battlefield had already justified. Further, given the fact that the two opposing forces were pretty much equally matched in troop strength, success depended on the ability of the commanders to aggressively press the attack. Although the tactical advantage of Morton's positioning to perhaps get at and turn the Union right provided some degree of hope for success, there were no frills in the plan, they were simply going to come out of the woods and run right over the Tories, or die trying.

It was now mid-afternoon. Earle and Morton returned to their regiments and made final preparations. With horses and their holders already to the rear, the troopers carefully checked pistols and carbines, stuffing extra rounds in their pockets and haversacks

all the while grimacing each time a shell burst into the trees overhead. Ferguson recalled the artillery blasts:

> The enemy in the meantime opened with two guns which I took to be six pounders from the noise they made and the way the splinters flew from a log house struck by them near me.[436]

When all was ready, the bugles crisply sounded the advance and Ferguson unleashed his men with a shout of encouragement. Guided by their officers, the Rebels swiftly pushed right through the trees and underbrush, not yet visible but certainly audible as the unconquerable Rebel Yell echoed from the woods. The unholy yelping forebode an ominous outcome for those on the receiving end and the enemy skirmishers wasted no time scrambling back from the tree-line.

If the Unionists waiting across the first line of defense were unnerved by the sight of their own skirmishers sprinting towards them — looking like so many scared rabbits — the long line of furious Southerners spilling out of the forest chilled them to the bone, particularly so for those unfortunates observing Morton's men aiming straight for their flank.

Even though the Tories were solidly set along both sides of the primary road with an open field that the Rebels were now exposing themselves without cover, they showed little deference for the safety of their returning comrades who were frantically shouting: "Here They Come!" "Here They Come!"

As if on some unspoken signal, the Tories across the entire front fired their weapons sending a deafening plumb of whitish smoke billowing out. Letting loose too soon and for the most part way too high, the effect was minimal.

Morton struck first. Materializing like phantoms on the Tory right flank, the Confederates poured a deadly enfilading fire into the surprised blue coats. Clearly more enthused with plundering the

civilian homes of their neighbors than actually fighting Confederate soldiers, this unexpected development completely unnerved them. Besides, a good number of the Tories were deserters from Confederate service and knew that if taken on the battlefield that they would not be treated as prisoners of war but rather introduced to either a noose or a firing squad. When one adds the floating rumor of 5,000 Confederates in the area to the shear audacity of Ferguson's attack, what occurred next was not unforeseeable.

In fact, long before any of Morton's boys actually reached the Union line, a great number of Tories jumped up and turned tail for the rear, as they had predetermined to do so should things *appear* to go badly, and seeing screaming Rebels rushing in a loop that would soon engulf them, they panicked. Morton wasted no time pushing this early success, directing his men to storm forward to keep the enemy from regrouping. For the Federals who chose to remain and fight, the point blank nature of things made it certain to everyone that it was either surrender, flee, or die.

In the meantime, while the Tennesseans were slashing through the Tories like a hot knife through butter, Earle's Alabamians on the right were having a much harder time of it. Their emergence from the woods put them in a face-to-face encounter and a hailstorm of lead projectiles portended an uncertain outcome of the contest. But the advantage was with the Confederates. As Morton's aggressive punch on his side of the road smashed apart the remnants of Tory companies E, A, and H, Earle entertained zero thoughts of giving up against his sector. General Ferguson spent little ink describing the scene.

> As rapidly as possible I formed my lines, had the men dismounted, and attacked the enemy, who were soon driven back [on the Confederate left] by the Second Tennessee, under the able and gallant leadership of Lieutenant Colonel Morton, and a portion of the Second Alabama.[437]

With the Union right turned and up in the air — though some continued to fire as they fell back — Tory companies B, F, and G on the opposite side of the road were isolated and cut off, a matter the very competent Morton immediately seized upon. In a brilliant move exhibiting an incredible sense of timing, the brave commander personally led two of his Tennessee companies through clouds of deep drifting gun smoke right across the road and head-on into this newly exposed flank. Pressed hard by Earle to their front and now Morton to their side, chaos gripped the three remaining companies and the order to retreat was obeyed without objection, albeit the movement backwards was anything but orderly.

It was over. The entire Union front crumbled and the Rebels drove the Tories across a field carpeted with dead and wounded, as fast as feet could carry them. Without supporting infantry, the Union artillery had no choice but to quickly follow suit, hitching up and pulling rearward. Confederate Sergeant Hancock's diary vividly recorded the initial Rebel thrust which disintegrated the Tory line.

> The Federal skirmish line ... was in a skirt of woods a short distance in our front, while their [Union] main line was just behind this skirt of woods in another old field. All things being now ready the whole [Confederate] line was ordered to charge [on foot]. Their [Union] skirmish line fell back through these woods as we advanced, and after heavy firing from both sides for a few minutes we drove them from their position on the [Confederate] left of the road .... Seeing that the ... Second Alabama had failed to move the Federals on the right Lieutenant Colonel Morton dashed across the road to their assistance with two companies of the Second Tennessee, and he soon succeeded in driving them from their position on the [Confederate] right also. Then our whole line moved forward a few hundred yards .... As soon as our horses could be brought up to us we mounted.

> Dashing forward a short distance we dismounted again, but as it proved to be only a few skirmishers we remounted again [heading now to the second Union line].[438]

On the Union side of things, Sergeant Major Dunn witnessed his fellows hesitate, falter, and then break in mad confusion. Fear was a convincing motivator and the rasp of heavy breathing along with the jingling clatter of cavalry spurs all mixed together into a general sound of madness so that any thought that the retreating Unionists might allay their panic and rally behind steadfast comrades in the second line set across the bigger part of its own open field was wishful thinking. With Rebel officers feverishly calling back for the horse holders to come up, even the most steady of the Tory men realized that all was lost and the screams of their wounded fellows on the ground did nothing to calm the atmosphere. There would be no stand at the second line! Not only were the first line of soldiers unwilling to rally around the second line and regroup, but large swaths of blue uniformed men in companies L and D of the second line simply joined in on a now cascading race further rearward, all bolting towards the nervously waiting reserve company. Dunn's self-serving explanation for all this shameful cowardice was that the Rebel attack was simply too long. He dryly wrote:

> Companies E, A, and H were soon driven out [first line Union right] and the Rebs began to fire on Companies L and D [second line Union right]. They stood the fire for a while and then retreated. I was letting down the fence at the time they began to fire on Company L and had some trouble to get on my horse …. Orders were sent to B, F, and G [first line Union left] to fall back and soon they came tearing [back]. Stenburg was killed, Swift wounded and Chandler killed.[439]

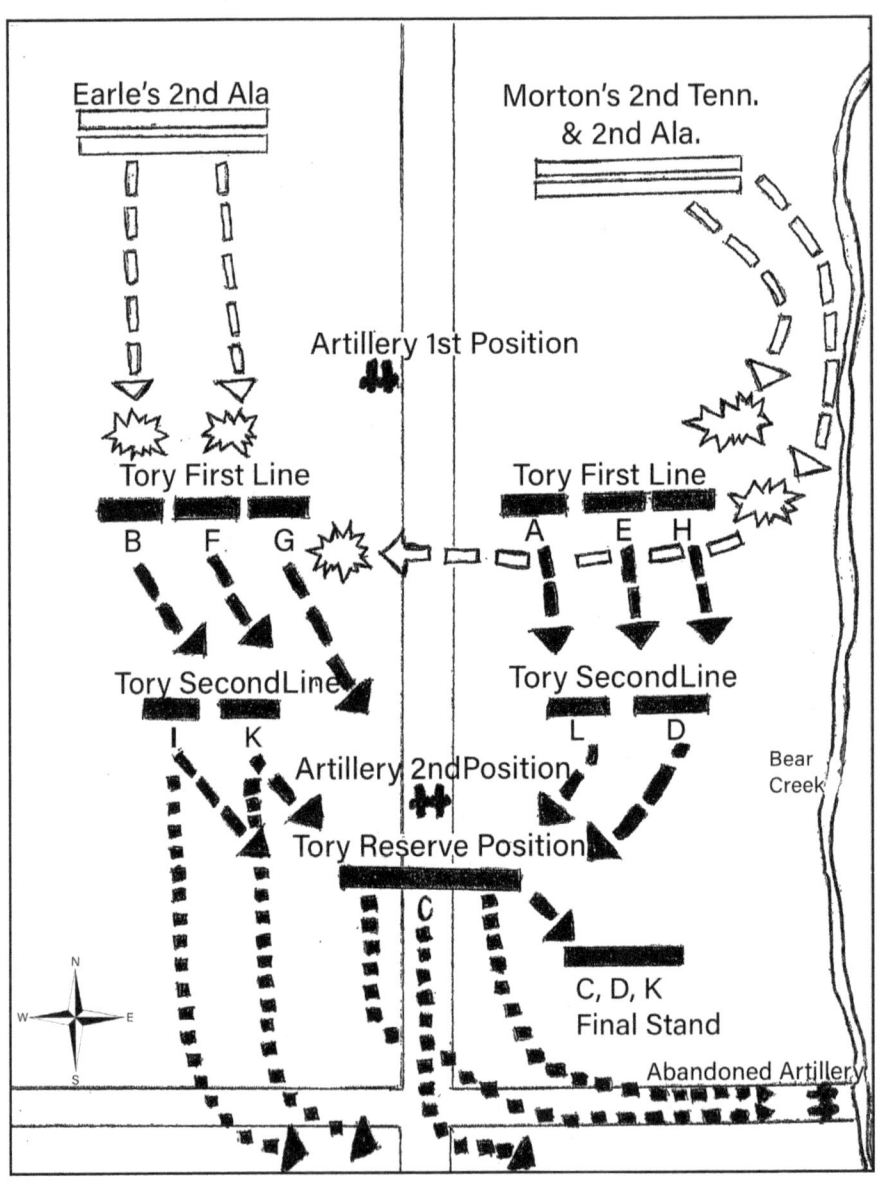

Battle of Vincents Crossroads.

And where was Colonel Spencer? It is difficult to explain the curious neglect exhibited by Spencer during the fighting at Vincents Crossroads except to note that as was the case with many a senior Federal commander during the War, they were generally nowhere to be found on the field of actual battle — what Southerners of the time called putting your "headquarters where your hindquarters" were. Such was the case of Spencer while all this melee was transpiring.

Instead of planting himself at the first or even the second defensive position to inspire and convey commands directly to his men, Colonel Spencer had elected to "lead" from the very rear of the regiment, with his reserve Company C.[440] Consequently, not only was Spencer totally unaware of the fatal error regarding the frontline alignment of his forces on his right, which had allowed Morton to shatter and then roll up his entire first defensive line, he was now unable to rally his panicked men stampeding through and from the second defensive line. Spencer could only see the jaw-dropping disaster through his binoculars, as if in slow motion.

The only positive development was that the Rebel advance had not been able to keep pace with the much faster retreat. Winded Confederates were scrambling about on foot looking for their horses while others had stopped to scoop up much-coveted Union weapons and equipment abandoned and strewn about. Spencer knew that his only hope to avoid complete annihilation was to organize an emergency formation to stem the chaos.

In tandem with the victorious attackers losing cohesion, Spencer was pleased to also see that the Union artillery had taken it upon themselves to reposition next to a single "house in the middle of the field"[441] and was once again firing shot and shell at the more advanced groups of pursuing Confederates causing them to temporarily halt. If a sufficient number of men could be pushed to rally around the guns the Rebels could be blunted, giving Spencer time to organize an *orderly* retreat.

In desperation, Colonel Spencer ordered remnants of Company L, which had run all the way back to his rear location, to regroup and advance to a "little strip of woods in the center of the field"[442]

next to the two artillery pieces. Sergeant Major Dunn also spurred his horse towards the precious guns shouting along the way for men to follow him. Dunn recorded:

> The Rebels were now in plain view in the corn field but the artillery soon drove them out and the column [retreating Tories from the first and second defensive lines] then fell back the length of the field. The [civilian] refugees tried to get by and the pack mules were running everywhere. I tried to get the men into shape and some of them would come and some would not.[443]

Sergeant John Phillips was one of those Tories who retreated in the initial onslaught and then returned to stand with the artillerymen. Phillips recalled:

> We had orders to fall back a quarter or half a mile south and were also ordered to dismount and form a line on the right, our artillery had fallen back also. The Rebels then came in sight, and we began to do some shooting in good earnest and held them in check for a while.[444]

Fortunately for the Rebels, while the guns kept Morton temporarily in check on the Union right, Colonel Earle and the larger part of the 2nd Alabama came pressing down hard on what remained of the dissolving Union left. Understanding that without sufficient infantry support to protect the artillery's exposed flank, the blue gunners servicing the tubes must fall back or be shot down, Earle sent a reinforced squadron to lick around to the far side, find good firing positions, and open up with their carbines.

It was now a fight for the artillery and time was running out for Colonel Spencer's beleaguered command. Dunn screamed

himself hoarse without effect, his imprecations to turn around a sufficient number of wild-eyed Tories to stabilize the ground were in vain. Soon enough, the intensified firing from Earle's well-placed bullets signaled to Dunn that he had no choice but to order the two cannons hitched up to their individual horses and hauled back. Phillips recalled the moment.

> We were then ordered to mount which we, or I, found difficult to do .... There was so much confusion and so much going on that it was some time before I found my horse. I was looking for Clint [the number four horse holder] and he was looking for me. When I got my horse, I was almost exhausted, as I was loaded down with ammunition.[445]

With no indication that the Confederates were going to let up, Spencer needed to find another place to make a defensive stand, ideally a piece of high ground further down the road and out of sight. For now, his only satisfaction was that the artillery had bought the time needed to see the bulk of the men and baggage flow out of the immediate battle zone giving him time to rally the remnants of two companies, D and K, and add them to his own reserve, which he then planted well down the road and hidden on a small rolling hilltop.[446] The Unionists on the hill deployed quickly knowing that they would soon see plenty of Rebs.

The largely one-sided fight had now gone on for well over three hours. While the Rebels were greatly invigorated by the sweeping success they had won thus far, Ferguson was anxious to finish the job. With the enemy cannon and all remaining Federals cleared off the field and on the run, Earle and Morton worked rapidly to regroup their men in order to continue the attack.

In the meantime, Ferguson ordered up the 2nd Alabama's D and I, which he had held in reserve, to spearhead the mission of making fresh contact with the vanishing Tories. Cheered on by scattered groups of comrades who were still picking their way

across the abandoned terrain, the gritty Alabamians of Pegues' D Troop spurred their horses forward at a brisk gait using the main road to center them along. However, after what seemed like only a few minutes, the riders were greeted by an unwelcomed volley raining down on them from the Tories perched on Spencer's hilltop. Rebel saddles emptied and the rest wheeled about at the double-quick to safety.

As always, Colonel Earle was in the thick of the fight directing and encouraging the men. He lost no time in deciding what to do. Simultaneously ordering a squadron to go around the hill and charge on horse up the far side, Earle directed Captain Pegues to dismount his men and go at the Tories on foot. Pegues smiled, smartly saluted, and personally led his troopers on a crisscrossing jaunt up the slope going straight into the face of what he assumed would be determined soldiers dug into good fighting spots. Many of his men fully expected to enter into their eternity executing such a desperate maneuver.

Amazingly, the task of wrestling the high ground from the three Tory companies would require nothing more than climbing up the thing. As it turned out, the very sight of the initial wave of mounted Confederates was all that was required to drive them off. After firing a single volley, the Unionists precipitously turned tail and raced down the back side with only a handful stopping to take cover behind some abandoned shacks at the base. Reaching the summit on foot, a surprised Captain Pergues could clearly see them and excitedly yelled to a fellow mounted officer to take his squadron of troopers who had horses and sweep down on the enemy. Cochrane wrote:

> As soon as the Yankees fired [on the mounted cavalry charge] we were ordered to dismount and charge them. They were on a high hill and ran straight off but we did not know it. We rushed up the hill on foot and another squadron of ours, hearing the firing, rushed up from another way [on horseback] and got

on the hill the Yankees had just left and dismounted like us. Captain Pergues, who saw them halloed to them not to dismount but to charge that old field and those old houses for they had just gone over there, and when the squadron would not charge he cried, "Give me your horses and I will charge." "Get down and give them to me" but they would not charge nor lend us the horses.[447]

After giving up the hill, and with the bulk of his demoralized regiment gone in hurried flight to the four winds, Sergeant Major Dunn and Colonel Spencer made one last attempt to slow down their pursuers, hoping to at least save the cannons and wagons from certain capture. Once again, Spencer was able to rally a rear guard together and deployed them into a line of battle. Some remained mounted and held the horses for their dismounted fellows who nervously formed up across the same road that the cannons had just tore down in great haste. All secretly wished that they were also running down that dusty exit instead of resisting what they knew was going to be another thrashing.

Interestingly, this final Union stand would constitute one of those rare moments in the War when a body of Confederate cavalry would *intentionally* charge directly into prepared, dismounted Federals. Informed of the new enemy formation, General Ferguson elected to personally lead the charge. In short order, several squadrons of horsemen were squared off next to one another under guidon bearers, with a second line formed up so that the attack would center on the road and hit the enemy in two consecutive waves. Ferguson was gambling that the dispirited Federals would break and run into the piney woods just at the sight of the thundering horses, as they had done more or less all afternoon long. Urged on into the risky maneuver by their own brave leaders, the Southern horsemen did not blanch when the charge sounded, although all knew that a frontal attack straight into a prepared dismounted enemy spelled certain harm. Working their spurs so that the animals moved at a pounding run, many used pistols instead of sabers, some even

rode with reins clenched in their teeth so both hands could wield a revolver.

Spencer's men were initially startled by this mad charge and at less than fifty yards out, the Rebels were engulfed by a sheet of flame which disabled many of them, but this time there was no veering off. The riders kept coming. Sergeant Major Dunn recalled the dreadful scene.

> Colonel and all of us that cared anything for the regiment were trying to get them to fall into the road. I succeeded in keeping some of them from going ahead of the guns [which were being drawn down the road]. Half a mile southwest of the field and just after the guns had crossed a little brook, the advance [rear guard] was fired into. I staid [sic] in the rear of the guns and did what I could to keep the men back [in a defensive line]. About this time the Rebels charged on the rear and the companies left there gave them a volley that disabled a great many.[448]

Private Cochrane was in the middle of it all and sent up a quick prayer to the Lord Almighty that the desperate hell-for-leather horse charge would spare his life and the lives of his friends. He marveled at the grace of God when neither he nor his comrades were hit, despite several of the horses torn apart with horrible wounds.

> The bullets came so close to my breast that I thought I felt the wind of them. I was in one man from the front of the company and the fire was directed at the front. [Private] W. Sanders belonged in my set of fours but he was behind [Private] C. Martin, who was behind me. The shots that killed Sanders' horse and wounded Charlie's [horse] passed to the left of me .... The bullets that came my way did no damage though

it seems a miracle how they could pass so close to so many and miss us all. I prayed that we should go through the fight and not lose a man [in his messmate group of four] and my prayer was answered.[449]

Others were not so blessed. As the Confederate cavalry rode forward on angry mounts, ears laid back and nostrils flaring, one of the casualties in the impetuous charge was the courageous Lieutenant Colonel George Morton who was flipped straight back off his horse by a Union slug striking him in the chest. Miraculously, apart from having the wind knocked out of a badly bruised body, Morton survived the event — the offending projectile was a spent bullet that left a terrible bruise yet failed to pierce flesh. Ferguson recalled the event:

> We soon were met by a volley from the rear guard posted in a well selected position. I heard a ball strike Muldrow [sic, Morton] and saw him fall backwards from his horse but kept on, supposing him killed. The [Union] rear guard ran after firing that volley which was the last stand they made.[450]

Morton's fall also caught the attention of his men and those next to him leapt off their horses in order to protect their leader while others dismounted and continued the attack on foot, pistols blazing away. Sergeant Hancock was right there.

> [T]hey poured a volley among us, and our daring leader, Colonel G.H. Morton, fell from his horse. Leaping from our saddles, charging on foot, we completely routed the Federals that they did not make another stand, but dashed through the woods to our right .... Remounting and dashing down the road we soon learned that none of the Federals had retreated along the main road.[451]

While the Federal volley that struck down Morton and so many others did horrendous damage, it failed in its purpose. The butternut and grey who slid off their mounts continued the final yards on foot while the still mounted Rebels came crashing in. For a brief moment, the scene was a melee of swinging sabers, colliding animals, and flying dirt. But only for a moment. With scared and hallow eyes, the Tories broke and expended their remaining energy chasing horses that had bolted into the brush. To avoid easy capture none of them took to the main road, it was everyman for himself and each fled where his own fright pointed, scattering like quail.

With Morton out of the fight and the Tories completely routed, Ferguson ordered a halt so that weapons could be reloaded and parched throats watered. After a short respite, the Confederates left the main road in squad sized groups and fanned out into the surrounding woods, causing the deepening forest to come to life with the heavy echo of gunfire crackling through the air, most shots clipping leaves and spraying splinters from trees but some hitting their marks. In every direction, puffs of sooty smoke hung about like so many dirty mushrooms.

Understanding that he had been pushed further back into Alabama to the east, Spencer funneled what troopers he could onto a spur trail that led due north towards Bear Creek, the same trail the artillery had taken. Finding lots of fresh tracks churning up the trail, to include the unmistakable imprint of cannon wheels, Pegues was first to follow Spencer and the artillery. Apart from capturing the enemy's flag, capturing a cannon was considered a great feat and a prize which Pegues was determined to have. Cochrane wrote:

> When we started after the cannon someone told the Captain [Pegues] that Co I was not along. He said, "Never mind Co. I. Let Co. D come on." He seemed like he had rather capture the cannon with our company …. We then found the cannon track and started at a gallop to overtake them and have the honor of capturing them.[452]

Unbeknownst to the Federals, the side road they had taken towards Bear Creek was a dead end which abruptly terminated at the water's edge revealing an exceedingly high bank on the opposite side. Imagining themselves hopelessly trapped, there was no choice for those still on horse but to plunge their mounts into the deep creek and hopefully spur them up the six to eight foot muddy embankment on the other side. Having earlier confronted the same obstacle, the artillerymen hauling the guns chose to cut their animals loose and without even spiking the tubes to render them inoperable, swam for their lives. Sergeant Phillips shared the panicked atmosphere.

> A little before sunset we came to a creek where the road seemed to give out. Here we found our artillery deserted and did not see any way of crossing the stream [Bear Creek]. The banks were from six to eight feet high and perpendicular. The Rebs were pressing us in the rear, charging us and shooting a continuous volley in the rear. Our men were shouting forward at every breath. I plunged my horse off a steep bank, into the creek and he commenced pawing and trying to go up on the opposite bank. I slide off of him in the water and assisted him all I could, and as he went up the bank, I caught him by the tail and went out with him. Lieut. Emerick's horse went into the creek a few feet below where mine went in and broke his neck. I do not know what became of Lieut. Emerick as I saw him no more during the engagement. I then mounted my horse and started up a long hill. Everyone that I saw seemed to be excited and confused.[453]

It was over. The Unionists had been thoroughly bested at every point. Staying close by his commanding officer's side throughout, Dunn recalled the final gasps of the 1st Alabama Tory Regiment as about seventy men huddled around their desperate commander

"who drew a pistol and tried [unsuccessfully] to form" another line.[454] However, multiple Confederate volleys found the group and blasted them apart.

> At this point Captain Shurtliff came ahead, McWright with him, and tried to get the men to halt. He told the Colonel [Spencer] the guns [artillery] had been left [at Bear Creek]. Spencer then drew a pistol and tried to form a line. As soon as I saw him, I whirled my horse and called the men that I knew to help form the line but there was no use …. We had only gone a short distance when ten volleys were fired from the right and rear of us. Several men were believed to have been killed at this place Lieutenant Perry among the rest.[455]

The retreat, which began as a rout, had now turned into a complete disintegration and Ferguson's only remaining enemy was the diminishing daylight. He ordered all horse holders to come forward so that everyone could join in the chase.

> As soon as the horses could be brought up the fleeing enemy were hotly pursued and their retreat converted into a wild panic. The chase was kept up for 10 miles through dense woods and over a mountainous country until dark.[456]

Sadly, with the Tories completely scattered, some individually and others in small bands, the Confederates had no way of following up on their stunning victory. By wisely staying off the road, the majority of the Tories were able to slip away into the thick timber and underbrush. While dozens of the enemy were killed or wounded, General Ferguson noted in his after-action report that over a hundred Federals were taken prisoner, but that the number

of enemy dead was unknown due to the fact that most were killed in widely scattered wooded areas that spanned a large geographic area.

> Their perfect knowledge and our ignorance of the country enabled most of them, however, to escape by separating into small squads and leaving the [main] road.[457]

Sergeant Hancock who fought alongside Morton, speculated that the results would have been even greater had Mooreland's Battalion been able to get behind the Tories as Ferguson had directed at the outset.

> I think that General Ferguson had failed to accomplish all that he designed. Mooreland's Battalion, from General Roddy's Brigade, was to attack the Federals in the rear about the same time that he (Ferguson) attacked them in front, and thus make a capture in place of a rout. But owing to some mishap or other Mooreland failed to appear in the rear at the proper time.[458]

Like the rest of the broken Tory regiment, or what was left of it, an exhausted Dunn traveled all night on horseback and part of the next day with a small contingent of other haggard Unionists before reaching the safety of their main camp at Iuka. Without mounts, Sergeant Phillips joined a group of "four or five" and took three days to walk back the 30 miles to Iuka.

> Our chance then was to go down that hollow far enough to avoid danger then go west far enough to avoid contact with the enemy, and then turn north to get back to our lines [Iuka]. We had to leave our horse and side arms as we did not see much chance of getting away without being captured with our horses.

> Before day we passed through a corn field and each of us secured an ear of corn, and that was about all we got to eat for the next three days.[459]

Given the unwillingness of the Tories to stand and fight, most of their losses ended up in the "unaccounted for" column indicating that many of those that sprinted into the forest chose to discard their uniforms and meander back to their homes in the mountains of Alabama rather than return to Iuka. Although the 2nd Alabama would face a reconstituted 1st Alabama Union again the following year during Sherman's March to the Sea, for now the Unionists were thoroughly crushed. Sergeant Major Dunn's diary entries for the next several days continued to record the extent of their inglorious thrashing.

> We went right into the woods away from the road of any kind. Had three or four shots fired at us once after leaving the hill. A man who was shot through the hand and body rode with us six or seven miles and then stopped at a house …. Henry Kelogg's boy [Tory civilians] guided us to Iuka …. Three miles from Iuka we halted and feed. It was four o'clock [a.m.] and we had rode 75 miles.[460]

> October 27: Went into Iuka in the morning, drew rations and forage for 122 man [sic] and horses. Colonel Spencer got into Glendale [Mississippi] a little later with about the same number.

> October 29: Nothing today. [Colonel] Spencer went to Iuka. The boys tell some funny stories of the affair. One man got thrown, jumped on behind another horse. The fellow in front said: "Oh Lord, do get off," but he could not push him off, nor coax him off and at last said: "Well if anybody is shot in the back it will be you."

October 30: Nothing of any consequence. A few men coming in all the time. Lieutenant Swift is still living.[461]

On the Confederate side, General Ferguson himself was almost killed in the fighting. Like all aggressive combat leaders, Ferguson was ever anxious to personally follow up and direct his men, something that can't be done from behind and as in many instances during the War, the attendant consequences for such bold leadership was often at great cost. With only two members of his staff accompanying him, the South Carolinian recalled his close call with the angel of death.

> Suddenly four men [Union troopers] stepped into the road about 40 paces in front of me, took deliberate aim with their carbines, fired, then jumped back into the thick bushes. Fortunately for me they missed.[462]

Casualties on the Southern side were amazingly light with less than a dozen for the entire 2nd Alabama. According to Captain Allen's report of the affair, one of the dead, Sergeant Croxton, and one of the wounded, Private Murry, were from his Company F.[463] Allen wrote:

> The company was engaged in a fight with the 1st Alabama Tory Regt. On the 20th day of October in which Sergeant Croxton [W.P. or W.J.] and Private [J.] Murry was wounded. Private Murry has since died.[464]

Captain Frank King recorded the following for his Company B.

> On the expedition to the Tennessee River, which left Pontotoc on the 6th of October, the Company carried in the aggregate 61-men, it was present in the battle which

> General Ferguson gave the 1st Alabama Troy Cavalry, fighting on the right wing in support of the Squadron of Capt. W.L. Allen and contributed it's proper share to the complete route of the enemy that day.[465]

In his after-action report dated October 31, 1863, written near Courtland, Alabama, Ferguson rightfully praised the brave and energetic Colonel Morton, who had rolled up the Tory front and skillfully lead his men throughout.

> I am indebted to the officers and men of the command for gallant conduct and cheerful endurance of hardship and hunger on this scout; but to Lieutenant-Colonel Morton and Maj. H.W. Bridges more than a passing tribute is due. The former led his gallant band with a cool skill and determination, admirable in the extreme, until knocked from his horse by a spent ball. The latter was, as usual, foremost in the fight, everywhere inspiring and encouraging the men and officers. With his own hand he killed 1 and wounded and captured several other Yankees. His horse was shot under him and his coat pierced by a bullet, an evidence of the close character of the fight.[466]

Having pursued the enemy for ten miles, Ferguson regrouped his spent but much satisfied men, set out pickets, and rested for the night. On the next morning the Confederates surveyed the lengthy battlefield. Along with rifles, cartridges, ammunition boxes, and clothing strewn in every direction, there laid the blood-stained and mangled forms of dead Alabamians in blue uniforms. The Tory dead that could be found were "buried" by throwing dirt over them where they fell, paying a silent salute to this bitter irony of the War where brother literally fought brother. Ferguson observed the strange, sad sight: "In the very center of the Confederacy [Southern] men

wearing the enemy's [blue] uniform killed as some were within half a mile of their own houses."[467]

After seeing to the dead and caring for the wounded, Ferguson's strike force packed up everything of value to start the long ride back. He proudly boasted about the captured Federal cannons as well as the many captured Union cavalry guidons and the enemy regimental flag which were sent to Richmond as war trophies. The only regret was that he was later obliged to relinquish the two mountain guns to the Confederate ordnance department because no ammunition was available to service them.

> Major Bridges distinguished himself greatly in this fight; I sent him on to Richmond with the captured flags .... The two guns captured were beautiful little steel guns, drawn by one horse each and firing lead balls of an inch and a quarter in diameter, as well as grape and canister. I tried to have ammunition made for them at our arsenals but failed and had to give them up [to the Confederate ordnance department].[468]

A triumphant Ferguson returned to S.D. Lee on October 29, 1863, and instead of resting, the men were immediately thrown into another vicious fight — they arrived just in time to assist Lee's troopers to fend off a massive Federal assault headed by Brigadier General Peter Joseph Osterhaus which consisted of two full strength brigades of infantry, two regiments of cavalry, and a battery of artillery (six field pieces).

The Union attack had hit Lee's command on the early morning of October 28, during a cold driving rain. The sheer numbers of Federals were more than enough to muscle the Confederates back, forcing a hasty retreat to a section of Cane Creek about nine miles southwest of Tuscumbia where S.D. Lee found good ground to dismount and dig in. After another two-hours of heavy skirmishing, darkness brought the fighting to a temporary standstill with the

Federals content to renew the question in the morning. However, S.D. Lee had other ideas.

Although heavily outnumbered Lee did the unexpected. Instead of finding satisfaction in delaying the enemy and then prudently falling back further to the south, he shifted the bulk of his troopers to the northwest near Little Bear Creek, about two miles west of Tuscumbia, taking up strong fighting positions behind fallen trees and mounds of dirt, supported by light artillery. Ferguson's cavalry arrived on the outskirts of Tuscumbia just in time to assist and with his characteristic resolve, Ferguson immediately pitched his men into the heavy fighting that day. The 2nd Alabama fought particularly hard, both on foot and in the saddle, losing 17 men in killed, wounded, and captured. Interestingly, part of the 2nd Alabama was able to dart around the Union rear and carry off several supply wagons loaded with military goods to include the divisional medical wagon of General Osterhaus, from which the 2nd Alabama surgeon was rewarded with a brand new surgical kit!

S.D. Lee knew by now that the massive Federal movement against him was designed to permanently keep the marauding Rebel cavalry from tearing up any more of the railroad running across north Alabama to Chattanooga. Moreover, Osterhaus was more of a mind to pillage civilian property in the area than to continue pursuing S.D. Lee's faster moving cavalry any further into the countryside. In any event, by October 30, 1863, Sherman's main body had abandoned the Memphis & Charleston and crossed the Tennessee River at Eastport (near Florence, Alabama), continuing on foot towards Chattanooga along the north side of the river.

Low on food, forage, and ammunition, the men and animals of Lee's command were in dire need of reconstitution and S.D. Lee advised General Bragg that he was no longer able to continue in the field. With the fighting now over, a reporter telegraphed back the long causality list for the 2nd Alabama Cavalry Regiment which was printed in the *Mobile Advertiser & Register* newspaper on October 31, 1863:

Action Around Tuscumbia, October, 1863

List of Wounded — [Second Alabama Cavalry] Confederate

General [S.D. Lee] has only brought enough supplies for a 10 day to 2 week operation, it has been raining almost every day, and it is a very cold rain. Supplies and ammo are running low as a result of the fighting around Tuscumbia.

Capt. T. Puryear .... Co. G .... thigh fracture

Sergt. B.F. Carmichael ..... Co. H .... thigh

[Private] E.B. Thomas ...... Co. C .... bowels

[Private] H. Stephens .... Co. C .... arm

[Private] J.R. Dickinson ...... Co. D ...... head mortally [sic]

[Private] T.W. Link .... Co. F .... thigh

[Private] J.T. Ferguson .... Co. H .... thigh

[Private] J.F. Stargis .... Co. H .... thigh

[Private] D. Carr .... Co. D .... thigh

[Private] George Skipper .... Co. K .... rip [rib]

All of 2nd Alabama, Dickinson, Carmichael, and Thomas were captured. The 7 other wounded were left in Tuscumbia. Information given a newspaper reporter by S.D. Lee's troops.[469]

Permission to return to Mississippi was granted on November 4, 1863, and the grand Confederate raid was over. Major General Wheeler met with S.D. Lee for a final conference while the troopers in the various regiments prepared for the march back to Mississippi. Ferguson would never forget the sad conditions in northern Alabama caused by repeated Union terror attacks, but he also recalled a farewell dinner he shared with his fellow general officers at a fine mansion owned by a retired old Army Colonel named James Sanders.

> The rich and beautiful valley of Tennessee [northern Alabama] was at this time a scene of utter ruin marked by blackened ruins; the torch had been applied [by Union troops] to everything that would burn. All the invading troops were brutal enough but the Germans, and those commanded by Germans, like Sigel and Osterhaus, were by far the worst. Before leaving the Tennessee valley, Gen. S.D. Lee, Gen. Wheeler and I met at the hospitable and elegant mansion of Col. [James Edmonds] Sanders near Courtland, and passed a delightful evening there.[470]

As fate would have it, Private Cochrane was also present at the dinner where Sanders graciously recalled Cochrane's father, a well-respected attorney, and even his grandfather, a Revolutionary War hero.

> I expect you are a little curious to know how it happened that I was so well treated by Col. Sanders. Gen. Ferguson wanted one of the most discreet, cautious, and trusty young men in the command with a good horse and turning to Captain Pegues told him he might have the honor of selecting from his company. (Now this is not to go out of the family). Captain Pegues told the Gen. he had one who would

suit him and then halloed for Cochrane to come to the front.... I was drenched with rain but I got a cheerful fire and told my name and my grandfather's and they knew them and at the table he said to General Ferguson, "Let me introduce you to Mr. Cochrane who, I find, is a descendant of one who was once a great benefit to me in politics."[471]

The 2nd Alabama moved out with the full brigade and by November 9, had reached Brown's Ferry, Alabama. By November 13, they crossed into Mississippi, fording the Tombigbee about one-half mile above Cotton Gin Port to then ride back to their huts and warm stoves about one mile north of Okolona, on November 15. To say the least, all were much fatigued and in need of rest and decent food.

— GETTING FORREST INTO TENNESSEE —

S.D. Lee's cavalry raid on the Union railroad did slow Grant's move to relieve the "siege" at Chattanooga, even if it was only a short reprieve. In the interim, General George H. Thomas had replaced General Rosecrans at Chattanooga and by mid-November the Federals were beefed up to 60,000 men and flush with supplies of all sorts.

Just barely 40,000 in number, the Confederates under Bragg still held the heights overlooking the city even if no real effort to do anything of note had occurred since the pyrrhic victory at Chickamauga. Incredibly, the dull headed general was more engaged in political infighting which resulted in running off the best cavalry commander in the Confederacy, Nathan Bedford Forrest, and "encouraging" General Longstreet with his 12,000 veteran troops on loan from Robert E. Lee to depart towards Knoxville. In short, Braxton Bragg had set himself up for another fiasco and everyone except Jefferson Davis could see it coming.

By this point in the War, Forrest was already a universally recognized genius in combat and given the nickname "Wizard of the Saddle."[472] Ever since the tactical win at Chickamauga, Forrest had openly voiced his disgust about Bragg's failure to capitalize on their hard-fought victory and also bristled at being placed under the Army of Tennessee's cavalry commander General Wheeler. Disgruntled and insulted, Forrest offered his resignation to Richmond which President Davis wisely rejected, suggesting instead a transfer of General Forrest to Mississippi, yet without Forrest's own cavalry forces. Accordingly, General Forrest (promoted to Major General on December 4, 1863) left Chattanooga bound for Mississippi in the second week of November with only a small entourage, anxious to add to his legendary status with new feats of wonderment.

One week later, the Army of the Cumberland launched a massive counter attack and swept Bragg's men right off the high ground of Missionary Ridge and back into north Georgia where the Federals half-heartedly pursued before returning to Chattanooga for the winter. The only encouraging development for the South was that Jeff Davis finally relieved his West Point crony, the inept Braxton Bragg (appointing him three months later as a "special military advisor"). General Joseph E. Johnston, certainly no friend of Jefferson Davis, replaced Bragg and immediately set out to revitalize the demoralized Army of Tennessee. Johnston's vacated command slot in Mississippi was filled by Lieutenant General Leonidas Polk, who formally took charge of the Army of Mississippi on December 22, 1863.

Joe Johnston used the ensuing winter months to burrow in at Dalton, Georgia, where he reorganized his army from top to bottom. Besides ordering up new and abundant rations, uniforms, and equipment, he allowed what his predecessor Bragg had never granted — furloughs. Operating on a rotating basis, huge numbers of men received permission to go home on leave and all those absent without leave were granted full amnesty upon their return to the ranks. Johnston's efficiency and attention to the troops resonated not only with the soldiers but with the entire State of Georgia.

Johnston also vigorously pressed Richmond for remounts, equipment, proper forage, and new weapons for Wheeler's cavalry so that within a few months, large portions of the cavalry were able to discard inadequate rifles for brand new British-made Enfield carbines or their Confederate made equivalents.[473] Pistols were also provided in large quantities.

Meanwhile, when General Forrest arrived in Okolona, Mississippi, on November 18, he had only 279 men with perhaps half of those effective for service. Around this tiny nucleus he intended to personally build an entire brigade or a division! A native Tennessean, Forrest's audacious plan to accomplish this task was to strike into Union held west Tennessee and raise new recruits from the loyal men across the farmlands, secure mounts, arm them with newly captured stores of Federal property, and then return to Mississippi. For the plan to work, however, the Rebel chief would first have to slip undetected into Tennessee. S.D. Lee ordered Generals Ferguson, Ross, and Chalmers to attack various points along the Memphis & Charleston in Tennessee to create a diversion so Forrest and his small band could enter unnoticed. To beef up his force, Forrest was temporarily given Colonel Richardson's much depleted "brigade" which was then only about 250 strong, with probably 175 effectives, the balance were on "leave" procuring mounts and warm clothing.

Ferguson and his far more robust brigade had not been back in Mississippi for two weeks before being ordered to attack the Federal garrison at Pocahontas, a Union held town in Tennessee sitting on the Memphis & Charleston. From their starting point in Okolona, where they had taken to winter quarters, the distance for Ferguson was about 90 miles due north, a hard but doable three-day march. A larger force under S.D. Lee and Chalmers would press out to the northwest feigning an attack on Memphis itself in hopes that the Federals would rush reinforcements in that direction. Behind this smoke-screen of feints and demonstrations would follow General Forrest and his horsemen.

Ferguson anticipated that he might have to fight Yankee cavalry during the journey through Mississippi to the border of Tennessee, but what he did not anticipate was the battle he would have with mother nature. As it turned out, it would take him a full eight days and nights of marches and counter-marches to reach the railroad in Tennessee.

At first things started out well. Ferguson made the standard preparations for the movement with several days cooked rations, sufficient pack mules, supply wagons, and two guns from Owens' light artillery. All the tents and much of the cooking equipment were left behind at Okolona along with the men and horses not fit for duty. On November 25, 1863, the Rebels got a late start and moved only about five miles north from Okolona on the Pontotoc road where they spent a comfortable night rolled up in blankets under the stars. On November 26, after marching over 20 miles, the command halted for the night just north of Pontotoc, again spending a rather pleasant evening. When they rode out early on November 27, it was another unseasonably warm morning, tempting those that possessed greatcoats to stuff them into their saddlebags. By noon, however, the temperatures dropped dramatically and the entire command was soon hit by a cold drenching rain that came out of nowhere. Rubber blankets were donned as the rain uncomfortably dripped off hats and necks. Then, as the soaked riders drew near to Ripley to find camp, the temperature plummeted.

Time and weather were against Ferguson and the new day dawned in the same manner as it had ended — bone-chilling cold. Acknowledging that the icy weather had rendered his command non-combat ready, Ferguson wisely ordered the brigade to turn around and return to New Albany being "convinced that by this time the enemy was informed of my coming and that with their numbed hands the men could not fight nor load their muzzle-loading pieces."[474] The grueling ride back to the promised shelter and warmth of New Albany was accomplished in a wet snow without halt throughout the day and the long night that followed. Sergeant Hancock noted:

We got back to camps [New Albany] a little after sunrise on the morning of the 28th, and a set of cold, wet "rebs" were we. It was an awful disagreeable night.[475]

Ferguson was right to turn his frozen troopers around. Union Colonel John K. Mizner had just moved into the vicinity of Ripley with part of his well-equipped cavalry brigade and staying in the area would have surely meant engaging in a fire-fight. As it was Ferguson's brigade "lost upwards of three hundred horses with lung fever contracted on this march, and some men."[476]

Along with their sister regiments, the 2nd Alabama was relived to be back at New Albany, until a frantic telegraph from S.D. Lee ordered Ferguson to leave New Albany and return to Ripley as soon as practicable to confront a reported Federal raiding party and to again move up into Tennessee to help Forrest as previously ordered. By then the temperatures had somewhat moderated and the snow turned back to heavy rain. In the middle of the following rainy night Ferguson set out once again for Ripley braving a deluge of water, his men hardly having the time to dry out their clothes from the previous movement. In addition, the number of effectives for duty was now lower by several hundred, some too sick and others without substitute mounts.

This time, Ferguson ventured out with only a small part of his command, joined by the artillery, which he personally led straightway into the darkness successfully crossing the nearby Tallahatchie River and then feeling his way slowly forward along the muddy roads while the larger part of the brigade — escorting the wagons — was ordered to trail along at first daylight. Ferguson calculated that the rain would let up some by morning allowing for the slower moving wagons to catch up.

Once again, Ferguson and his smaller column of Confederate riders could not get past Ripley. The culprit now was the extreme flooding. The night had brought heavy downpours across the Mississippi countryside, saturating it and transforming the usually calm rivers and streams into raging deathtraps. Since the rain-

swollen river had washed out all the bridges to his front, Ferguson could find no way to get the cannon and the horses over the now completely flooded Town Creek that extended just to the south of Ripley. Usually, if no bridge was available and the water was not too deep, the horses would be forced to swim in groups led by a trooper in a skiff holding the bridle of a lead animal, the rest of the men would then make rafts or swim across. This time, the waters were of such force and depth that this could not be accomplished.

Again, there was no option. Ferguson was obliged to countermarch with his advanced party back to New Albany. However, he quickly discovered that not only was it impossible for him to recross the Tallahatchie, just north of New Albany, but that the larger part of his command accompanying all the supply wagons was now stranded on the south side of the Tallahatchie, also due to the flooding. In short, Ferguson's main body had not been able to even get out of the outskirts of New Albany.

For the rest of that day and most of the following, Ferguson was trapped between the two swollen rivers and could do nothing other than to wait for the waters to subside, very happy that he was not attacked by the enemy while his vulnerable command stood divided. On December 1, the main body was able to repair a bridge and get over so that the full brigade was finally consolidated. Determined to fulfill his orders, Ferguson moved north once again, slipping and sliding in treacherous mud towards Ripley, now for the third time. The only favorable news in all the various delays was that Ross' brigade and Forrest's small command were able to close up and both bodies of cavalry now trailed along about a half day's ride behind Ferguson.

In the meantime, Colonel Mizner's blue horsemen were still hovering near Ripley where Ferguson bumped into them about six miles south of town. He ordered the 2nd and 56th Alabama to charge into the enemy and drive them back. Ferguson chose the "gallant Earle,"[477] as he took to calling Colonel Earle, to spearhead the combined assault. In keeping with the general theme for Union raiders, the Yankees showed little fight and much flight. A double

line of charging gray riders, revolvers blazing, drove all indecision from Mizner and the blue horsemen simply raced off. The two Alabama regiments chased them with great vigor for many miles, stopping and dismounting for battle only when the Federals formed defensive lines to slow them down. Ferguson recalled:

> I found the enemy there [Ripley], deployed two Regiments and charged, when they broke and fled, throwing a strong rear guard from time to time. After routing one of these I met Wm. Baker, my ordnance officer, who had been with the advance all the time. He was much excited and exclaimed "such fun! To flush them and see them run."[478]

After pushing the Yankees for some miles north towards Ruckersville, Mississippi, Ferguson placed a strong picket on the main road to shield his true movement which was now redirected towards Saulsbury (also known as Saulsberry Depot), Tennessee, sitting squarely on the rail-line about 17 miles due east of his original target of Pocahontas — couriers had informed him that Forrest intended to pass from Mississippi into Tennessee through Saulsbury.

Although Saulsbury was a small town, the Federal fort located there was a different story. Nevertheless, only minutes before Ferguson's cavalry rode in on the afternoon of December 2, on the west side of the town, the entire garrison fled east by train in great haste headed for the larger post at Pocahontas. A greatly disappointed Ferguson had come within "an ace" of capturing them all, to include a locomotive.

> I arrived there [Saulsbury] in the afternoon and found the garrison had evacuated the place and gone to Pocahontas to which place the Brigade [Mizner's] from Ripley had fled. I at once sent a Regiment to obstruct and guard the RlRd in that direction, and

they came within an ace of capturing a train with part of the returning [retreating] garrison, before they [the Confederate cavalry] reached the track, the engineer saw them and was able to back his train quick enough to save it.[479]

Satisfied that he had shoved the Yankees completely out of the area and opened a rather significant hole, Ferguson ordered his men to confiscate all Federal supplies abandoned at the Saulsbury depot and set fire to the rest. The government buildings, warehouses, and wooden barracks were torched.

Next, assuming that the Federals were rapidly organizing a counterattack which could soon be upon them in great force, the black-bearded commander prudently fanned out his ablest scouts in both directions on the east/west rail-line to keep him informed of developments. He also sent additional riders to his south to guide Forrest and the others forward. It was then shovels and spades as the troopers set up barricades across and adjacent to the tracks in both directions and waited for General Forrest to arrive. Just after nightfall, as the 2nd Alabama and her sister regiments watched by light given off from the still burning Federal storehouses, the great warrior Forrest arrived with his small cavalry force of less than 300, accompanied by S.D. Lee and Sul Ross. Forrest himself seemed to brighten up the gloomy night simply by his presence and he wasted no time crossing over the railroad tracks of the Memphis & Charleston heading straight into the heart of his beloved Tennessee. After such a horrendous battle with mother nature, Ferguson's boys took great pride in their eminently successful blocking mission and saluted Forrest's troopers with heartfelt words of encouragement, watching with satisfaction as they trotted by unmolested through Saulsbury. Bolstered by Ross and S.D. Lee, the Confederates had now only to stay a bit longer in order to stir up as much noise as possible before turning back into Mississippi. Ferguson wrote:

> The object of our movement was to allow Gen. Forrest to cross with a small force into Tenn. He reached

Saulsberry at dark and at once crossed, between the burning depot on one side, and some stores on the other, fired because they were used by the Federal troops. The bright light made the darkness beyond seem impenetrable, and it looked as though he was going to certain destruction. The line of Rail Road was heavily guarded, there were many [Yankee] troops in Memphis, so his return appeared impossible .... The rear of his column was brought up by an elderly negro woman in a dilapidated looking buggy, and wearing a long old-fashioned sun bonnet, and driving with a rein in each hand. This was Forrest's cook. My men cheered her loudly, but she passed on, perfectly unconcerned.[480]

After crossing into Tennessee, Ross' brigade continued ahead to Grand Junction and La Grange, Tennessee, where they aggressively demonstrated outside the two Federal garrisons there, but made no real attempt to assault them. Meanwhile, as expected, Union soldiers came pressing hard toward Saulsbury totally unaware that Forrest had already slipped past and was camped for the night at Van Buren, seven miles into Tennessee, and headed for Jackson. A little after midnight, Ferguson was alerted to the approach of a large body of enemy troops tramping down from the east and sent the 2nd Alabama and 12th Mississippi out on the Pocahontas road to confront them. Their orders were to slow down the Yankees, but not to attack them. About five miles down the potholed road, the two regiments found the enemy front and engaged in heavy skirmishing, shooting mostly from horseback. In the darkness, neither side could determine the strength of the other, although the Confederates knew full well that they were badly outnumbered and wisely avoided a general engagement as ordered, slowly giving ground as required. In this manner, mounted Rebel squadrons would rotate with each other, shooting and falling back, shooting and falling back, all the time making as much racket as possible.

By daybreak of December 3, the 2nd Alabama and 12th Mississippi were instructed to break off and hurry back to a well prepared defensive line about a mile from town consisting of fallen trees and narrow ditches, where they quickly dismounted and anchored on either side of the already entrenched and waiting 2nd Tennessee Cavalry.

Ferguson had chosen the ground perfectly; it was a splendid blocking position set out on a half-mile or so of open ground to the front with more than sufficient foliage behind to properly conceal the horse holders. Although exhausted from sniping at the Federals all night long, the powder-begrimed faces of the 2nd Alabama under Colonel Earle showed no signs of fatigue as they watched a gigantic blue wave tramp out of the tree line and align in a long line of battle bordering the open field. Sergeant Hancock proudly described how the three cavalry regiments held the enemy back for a time and the effects of a delightful, artillery duel before a worried General S.D. Lee ordered Ferguson to fall back, mount up, and break contact altogether.

> By daybreak the skirmishing was in sight of our position; soon after which those two regiments [2nd Alabama and 12th Mississippi] fell back and formed, one to the right and the other to the left [of the 2nd Tennessee]. There was an open field for half a mile to our left and right, and also in front, so we had a splendid view. It was a beautiful, clear morning. The Federals moved their artillery out into the opposite side of this old field, in plain view of our position, unlimbered and opened just about sunrise .... We still had the two pieces of artillery that we brought out on picket with us the evening before .... Our artillery opened. "Look! Boys, look! That was a good shot." The Federal column moving to our right was cut in twain. "That beats anything the Federals have done, for they have not yet thrown a single ball to our line."

> By this time we could plainly see that the Federals were outflanking us, both right and left .... However, [S.D.] General Lee, taking in the situation at a glance, addressing General Ferguson, said, "General, withdraw your brigade immediately!"[481]

If S.D. Lee was not willing to engage in a stand-up fight against overwhelming masses of blue infantry, he was still not ready to return to Mississippi either. Lee decided to move Ross and Ferguson 20 miles further to the west following the railroad as far as Moscow, Tennessee, on the Wolf River. S.D. Lee was desirous to do additional mischief and knew that the slow-moving Yankee infantry to his east could not keep up with his cavalry riding to the west, even when the Rebels occasionally stopped to tear up sections of track along the way. By then, General Chalmers' brigade had also come up to support Lee, surging the roving Rebel force to three brigades of cavalry.

Confident that every Yankee from miles around was converging against his command and not Forrest's, S.D. Lee's final objective was to destroy the sturdy wooden railroad bridge which crossed the Wolf River about one mile west of Moscow. Chalmers and Ferguson were tasked with taking the structure out and on December 4, they hotly engaged a body of Federals dug in along the central road on the east side of the bridge. The fighting was on foot and extremely stubborn, taking over an hour to drive the enemy back across the wooden structure. Not all the Federals were able to get away, however, and dozens of them drowned trying to swim for it, with over 40 scooped up as prisoners. But the bridge itself was never taken. The hour-long fight had given time for the Yankees on the opposite side to collect a heavy force, well barricaded and backed by artillery loaded with deadly cannister shot. They dared the Confederates to attack them. S.D. Lee wisely called off the assault.

Private Cochrane wrote of his part in the fighting near Moscow and the tragic death of a much-respected officer in the 2nd Alabama by friendly fire.

I suppose you have heard that our division had gone to West Tennessee to carry Gen. Forrest through the lines. We had a fight at Moscow, Miss. [Moscow, Tennessee] and drove the Yankees over [the bridge at] Wolf River [in Tennessee], killing and drowning a good many, captured 40 and a good many horses. A man who belongs to Captain Pegues' squadron in Co. "I" had his horse wounded in the leg and has returned to the slow train. He only reports one man killed in our regiment. That is Lieut. Todd from North Ala. one of the bravest and best officers in the regiment. He was loved by every soldier in the regiment. Whenever there was a dangerous scout on hand he got in it. Whenever the Yankees were near he usually led the advanced guard. He was returning from one of these scouting expeditions and coming to our pickets they fired on him (without halting I suppose) and shot him through the forehead, killing him instantly.[482]

Content with the overall results of the "grand distraction," Lee moved all three brigades due south on December 5, camping about eight miles west of Holly Springs, Mississippi. By December 7, the Confederates were at Grenada (Tullahoma) and stopped there to endure a very rainy night. Leaving Ross' brigade to take up scouting patrols, S.D. Lee then crossed the Tallahatchie River at Wyatt — "that is, where Wyatt had been; every [civilian] house had been burned by the Federals."[483] The Rebels needed no reminder of Yankee depredations against innocent civilians, the evidences of their barbarity were everywhere.

Chalmers was left at Wyatt to take up his old position along the south-east side of the Tallahatchie and Ferguson marched to Oxford (December 8), then to Pontotoc (December 10) where he rested his command one day, then to Verona (December 12) where

the brigade's wagons were waiting with their tents, supplies, and decent chow. After resting at Verona, the brigade arrived at Okolona (December 20) where the horses were glad to be brushed out and tucked into their wooden stables and barns.

Not only was the overall operation a glorious success, despite the bad weather encountered at the outset and the failure to destroy the bridge at Wolf River, the men in Ferguson's brigade were ecstatic about the seizure of large quantities of Union booty, primarily from Saulsbury, some of which proved to be a source of great amusement. Ferguson wrote:

> Among the things captured in the depot [Saulsbury] were two large dry goods boxes filled with all sorts of things, the distribution of which caused much merriment. Kate [General Ferguson's wife who was related to Robert E. Lee] received as presents from their contents, a roll of black sewing silk, which lasted her through the war, and a pair of button hole scissors she still uses .... Col. McFarland of Gen. [S.D.] Lee's staff, a great red headed six footer, got hold of two pairs of knit drawers, these he considered a great prize. I happened in the room when, standing before a blazing fire, he opened them, his long arms stretching out the legs to the full extent, and they proved to be woman's drawers. A shout went up from the assembly, and he kept that position with his prize exposed for some time amid a volley of pleasantries at his expense .... The driver of Gen. [S.D.] Lee's ambulance got a hoop skirt; this he tied to the roof of the ambulance on the inside, and it was the source of wonder and amazement to some of the natives and of merriment to the soldiers. The Gen was furious when he discovered it and ordered its instant removal.[484]

— Getting Forrest Out of Tennessee —

The troopers of the 2nd Alabama anticipated at least a few weeks to hunker down in winter quarters to recuperate. It was not to be. Just days before Christmas 1863, Lee called on Ferguson and his other brigade commanders to saddle up once again and proceed north in order to now help Forrest get out of Tennessee and back into Mississippi. As before, Ferguson was ordered to conduct a diversionary attack on the Memphis & Charleston in the vicinity of Pocahontas. After making all the usual preparations, Ferguson left Okolona with his brigade at 2 p.m. on Christmas Eve. He had proceeded only two miles before a courier delivered new instructions to return to camp. The men were delighted, much preferring to celebrate Christmas Eve in their warm barracks at Okolona and not in the blasted saddle. And celebrate they did — firing off weapons, singing, and drinking so that by the next morning, Christmas Day, many were too drunk to make reveille. Sergeant Hancock described the revelry.

> This is Christmas Eve, and plenty of whisky in camp. The boys were cutting up at such a terrible rate, and shooting so much all through the brigade [all four regiments], that, awhile after dark, Ferguson ordered the commanders of regiments to send the next man who shot a gun to his headquarters, if he could be found; but if he could not be found, the whole regiment must be ordered into line and stand for one hour. There was not much more shooting after that. CHRISTMAS DAY was a noted day .... Well, I shall not accuse any of the boys of being drunk, but I hope that they will excuse me for saying that some of them had either smelled or tasted of something that made them appear a little "funny."[485]

When the full brigade finally did move north, mother nature once again proved to be their greatest obstacle. Just as the weather refused to cooperate when Ferguson went to help get Forrest into Tennessee a month ago, it again hampered him on the mission to get Forrest back out.

On December 29, Ferguson moved his troopers to Pontotoc. The next day the men marched to New Albany where they "drew seven days' rations of crackers — hard tack — at the later place, something unusual;"[486] it was captured Union foodstuff which at least replaced the monotonous cornmeal. In addition, the men also enjoyed an eight-hour rest.

Early on New Year's Eve, the column moved out towards Ripley with the 2nd Alabama in the lead and the 2nd Tennessee in the rear. At first the weather was mild, but by the late afternoon it deteriorated dramatically. Preceded by a huge rain storm which thoroughly drenched the men and animals, a cold blistering wind quickly followed and turned absolutely everything to ice. The intensity of the cold struck so suddenly that the soaking wet garments froze rock hard with the mains and tails of the poor horses likewise turning stiff. Ferguson wrote:

> [I was] ordered in December to attack the federal garrison at Pocahontas [Tennessee], a small town on the Memphis and Charleston RlRd [sic]. When I left in the morning it was foggy and so warm that a light rain coat was disagreeable, it next rained hard so as to wet the men thoroughly, then, as I entered the town of Ripley, the wind switched around to the north, there was a flurry of snow and before the head of the column had reached the other side of town, every particle of wet clothing had frozen stiff.[487]

Realizing that it was literally a matter of life and death to dismount and start fires in order to prepare for the plunging temperatures that were sure to come at darkness, Ferguson pushed

the brigade a few miles past Ripley to a stand of timber just to the north and called a halt. Some of the men without the benefit of overcoats were frozen so stiff in their saddles that they had to be pulled free. Ferguson recalled:

> I had to push on a few miles to reach a camping ground with timber; when I reached it some of the troopers had to be taken off their horses. Poor fellows, they had cotton clothing only, and no overcoats nor blankets.[488]

Along with the other regiments, the 2nd Alabama immediately went to work dismantling nearby rail fences, gathering dead wood, and cutting down trees, as others sought out any resinous pine knots to quick-start and fuel the fires. Smoke soon swirled into the snowy sky and the troopers eagerly circled around the flames warming themselves as best they could, constantly rotating some frozen portion of the body towards the heat. Hundreds of fires were kept blazing all night long with the men wrapped in blankets like Indians and packed so closely around the flames that their garments singed. Wood smoke may have burned the eyes and permeated skin, hair, and clothes, but at least the flames kept them alive as they prayed for dawn. Pooling their blankets and saddle blankets some messmates bedded down en masse "hog fashion," mindful to take turns keeping the precious fires burning bright through the long night. "All the time it got colder and colder," Ferguson wrote, "and the night was one of great suffering."[489] Sergeant Hancock recorded it as the coldest night of the entire War, something all the men would recall for the rest of their lives.

> It rained in the morning, but just before we got to Ripley in the evening there was a very sudden change in the weather, and as we passed through the above named place it began to snow; nor had we gone far beyond before our wet blankets and clothing were stiff frozen .... As [the] horses were about given out

and the men were about frozen out, they halted for the night .... The wind blew a cutting blast all night. There was not much sleeping done by us that night. By standing by good fires, with our blankets around us, we did not freeze, though some were frost-bitten. This memorable night, in which the old year (1863) stepped out and the new stepped in, was the coldest night of the war.[490]

Those few that managed to get some sleep awoke the next morning much like the way they had ended the previous day — bitterly chilled and utterly numb. The men painfully huddled in front of small firepots consuming a quick breakfast and tending as best they could to the stupefied animals.

The raw winter sun on the unholy morning of the first day of January 1864, revealed the 2nd Alabama saddled up and moving out, still 17 miles south of the Memphis & Charleston, approaching somewhere between Pocahontas and La Grange, an area spanning about 25 miles. Hopes of a brief break in the weather was once again dashed by an unforgiving cold that cut straight through them meaning that the nightmare was not over. All now wore their blankets as capes and tucked ice-cold hands under garments as best they could. The horses were so shaken by the extreme ice and snow that the riders were obliged to dismount and walk them — both to comfort the animal and to stamp their own feet in hopes of shaking off the effects of extreme cold on human flesh. The command was now strung out as far as the eye could see with scores of animals slipping and stumbling, dangling bloody icicles on their knees bearing silent testimony to their torment. The frigid temperatures showed no mercy and to make matters even grimmer, everyone sensed a growing heaviness in the atmosphere which meant another killer storm was coming.

Miraculously, there was something else that greeted them. A hard riding courier covered head to toe in snow covered blankets brought welcomed news. Forrest had already safely passed the

remaining portion of his command out of Tennessee a week earlier (a separate group of 1,200 unarmed recruits left Tennessee around December 18), weaving around the Federals between Moscow and Memphis with forty supply wagons, 200 cattle, and 300 hogs!

Rarely did the men agree on anything, but this time every trooper was ecstatic. Ferguson called back the 2nd Alabama from its lead position and moved them towards Okolona as rapidly as possible. Still, the horses were so used up that the men mercifully walked the suffering animals a good portion of the way over ground so stiff that the frozen roads left absolutely no imprint of their passage. When they encountered bridges, volunteers broke out of the column and threw dirt on the wooden planks to keep the animals from slipping and breaking their legs.

In the larger picture, Forrest's mission was a complete success. In less than 30 days, Forrest had brought out 3,500 new recruits on horseback. Passing within nine miles of Memphis and straight through or around 10,000 Union soldiers, Forrest not only captured and carried off over a hundred wagons full of supplies, he burned down numerous depots and tore up miles of railroad track. The Yankee high command was furious.[491]

One of the other benefits of the extreme cold was a break in the Federal terror raids into Southern held territory. On January 7, 1864, Ferguson moved his used-up command nine miles south of Okolona near Pikeville so that the men could scatter out to get forage for the surviving horses and obtain replacements for the hundreds that had perished over the recent month of grueling duty.

Normally, inactive camp life in a prosperous countryside unspoiled by enemy depredations meant an abundance of good food where the men could barter, buy, or be gifted both the basics and other delicacies. Sadly, however, the conditions across north Mississippi at this stage of the War offered no such opportunities, the land had been razed by the Federals and the troopers could expect little. Nugent described the civilians as hospitable but absolutely destitute.

> A great many of them are in such a deplorable estate of destitution that it is utterly impossible for them to supply even a single person with a meal, without stinting themselves almost to the point of starvation. For an instance of this great destitution, I called at a little log cabin by the road side and counted thirteen children besides four or five grown persons. The house was rudely constructed at the base of a long and dreary looking hill, whose sides were covered with the withered sedge so common to old fields in this country and a few scattered pines. At the point where the hill flattened into a mirey bottom there was a corn field of about ten acres, the stalks of maize resembling — to use a familiar phrase of my Father — pipe stems. This was, as far as I could discern, the only source of supply for bread they had.[492]

Still, for a full 20 days it was a period of welcomed rest as the weather ever so gradually warmed up, allowing ample time for the magic of boiling hot water, lye, and soap to remove the legions of lice which infested man and beast alike. But on January 27, 1864, the "winter quarters" abruptly ended. Ferguson was instructed to pack up and move his brigade about 160 miles south towards Jackson, Mississippi. Rumors were that Sherman was preparing a large infantry movement out of Vicksburg, perhaps intending to attack the vital port city of Mobile. If the intelligence proved accurate the 2nd Alabama would be in for much hard fighting.

Ferguson's spot was filled by General Forrest's new command which was headquartered at Oxford. In addition, to compensate for the additional responsibility placed on Forrest's raw recruits, Lieutenant General Leonidas Polk approved the transfer of Barteau's 2nd Tennessee Cavalry regiment from Ferguson's command to Forrest, a move the Tennesseans absolutely cheered[493] and Ferguson openly lamented. When Ferguson headed south on January 28, he was minus the hard fighting 2nd Tennessee and

very apprehensive about the still horrid conditions of his horses. He did, however, take great comfort that his best regiment, the 2nd Alabama, was still present for duty under the able leadership of the gallant Colonel Richard Earle.

Chapter Six

MERIDIAN: PRELUDE TO TERROR

"Next year their lands will be taken; for in war we can have them, and rightfully, too, and in another year they may beg in vain for their lives."[494]
— *William T. Sherman*

IT WAS NOW A NEW YEAR, 1864. The situation for the Confederacy was bleak, but not entirely hopeless. To be sure, the opportunity for large scale offensive operations onto Northern soil were gone, but if the embattled Confederacy could hold its own on Southern battlefields until the November elections, Lincoln and the Republicans might well be voted out and a peace treaty would follow. Due to a war weariness that had set in all across the Union, Lincoln himself shared this assessment causing the *New York Times* to write about a "manifest ebb in popular feeling throughout the entire country ... a regular period of despondency."[495] Not only had the Union military suffered 100,000 more casualties than the Confederacy, desertions were rampant spurred by a hatred of the unpopular draft and a laundry list of other concerns to include:

> [H]arsh suppression of dissent resulting in the suspension of the writ of habeas corpus in several states, imprisonment and even exile of opposition

figures, and other constitutional infringements ... [along with Lincoln's] Emancipation Proclamation, [which] many outside New England rebelled against fighting other white men to free black slaves.[496]

Prone to boughts of deep depression and extreme pessimism, Lincoln actually wrote individual letters of apology to his cabinet members and tucked them away in a desk drawer, anticipating his defeat at the polls. Something had to be done.

Of course, the South prayed that they might yet fend off the Yankee war of conquest. Depravations were all too real and limited resources stretched to the breaking point, even though the spirit of resistance burned bright. After all, they still had the indomitable Robert E. Lee. The people remained absolutely confident that Marse Lee would continue to pull off stunning victories as he had done so many times before against Lincoln's invading armies. While it was true that the much-vaunted Army of Northern Virginia had been forced back from Pennsylvania in July 1863, the Confederates still held onto much of Virginia and their capital at Richmond remained as defiant as ever. Every Union general that had come after Lee had been soundly whipped and sent scurrying back to Washington so that the *New York Tribune's* war cry of "On to Richmond" was replaced with the ground soldier's more accurate assessment, "It's a long road to Richmond."

In the Deep South, General Johnston protected the vital city of Atlanta with the battle-hardened veterans of the Army of Tennessee firmly set at Dalton, in northern Georgia. In the wake of Bragg's debacle at Missionary Ridge, the men were undeniably better commanded and more importantly, ready and eager to fight.

In short, the South was not about to quit. But the Union had a new war strategy and nefariously evil tactics to accompany it — attack the Confederate armies in unison and brutalize the Southern people with scorched-earth terror.

— Grant's Grand Strategy —

Lincoln looked to hard drinking, cigar chomping, Grant to save his presidency. In reward for taking Vicksburg and the striking victory at Missionary Ridge, Grant was catapulted to the top of the Union military's command structure, culminating with a promotion to Lieutenant General and the position of General-in-Chief of all United States forces (effective March 1864).

Always impatient in temperament, Grant had actually cut down on the alcohol, but not the cigars and in late 1863, he formulated a grand strategy to subjugate the South. Unimaginative in design, the plan was not a swift knock-out blow as had been attempted in the past by so many other overconfident generals, just a long game of *strangulation*. The strategy centered around employing the tremendous advantage the Union held in manpower and resources to simply grind down the Confederacy in a bloody war of attrition. No one quick victorious thrust to the heart, just a series of deep gashes all across the corporate body until the Southern armies literally bled to death. Regardless of the number of casualties required to accomplish the goal of annihilation, Grant intended to launch simultaneous attacks by all the major armies in the field, then 21 army corps consisting of approximately 533,000 men, against the two major Confederate armies. Nothing fancy or brilliant in the plan or the execution, each Federal force would just bunch up in a tight porcupine-like mass and move slowly forward against their far weaker opponents. Furthermore, with these huge movements synchronized, each Confederate army would be individually overwhelmed making it impossible for Richmond to shift forces from one army to another as was done with its victories at Manassas in 1861, and Chickamauga in 1863. One historian described Grant, who many considered a long ways from smart, and his method of warfare as follows:

> Grant was not a particularly imaginative strategist. Grant believed in increasing the weight of the army he brought to bear upon the enemy's defenses until

they snapped like an overburdened shelf. He plotted the eruption of men he would need to overflow the landscape.[497]

The main drawback to Grant's all engaging plan rested in the horrendous casualties that were sure to follow. However, this calculation did not faze Grant in the least because he knew that they could easily replace the losses — immigrants were pouring off the boats in New York by the tens of thousands — while the Confederacy could not. In fact, Grant's Union Army of the Potomac almost drowned in its own blood during the summer of 1864, losing in combat more men than Lee had in his entire army! Although Grant would never admit it, even to himself, he pragmatically understood that Lee was by far the superior general. It was simply that Grant understood that he could afford to lose battles longer than Lee could keep winning them. Impervious to Northern cries that he was a butcher of his own men, he coldly calculated that Lee would eventually run out of men and material. Lee's generalship was like the fox, but Grant would plod ahead and crush like the elephant.

In any event, the entire premise for the coming slaughter of 1864, would require far more blue-clad men than was currently on hand and Lincoln was obliged to call up another half million draftees, right on the heels of the hated Federal Draft Act of March 1863, which had sparked massive riots in New York City and witnessed the largest number of lynching's of black Americans in U.S. history.[498]

Consisting of three legs, the grand movement would kick off in the spring of 1864, when the weather sufficiently warmed. It would play out as follows: (1) In the far west, Union General Banks would move out from New Orleans with the limited objective of capturing the blockade running port city of Mobile; (2) Sherman would strike out against Johnston who was covering Atlanta; and (3) Grant would go after the main prize of R.E. Lee, who was protecting Richmond from the Rapidan River.

Grant personally commanded the two large Federal armies in the east, the Army of the Potomac, commanded by General Meade, and the Army of the James, commanded by General Ben "Beast" Butler. As a collateral effort against Lee, Grant also ordered Union General Sigel to advance another smaller army into the Shenandoah Valley to prevent any foodstuffs from going to Lee's embattled troops. Instead of remaining as a blocking force to choke off the food supplies, permissible under the law of war, Sigel was specifically authorized to employ terror tactics on all Southern farmers which included burning down any and all civilian crops, barns, and homes in the farm rich Shenandoah Valley.

In the lower South, General William T. Sherman bundled three separate Union armies in Tennessee into a massive "army group" of 100,000 plus. This force would drive straight into northwest Georgia to attack Joe Johnston's much smaller Army of Tennessee consisting then of only two depleted corps totaling about 40,000 — one under Lieutenant General William J. Hardee and the other under Lieutenant General John Bell Hood.[499]

General Banks, who was initially ordered to attack Mobile, requested and was given permission to instead move into Louisiana and east Texas with a joint land and naval force on what would be called the Red River campaign. It did not go well for Banks who was soundly defeated in the spring of 1864, by a much smaller Confederate force under General Richard Taylor. This meant that it would be up to Sherman and Grant to deliver on the ultimate conquest.

— Lincoln's Two Policies of Suffering —

While readily approving Grant's military strategy, Lincoln chose to look the other way when Grant implemented two other collateral policies — each one a horrid construct of heartlessness that shocked the conscience. First, in order to further weaken the ability of the Confederacy to replenish their numbers in the field, Grant drastically reduced the volume of prisoner of war (POW) exchanges with his

Confederate counterparts. Grant knew that with over 85% of the white male population in the South already in uniform, prisoner exchanges were the only source the Confederacy had to replenish their depleted ranks, unless they enlisted black Southerners to bear arms. In contrast, the Union had no such manpower problems and simply drew from an endless supply of young fresh-faced draftees, many foreign born. In addition, the Lincoln Administration had finally agreed in 1863, to enlist tens of thousands of black Americans into active military service, a brilliant move that greatly assisted the Union war effort. Though the Confederate Congress finally followed suit in March 1865, authorizing the arming of 300,000 "volunteering" Southern blacks in return for their freedom, it was by then far too little and far too late.[500]

Without debate or objection from Lincoln, the new Union policy of halting POW exchanges was implemented with a cold and heartless calculation and little regard to the deadly impact on its own soldiers. Everyone absolutely knew that such a move would spell horrible suffering and miserable death to thousands upon thousands of Union prisoners — the South could not feed and care for its own troops in the field let alone the multitude of new Union prisoners that flooded into their hands. Accordingly, Lincoln's policy directly contributed to the misery at Andersonville and other Southern POW camps.

Lincoln's willingness to sacrifice his own soldiers meshed perfectly with the second newly approved policy to prosecute the War. Designed to inflict unnecessary pain and suffering, the Union openly sanctioned the use of wide scale terrorism on innocent Southern noncombatants in the belief that the families, soldiers, and government would stop resisting the Union invasion and surrender.

Without question, Grant and others in the hierarchy of command were always careful to disguise the new terror policy with colloquialisms, but the facts attest that civilians and their property were now fair game for "total war." Sherman knew exactly what Grant was suggesting, for example, when his boss slyly substituted

the normal term "war materials," used for the lawful activity of destroying such things as military warehouses, supply depots, railroads, and forts with a new term he coined — "war resources." Not found in any civilized law of war codes and in point of fact specifically outlawed by the Union's own Lieber Code, the Union's intentional targeting of so-called war resources simply authorized the use of raw violence against civilians. Grant telegraphed Sherman:

> [G]et into the interior of the enemy's country [Georgia] as far as you can, inflicting all the damage you can against their war resources [emphasis added].[501]

As covered in the companion book *Union Terror*, war resources included every man, woman, and child and every piece of private property they used or lived on. The ad hoc Federal cavalry terror raids against civilians and their property that the 2nd Alabama had been so busy blunting across northern Mississippi and Alabama for the past year would seem like child's play to what was about to unfold across vast swaths of Dixie. Widespread terror as an acceptable war tactic had now arrived and would soon reap an unholy harvest of suffering and destruction.

— Trial Run for Terror —

For several months after New Year's Day of 1864, all was fairly quiet on the eastern front in Virginia where Robert E. Lee held his army firm and defiant. Similarly, during the first few months of 1864, General Johnston's Army of Tennessee on the western front at Dalton enjoyed the uncommon luxury of relative inaction. On the other hand, S.D. Lee and his cavalry in far off Mississippi had no time to rest as they experienced first-hand the inauguration of the Union's new policy of large-scale terror attacks against civilians.

As it turned out, General Sherman was not content to simply gather men and supplies in the hub of Chattanooga to later go

against Joe Johnston in the spring. In the interim, both he and Grant hoped to enlarge the scope of Union occupation by taking the strategic port city of Mobile (a topic of constant discussion for them) or the important manufacturing town of Selma, Alabama.

The two met face-to-face in Memphis to plan a limited wintertime offensive and agreed to try a double envelopment movement against the key Confederate supply center at Meridian, Mississippi, immediately followed by a quick thrust into Alabama. The plan called for Sherman to head out from Vicksburg in early February 1864, with over 20,000 men in 12 infantry brigades plus some 5,000 cavalry and artillery, and head straight east to Meridian (just over 150 miles away), where he would rendezvous with General William Sooy Smith's 8,000 horsemen riding down from Collierville, Tennessee (30 miles east of Memphis). Sooy Smith, who had recently been promoted to command all the Union cavalry in the Army of the Tennessee, would arrange his departure a day or two earlier than Sherman's so that he could both cover the longer distance of over 200 miles to Meridian and also have time to do as much destruction as possible to civilian homes along the way. Once the two linked up at Meridian, the powerful combined force could then easily push its way into neighboring Alabama targeting either Selma or Mobile, both well within striking distance. Then, by late March 1864, Sherman would hurry to his main command force of over 100,000 camped in and around Chattanooga to lead them out on the spring assault against Johnston. Being on time to launch the Georgia campaign was the only pre-condition set by Grant.

Since the Union burning of the State capital of Jackson and several other nearby towns in the summer of 1863, Meridian, which came into existence as a small railroad stop in 1860, had been hastily rebuilt and beefed up where it now served as a vital regional Confederate command center with supply depots, arsenals, and hospitals. Three functioning Southern railroads intersected at Meridian transporting government grain, livestock, ammunition, and other supplies all across the South.

To oppose Sherman's infantry out of Vicksburg, was the well liked but rather mediocre Lieutenant General Leonidas Polk who commanded the Army of Mississippi as well as overseeing the Department of Alabama, Mississippi, and East Louisiana. His small force was stationed at various locations across the sprawling region and consisted of about 10,000 infantry effectives, the cavalry of S.D. Lee, and now Forrest's untested 3,500 new recruits from Tennessee. Polk, a member of the clergy and a graduate of West Point was also an old friend of Jefferson Davis and while he solemnly pledged to Richmond that he would hold Meridian at all costs, Polk's real strategy was to save as much government property as possible from Meridian and fall back into Alabama. As it turned out, during the entire Federal incursion not a single rifle shot from Polk's infantry was ever fired at Sherman or Smith! All resistance came from the Rebel cavalry only.

Sherman's February 1864 campaign to Meridian was not just another military maneuver to battle Confederate forces, it was also meant to cut an arid path of total destruction across middle Mississippi with the premeditated goal of terrorizing noncombatants. While Union raiding parties had engaged in depredations against civilians for quite some time now, those atrocities had been relatively small in size and purpose, carried out mostly via hit and run cavalry raids. This was different. Indeed, Sherman's Meridian brutal foray would serve as a dark harbinger of things to come for thousands of Confederate civilians during the remainder of the War — entire Federal armies would now pick clean as a hound's tooth huge swaths of Southern landscape and put them to the "Sherman torch."

Rubricated by a nervous personality, General Sherman was perfectly suited to kick off this grotesque orgy of real and physiological terrorism. Even the friendliest biographer of William T. Sherman concedes that he was haunted by a plethora of personal demons and by this stage of the War the wild-eyed scoundrel had convinced himself that command directed terror against women and children was completely justified. Sherman embraced the evil and proudly offered himself as the Union's chief instrument of

terror boasting in a long rambling letter to a subordinate stationed at Huntsville, Alabama (he asked his U.S. Senator brother in Ohio to republish the letter in the newspapers), of the need to treat all Southerners with unrelenting viciousness.

> The Government of the United States has ... any and all the rights of Sovereignty which they choose to enforce in War, to take their [Southerners] lives, their homes, their lands, their every thing, because they cannot deny that War does exist by their acts, and War is simply Power unrestrained by Constitution or Compact.[502]

In short, the Mississippi march was Sherman's dry run for the ground shaking war crimes he would commit in Georgia and the Carolinas later that year and into 1865. The miscreant Union commander gleefully got things rolling during the month-long movement to Meridian by allowing his infantry to steal or destroy all food and livestock they encountered along the way as well as burn families out of house and home, black or white, from the largest plantation to the smallest cabin. Sadly, coterminous with the command sanctioned destruction of civilian property, subordinate officers routinely turned a blind eye to felony crimes that occurred to include robbery, assault and battery, and in not a few instances, sexual assault.

— Fighting Sherman's Meridian Raid —

Confederate spies warned in January that the Federals were planning to attack east from their new base at Vicksburg and on February 3, 1864, Sherman's Sixteenth Corps under General Stephen B. Hurlbut and his Seventeenth Corps under General James B. McPherson moved out of the river city configured in two large columns with a cavalry brigade of four full strength regiments commanded by Colonel Edward F. Winslow riding ahead on point.[503]

Sherman was lumbering forth to Meridian with over 25,000 troops and terror was on his mind.

As their nominal pathfinder, the Yankees simply guided themselves astride the tracks of the Southern Railroad which led straight to Jackson and then on to Meridian. Until they reached Jackson, McPherson's troops marched to the south of the rail and Hurlbut to the north. Even though Sherman had stripped his well-dressed infantry of tents and other extra baggage, over 1,000 supply wagons trailed behind hauling ammunition, food, and artillery. With dry weather the Federals made excellent time.

Like a swarm of locusts, Sherman's marching infantry ravaged and razed everything in their direct path of march, civilians on the periphery were spared the torch only because Sherman was intent on getting to Meridian on time to meet Sooy Smith. Within four days they were just a dozen miles away from the only natural obstacle that might pose a problem should the Confederates choose to make a fight of it — the formidable Pearl River. Situated just to the east of Jackson, the Pearl flowed north to south providing Polk with a marvelous opportunity to dig in on the opposite bank and punish Sherman when he attempted to cross. Inexplicably, instead of organizing a defensive stand at the Pearl, Polk refused to even try, content to mark Morton, about half-way between Jackson and Meridian, as his point of resistance.

General Smith, who was supposed to have left Collierville on February 2, did not trot his heavy cavalry command out of that city until February 11, alleging that bad weather had delayed one of his smaller brigades. With 8,000 horseman and the accompanying artillery and wagons pushing down into north Mississippi, it was not long before Confederate scouts spotted him and since Ferguson had been hastily transferred to Red Jackson's division to confront Sherman, the only Rebel cavalry to oppose the Yankees was Forrest's untested Tennessee recruits, about 3,000 effectives.

Polk's first move in this chess game was to send out part of S.D. Lee's cavalry under General Red Jackson to do all that was practicable to slow Sherman while Polk busied himself consolidating

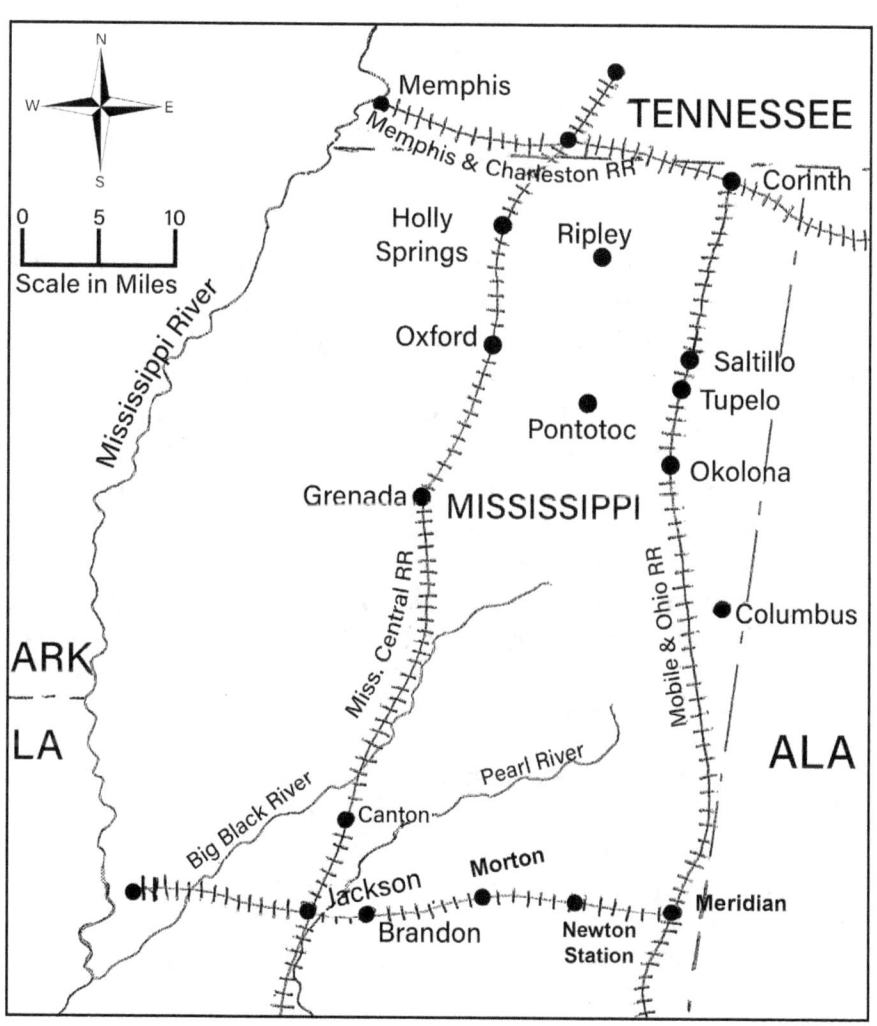

Route of March — Vicksburg to Meridian.

his infantry at Morton. After a long and arduous ride from Aberdeen in northeast Mississippi, most of the Ferguson brigade crossed the Pearl at Cullum's Ferry near Canton on February 3, where Ferguson received orders from S.D. Lee to help screen Major General William Loring's Division as it converged on Morton.

Since Christmas of 1863, Lieutenant Colonel J.P. West had temporarily commanded the 2nd Alabama while Colonel Earle recovered from an unspecified ailment. However, with fresh orders to confront Sherman, the indefatigable Earle immediately returned to his command[504] to join Ferguson's tired but determined brigade as it headed straight to Clinton to engage the advancing Federals.[505] Ferguson wrote:

> I had not been in Clinton more than an hour before I was engaged with Sherman's advance guard with which I fought until nightfall [February 4-5]. I remained in Clinton during the night and had a man killed by a stray bullet fired from an amazing long distance. Next morning I was directed to fall back, fighting [as we did].[506]

Sherman's advance, commanded by Colonel Winslow took possession of Jackson on the late afternoon of February 5, where the Federals once again re-burned the city (for the third time). Sherman's infantry soon arrived and crossed over the Pearl on February 6-7, using pontoons that had been carelessly left behind by the retreating Confederate infantry. The Yankees wasted little time lingering in that place so that by the afternoon Sherman entered the neighboring town of Brandon and burned it to the ground. A foot soldier in McPherson's wing recorded:

> This place [Brandon] like Jackson was none the better nor richer for our occupation, foraging and fire doing fearful work, and as usual attacking the loveliest and costliest first.[507]

Almost simultaneous with the Federals passing through Jackson, Ferguson and two other cavalry brigades — Wirt Adams' and Peter Starke's — rode into the devastated city, swimming their horses at Smith's Ferry. Many of the Rebel horse soldiers swung around the enemy's flanks to continue skirmishing, but Ferguson was ordered to take his brigade directly to Morton.

As the enemy marched steadily forward towards Meridian, the Confederate foot soldiers began to coalesce at Morton as directed, all the while Polk straining the telegraph wires calling on both Johnston and Richmond for reinforcements. Only squadrons of butternut horsemen continued to vigorously skirmish with Sherman's front and flanks, also becoming adept at picking off any Yankee straggler or looter that strayed too far from their columns seeking to "live off the land." The Rebel troopers were so successful that Union officers were obliged to order their men to stop "foraging" the outlaying civilian homes that were not directly in the line of march.[508]

Like Sherman and his generals, Ferguson and S.D. Lee fully expected Polk to make a fighting stand at Morton. True to character, Polk lost his nerve and ordered a retreat, expecting the cavalry to cover the movement. And so, on the early morning of February 9, Ferguson's brigade found itself heavily skirmishing against Winslow's cavalry a couple miles west of Morton. Seeing that he could do no more, Ferguson broke off the fight and wisely fell back and positioned himself on the road to Hillsboro, to oppose the oncoming Federals between Morton and Shockalo Creek. Once set on the road, he left a small contingent behind and took the bulk to Hillsboro to meet with General Polk, this being the imagined next stop for the Union advance. Because Polk was still unsure if Sherman intended to turn south and move to Mobile or go to Hillsboro and then straight to Meridian, he ordered Ferguson to march to Newton Station to screen the retreat of French's division as it boarded the cars to Meridian. Leaving a small portion of his brigade near Hillsboro, Ferguson arrived at Newton Station to see French's troops safely off.

By the afternoon of February 9, it was clear to Polk that the full Federal army was heading to Hillsboro and Mobile breathed a sigh of relief. As usual, this new intelligence had no positive impact on the portly general and the infantry was ordered to retreat even further east. By February 10, only a portion of Ferguson's brigade commanded by Lieutenant Colonel William Maxwell was at Hillsboro to offer any resistance. A Federal trooper recorded the ensuing hard skirmishing in his diary:

> Early on the morning of the 10th [February] moved forward through Hillsboro and over Ontoxaloo [Hontokalo] Creek. Skirmishing went on fitfully all day, at times obstinately. Some prisoners were captured and the column that followed the skirmishers [Confederate cavalry under Ferguson] saw 13 dead rebels along the road.[509]

By fighting dismounted and then galloping back to the next ridge when the pressure was too great, Maxwell's troopers put up a stubborn show of it, also felling trees and digging up the road, yet Hillsboro too was desecrated and turned into a pile of ash by the Yankees.[510] By 3 a.m. of February 12, Maxwell was able to reunite with Ferguson near Chunky Creek on the Decatur-Meridian road to shield the march of the Confederate infantry to Meridian.[511] After placing pickets out covering all the approaches to Newton Station, the brigade moved south a few miles to Joseph Moore's Plantation, just above Garlandsville. Then, on February 11, S.D. Lee countermanded instructions from Polk that would have sent Ferguson further southeast to guard the Mobile & Ohio, and ordered him to wedge himself between General Hurlbut's Federals and a wing of the Confederate infantry then passing through Decatur.[512] The gray horse soldiers grabbed only a few hours of sleep and then rode most of the night through dense pine trees "over roads little traveled and covered up with pine straw"[513] before settling on the east bank of Chunky Creek, about 5 miles east of Decatur.

Ferguson set out some advanced skirmishers to the Patterson Plantation on the west bank of Chunky Creek, destroyed the bridge by throwing a huge tree over it, and then set about organizing an ambush designed to strike confusion on any exposed portion of Winslow's cavalry, who was spearheading the infantry advance. He messaged General Loring at 10:45 a.m.[514]

Decatur & Meridian Road,
At Crossing of Chunky Road
February 12, 1864

Maj. Gen. W.W. Loring:

General: The enemy are advancing from Decatur. I shall skirmish with them here and all the way back [to Meridian]. Please send me Croft's battery and a wagon load of ammunition. My ordnance officer has written a note for the kinds needed. I have also sent to wagon train to have provisions cooked and sent to me. Please order all serviceable horses to come with or follow Croft's battery.

Respectfully,

S.W. Ferguson

Brigadier General

By the time Ferguson sent the message to Loring, Winslow's cavalry had long since entered Decatur, followed shortly thereafter by the infantry, where the accompanying looting and burning once more played out its ugly tale. As expected, the blue cavalry moved out by mid-morning and later that afternoon the bulk of the Federal infantry followed. Soon thereafter hundreds of wagons lumbered into the fire-gutted town along with General Sherman and his aides.

Covered with dust and grime, Sherman requisitioned one of the few dog-trot cabins that was still standing and fell fast asleep, unaware that a regiment of infantry that was supposed to be guarding the place had inexplicably marched out of town, leaving a sleeping Sherman and a long line of parked wagons, most still hitched to their mules, in a most precarious spot. Informed only about the vulnerable wagons, at about 6:30 p.m. S.D. Lee sent his escort troopers (Nelson's Georgia Partisan Rangers) and a undersized regiment from Adams' brigade to attack them. Needless to say, the ensuing fighting awakened Sherman and caused great panic in the darkness before sufficient numbers of Federal infantry could be rushed back to repeal the attackers. Still, the Rebels torched 20 wagons, sabered to death 24 mules, and killed four of the enemy,[515] all the while totally unaware of the fact that Sherman himself had been within their grasp!

Ferguson's day would be just as eventful. Informed by scouts that Winslow was approaching his position, Ferguson gave orders to the dismounted portion of his brigade concealed on the opposite side of the water to fire into the approaching Yankees once a sufficient number had crossed. Coterminous with any opportunities that might materialize once the shooting started, Ferguson intended to conduct a bold charge with a mounted portion of his command. As fate would have it, just such a window opened and the resulting fight was reported in vivid terms by Northern newspapers all the way back at Saint Paul, Minnesota.[516]

Unable to efficiently traverse the water by use of the badly damaged bridge, most of the arriving Federals waded across at shallow spots and scrambled up the far bank under the watchful eyes of well-hidden dismounted Confederates in the tree-line. Then, at a given signal, Ferguson's boys greeted the Yankees with a barrage of well-placed bullets while swarms of Rebels came storming out of an adjacent section of the woods on horseback with shouts, pistols, and sabers, Ferguson leading the way. The ensuing close quarters clash, which began about noon, was a bloody affair. "I was wounded in the arm in a hand-to-hand encounter," Ferguson wrote on a pension application and "I killed three of the enemy, one

an officer, using both my pistol and sword, and my horse was shot under me."[517] Ferguson wrote in his memoirs:

> Near Chunky River [Chunky Creek] I prepared an ambuscade which, I learned from a Northern newspaper's account of it, proved very successful. Here I received a wound in the arm so slight that it did not cause me to dismount; this was my only wound, though I had three horses shot under me [in the course of the entire War].[518]

After about an hour of combat, Winslow was able to amass enough men to force the Confederates back. Still, for the next several miles the Rebels continued to do all that could reasonably be expected to slow the blue juggernaut. With only about 17 miles to Meridian, axes and trenching tools went to work all along the road felling trees and digging ditches to give Loring's troops time to pass through unmolested.[519] Later that afternoon at the Reynolds Plantation, four companies of the 2nd Alabama under Earle's leadership engaged in another sharp fight with Winslow's troopers. Twice the Federal cavalry regrouped and charged at Earl's dismounted men, and each time were hurled back with heavy losses.[520]

Indeed, as Winslow's cavalry, supported by two full divisions of infantry, pushed ever closer towards Meridian, the fighting became more desperate. Luckily for the Rebels, the landscape heading into the city now turned in their favor as the area was thickly covered with virgin timber, heavy underbrush, and rough mountainous hills. Nevertheless, on February 13, only Ferguson and a single pioneer corps were there to degrade the paths from Tallahatta Creek all the way back towards Suqualena by felling pine trees across the roads and using spades, clam bars, and pickaxes to dig out gaping holes. Outnumbered 20 to 1, Ferguson skillfully rotated each of his four regiments to strike at the front and flanks of the advancing Federals, withdrawing them in turn so that he was able to retard the enemy's rate of advance all day long, causing a

frustrated Sherman to directly message Winslow to continue his movements forward into the evening hours. The only mishap for Ferguson's brave troopers occurred near Suqualena, where a line of his own skirmishers inexplicably fired a scattered volley into an advanced portion of a dismounted line wounding several and killing at least one Alabamian, Private Coleson.[521]

Ferguson and the rest of the Rebel cavalry were clearly doing all that Polk required, even if Polk could not bring himself to fight. Still, it was not just Sherman that worried him. Since February 11, when the old general first received word about Federal cavalry pouring down from Tennessee into Mississippi, he had become increasingly worried about being attacked from the north and now with the Sherman so close to Meridian, he elected to abandon the city altogether and shift his infantry southeast to Demopolis, Alabama. With the Rebel cavalry's unparalleled success in slowing Sherman's army to a crawl, Polk was able to take two full days to evacuate everything of value from Meridian so that by the morning of February 14, the Confederate infantry had vanished, removing by train and wagon over $12,000,000 in military property.

Up until the very last moment, Ferguson's troopers guarded the upper and lower roads leading into Meridian and fired the first shots in defense of the town, skirmishing heavily with the 5th Illinois Cavalry. Fighting in staggered lines of battle, the weight of increasing numbers of Union cavalry pressed Ferguson back into Meridian proper resulting in several casualties for the 2nd Alabama to include the death of Private Alexander West (Co. B), the young son of Lieutenant Colonel John P. West. Ferguson was the last to fight for Meridian and having been muscled eastward out of town, by 4 p.m. the Federal infantry simply walked into the empty city. Ferguson retreated along the Mobile & Ohio north to Marion where he joined the rest of S.D. Lee's command and hovered about for the next several days striking back at Winslow's probing scouts around Marion and Old Marion. Ferguson recalled:

> From this time [the skirmish at Chunky Creek on February 12] until I left the vicinity of Old Marion, on the afternoon of February 18, my command was almost continually engaged with the enemy, the skirmishing at times being kept up until after dark.[522]

When Sherman himself rode into Meridian, he discovered to his great disappointment that all the warehouses were yawning empty and the rolling stock of the three railroads long gone. Having missed his chance to take the city whole, thanks in large part to the work of the stalwart Rebel cavalry, the disheveled Sherman was absolutely livid and blamed it all on Sooy Smith who should have arrived from the north days ago as agreed in their Memphis battle plan. To compound his frustration, the Yankee general had absolutely no idea where Smith actually was, not a single courier had been sent to Sherman since he left Vicksburg. With little choice but to stay put until word from Smith might arrive, an angry Sherman turned his army loose to pillage and burn the civilian property in the city and its environs to include destroying the infrastructure. Literally every house in the town was burned to the ground. For seven full days — February 14-20 — it went on. One section of 10,000 men set about tearing up the railroads and bridges north and south of Meridian, while the rest targeted the city itself. Sherman bragged in a dispatch:

> For five days [the Federals stayed for a week], 10,000 men worked hard and with a will in that work of destruction, with axes, crowbars, sledges, clawbars, and with fire, and I have no hesitation in pronouncing the work was well done. Meridian, with its depots, storehouses, arsenal, hospitals, offices, hotels, and cantonments, no longer exists.[523]

On March 27, 1864, *The New York Times* reprinted a letter from a Mobile newspaper of a Southern woman's account of the atrocities. A resident of the place, the mother and her children

had the good fortune of having their home occupied by Brigadier General Mortimer Leggett and his staff, so that it was spared the torch. After the Yankees left, she wrote her mother in Mobile:

> My Dear Mother: The Yankees came in [Meridian] at 4 P.M. in full force. They skirmished a little [with Ferguson's Confederate cavalry] in our yard which frightened us very much .... After the skirmishing stopped, the mob ran around going into houses, breaking open doors, trucks, locks &c. tearing up and destroying everything they could. Caught all the chickens in the place in half an hour .... Only five men entered my house and demanded my keys ... they wanted all arms and gold and silver .... Our store was burned to the ground, and so was another one of our new houses. My two milch cows were killed, and every one in the town; and for eight or ten miles around all cattle and horses. Our horse was not at home. The printing office and all public buildings were burned up, and Mr. Ragsdale's Hotel, Terrills' and Burton House .... Oh, such destruction.[524]

But where was Sooy Smith? The answer was that Smith's "flying column" of 8,000 blue troopers armed with those wonderful breech-loading carbines and 20 pieces of artillery had encountered Nathan Bedford Forrest. While it is true that Smith got a very late start from Tennessee, he delayed himself even further when he reached the Memphis & Ohio and lingered to tear up track between Okolona and West Point. This allowed time for Forrest to pull his much smaller command together and to also discern that Sooy Smith was going to Meridian to join Sherman, then only 80 miles away.

It was February 20, and the Wizard of the Saddle thought to set a trap somewhere just below West Point which he intended to bait with his younger brother's brigade. Although vastly superior numbers of the enemy pushed Colonel Jeffrey Forrest back through

West Point that late afternoon, Smith inexplicably stopped his pursuit at Ellis Bridge on Sakatonchee Creek and camped for the evening.

The night was long and Sooy Smith's imagination got the best of him. Believing exaggerated reports of Confederate reinforcements and a looming Rebel counterattack, Smith nervously fretted on his cot that the invincible "devil Forrest" would destroy him. Amazingly, he decided to retreat back to Memphis come first light! True to character, once informed of Smith's retrograde movement, General Forrest immediately grabbed the closest troopers on hand, a mere 150 men, and launched what can only be described as a reckless assault on the rear of the Federal horse column. The rest of his men would have to catch up!

In a running 50-mile gun battle that lasted two days and would see the Federals make successive stands and then fall back each time they were attacked; many brave men died on both sides to include Colonel Jeffrey Forrest. With a path marked by exhausted horse flesh and abandoned Federal equipment of every description, by the time the much-frazzled Yankees reached the safety of Memphis on February 26, Sherman was well on his way back to Vicksburg having left Meridian, or what was left of it, on February 20. For his part, Smith's command was absolutely demolished. Out of 8,000 troopers, no more than 2,200 men were still on serviceable mounts, the other 5,000 that made it back either had no mounts, rode double, or were astride broken-down horses.

— Escorting Sherman Back to Vicksburg —

When it became clear that Sherman was intent on remaining stationary at Meridian to wait for Smith, S.D. Lee rushed several brigades north, to include Ferguson and Adams, in order to help Forrest fend off Sooy Smith. Ferguson was temporarily named a "division" commander with Adams' brigade under his immediate command, so that Colonel Earle took over as the temporary brigade commander for Ferguson. Having shifted from Marion to nearby

Alamutche, Ferguson departed on the morning of February 20, and arrived in Starkville, 40 miles south of Okolona, on February 22, only to discover that Forrest had already routed Smith. A beaming S.D. Lee wired Polk at Demopolis of the phenomenal victory and after resting his men and animals, Ferguson and Adams countermarched their worn commands on February 24, to assist Red Jackson who was ordered to engage Sherman's now Vicksburg bound returning army.

Disgusted and unwilling to wait any longer for Smith, Sherman finally left Meridian on February 20. Given that the countryside on the outbound trip was thoroughly gutted out, the Federals embarked to the northwest stopping only at the prosperous town of Canton, located 25 miles above Jackson on the Pearl River, to again wait on word from Smith. Ever the duplicitous hypocrite, before leaving Meridian to march the 95 miles to Canton, General Sherman issued his standard pro forma orders banning the burning of property and any outrages on civilians along the way, but everyone knew such orders were irrelevant. One Union soldier with the 15th Illinois Infantry candidly told the truth about the abuse — even taking food from starving children — when he wrote:

> Sherman's army left fire and famine in its track. The country was one lurid blaze of fire; burning cotton gins and deserted buildings were seen on every hand. I regret to say it but oft times habitations were burned down over the heads of occupants, but not by order .... I have seen the cabin of the poor entered and the last mouthful taken from almost starving children. No one, who has a heart that beats in sympathy for the sorrows of others, can look on these things without the strongest feelings of compassion for the victims.[525]

However, just before the Union Army entered the large town of Canton on February 26, something unexpected occurred. In stark

contrast to his open policy of fire and terror on civilians, Sherman issued new orders which were detailed and crystal clear — no arson, no looting, no depredations of any kind were to be committed while the troops waited in Canton. Unlike the horrible fate of every other town which Sherman's army entered, only Canton's railroad tracks were destroyed. The reason for this most unexpected turnabout had nothing to do with humanitarian concerns or the Federal commander's desire to actually follow the law of war. The only reason Sherman spared the town was because he had decided to return by an escort of cavalry to Vicksburg on February 28, and leave his army behind to march the remaining 70 miles by itself. As previously covered in *Union Terror*, these "real" orders to respect civilians and their property as required by the law of war did not sit well with Sherman's troops who were accustomed to the "fake orders" which allowed the atrocities. One Union Soldier noted the contradiction.

> It seems to me that here is something wrong in this expedition — for [the towns of] Brandon, Morton, Hillsboro, Decatur, and Meridian were burned to the ground — not a building to tell where they stood, the country was very poor, and the inhabitants ditto. I don't believe there were really half a dozen rich men east of the Pearl River — of course — all men [off] in the [Confederate] army as nearly as I could find out .... But as soon as we reached the neighborhood of Canton where the country was rich and the plantations large, where the inhabitants were not only influential and men of wealth but were to a man avowed rebels and told our soldiers so and in some cases the women spit in our boys faces, no sooner had we reached there than Sherman issued an order prohibiting under penalty of being marched to Vicksburg tied behind a wagon with a placard on his back for the same burning and plundering that heretofore had been encouraged. Even the wells

and cisterns were guarded and we were forced to drink stagnant water enough to make anyone sick [emphasis added].[526]

By February 29, the main Union supply wagons — stolen and government issue — began the long bumpy journey back to Vicksburg out of Canton. From the huge stolen Conestogas to the tiny ox carts, the transports were crammed full with miscellaneous plunder (the officers would get their division of the stolen property upon return to the post) so that by March 1, Mississippi was once again subjected to new outrages of every sort by marauding groups of Yankee "foragers." Sherman had only exempted Canton from terrorism, not the small farms and families in the countryside between Canton and Vicksburg. The soldiers were allowed to loot private property, glut themselves on stolen civilian foodstuffs, burn down dwellings, and shoot at will all the domestic animals in the yards, pens, and fields.

Tasked with "escorting" the Yankees, General Red Jackson moved quickly to do just so, mindful that the main goal of the cavalry was to minimize the pillaging. Jackson was then headquartered at Sharon, 7 miles to the northeast of Canton and could count three brigades of cavalry at his disposal — Starke, Adams, and Ferguson (Sul Ross' brigade had been sent to target Federal transports on the Yazoo River). Red Jackson placed Adams to the south to flank the Federal left, Starke to the north to do the same and Ferguson to the rear, with all three instructed to keep up as much pressure as practicable, picking off any of the blue thieves that wandered from the main body as well as capturing Union stragglers. The three Confederate brigades divided out by their individual regiments hopscotching and taking turns in order to get at as many looters as possible. Red Jackson described the movement as follows:

> The enemy was scattered in parties of thirty and forty, foraging and pillaging through the country. I [General Red Jackson] therefore adopted the plan of detaching regiments to operate against them. This

succeeded admirably .... In this manner they pursued the enemy ... capturing fifteen wagons and teams and one hundred and fifty prisoners, killed and wounded [many] numbers, also captured fifty cavalry horses and equipments .... The effect was to confine them [the Union forces] closely to the road on which they were moving [to Vicksburg].[527]

After crossing the Yokahockany River at LaFlore's Ferry, on February 24, Ferguson engaged in his first contact against foraging parties belonging to the 10th Missouri Cavalry. "[I] soon encountered the foraging parties of the enemy, which were at once driven in, with a loss to them of 7 killed and 38 captured; to me of 1 officer and 1 man wounded.[528]

While the Confederate cavalry captured scores of Federals, many of the Yankees found in the act of pillaging and burning civilian homes were summarily lined up and shot on the spot; the Union rosters would later list them in that catch all category called "missing." In his own report, Red Jackson briskly confirmed the hard realities of dealing with the thieves. "The number of their killed will never be known," he recorded in his after-action report, "as a great many were killed while out from the main body, plundering and burning houses."[529]

— THE TALLY —

On March 4, 1864, the bulk of the Union army reached their barracks at Vicksburg having traveled about 360 miles (round trip) in 30 days. The official casualty count was 341 killed, wounded, and missing. As stated, since the return trip from Meridian to Vicksburg was about 20 miles to the north of the outbound path, this previously untouched territory was also left desolate of any domesticated animals, food stuffs, or structures. The tears of the women and children were all that remained. Thus, although Sherman fought only the Confederate cavalry and missed capturing any of the large stores of Confederate supplies

at Meridian, he could still brag that he had burned out a path of desolation that encompassed an area 50 miles wide on his trip up and back. The despicable general freely admitted to the atrocities against the civilian population, some of which were recorded in Union controlled newspapers to include the drowning by Union troops of over 20 black children thrown into Chunky Creek.[530] "We *lived off the country*," Sherman boasted, "and made a swath of desolation fifty miles broad across the state of Mississippi, which the present generation [of civilians] will not forget."[531]

On the other hand, General S.D. Lee summed up the raw truth about Sherman's heartless use of terror tactics during the Meridian campaign:

> There never was an army in a civilized country that laid waste and destroyed public and private property as did Sherman's army. They burnt nearly every town they passed through, and their route was marked by the smoke of burning buildings and desolate homesteads .... Sherman's expedition is almost inexplicable.[532]

It is true that Polk had saved much valuable government property and the cities of Mobile and Selma were safe thanks to Forrest, yet the only opposition Sherman faced during the entire movement was from the ever-present gray cavalry. The total for killed, wounded, and missing on the Confederate side is conflicted, with estimates ranging from 109 to 288. According to one source, Ferguson's brigade suffered 4 killed, 14 wounded, and 20 missing.[533] Whatever the true number, Ferguson continued his harassing attacks until March 4, and was justifiably praised by General Red Jackson "for his gallantry, energy, and prompt compliance with all orders while temporarily serving under my command."[534]

During the Meridian campaign, the 2nd Alabama covered well over 400 miles in just under a month's time, moving in a giant triangle across the map before settling down at Madison Station and

then to a camp near Canton for a well-deserved reprieve. Ferguson admitted that the difficulties of constant skirmishing with superior enemy forces proved to be a severe strain on his detached brigade.

> [The 400 mile operation] severely taxed the fortitude and patriotism of my men. At all times prompt to respond to every order, they boldly engaged the advance of a large and confident army and unflinchingly held their position until ordered off the field.... I append a list of casualties.[535]

Mercifully, the men and animals stayed put at Canton for about three weeks to recuperate. In fact, conditions were so stable that Ferguson's beloved wife Kate made the 180 miles on horseback from Tuscaloosa to join him there. No doubt, other wives and sweethearts visited the men of the 2nd Alabama as well, but these pleasant scenes were always overshadowed with concerns about how long the ruthless war of Yankee aggression would continue to go on.

— Hunting Down Tories and Deserters in North Alabama —

In the wake of the heretofore unprecedented acts of command directed vandalism and arson carried out in the Meridian campaign, the Confederate cavalry in Mississippi was in no mood for leniency on Union raiders and Tories. In early April 1864, Ferguson received new orders to rejoin Red Jackson's small division of horse soldiers to confront a reported enemy pillaging raid heading to the rich iron and coal fields around what is today Birmingham, Alabama. By April 8, Ferguson's independent brigade reached Tuscaloosa which was a welcomed sight for the men who hailed from that university town. However, when the supposed Union intrusion failed to materialize, General Polk instructed S.D. Lee to keep Jackson's division, along with Ferguson's brigade, in the area for a new mission.

Local law and order in north Alabama had greatly deteriorated causing Alabama Governor Thomas Hill Watts to note that "[t]he cries of the starving people are coming to me almost every day [from north Alabama]."[536] Even though the 2nd Alabama had vanquished the 1st Alabama Union Cavalry at Vincents Crossroads just six months ago, "bands of thieves, deserters, and draft-dodgers increasingly waged guerilla style warfare"[537] throughout the region and Polk desired to flush these undesirables out of their hiding places in the forests and rocky hills. Reacting to the recent news that some Alabama Tories had hanged a Confederate home-guard commander by his feet and then roasted him alive over a fire, Polk especially ordered the gray cavalrymen to punish any *armed* Unionist or deserter that was caught "with death upon the spot."[538] The bishop turned general was absolutely clear in his succinctly worded directions to S.D. Lee.

> [You] will arrest them [armed Tories, deserters, and fugitives] and will deal with all such as may be banded together for resistance in the most summary manner.[539]

Red Jackson's 2,500[540] troopers, to include Sul Ross' brigade, settled into camp at Tuscaloosa while Ferguson moved his brigade of about 1,200 effectives to Elyton Cross Roads, 50 miles from Tuscaloosa. By April 30, Ferguson shifted his headquarters back closer to Tuscaloosa, bivouacking at the small town of Centreville. From these central spots, the commanders sent out rotating patrols on far ranging scouts north into no-man's-land where there were few laws or men to enforce them.

The police duty to round up absentees, arrest deserters, and capture armed Tories and spies was an unpleasant one. Not only did it require making wide ranging manhunts to track down and deal with the various categories of malefactors, but the terrain was extremely rough requiring the troopers to toil over rocky mountains with narrow ravines, often in single file and constantly shut in by dense forests of impenetrable pine. In addition, good intelligence

was hard to gather and many of the pro-Unionist homes had to be individually searched looking for evidence of Tories and deserters. While many who were caught bearing arms were shot for treason, most of the detainees were turned over to local authorities. Ferguson never mentioned the numbers that his men executed but his fellow Brigadier, Sul Ross, acknowledged in a letter to his wife that his men "have caught & hung several of the "Robbers — Deserters &c."[541] In a May 4, 1864, letter written to his mother from Tuscaloosa, Major James C. Bates, of the 9th Texas Cavalry, Ross's brigade, provided his insight.

> I just returned from a ten days hard scout in the northern portion of the State catching deserters — not a very pleasant business. Deserters in the mountains of Ala[bama] are very plentiful. It seems to be the rendezvous for them from all parts of the Confederacy.[542]

Within a month, the Confederate cavalry patrols had made a significant impact in scattering the disloyal reprobates causing one Unionist leader, a cousin of Mark Twain, to appeal in a panic filled letter to President Lincoln for immediate Federal protection.[543] Despite the distasteful nature of the duty, the men of the 2nd Alabama were nevertheless in an upbeat mood. Because the patrols were rotated amongst the companies, at any given time half the regiment was in the main encampment which was alive with all sorts of amusements capped by a steady flow of local women who brought with them boxes of food, clothing, and other delicacies. Furthermore, their beloved Colonel Earle freely granted the men short furloughs so that they could go home to get fresh horses or just visit loved ones.

With the start of May 1864, it was an undeniable fact that the 2nd Alabama had endured much hard duty in the past year earning an enviable reputation for courage, endurance, and dependability. None could know how sorely that reputation would be tested when Sherman and his 100,000 came flooding out of the mountains of

Tennessee into north Georgia. Herculean tasks awaited the 2nd Alabama as they were soon to struggle mightily to protect the flanks, front, and rear of the retreating Army of Tennessee across the Georgia landscape. The regiment would be bathed in human and horse sweat for weeks on end with no permanent base to rest and little opportunity to recruit new horses or men.

Chapter Seven

THE DALTON/ATLANTA CAMPAIGN

"I observe my own feelings on the subject, and I think Atlanta will fall."[544]   — Henry Watterson

THE DALTON TO ATLANTA CAMPAIGN, or simply the Atlanta campaign, refers to a grueling four-month period of maneuvers, skirmishes, and battles fought from the city of Dalton to Atlanta, which pitted a well-armed and well-supplied army group of well over 100,000 Yankees under General Sherman against a bare-knuckled Confederate force which started at 40,000 and expanded to perhaps 55,000 (with the arrival of General Polk's army from Mississippi), commanded by General Joseph E. Johnston, and later John B. Hood. The 100-mile campaign was certainly the largest, longest, and bloodiest series of engagements that the 2nd Alabama faced during the War. Indeed, it was actually one multi-month battle that began on May 7, 1864 (on May 14, for the 2nd Alabama), and ended with the surrender of Atlanta on September 2, 1864. As a part of Ferguson's brigade, the 2nd Alabama fought continuously in innumerable skirmishes and battles, culminating with the distinction of being the very last Confederate soldiers to leave the city of Atlanta.

The Alabamians took heavy causalities during this period of service, particularly in the bloody fighting outside the city on July

21-22, called the Battle of Atlanta.⁵⁴⁵ A snapshot amplifying the extent of the losses was printed in a Montgomery newspaper report sent in by Dr. Hill, the 2nd Alabama's surgeon, covering only the period of 1-15 July, listing 22 dead and wounded:

> Mr. Ed. Will you please publish the following list of casualties in the 2d Ala. Cav., from the 1st to the 25th of July [1864]. Our regiment has been constantly engaged with the enemy, either on the right or left flank. Most of the casualties occurred on the 17th and 22nd. The 2d Alabama has become quite notorious for gallantry in the army, they "never skedaddle."⁵⁴⁶

The toll on the regiment's officers during this period was particularly telling. Major J.J. Pegues, wounded in the side; Captain J.A. Anderson, wounded severely in the side; Colonel Richard Earle, killed in combat at Kingston; Captain Whisenhant wounded at Kennesaw; Captain James Andrews wounded at Nickajack; Captain William Ashley wounded at Decatur; and Captain Bill Allen perished by disease in service, Atlanta.⁵⁴⁷

Like all large-scale engagements, the extended contest meant confusion, intermingled forces, loss of direction, false information, bad orders, and all the other maladies associated with the fog of war. On top of this, the troopers were perpetually in a state of extreme fatigue operating under unusually rainy weather that summer, sometimes as cavalry and sometimes as dismounted infantry, all the while facing the unpleasant prospect of being killed or maimed at any given moment. In turn, the number of effectives in the brigade constricted dramatically from the loss of horses and men who were killed, wounded, diseased, or simply worn out. Furthermore, while some of the dismounted men were allowed to remain with the "slow train," hundreds of others were sent back to Alabama to obtain replacement mounts or detached to new duty stations as far away as Mobile.

The Dalton/Atlanta Campaign

After the fall of Atlanta, surviving records show significant contingents of Ferguson's troopers, perhaps over 500 in number, stationed in western and central Alabama at Carthage, Dayton, Grove Hill, Selma, and Mobile. Many of these men where simply kept at these new assignments, never to return to the brigade. In fact, at the beginning of the Atlanta campaign,, Ferguson's effective strength at a roll call taken in Rome, Georgia, on May 10, 1864, was 1,575 men,[548] but when his brigade was assigned to General Wheeler on October 25, 1864, it had been reduced to 547 effective for duty![549] Then, by December 16, 1864, when Ferguson's brigade was ordered into the trenches at Savannah to supplement the garrison's infantry, he drew just 568 rations for *all* the men in *all* the regiments in his skeleton-sized brigade.[550]

— Sherman's Orders —

In March 1864, Grant gave Sherman formal command of a sprawling military department in the western theater called the Military Division of the Mississippi, which put well over 200,000 Union soldiers under his direct authority. Within two days of his appointment, which vaulted him over several more senior generals, the two met in Cincinnati, Ohio, to fine tune Grant's vision to subjugate the Confederacy. In early April, Grant again messaged instructions for Sherman to not only destroy Johnston's army but to also inflict "all the damage you can against their *war resources* [emphasis added]."[551] Sherman understood what Grant intended for him and replied in writing that he would "knock Joe Johnston and do as much damage to the *resources of the enemy* as possible [emphasis added]." They both knew full well their code language for brutalizing women and children.[552]

Sherman's massive force, which he called his "grand army," actually consisted of three veteran armies — the Army of the Cumberland, the Army of the Tennessee, and the Army of the Ohio. All totaled, Sherman had 19 infantry divisions and 4 cavalry divisions at his disposal, with the ability to quickly replenish his losses by rail from Tennessee.

Although the disheveled Ohioan wielded a power that was far superior to that of his opponent Joe Johnston, his tactical battle plan was designed above all else to avoid failure. By more or less tracking close to the Western & Atlantic which led directly to the vital manufacturing and rail hub city of Atlanta, Sherman's vastly superior army would simply elbow Johnston back through the mountains and dense forests of north and central Georgia.

More than any other campaign in the entire War, this long fight would be tied directly to a single railroad. As such, the weak link in Sherman's plan was the logistics. All his arms, ammunition, rations, forage, and equipment would have to follow his army by a single rail-line, the Western & Atlantic. While the Confederates had to protect the several railroads that fed into Atlanta which provided the Southern armies with their primary means of supply, Sherman just had one supply source.

Sherman knew that Johnston was an able commander but given the general's mediocre performance in 1862, in retreating from McClellan's peninsular movement on Richmond and again at Jackson, Mississippi, in July 1863, when Johnston simply refused to go on the attack, Sherman correctly concluded that the always smartly dressed Confederate would be extremely reluctant to take offensive operations against him. When given the option, Johnston would invariably choose to fall back instead of fight.[553] Still, Sherman anticipated two things: (1) Johnston would gather every available man he could lay his hands on; and (2) Johnston would try to get the cavalry behind the Federals and tear up the Nashville & Chattanooga and/or the closer Western & Atlantic to choke off the Federal life-line. Sherman proved correct about the first assumption and wrong on the second.

Ever the bean counter, in preparing for his mammoth campaign Sherman meticulously ensured that he had plenty of everything.[554] In the winter of 1863-1864, he turned the city of Nashville into a gigantic commissary depot stuffing it with tons and tons of supplies, to include 24 million rations shipped down from Louisville, Kentucky, and stored at innumerable warehouses. The supplies were

The Dalton/Atlanta Campaign

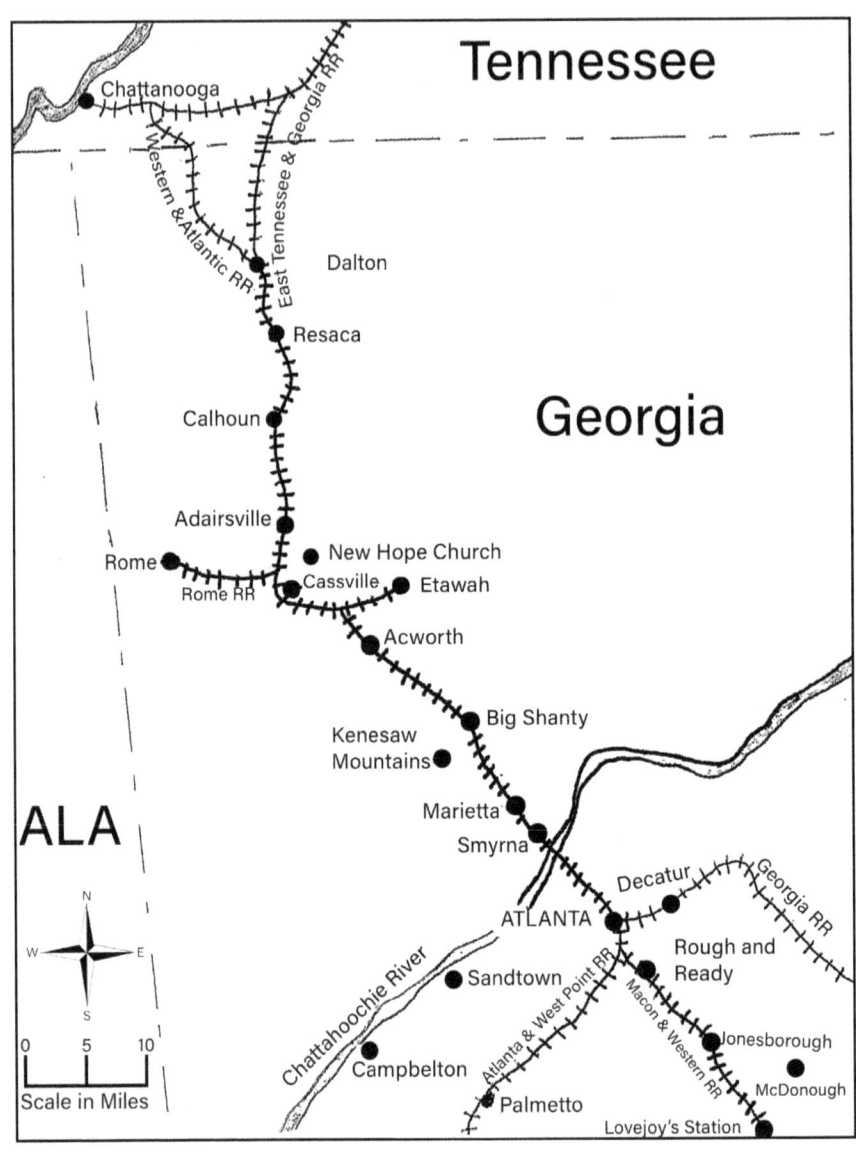

Western & Atlantic Railroad.

carefully categorized and then transported by train to the forward Union base at Chattanooga, so that when Sherman marched into Georgia, full trains could shadow his every move down that single track. Again, if the Western & Atlantic was significantly cut, his army would be stuck in the woods and high mountains of north Georgia unable to advance.

Since all depended on this single unfettered rail-line, Sherman shrewdly prepared for worst case scenarios. First, the Union commander constructed hardened blockhouses to protect the many bridges all along the railroad from Nashville to Chattanooga. Second, he created a massive sub-army of skilled engineers and unskilled laborers who were provided with everything necessary to quickly repair any breaks on the rail. Third, and most importantly, to address the fear that was foremost in Sherman's mind — that Confederate cavalry in Mississippi, particularly Forrest's, would tear up the Nashville & Chattanooga in middle Tennessee — he dispatched four separate expeditionary forces into northeast Mississippi between April and August of 1864, to eliminate, or at least to tie up, General Forrest. While none of these Union armies disabled Forrest, they did keep his Rebel cavalry away from the railroads.

Of course, Sherman was greatly assisted in all this due to Jefferson Davis' absolute refusal to order Forrest into Tennessee, being obsessed with keeping him in Mississippi, the home State of the president. Besides, many in the Confederate brass were jealous of Forrest, resenting his unpolished demeanor and wild popularity. Lee most certainly understood the gravity of inaction and also called for Davis to send sufficient cavalry, preferably Forrest, to destroy the railroad behind Sherman. Davis still refused. Throughout the entire summer months of the long struggle between Sherman and Johnston, even General Joe Wheeler's larger and extremely capable cavalry corps was never sent out to get behind Sherman and smash up the Western & Atlantic immediately in his rear. Only when it was all too very late — when Sherman was on the outskirts of Atlanta

— did Wheeler's thousands sally into Tennessee, accomplishing nothing except to wear out horses and men.

While it was true that the Rebels never cut the 138 mile Western & Atlantic stretched out behind the advancing Federals, they did as much damage as possible to it when retreating southward towards Atlanta. Unfortunately, Sherman's railroad crews were extremely adept at repairs and often had trains up and running in a days' time. One Union officer observed the following in his diary entry of May 21, 1864, from Kingston, the Federals having taken the town only a day prior:

> This Kingston has been a gem of a little town, but the Rebels burned most of it when they left. Our railroad men are very enterprising. The cars got here the same night we did, and a dozen or 20 trains are coming per day, all loaded inside with commissary stores and outside with soldiers.[555]

Finally, the fact that Sherman was concerned about food and forage requirements did not mean that he intended to suspend the use of terrorism on the noncombatants of Georgia. Breaking the morale of Southern civilians by terrorism was by now a fully accepted goal of the Lincoln Administration and after his easy accomplishments in Meridian, Sherman happily fancied himself as its chief herald using the sinister slogan "live off the land" as his moniker.[556] The only bright spot for the inhabitants of northern Georgia was that it was an area of few farms and extremely rough terrain. The pickings were far better from Atlanta out and when Sherman came there no family, black or white, would be spared from some level of violation.

One illustration of the countless episodes of pure terror visited on the innocents occurred on July 13, 1864, when Union cavalry encountered the home of master carpenter Horace King. King was a hard-working and prosperous free black Southerner who had

developed a thriving carpentry business just west of Palmetto, Georgia. Mr. King was away when one of Sherman's unrestrained cavalry regiments galloped onto his private property yelling and firing pistols into the air. The vandals gleefully sprang from their horses and ransacked the main house and barns while King's traumatized wife and children were forced outside. The family watched in stark fear as the roughly behaved Yankees stole "200 pounds of sugar, 400 pounds of bacon, 1,500 pounds of flour, 100 bushels of corn, a brand-new wagon, two mules and a saddle, and all the clothing, bedding, cooking utensils, and tableware they could carry."[557] Pleading that something be left for them to eat, one Union officer took pity on the mother and allowed her to keep two small sacks of flour. Still, the King's were more fortunate than most in that their home was not burnt to the ground.

— Johnston's Plan —

Joe Johnston knew that Sherman would be coming after him in the spring of 1864, even if Jefferson Davis had doubts. In fact, Davis never really entertained any thoughts about a defensive battle, he fantasied all along that Johnston's small force would take the offensive and go north into Tennessee.

Davis was an optimist and Johnston was a realist. What they did have in common, however, was a deep distrust and even dislike for one another. Thus, Davis' view of things had no impression on Johnston who intended all along to operate on the defense and wait for Sherman to make a mistake at which time he *might* attempt a counterblow. In fact, Johnston hoped against hope that Sherman would perform another spectacular tactical error as he had done at Chickasaw Bayou on December 29, 1862, the opening engagement of the Vicksburg Campaign, where Sherman foolishly ordered a full-frontal assault by 30,000 blue soldiers against firmly entrenched Confederate forces. The Federal infantry was mowed down like dry grass losing 1,779, compared to 187 for the Confederates.[558] Speaking of his failed generalship at Chickasaw Bayou, Sherman

merely noted: "I reached Vicksburg at the time appointed, landed, assaulted, and failed."[559]

Unlike Robert E. Lee's victory at Fredericksburg, where Lee soundly punished a gigantic Federal army in December 1862, by holding a strong defensive position against repeated frontal attacks, Johnston would have no such opportunity against Sherman, with the exception of a foolish assault at Kennesaw Mountain where the Federals were slaughtered across vacant up-hill terrain by well-directed fire from well-serviced fighting positions.[560]

Still, one thing that Johnston fully understood was the art of delay. By the time Sherman arrived in Nashville in mid-April 1864, to personally arrange the final details of the pending campaign, the Rebel commander had carved out an impregnable "Rocky Face" defensive line at Dalton less than 30 miles from Missionary Ridge, all the while pleading with Richmond for more troops, especially asking for all the idle garrison soldiers spread out across the lower South. Since the only large sized support that could immediately assist the Army of Tennessee was Polk's Army in Mississippi which consisted of three undersized infantry divisions and a grossly undersized cavalry division commanded by Red Jackson, Johnston sought and received pre-approval from Richmond to have Polk placed on standby to rush his infantry and the better part of Red Jackson's cavalry directly on should Sherman move against Dalton. Interestingly, the contingency plan approved by the War Department called for Ferguson's brigade, still in Alabama, to stay behind and remain under General S.D. Lee, who would take over command of the entire geographic department should Polk leave with his army.

As the warm weather days of April ticked off, spies reported a spike in preparatory activities in Tennessee causing Johnston to urge Polk in the first week of May to immediately send him all three of Jackson's cavalry brigades. Polk agreed and on May 6, 1864, Red Jackson ordered his brigades in Alabama to proceed to Rome, Georgia, about 50 miles south of Dalton. Furthermore,

knowing that Ferguson's independent brigade was also in Alabama and could reach Georgia in a few days ride to assist in providing reconnaissance, Johnston telegraphed Polk on May 8 to ask that they also be sent to Kingston.

> If [additional] cavalry, for instance Ferguson's, can be spared from your department, its presence near Kingston [Georgia] would be most valuable in giving security to our communications.[561]

Polk again agreed. Ferguson was formally assigned to Red Jackson's division and directed to move out.

Later that same day, telegraph wires to Polk buzzed with urgent pleas by Johnston to now dispatch the infantry by train with all available speed. To his great credit, Polk loaded the better part of 15,000 troops in and on top of boxcars and immediately moved to Johnston's aid, arriving just in the nick of time to stave off a Federal flanking thrust at Resaca, Georgia, in the fighting from May 13-15. This left S.D. Lee alone in Mississippi to command the remaining troops which included Forrest's and Chalmers' cavalry.

— The Campaign Begins —

Marching down out of Tennessee, Sherman had no intention of conducting a frontal assault against the well-prepared positions at Dalton. Engaging in a pattern of feints and side moves that would come to characterize his entire campaign, the Union commander sent one part of his army group, the Army of the Tennessee under General McPherson, in a wide arc 13 miles to the southwest in hopes of sneaking behind the Confederates and flanking them, while he made noisy demonstrations with the rest of his force at Dalton to keep Johnston ignorant of the move. Though McPherson reached his objective by May 9, easily passing through the unguarded mountains at Snake Creek Gap, he inexplicably failed to press on the few remaining miles to destroy the railroad and swallow up the

small Confederate garrison at Resaca. Such a move would have put Johnston in a tight spot, but encountering some aggressive Rebel cavalry to his front, McPherson succumbed to his ever-present fears of falling into a trap and decided to pull back and wait.

For his part, alerted to the danger posed by McPherson, Johnston sped three of Hood's divisions to Resaca on the night of May 9. It was not until May 13, however, that Johnston discerned Sherman's true intent and abandoned the splendid battlements at Dalton, shifting everything to Resaca. Desperate fighting ensued at Resaca after which Johnston easily slipped away and by the last week of the month the Rebels were strongly entrenched in favorable positions along what was called the Dallas-New Hope Church line. Still, in just about two weeks of hard fighting the Federals had managed to cover almost half the distance to Atlanta!

— Ferguson Joins the Atlanta Campaign —

In obedience to orders, Ferguson moved out of his Alabama camps under heavy springtime rains taking a separate route from the other brigades of Jackson's cavalry so that by a day's jump his troopers were the first of the cavalry reinforcements to arrive, reaching Rome on May 13. At this time, Ferguson's command consisted of the 2nd Alabama, 56th Alabama, 9th Mississippi, 11th Mississippi, and 12th Battalion Mississippi, with a total effective force just shy of 1,600 men,[562] the best regiment being the ever-reliable 2nd Alabama under Earle.

The arrival of Red Jackson's horsemen to the Army of Tennessee created a disjointed command arrangement. Major General Joe Wheeler, in charge of a cavalry corps, was superior in rank and structure to Brigadier General Red Jackson's small division, but because Jackson originated from a separate army he was allowed to operate independently from Wheeler's immediate command authority. It was only when their two forces were operating jointly on a particular mission that Wheeler would assume supreme command.[563] This shifting chain of command arrangement proved

difficult at times particularly when it came to Ferguson's brigade, which heretofore had generally been treated as an independent body apart from Red Jackson's authority.

— The Death of Colonel Earle —

On May 14, as Red Jackson's cavalry brigades were riding into Rome, Ferguson's brigade was already busy scouting the area to the east and north where they encountered a strong mounted enemy force consisting of two full strength cavalry brigades, one of them the famous "Lightning Brigade," so named for its achievements in Tennessee in the summer of 1863. The enemy brigades were on their way to cut the telegraph wire between Adairsville and Kingston and tear up track on the railroad spur that ran from Rome to Kingston.[564]

Even in the face of superior numbers, Ferguson did not hesitate to act and ordered a full scale attack straight at the enemy — horse meeting horse. Shocked by such boldness, the Yankee cavalry unceremoniously retreated from what one unit historian erroneously called overwhelming swarms of Confederates consisting of Nathan Bedford Forrest's cavalry as well as General Polk's infantry.[565] Of course, Forrest was far off in Mississippi and the bulk of Polk's infantry were fighting that day at the Battle of Resaca 35 miles to the northeast. It was Ferguson's single brigade that had routed them from the field and it was here that the 2nd Alabama received its first taste of the long fighting to come. Indeed, after other heavy skirmishes around Kingston over the next few days, Major Giles wrote his wife that the troopers had high confidence in General Ferguson.

> Gen Ferguson is very gallant & we like him very much, since writing the above we were ordered to charge the Yanks. Col Perrin [11th Mississippi Cavalry] made the first charge with our Reg & routed them. The balance of our Brig followed him & we run the Yanks five miles killing some & taking 12 or 15 prisoners.[566]

After Ferguson's engagement on May 14, Red Jackson's division received orders to move northeast to help shield the Confederate left flank as the Army of Tennessee fell back to Adairsville after the bitter fighting at Resaca. The cavalry moved out quickly and picketed itself along a ten mile stretch of territory so that by May 17, Ferguson was patrolling near Adairsville where his brigade camped for the night near the fabulous Woodlands plantation, about six miles north of Kingston.

The owner of the plantation, an Englishman by the name of Godfrey Barnsley, first settled in Savannah and made his fortune in shipping and cotton before moving to Cass County, Georgia, where he purchased thirty-six hundred acres of virgin land (formally Cherokee populated) and built a three-story, twenty-eight room, eclectic castle he named Woodlands.[567] The mansion was truly a wonder of its day, particularly known for the extensive botanical gardens which boasted exotic plants imported from all across the globe. Upon occupying the plantation, one Union officer described it as "the prettiest place I ever saw ... the house is excellent, the grounds excel in beauty, anything I ever imagined."[568]

Although Mr. Barnsley had several sons in the Confederate military and owned blockade runners which operated in and out of Confederate ports, he claimed neutrality and wistfully flew a large British flag prominently over the home. Like many Southerners, Barnsley believed the institution of slavery economically unsound and morally wrong, causing him to primarily employ Irish workers to run his estate and household. The senior housemaid for the Woodlands was a fetching Irishwoman by the name of Mary Quinn.[569]

On the morning of May 18, 1864, the 2nd Alabama was placed in the vanguard of Ferguson's column which cautiously headed towards Kingston where they once again ran into Federal cavalry near an unguarded wooden bridge. This time, however, the several brigades of Federal cavalry, to include the Lightening Brigade, were no longer probing about to ascertain enemy strength, they were screening to protect over 16,000 advancing Union infantry

under General McPherson, swarming through the rolling countryside with their center of gravity heading straight towards the Woodlands estate.

Formed in February 1863, the Lightning Brigade was commanded by the charismatic Indianian Colonel John T. Wilder. Designated as the 3rd brigade in General Kenner Garrand's cavalry division, the brigade consisted of an artillery battery and three regiments — the 98th Illinois, the 123rd Illinois, and the 17th Indiana. The brigade was also distinguished due to the fact that each man owned a Spencer seven-shot repeating rifle, which provided a wonderful advantage of firepower relative to the standard single-shot cavalry carbine. In addition, Wilder's men were almost completely mounted on thoroughbred horses "commandeered" by raiding Southern homes and farms in the heartland of Tennessee.

Both the Union and Rebel cavalry were equally surprised at this second serendipitous encounter, but this time it was Ferguson who gave ground to better ascertain the exact size and disposition of the enemy. Ferguson noted that the terrain he had just traversed was mostly open fields, well suited to cavalry battle, and that the Federals had been content to see him pull back without giving chase. Aggressive by nature, Ferguson decided to try a daring counterattack to see if he could spook the Yankees into another retreat and looked to his best regimental commander, Colonel Richard Earle, and "his famous 2nd Alabama"[570] to pull it off. Time after time, Earle had proven himself to be an invaluable warrior and neither the well-oiled 2nd Alabama Cavalry nor its courageous colonel needed a pep talk. With his usual confidence, Earle ordered the regiment readied in double rank formation waiting only for his scouts to chart the best ground for the pending horse charge. Within a half hour the scouts returned with welcomed intelligence, the Yankee cavalry was mounted and only tepidly moving forward.

Satisfied with the news, the rattle of bridles and pawing of ground signaled to all an impending rapid advance. It was easy for the anxious troopers to spot their beloved commander as he dashed about on his white horse inspecting the formation one final time. As

always Earle looked the epitome of a cavalry officer. Along with his full length gray uniform fitting perfectly over a thin but muscular frame, a flowing red sash and handsome leather belt firmly secured his pistol and saber.

Earle signaled the "Forward," buglers rang out the "Trot," and the regiment was off, gobbling up yard after yard until the enemy's advanced guard spotted them in the distance and frantically signaled the alarm. With the Yankees in sight, Earle spurred his warhorse to full gallop complemented by the regimental battle flag of the 2nd Alabama Cavalry proudly waving along with the many company guidons whipping about. Despite possessing vastly superior numbers, the surprised Federals turned their mounts and raced rearward, interpreting the bold charge as a sure sign that they were outmatched.

Earle cut an imposing figure that day as he basked in the promise of another splendid victory to add to the battle honors of the 2nd Alabama. Rubricated by the all too familiar crackle of gunfire and Minnie balls whistling in the air, the regiment chased the enemy right back across the original bridge and several miles beyond, all the way to the rolling green fields of the Barnsley plantation. By then, however, due to the great distance covered and the requirement to stop and secure large numbers of prisoners and horses, the pursuit had lost cohesion. In addition, hordes of Union infantry could now be seen off in the far distance streaming like ants across the surrounding ridges. Accordingly, just as the Woodlands home came into view, Colonel Earle had no choice but to pull up his command in order to reform and assess his next move.

Although Earle sent his prisoners and other captured booty back under close guard to Ferguson, he had no intention of returning the regiment just yet and instructed his company commanders to hasten the men back into order for a continued attack. In the meantime Earle galloped his steed over to the mansion to warn the Barnsley's to take cover in the basement to shield themselves from a battle that might soon be fought on their property.

As was so often the case amongst the Southern aristocracy, Earle was already familiar with the Barnsley family. Not only had he engaged in close business dealings with Mr. Barnsley throughout the 1850's, Earle had lodged at the renowned estate on several occasions, enjoying the beautiful environs.[571] The headmistress Mary Quinn stood in the basement door of the kitchen wing of the mansion gazing into Earle's dark eyes one last time before he gallantly swung into the saddle and raced back to rejoin his regiment.[572]

Earle was determined to keep the enemy from despoiling his friend's beautiful home. Apparently, he was either unaware or grossly overconfident about the whereabouts or disposition of the Union cavalry, out of sight, but surely somewhere up ahead. For their part, the retreating Federals had no desire to counterattack on horseback and instead used the pause in action to dismount and establish good firing positions designed to halt any further Rebel horse charges that might materialize.

When Earle returned to his command the officers had already arrayed the men in attack formation and the red crossed battle flag fluttered once more as the Alabamians deployed at the trot. Within minutes, the gray-clad riders encountered the usual mounted Union skirmishers, signaling proximity to larger numbers up ahead. The bugler blared out the command and another glorious charge gained steam, the ground rumbling with the sound of hundreds of hooves pounding and tearing up the sod. At the head of his men and throwing all caution to the wind Colonel Richard Earle never looked back.

Such bravery has its price. This time the Rebels were met by a hellish fusillade of lead spewed out from hundreds of well-serviced Spencers. Able to shoot 20 bullets in a minute, the dismounted bluecoats worked the carbines fast with withering effect emptying saddles and tumbling horses so that the doomed charge collapsed and veered off left to right.

Witnesses recall that Earle seemed oblivious to the murderous hail of gunfire. Instead of recoiling and spinning away with the rest,

he spurred his horse even faster, straight ahead into the thick of the fight. It was here, seated deep in the saddle and far in advance of his disintegrating regiment, that the gallant Colonel Richard Earle disappeared into blueish clouds of rifle smoke, within a stone's throw of the Barnsley home.

Precisely how Colonel Earle perished is unclear. While one version holds that he was called upon to surrender before being shot down,[573] the most likely scenario is that he was shot off his horse leading the attack just ten feet from breaching the Federal firing line, as documented by the regimental historian of the Lightning Brigade.

> We moved on the morning of May 18th [1864] — and in the (afternoon) the Johnnies came on like a whirlwind — the colonel (Earle) leading the regiment fell dead from his horse within ten feet of our lines.[574]

Union General Garrard also confirmed through his own sources that Earle was killed in the final charge, even identifying the soldier that shot him. Garrard wrote:

> Col. Earle, 2nd Alabama Cavalry, was killed by Private Bonner, Company "A" 98th Illinois Volunteers [a regiment in the Lightning Brigade], in a charge made by the enemy against my dismounted line.[575]

Sources supporting the call to surrender chain of events for his death come primarily from third party testimony to include Private Cochrane who wrote to his mother about three weeks after the fact that some prisoners reported Earle was killed after refusing to surrender.

> Col. Earle is missing. He routed a brigade of cavalry and pursued them so rapidly that the regiment did

not keep up and we have not heard from him except through prisoners who say that "a gray-haired Colonel rode up on four Yankees and ordered them to surrender and they shot him."[576]

An article on page two of the *Alabama Reporter* out of Talladega dated September 22, 1864, printed the testimony of "two ladies who recently escaped from the enemy's lines, and who were living in the immediate vicinity of the scenes which they describe [although they were not eyewitnesses to the death of Colonel Earle]."[577]

On the afternoon of the 17th day of May [it was May 18, 1864], our men drove the enemy [Wilder's cavalry] ... for five miles, killing a number of them. The pursuit ceased at Woodland, the residence of G. Barnsley, where 135 of the enemy were captured. Col. Earle was not appraised when our men retired. While at the spring a party of eight Yankees surrounded him and demanded a surrender. His only reply was the killing of one of the enemy — he [Colonel Earle] fell pierced by seven balls. He was buried by the enemy on the terrace immediately in the rear of the Barnsley's house.... His [personal] papers were given by Gen. McPherson to Mr. Barnsley, and are now in safe hands to be conveyed to his widow. The Second Alabama, while it mourns a gallant leader, cannot but be proud of his heroic death.[578]

One Southern family residing near the Barnsley's published their own account in 1905,[579] which provided both versions about Earle's death! Relating how they were able to see the running cavalry fight with "our old nurse ... in the kitchen door waving a large iron ladle as she shouted to the Confederates, "Go it, my brave boys, go it,"[580] the story notes that at first the Confederates were successful in driving the enemy cavalry with great loss but when the Federals

formed a dismounted firing line and opened up with deadly effect, "our men beat a hasty retreat, unfortunately leaving behind them Colonel Earle, the commander of an Alabama regiment."[581] The family then went on to include additional information as told to them by a member of the 2nd Alabama riding "a wiry little mountain pony, almost concealed by an enormous cavalry saddle, with a bright blanket and a broad gilt breast-strap who returned to speak to us [days after the fight] a boy about seventeen or eighteen years of age."[582] The Rebel trooper related the following:

> He [Colonel Earle] had sworn never to be captured, and when surrounded and ordered to surrender, he shot the man issuing the order. Of course he was instantly killed. The next morning he was buried, in his trousers and shirt, on the terrace near Mr. Burton's [sic] [Barnsley's] window."[583]

Other sources, like Ferguson's overview, spoke of the loss of Earle in general terms, unsure exactly how he had died. Concentrating on the success of how a single regiment — the 2nd Alabama Cavalry — had routed a full enemy brigade, Ferguson wrote:

> I spent one night in Rome and on the next day [Ferguson mistakenly implies that the date was May 14, but it was May 18] encountered [Colonel John T.] Wilder's Lightning Brigade, as it was called. They were approaching a bridge which was unguarded. The 2nd Alabama was at the head of my column. I ordered it to deploy and charge; this they did in handsome style, routing the enemy and chasing them for several miles, and capturing about fifty of their white horses. When they [the 2nd Alabama] started back it was found that their Colonel, the gallant [R. G.] Earle, was missing. His fate was not known for months, when some exchanged prisoners reported

that he was killed a considerable distance ahead of his regiment. His loss I feel greatly.[584]

Besides bagging 50 white horses from the enemy, Ferguson noted that many Federals were captured by Earle's 2nd Alabama to include the brigade adjutant, Leander Hamlin.[585] Major Pegues also wrote that the Alabamians scooped up a large number of surrendering troopers.

> [The 2nd Alabama Cavalry] met Gen. Wilder's famous Lighting brigade routing and driving it from the field and capturing many of its officers and men."[586]

Along with the tragic loss of Colonel Earle, the Confederate losses were substantial. Cochrane wrote that in his company alone: "We have had seven wounded horses and three wounded men, two of them severely. But this was done at Kingston [May 18, 1864]."[587]

Finally, Molly Curtis, a young girl at the Woodlands, vividly recalled the confusion of the brisk fight that felled Earle without detailing particulars:

> Me and Mammy was lookin out the kitchen window when the soldier mens hossess came jumpin over the fences and runnin every which way. And Mammy say, "Looks like bad trouble, get on the floor child!" and I did! She was afraid they'd set fire to the house and so everybody went down to the cellar and stayed ... and pretty soon we heard lots o'racket and fighten goin on down the hill there. Folks was hollering, and guns firin ... and some got shot too.[588]

In any event, Earle was gone forevermore, killed in action at the front of his command. As the smoked cleared heavenward across a silent field the Federals ventured out to view the thrashing horses

and bleeding men and after taking selected equipment and gear as souvenirs, the Rebel dead were buried in shallow graves and the wounded carted off to field hospitals as prisoners of war. Colonel Earle's weapons and personal possessions were lifted and his lifeless body carried the few yards to the Barnsley mansion where he was laid out on one of the manicured gravel walkways leading to the gardens. Union Lieutenant Colonel Charles Wills, 103rd Illinois infantry, recorded the sight, counting five bullets holes that had pierced the now lifeless body.

> Our division has had to advance today [May 18, 1864], but no infantry fighting. At noon we get into Adairsville and meet the 4th Army Corps .... We camped five miles southwest of town and by the prettiest place I ever saw [the Woodlands]. The house is excellent, the grounds excel in beauty [beyond] anything I ever imagined .... Our cavalry had a sharp fight here this p.m., and on one of the gravel walks in the beautiful garden lies a Rebel colonel, shot in five places. He must have been a noble looking man looks 50 years old, and has a fine form and features. I think his name is Irwin [Earle]. I think there must be a hundred varieties of the rose in bloom here and the most splendid specimens of cactus. I do wish you could see it.[589]

Curiously, along with a daguerreotype of his strikingly attractive blue-eyed wife, a second photo of "Mary L. Quinn the [Irish] housekeeper for the Barnsley's,"[590] was found tucked inside his uniform coat pocket. Whatever the nature of his relationship with Miss Quinn, there was never a charge of unfaithfulness lodged against Earle by any of his contemporaries.

Colonel Earle was buried by the Federals in a shallow grave directly under one of the windows of the mansion. Given the stench from his remains, however, the family reinterred the body

*Mary Quinn, Irish Head Mistress at the Woodlands.
Photo Courtesy of Alabama Department of Archives & History.*

Grave of Colonel Richard Earle at the Woodlands. Photo by Jeffrey Addicott.

in the rear rose garden terrace and erected a marker over the spot, which remains to this day.[591] According to a Barnsley descendant interviewed many years after the War, Colonel Earle's death and burial occurred as follows:

> The brigade [Ferguson's] moved over to Johnston's left (west) flank, and was in front of Woodland — which is the [Godfrey] Barnsley estate — about six miles north of Kingston the morning of May 18, 1864. The Federals [Wilder's Lightning Brigade] drove the Confederates back to Kingston (Ga) where the Confederates [2nd Alabama Cavalry] reformed their lines — drove the Federals back to Barnsley — and on beyond. Colonel Earle warned the Barnsley's that a battle was taking place and for them to get in the basements and out of the range of bullet fire. In a few minutes he was shot dead by Private Boner ... and his body brought back to the Barnsley estate. He was buried under one of the windows — but the odor from his grave was so terrible, that permission was granted by the Federals to move his body away from the window. He is buried back of the main Barnsley house, and between the wings of the house. His grave is marked by a nice white marble marker — with his name and rank on same.... Col R.G. Earle, 2nd Reg. Alabama Cav. C.S.A. Killed near this spot by U.S. Forces May 18, 1864.[592]

Regardless of exactly how Earle was killed, the 2nd Alabama's assault came to an abrupt halt with the remaining troopers racing away to safety followed that late afternoon by the arrival of thousands of Federal infantry under General McPherson who came sweeping onto the Woodlands where they observed with great amusement the British flag flying above the house. With his army camped on the grounds the night of May 18, McPherson dined with

Mr. Barnsley enjoying his host's pronounced English accent and the impressive wooden and marble furnishings of the well-stocked mansion. Before departing the next day, General McPherson issued specific orders that the plantation house should not be burned or looted. Quite expectedly, as often was the case when it came to dealing with Southern civilian property, this order was largely ignored when it came to looting, although the mansion was not destroyed and still stands.

> [On] May 18, [it was May 19, 1864], the general and the main Federal body continued on south, and stragglers broke into the cellar where they consumed a reported two thousand bottle of wine. The drunken men then started a large bonfire, fueling it with exquisite furnishings, while objects of marble and porcelain were smashed. What survived, along with all the food, was looted.[593]

— SKIRMISHING ALL SUMMER —

Lieutenant Colonel John Carpenter replaced "the gallant Earle" as the new regimental commander of the 2nd Alabama. Lieutenant Colonel John West, who had periodically served as acting commander had recently resigned his commission and returned home to the pleas of his family.

Pushed back on his heels, Johnston's retrograde movement out of Resaca now cast the dye for the entire campaign. Enduring heavy casualties in the process, the Federals would advance and the Confederates would retreat. General Johnston's first new defensive position in this dance of death was set along the Dallas/New Hope Church line with Red Jackson's cavalry fanned out in a wide arc to the left of the army and Wheeler's troopers doing the same on the right. Added to their traditional mission of protecting the flanks of the infantry and gathering intelligence would now come the disagreeable task of fighting in the trenches alongside the infantry. Nevertheless,

the gray troopers became expert at crouching in hastily dug rifle pits or temporarily holding the line in more formidable trenches in order to allow the foot soldiers to pull out and all get away safely. Of course, while they became quite adept at the tactic, there was nothing the cavalryman hated so much as to fight as a foot soldier. Before it became more commonplace, Private Cochrane complained to his cousin the bitter consternation felt by all in the 2nd Alabama about trench warfare.

> When we came here [to the left flank of Johnston's army] and were told we would have to fight in the breastworks we thought it awful. The idea of a Cavalry man dismounting, sending his horse a half mile off and he going into the trenches like an ordinary Webbfoot! But there was no way of getting off and now our Brigade marches to the trenches with a very good grace and woe will be the Yankee brigade that tries to drive them out.[594]

Within two weeks of Earle's death, the 2nd Alabama was directly involved in a string of bloody encounters around the important road junction of New Hope Church on May 25-26, Pickett's Mill on May 27, and Dallas on May 28. On several occasions therein, Ferguson's brigade was ordered to dismount and fight as infantry against savage Federal assaults. Along with a long list of casualties in the 2nd Alabama, three troopers from Company E were killed on the very first day — Private E.H. Morgan, Private Henry H. Moseley, and Private Marion Moseley.[595] Still, Sherman's Federals received the worst of it. At New Hope Church, Sherman engaged about 16,000 of his troops and suffered a galling 1,600 casualties. Johnston's Confederates fielded 4,000 and lost 400.

The Alabamians had long since learned the privations of war, but the harsh realities of this type of combat was something entirely different. Not only were the dead and dying everywhere, there was literally no letup in the fighting. In addition, wet weather contributed

to the misery with much of the bitter fighting at New Hope and Dallas taking place in heavy thunderstorms making conditions even more detestable for the outnumbered and outgunned Rebels who had to maneuver quickly on jaded horses to blunt each new enemy thrust.

None could know that the bitter week of blood-letting was only the beginning. In fact, from mid-May until mid-July, the men of the 2nd Alabama rode and fought, mounted and dismounted, in sweltering Georgia heat accompanied by unusually heavy downpours of rain that lasted for days and soaked every inch of their being. The roads disintegrated into wildernesses of mud so that wagons and heavy guns settled to their axles with men and horses not much better off. Ferguson recollected the hardships as extreme.

> I was engaged almost every day, never out of range of bullets day or night. Not in any great battle, but in many affairs that at the end of the month the muster roll showed a greater number of men killed and wounded than would reasonably have been the case in a severe pitched battle. Generally, when the [Confederate] infantry fell back from an entrenched position, the cavalry dismounted and, with horse holders a little in the rear, occupied the trenches with an exceedingly thin line to mask the movement until the infantry had time to fortify a new position, then fall back defending their rear. Many were the sleepless nights. I recall particularly one when I occupied the trenches at New Hope Church where had been some of the bloodiest fighting of the war. The enemy's line was so near that I expected to be attacked at every moment. The rain poured in torrents and the mud was deep. I lay on two fence rails placed in the middle of the road and which sunk in the mud until it was

flush with their tops. Holding my horse by the bridle in this situation I had a sound nap of an hour or so.[596]

For two grueling months the Alabama horsemen experienced the fiercest fighting as well as the heaviest casualties of the entire War. Under fire practically every single day, Ferguson's brigade operated generally on the western wing (the left flank) of Johnston's army as the infantry fell back from one defensive position to another through the rugged and mountainous Georgia landscape. Again, Ferguson's job consisted of two things: (1) determine the movements of the enemy; and (2) protect the front and flank of the gray infantry. This he did by rapid maneuver on horseback and lots of skirmishing on foot. In the case of the former, the mounted troopers would charge up to the enemy, fire their carbines and pistols, then spin about and fall back. In the latter, they would pick a spot to dismount and throw up defenses, fire their carbines into the advancing columns of enemy infantry and when pressed with overwhelming numbers, fall back to pick another spot where they would repeat the exercise all over again. In this manner the Rebel cavalry could both slow and then determine Union movements in order to allow General Johnston the ability to calculate when and where to select new lines of defense for his army. Ferguson recorded:

> My orders were to skirmish with the enemy [infantry] sufficiently to make him develop his force and prevent reconnoitering parties [enemy cavalry] from advancing and to fall back slowly, fighting just enough to accomplish those purposes.[597]

Since Sherman generally preferred moving to his right it meant that the cavalry on the Confederate left, to include the 2nd Alabama, bore the brunt of the action. Demanding more and more from their suffering mounts the poor animals broke down in alarming numbers and many simply expired of sheer exhaustion. The only

saving grace was the general ineffectiveness of the Union cavalry, which Sherman seldom used, to hinder the Confederate cavalry,.[598]

A letter from an Alabama horseman describing the work of the cavalry was printed in the *Montgomery Daily Advertiser* in June 1864.[599] The trooper described the horrendous conditions of this never-ending type of warfare and its impact on man and beast.

> We have participated in every engagement that has taken place ... though about one third of the brigade has been obliged to succumb on account of their horses giving out. I have nothing to say about the men, they are expected to travel and fight at least twenty-four hours in each day, and after this work is done, they are required to groom their horses for two hours, and employ the rest of their time eating and sleeping.[600]

The same Alabama cavalryman also explained to the folks back home:

> Think of a man starting out with a fine suit of clothes, enduring clouds of dust for twenty days, torrents of rain for three nights, besides the injury to his clothing from lying on the ground at night, exposed to the sun all day, his face begrimed with dust and sunburn, half starved, exhausted with hard marching [riding] and fighting day and night.[601]

On June 6, 1864, Cochrane wrote to his mother about the fighting.

> I am afraid that you have been uneasy about my not writing but I have heard that letters were not allowed to leave here [Marietta, Georgia]. We have been in a

great many fights and the cavalry of the Mississippi [Red Jackson's division] report that we have a better name for fighting than any in the Confederacy, among the highest Generals I'm told. Some part of my brigade [Ferguson] has been engaged nearly every day since we got here and part of the time the brigade has been in the ditches as infantry.[602]

A week later, Private Cochrane wrote his cousin about the constant strains of combat observing that his previous assessment, "that the war had not worn us much," was no longer true.

We have been in the front for the last three days and have just been relieved by Ross's [sic] Brigade in order that we may rest. The Miss. Cavalry [referring to the fact that all three brigades had been drawn from Mississippi to support Johnston] form a part of the left wing of Johnston's army and we three Brigades, Armstrong and Ross and Ferguson's, relieve each other by turns. When either Brigade is on duty we have to keep the strictest watch over every bush, tree, stump or anything that could conceal a Yankee.... Our Brigade was on two days and three nights and I don't think there were ten minutes passed during the time that you could not have heard a gun fired.[603]

Major Giles also wrote his wife about the heavy losses in Ferguson's brigade in fighting around Marietta, Georgia, during the middle part of June 1864.

Our Brigade had a very heavy fire poured into it on yesterday [June 17, 1864], in which we lost considerably in killed, wounded & missing. Ed Jackson was wounded in the left hand a severe wound

but will not have to be amputated. The rest of our friends are all safe. I enclosed you a rough diagram of our line of Battle. The Yanks came on us yesterday morning in considerable force. We were Fergusons Brig unprotected & had to get out as best we could & were consequently thrown into some confusion, but the playing of small arms & artillery directly on our lines. I am surprised that we even escaped as well as we did, our loss in killed, wounded & missing will perhaps be 75 or 100 men & 50 horses in the Brig. ... Time passes very rapidly here ....[604]

Whenever practicable, the cavalry brigades would rotate the duty of protecting the Rebel army in order to provide at least some limited relief for the horses and men. In Red Jackson's division, the cavalry brigades alternated between generals Ferguson, Ross, and Armstrong. All three of the generals where excellent at their jobs and respected one another with Ferguson often voicing special praise for Brigadier General Lawrence Sullivan "Sul" Ross who commanded four Texas regiments. Sul Ross was raised in Texas and distinguished himself before the War in fights with the fierce Comanche warriors that roamed freely across large portions of the Texas hill country, on one occasion rescuing a little white girl whose parents had been killed by the Indians. Sul adopted the girl and raised her as Lizzie Ross.

Major George L. Griscom, the adjutant of the 9th Texas Cavalry Regiment, Ross' brigade, kept a detailed record of the rotating cavalry duty in his personal diary, putting his own spin on what was obviously a healthy rivalry between his brigade and Ferguson's.

June 1: To Dallas.

June 2: Move in rain to vicinity of New Hope Church.

June 3: Move via Dallas on S. road to Pumpkin Vine Creek.

June 4. Move ¾ miles beyond New Hope Church.

June 5: Skirmish. Fall back on Dallas and Powder Springs Road.

June 6: Go to Ebenezer Church and rest.

June 7: Remain in camp.

June 8: Move at 7 AM to relieve Ferguson's Brig. on picket [near Ebenezer Church].

June 9: Skirmish.

June 10: Skirmish. Relieved at 11-1/2 AM by Ferguson's brigade. Move back on Lost Mt. and Marietta Rd. 4 mi. below Lost Mt.

June 11: Saddle at 6 AM and remain so till noon. Heavy rain.

June 12: Tremendous rainstorm all day.

June 13: Hard rain all night. Relieve Ferguson and keep up continual skirmishing.

June 14: Skirmishing day and night. [Confederate] Gen. [Leonidas] Polk killed by a shell.

June 15: Relieved at 11 AM by F [Ferguson]; ordered back into line to reinforce Ferguson whose skirmishers are driven in. F's [Ferguson] artillery drives enemy back.

June 16: Take positions left of Ferguson who joins the infantry. Heavy skirmish.

June 17: Heavy skirmish — two divisions of [enemy] infantry, one playing a full brass band.

June 18: Remain in camp. Heavy rainstorm.

June 19: Infantry [Confederate] has fallen back — we fight as rear guard. Relived by Armstrong.

June 20: Brisk skirmishing. Drive them beyond Powder Springs. Rain.

June 21: Move at noon to Powder Springs. Rain.

June 22: Skirmish.

June 23: Brisk skirmishing.

June 24: Skirmish. Can hear [Union General] Schofield's band playing "Dixie."

June 25: Skirmish.

June 26: Skirmish. At night their band plays for us again.

June 27: At 7 AM the 9th [Confederate infantry] is ordered to hold a position Ferguson's brigade has failed to hold. Encounter a division of Federal infantry.

June 28: Skirmish.

June 29: A continual fire kept up. Go fishing and get a fine mess.

June 30: Skirmish all day.

July 1: The enemy press Ferguson's brigade back and expose our left ... federals get within 30 yards ... and pour in deadly fire ... hottest days work of the week ... retire to Nickajack Creek.

July 2: [B]oys go swimming and remain there till 10 AM — are then ordered to Armstrong's left ... in camp 2 PM in a tremendous storm.

July 3: Skirmish and battle ... hard day's work.

July 4: Two skirmishes ... brisk fighting ... at 10 AM Ferguson gives way again on the right. Charge and countercharge.

July 5: Two skirmishes. Hard fighting. Enfiladed, forced to pull back.

July 6: Move farther down river to Baker's ferry.

July 7: Desultory skirmishing ... men go bathing, berrying and grazing.

July 8: Skirmish briskly all day ... shells close ... graze horses and go berrying.

July 9: [S]kirmishing kept up all day ... Ferguson's Brig. relieves us.

July 10: Slight skirmishing all day ... Preaching in the AM.

Trampling Union Terror

Western & Atlantic Railroad.

> July 11: Brisk skirmishing all day ... Ferguson's brigade moves to the right.[605]

Sherman's dogged use of his massive numerical superiority to press ever forward versus Johnston's skillful use of the cavalry and terrain to block him could not go on indefinitely. To break the pattern in the Confederate's favor, both Joe Wheeler and Red Jackson pled anew with Johnston to allow them to strike out behind Sherman's lines and disrupt the Atlantic & Western connection to the Union supply base. If the trains could be halted for even a week or two, Sherman would have to retreat or starve.

Still, Johnston refused. As shortsighted as Johnston was in this regard, Davis also proved totally myopic in his mistaken belief that Sherman could be halted without going after his supply-line. After the War, Jeff Davis finally admitted that keeping Forrest back from Sherman's rail-line was perhaps his greatest mistake of the War. "I saw it all after it was too late,"[606] he lamented.

Although Johnston had resisted Sherman's attacks and inflicted significant losses while suffering far fewer, he had given up miles

and miles of precious territory to do so. When the rank and file realized that they were less than twenty miles away from the great barrier of the Chattahoochee River, a deep frustration took hold. Johnston's Fabian strategy was wearing dangerously thin causing the personal politics between Davis and Johnston to come to a boil.

Sadly, coterminous with the Davis/Johnston tensions, a serious command dispute also flared up between generals Red Jackson and Ferguson. Jackson, who had previously praised the leadership abilities of Ferguson during the Meridian campaign, now falsely charged him with acting "disgracefully" at the battle of New Hope Church[607] for not properly handling his Mississippi regiments during the fighting.[608] Ferguson called Jackson a "damn liar" which in turn prompted the hot-tempered red head to challenge his fellow brigadier to a duel, which in itself was a violation of Article 25 of the Confederate Articles of War.

> No officer or Soldier shall send a challenge to another officer or soldier, to fight a duel, or accept a challenge if sent, upon pain, if a commission officer, of being cashiered.[609]

Jackson soon calmed down and refused to follow through with his false bravado, instead preferring formal court-martial charges against Ferguson charging him with the petty offense of "not furnishing inspection reports,"[610] saying nothing about the initial allegations of battlefield misconduct. Per standard protocol, Ferguson was temporarily placed on "leave" from his brigade, but reinstituted after a quickly convened court-martial found him not guilty. The tension was far from over however, and a furious Ferguson formally petitioned Richmond to conduct a complete investigation into the matter.

Under the Confederate Articles of War, courts of inquiry were established to investigate accusations of wrongdoing and make recommendations to the commanding general.[611] More like an administrative fact-finding body than a court, it consisted of

appointed officers with a judge advocate who served as the recorder with full authority to examine any witnesses he desired. Amazingly, even with all the catastrophic challenges facing the nation to include the capture of Atlanta on September 2, 1864, the Richmond bureaucracy found time to schedule a formal court of inquiry to look into Ferguson's complaints. By command of the Secretary of War, Special Orders No. 220, dated September 16, 1864, the following order was cut:

> At the request of Brig, Gen'l S.W. Ferguson, a Court of Inquiry composed of the following named officers ... [one of the three was his old boss General Daniel Ruggles], will be convened at Headquarters, Army of Tennessee, on the 27th Sept. 1864, to inquire into the differences existing between Br. Genl S.W. Ferguson and Br. General W.H. Jackson. The court will report [the] proceedings and their opinion to Gen'l Jn. B. Hood.[612]

Meanwhile, the maneuvering of the two armies continued unabated. By June 10, the constant rain and drizzle that had lasted for almost two weeks finally broke to reveal Johnston's latest fortified battle line which stretched for an incredible ten long miles from Brush Mountain on the right to Lost Mountain on the left. Ferguson's men were dismounted and "put into the trenches between Gilgal and the base of Lost Mountain"[613] where they saw heavy action repelling numerous probing attacks from enemy cavalry and infantry skirmishers.[614]

After ten days of intermittent wrestling Sherman pushed his infantry further around the left side and Johnston shortened his line to about six miles to again check Sherman with a new defensive placement girding Kennesaw Mountain. Frustrated with not being able to pin down his ever-elusive opponent, Sherman deluded himself into believing that he could annihilate Johnston's army with one knock-out punch. He decided to change tactics and

ordered simultaneous frontal assaults straight up the middle and to the right of the Confederates to smash through what he believed were thinly stretched areas held by demoralized soldiers.

On June 27, with temperatures topping 100 in the shade, Sherman hurled eight full brigades up the slopes of the boulder strewn mountains with orders to destroy the entrenched Rebels. While these troops were the same men who had stormed right over Bragg's men at Missionary Ridge seven months earlier, they were now cut to bloody shreds against the well-prepared Confederates at Kennesaw Mountain. This time the butternut infantry was competently led, dug in on high ground, and waiting for the Yankees with plenty of ammunition and itchy trigger fingers. Along with Red Jackson's other cavalry, Ferguson's brigade was about eight miles to the west protecting Johnston's flank in heavy skirmishing which saw the 2nd Alabama's Captain Whisenhant severely wounded.

Sherman's frontal assaults in the sweltering summer heat at Kennesaw were pure slaughter and cost him 3,000 in dead, wounded, and missing. Confederate infantryman Private Sam Watkins was one of the men who helped hold back the blue waves and recalled the fight as one of the most traumatic of the War.

> I never saw so many broken down and exhausted men in my life [Confederate defenders]. I was sick as a horse, and as wet with blood and sweat as I could be, and many of our men were vomiting with excessive fatigue, over exhaustion, and sunstroke; our tongues were parched and cracked for water, and our faces blackened with powder and smoke ....[615]

When it was over and the Union soldiers staggered back to their own lines, Sherman brushed aside any hint of regret or responsibility for his foolhardy attacks. Arrogantly suggesting that his army needed blooding for the sake of increasing their fighting spirit he self-righteously claimed: "The assault I made was no mistake ... I had to do it."[616] "Old Billy" buried the dead and went back to his

standard fare of flanking movements, shifting his army once more around to the west where he encountered the ever-present cavalry brigades of Red Jackson.⁶¹⁷

Always concerned about getting strung out too far and overwhelmed, Red Jackson wisely dug in his dismounted troopers on the north bank of Nickajack Creek. By July 2, Johnston had successfully slipped out of the Kennesaw mountain range and made his way south to Smyrna just north of the Chattahoochee River where he set about entrenching a new line, fully aware that Sherman sorely wanted to attack before they could finish digging in. Once again the Rebel cavalry stood in Sherman's way — Red Jackson to the Federal right and Wheeler to the Federal left. Buttressed by some Georgia militia coming up from Atlanta, Jackson's dismounted troopers put up a stalwart resistance at Nickajack Creek significantly slowing both General McPherson's Army of the Tennessee and General Scholfeld's Army of the Ohio.

By July 4, McPherson's 30,000 blue infantry forced their way across Nickajack Creek, but not in time to catch Johnston in an unprepared state. Indeed, before the 2nd Alabama was able to torch the main covered bridge over Nickajack Creek and escape to the other side, many of the Alabama troopers were badly wounded to include Private James Gould, Company B, who was shot clean through the shoulder.

Sherman came up short and still stinging from his disastrous charges at Kennesaw; he was in no mood to assault another strong force of energized Confederates at Smyrna. Leaving part of his infantry to demonstrate, the Union commander unexpectedly switched his flanking movements from the west, which were guarded by Red Jackson, and moved the main body of his army group due east, seeking to cross the Chattahoochee at some point far above Johnston's right flank to perhaps get behind the Confederates. Johnston immediately responded by ordering his cavalry to scout and defend all the river crossings for an area that stretched over 40-miles! Of course, the hefty assignment was simply

too great to accomplish and on July 8, Schofield's army crossed the Chattahoochee River to the east near the mouth of Soap Creek.

Predictably, once Johnston discerned what had happened, he abandoned Smyrna and crossed his soldiers over to the south bank of the Chattahoochee during the night of July 9-10, where he set up a new front. The cavalry covered the move and Ferguson's brigade was the very last to get over the Chattahoochee, burning the pontoon bridge behind them. Ferguson wrote that the mission was made difficult by the increasingly accurate explosions of Union artillery.

> I was even more sleepy the night before we crossed the Chattahoochee River [July 8-9, 1864]. I had lain down with my saddlecloth under me and my head on my saddle and gone so sound asleep that when some dispatches of importance were brought in it was found impossible to rouse me so my Adjutant forwarded them .... The next day I brought up the rear of the army and crossed the pontoon bridge, at the time the enemy had got a battery in position and the shells were bursting very close by.[618]

With his back literally at Atlanta, there was no place left to go. After swarming over the Chattahoochee River at various crossing points, the Yankees were about ten miles from Atlanta. The Army of the Cumberland was moving down from the north, the Army of the Ohio from the northeast, and the Army of the Tennessee from the east. For his part, Johnston seemed oblivious to the gravity of the situation and blissfully set his engineers to further strengthen the outer perimeter defenses surrounding Atlanta. In addition, since Sherman had shifted the bulk of his three armies to the north and east, more Rebel cavalry was needed on the Confederate right and on July 12, Ferguson was instructed to pass his cavalry brigade from the left flank of the army to the right flank where he would now serve alongside General Wheeler.

At five feet five inches tall and 120 pounds, the twenty-seven-year-old Wheeler was not imposing physically, but was a tenacious leader known as "Fightin' Joe,"[619] a name he earned fighting Indians as a freshly minted West Point graduate. Hailing from South Carolina, Wheeler was one of the South's ablest cavalry leaders, participating in well over a hundred battles and skirmishes, suffering three wounds, and sixteen horses shot out from under him. His boundless courage, dignified bearing, and pure enthusiasm earned him the devotion of his men causing one of his cavalrymen to remark:

> General Wheeler never asked his men to go where he would not lead, and for this we loved him, and gladly rode with him into places where we knew all would not come out alive.[620]

Recognizing the continued animosity and bickering between Ferguson and Jackson, Johnston's decision to shift over Ferguson's small brigade of no more than 1,000-1,200 effectives, was also driven by political/personal concerns. Unfortunately, the ill feelings between the two cavalry generals was only aggravated by the move with Red Jackson soon thereafter preferring new court-martial charges against Ferguson for disobeying a direct order to leave behind the horse artillery assigned to his brigade when he left to join Wheeler (Ferguson was not officially assigned to Wheeler).[621] Like the first one, this second court-martial went nowhere and Jackson's only lasting satisfaction was to "bad mouth" Ferguson's reputation to General Joe Wheeler, which he freely and frequently did. Major Giles was very frank to his wife about the enmity.

> Owing to the disagreements between Gen. Jackson & Ferguson we have been turned over to Gen Wheeler, our future operations will be under his control, so when you look for our names in the papers you must look among "Wheeler's Cav" for it. Gen Ferguson has been displeased with Gen Jackson for sometime &

Lieutenant General Joseph Wheeler.

accuses him of treating our Brig. With disrespect and applied to Gen Johnson to be relieved or have our Brig transferred to some other command. Gen. Johnson yesterday ordered us to report to Gen Wheeler. Now you have the whole matter. Many of us do not like this but the majority are delighted to get from under Gen Jackson's clutches. He is very unpopular [Gen Jackson] with everyone & I expect very inefficient.[622]

Ferguson seemed to take it all in stride and when writing of the transfer he focused his recollection on the high morale of the embattled gray infantry as he trotted his horse soldiers with his "stolen" artillery battery through the entire Army of Tennessee.

> The next day I was transferred from our left flank to the right flank in going this distance I passed through the entire army. Never had I seen troops in higher spirits and more confident in their General and in

the victorious result of the great battle all felt to be impending.... They were amusing themselves playing cards &c. All the little pleasantries usually exchanged when cavalry and infantry passed each other were of a kindly nature as between those who might not meet again. In this army which had retreated all the way from Dalton were hundreds of soldiers, nay thousands, who had been wounded in the campaign gone home and recovered enough to come back to their colors. No demoralization here, surely no other volunteer troops in all history have equally the Americans in this particular. For, generally, retreat, except with tried veterans, had been synonymous with demoralization.[623]

— Atlanta —

If someone were to view the modern city of Atlanta from one of its many skyscrapers, the eye would take in the urban sprawl of a huge Southern city. But in 1864, the outskirts of Atlanta looked like the face of the moon — only barren landscape for as far as the eye could see.

Although the city proper was crowded with houses and warehouses of every description and intersected by an impressive railroad system running through its heart, the Confederates had long since cut down the surrounding trees and in their place built impenetrable defenses that required only a minimal force to hold. Buttressed by 36 cannon emplacements set out as individual redoubts, the line circling Atlanta was defended by deep trenches, thick wooden walls, and *cheval de fries* (X shaped wooden barriers). The fortified perimeter stretched for over twelve miles around in circumference, generally lying about a mile outside the city's edge,[624] with the northern approaches boasting a double line of embattlements. A secondary inner defensive wall within the city itself covered a circle of about four miles.

Atlanta Landscape in Front of Confederate Defenses.
Photo by George N. Barnard.

Like all Southern cities, Atlanta had a mixed population of whites, slaves, and free people of color. The population in 1864 was about 30,000 and over 5,000 buildings and houses were sectioned out, most of them private dwellings, but many businesses and hospitals as well. In fact, with six hospitals and the Atlanta Medical College (located on Butler Street) which specialized in surgical cases — "the laboratories were operating rooms and the classrooms were the wards"[625] — Atlanta was the premier medical center for the Confederacy and thousands upon thousands of wounded were shipped in and cared for at the various facilities.[626]

Atlanta was also an important packing plant and manufacturing center producing all kinds of weapons, clothes, leather goods, and transportation vehicles. Most importantly, from the fertile farmlands of Georgia, Mississippi, and Alabama, the trains brought in a steady stream of food crops and animals. Along with war materials, these foodstuffs were funneled through Atlanta and shipped out to Lee's Army of Northern Virginia as well as the Army of Tennessee. Lined up beside the tracks inside Atlanta, hundreds of warehouses were constantly filled and then emptied by a nearly continuous stream of trains.

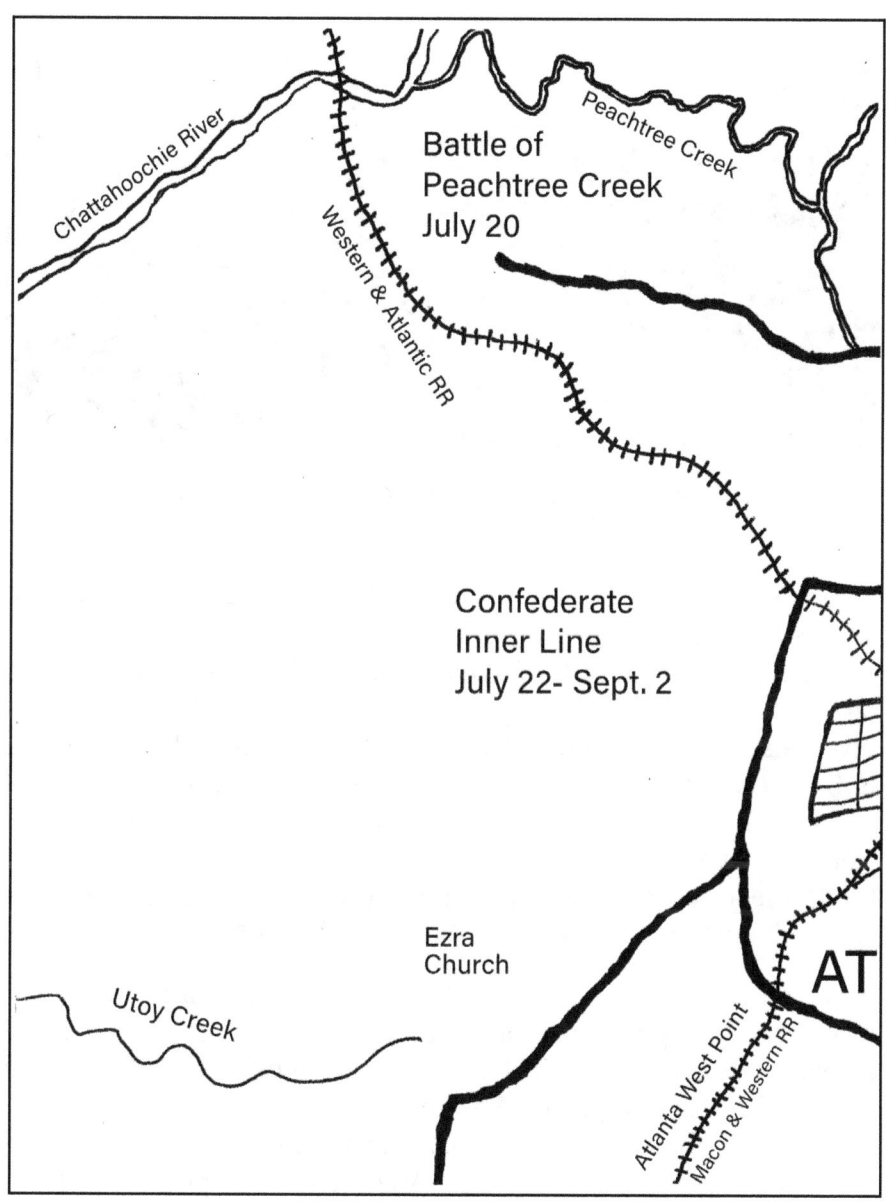

The Dalton/Atlanta Campaign

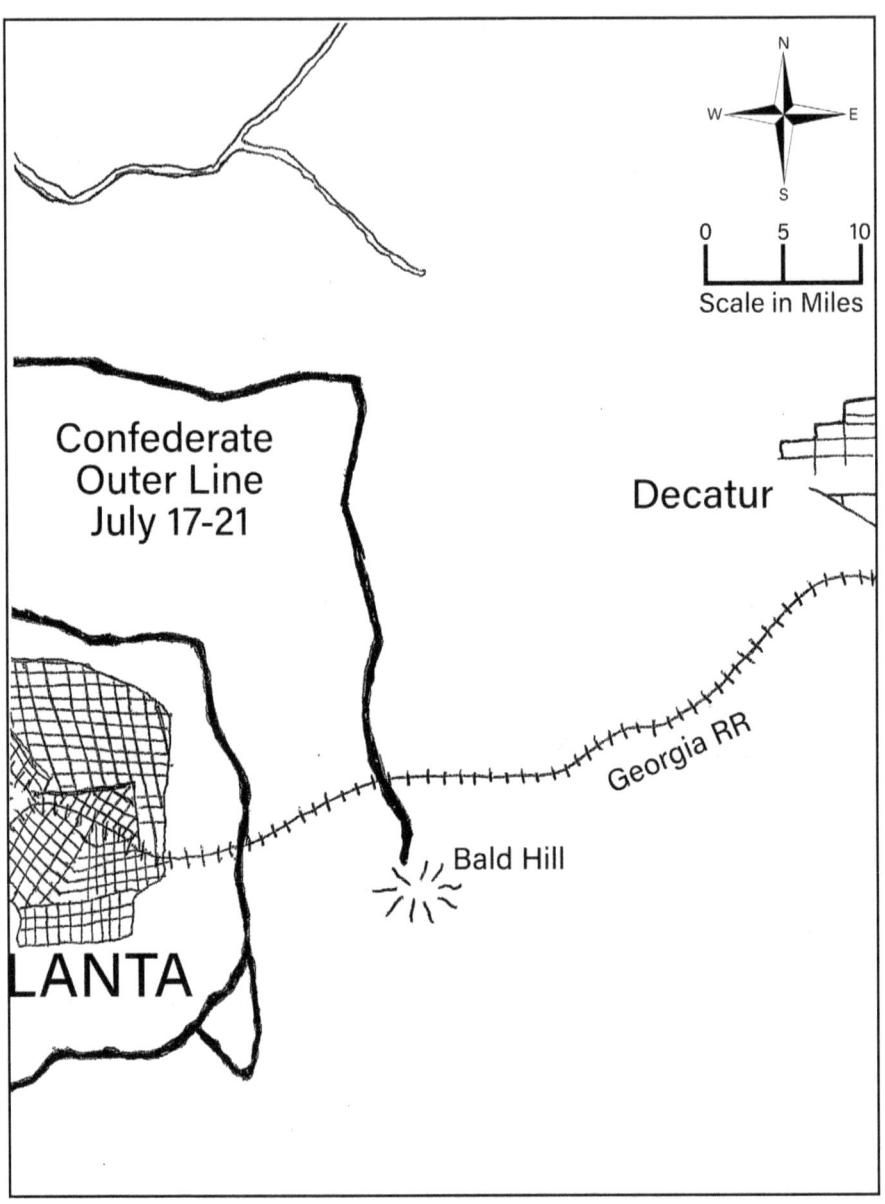

Confederate Defensive Lines — July to September 1864.

Indeed, Atlanta was called the gateway city because four major railroad lines intersected there, making it a linchpin for the South's transportation system and the primary center of gravity for all that remained of the Confederacy east of the Mississippi River. The three main rail-lines that radiated out from the impressive Union Passenger Depot were: (1) to the north, the Western & Atlantic, going to Chattanooga; (2) to the east, the Georgia Railroad, running to Augusta; and (3) to the west, the Atlanta & West Point, running all the way to Montgomery, and the accompanying Macon & Western, which shared a six-mile common track out of Atlanta to Eastport where it then broke off and ran south to Macon and then east to the Georgia coast. Without a doubt, capturing Atlanta would paralyze the South.

— Hood Replaces Johnston —

Things were now at the breaking point and for Johnston it was do or die. No one can dispute that Johnston's army "never broke [and] never gave up a line without determining of their own accord to retreat to a more defensible location,"[627] yet they were now pressed back beyond the Chattahoochee River to its smaller tributary Peach Tree Creek, only a few miles from Atlanta. Convinced that Johnston would give up the city and retreat without a fight, Jefferson Davis relieved him on July 17, 1864, and elevated the ambitious thirty-three-year-old corps commander in Johnston's army, John Bell Hood, to take his place.

Hood had previously served with great distinction under Robert E. Lee, but at a terrible personal price. At Gettysburg, shell fragments tore apart his left arm leaving it limp and useless and then at Chickamauga, a bullet shattered his right leg mandating amputation at the thigh. No one questioned that Hood was a brave and aggressive fighter, only that he was not up to running an army. General Lee certainly did not think so and strongly advised President Davis against elevating Hood to the position. Davis would not listen and Lee, who should have been given the authority and autonomy Lincoln had bestowed on Grant, could only resign

himself to Davis' constituted authority. Imagining himself as the outstanding military mind in the Confederacy, only begrudgingly admitting that Lee was his equal,[628] Davis ignored Lee's sound advice and Hood was promoted, as it tragically turned out, far beyond his capabilities.

The impact of the change in leadership on the Army of Tennessee was overwhelming negative. Still, the men would fight hard for the South, if not for Hood. Ferguson recalled the moment he learned of the appointment of Hood.

> By sunrise the following morning [July 18, 1864] I was pretty warmly engaged so much so that when a courier handed me a dispatch I rode a few steps and got behind a small jug factory to read and answer it for the bullets were coming so fast and thick. It was the order relieving General Johnston and placing General Hood in command. For the first time in the war my heart failed me and I doubted of our ultimate success. I had known Hood in the Corps of Cadets and I did not believe him capable of filling the place. I believed General Johnston one of the greatest of soldiers and think so today.[629]

Hood had about 35,000 infantry, 7,000 cavalry, and 1,500 Georgia militia. On the other hand, Sherman was flush with replacements possessing over 88,000 infantry and 12,000 cavalry, with more troops arriving daily.[630] Nevertheless, despite his numerical superiority, Sherman had no intention of immodestly attacking the city's outer walls head on, content to maneuver about to perhaps find a weak spot while targeting the various railroads that fed into the city.

Since July 10, the Confederate infantry had been kept busy digging new trenches about two miles south of Peachtree Creek on a line nine miles long. Jackson's cavalry was still spread out along the crossings of the Chattahoochee to the west and Wheeler's cavalry, now with Ferguson's brigade, covered the eastern approaches

to Atlanta via Decatur. Major Giles hastily wrote a letter to his wife on the morning of July 19, indicating that things were fairing quite well with Ferguson's brigade, despite the fact that the horses and men in the regiment were broken down with sickness.

> We [Ferguson's brigade] made a force march to this place [Decatur, Georgia] last night [July 18, 1864] — got here about 11 O'clock. Our purpose is to protect the R.R. in this vicinity. We are 8 miles from Atlanta & have a good camp & I think we will have but little to do for the next few days, if we remain here. We are all in deep distress, because Gen. Johnson has been relieved from duty.... Our Reg [11th Mississippi] Has had no fighting to do for the past 10 days & we are now "spilling for a fight!" The last 20 days has reduced our number very much from sickness & sore back horses.[631]

Interestingly, the ink had barely dried on Giles' letter before Ferguson's command was ordered to saddle up with the other cavalry brigades under Wheeler to resist the advance of over 30,000 Yankees storming into Decatur, about seven miles to the east of Atlanta. Union Lieutenant Colonel Wills dryly noted the lopsided engagement which followed and the subsequent disgusting practice of pillaging civilian property.

> To-night [July 19, 1864] we are in Decatur, six miles from Atlanta .... A citizen says there was nearly 4,500 Rebel cavalry here. A small portion of our mounted forces made a half-charge on the Johnnies just this side of town, and the Rebels stampeded. They knew we had a large force, and, of course, could not tell just what number was coming on them .... Our men, as usual, all stopped in town to flank [steal] the onions, potatoes, chicken and sundries, in which they were

busily engaged when the Rebels, who had rallied and got a battery in position, opened right lively. Our men drove them away, and then all hands went to foraging [stealing] again.[632]

Coterminous with the close proximity of the enemy, Hood saw that Sherman's forces were split apart into three main groups each sliding forward at a slow but steady rate of about one mile every three hours towards Atlanta. He correctly thought that this oversight, or over confidence, offered a prime opportunity for him to attack some isolated portion of the enemy. The largest, General Thomas' Army of the Cumberland, was moving from the north of Atlanta and General McPherson's Army of the Tennessee and General Schofield's Army of the Ohio were coming from the east by way of Decatur, although Schofield would soon shift to the center and McPherson a bit to the left following down along the Georgia Railroad. Hood also noted that Sherman was without sufficient cavalry to screen or gather intelligence, since General Garrard had ridden his division out on a three-day raid towards far off Covington and Stone Mountain, leaving Sherman temporarily blind.

Seeking to take advantage of the significant gap that had opened up between the plodding armies, Hood wasted no time in throwing out his men on the offense in a desperate gambit to cripple General Thomas as he crossed Peachtree Creek. Hood's plan was fundamentally sound except that he foolishly chose to strike the largest of the three Federal armies.

The attack took place during the late afternoon of July 20. Unfortunately, as one might expect given Hood's newness to the job, command and control fell apart. Not only were the Confederate assaults piecemeal in nature, but the dense woods and heavy underbrush north of Atlanta presented unforeseen impediments. In turn, in many of the key spots of contact, the Confederates ran into larger bodies of infantry than Hood's attacking force. After desperate fighting that lasted until sundown, Hood was obliged to retreat suffering lopsided casualties of 2,500 compared to 1,750 for Thomas.[633]

Ferguson's brigade was not in the horrid brawl at Peachtree Creek on July 20. Nevertheless, to the immediate east of Atlanta, they performed astonishing service during July 19-21, which unquestionably prevented a catastrophic disaster to Hood's entire army. Through sheer grit and stubborn fighting, they helped to significantly delay the 30,000 troops of McPherson's Army of the Tennessee as it streamed out from Decatur and then single-handedly held a key hill on the exposed Confederate right at the very outskirts of Atlanta against two Yankee divisions at a place called Bald Hill. By pulling off these two critical achievements, McPherson was prevented from overwhelming Hood's weakened right flank and destroying in detail the entire Confederate army from behind.

Ferguson's cavalry started the fighting on July 19, when his brigade and Iverson's were ordered into the city of Decatur to contest the thousands of incoming Yankees. Though the gray troopers were driven out of the city, they dug in at nightfall about two miles distance to wait on what the morning would bring. Major Giles described the action.

> Instead of the nice quiet time we expected to have, we had one of the hardest days we have ever had [July 19], we were ordered to saddle up to meet the Yanks [McPherson's Army], they came on us in heavy force [into Decatur]. Two Army Corps, 30,000 strong, we had 2 Brigades [Ferguson and Iverson] & had to fight a pull back all day — the Yanks got the RR at this place [Decatur] later in the evening. We have fallen back 2 miles towards Atlanta.... We are all well this morning [July 20] & waiting to be ordered out for the days fight.[634]

— Bald Hill —

The morning of July 20, 1864, was hot, bright, and clear with high clouds. As Hood hastily prepared for the horrendous fighting that would soon rage along Peachtree Creek, Wheeler's cavalry division was asked to screen to the front of Major General Benjamin Cheatham's Rebel infantry corps thinly aligned on Hood's far right. Cheatham's line extended all the way from the east side of the city and anchored just on the outskirts at the Georgia Railroad with his troops stretched so thin that a mile long section in the middle had only a single rank of soldiers. Facing him off in the distance was McPherson's entire army which was expected to march from Decatur that very morning. Only Wheeler's cavalry was positioned between the two opposing forces.

Specifically, Wheeler's orders were to make contact with and secure Cheatham's far right at the Georgia Railroad, create a further line of defense on the city's extreme east side, and watch and/or contest the advance of the Army of the Tennessee's 30,000 soldiers.[635] To do all this Wheeler had only one haggard and worn cavalry division under Major General William T. Martin (Iverson was temporarily in command of General Martin's division who had fallen ill) consisting of two brigades and Ferguson's small undersized brigade. General Humes' cavalry division was on Hood's left at this time.

When dismounted, the Confederates could only field an effective fighting force of barely 2,500 troopers and a single four-gun battery,[636] which meant that they were outnumbered well over ten to one. The only available help for the fifteen regiments (counted from the three brigades of Ferguson, Iverson, and Allen), was behind them where 800 militia nervously huddled behind Atlanta's inner fortifications. Without question, once the Yankees brushed the cavalry aside, the Georgia militia and Cheatham's thin line would be nothing more than a nuisance.

The day of July 20, had barely begun when Ferguson's hard riding scouts breathlessly brought back the bad news to Wheeler

— McPherson's entire force was rumbling out from Decatur leaving behind only 1,000 supply wagons, parked under a strong guard. The Confederate cavalry fell back and by late morning Wheeler notified Hood's headquarters of the looming threat followed up by subsequent messages in the early afternoon that McPherson's full army was now closing in from the east. Indeed, by the time Hood launched his attacks at Peachtree Creek around 4:00 p.m., McPherson's three corps had moved down quite a distance via two parallel approaches to a point just two short miles east of Atlanta. The powerful Fifteenth Corps followed the line of the Georgia Railroad on the Decatur road and the Seventeenth Corps took the harder route via farm roads to the left. The smaller Sixteenth Corps followed behind as the reserve force.

For the first time since the War began, Atlanta now stood in plain view of Yankee eyes and an opportunity for a stunning victory was set out on a silver platter. For the cautious McPherson, however, it was Snake Creek Gap all over again. All Sherman's favorite general had to do was to march forward just a couple more miles and aggressively strike Cheatham's Confederates at the Georgia Railroad and Hood's entire line, then spread out in an elongated arc above the city facing Thomas at Peachtree Creek, could be rolled up counterclockwise and Atlanta would fall. Again, the sole blocking force that stood between Atlanta and McPherson's blue hordes were the cavalry brigades of Ferguson, Iverson, and Allen.[637]

Troubled by emergency requests from Wheeler for immediate infantry support to be sent forward, Cheatham was also quick to appreciate the brewing crisis but told Wheeler that he could spare no troops adding with an open air of despair that he would be unable to stop McPherson from crushing his vulnerable right flank. They must prepare for the worst.

Given the circumstances, the probable choice would have been for Wheeler to race back as quickly as practicable to Cheatham's line, dismount, and fall into rank shoulder to shoulder with the gray infantry to face the onslaught. Of course, Wheeler had no intention of falling back to Cheatham's line, retreating into Atlanta's trenches

(as Hood himself had suggested to the Rebel cavalry chief earlier in the day), or anywhere else. To do so would have opened up the entire eastern approach to Atlanta. Instead, depending on deception and mobility, Wheeler elected to aggressively pitch into the Yankees in hopes of stalling them until Hood could send reinforcements. His intent was to fight for every inch of ground, trading ground for time, until his men shot away their last rounds.

And so, Wheeler led out a strong mounted screen consisting of Ferguson and Iverson and at a selected point "half-mile west of a north-south road known for the Clay residence off to the side of it,"[638] Wheeler ordered the troopers to count off by fours and prepare to fight on foot. Skillfully concealing his four-piece artillery battery in a thick belt of timber, the tubes opened up with a deafening barrage on the lead elements of Major General Frank Blair's Seventeenth Corps as they came into view. With the horse holders at the rear, the well-hidden Rebels joined the artillery, firing their carbines, moving from one spot to the other, and making as much racket as possible.

It worked. Having all along anticipated stiff resistance, the Federal infantry reflexively halted and spread out in a strong line of battle parallel to the seen and unseen Rebels to their front, running up two of their own artillery batteries to reply in kind. During the ensuing hour-long artillery duel that sent trees splintering and animals bolting, Wheeler skillfully pulled the larger part of his dismounted troopers back to new positions using the rest to demonstrate loudly so that by late afternoon the dust-covered Rebel horsemen had successfully reduced the Yankee advance to a crawl until, of course, they ran out of ground. Now with their backs literally to the wall, General Wheeler formed a last-ditch line of defense running from a commanding eminence known as Bald Hill to the nearby Georgia Railroad connecting with the extreme end of Cheatham's infantry, a total distance as the crow flies of about three-quarters of a mile.[639] At 6:15 p.m., with almost three hours until dark, Cheatham frantically wrote Wheeler that he was also in a very tight spot: "[The] enemy are pressing my center, which is only a single line for one mile.

I am afraid it will not sustain itself. I have weakened my entire line to fill up the gap of one mile."[640] Luckily for Cheatham, the Federals were only probing him, McPherson's attention was laser focused on capturing the only high ground around — Bald Hill.

Ferguson's brigade was dismounted and placed on the very summit of Bald Hill, so named because the top had been largely cleared of trees, and Iverson's brigade took up positions below the hill stretching on out and connecting to Ferguson's left.[641] In turn, Allen's troopers were aligned on Iverson's left and they extended their reach to the Georgia Railroad connecting with Cheatham's infantry. All three brigades were dismounted and immediately set to digging shallow firing positions and throwing up log breastworks, with the horse holders anxiously waiting behind.

As part of Ferguson's brigade, the 2nd Alabama did not draw the long straw in this final stand. Perched atop the high ground, Ferguson's brigade of perhaps 800 fighting men (the other one-quarter remained with the horses far behind) had a very frightening bird's eye view of the entire Seventeenth Corps under General Blair. Everyone knew that Bald Hill was the key section of ground and defending it meant the inevitable concentrated attack by overwhelming numbers of veteran enemy soldiers.[642] With no artillery support to back them up, the dismounted cavalrymen had only their carbines and side arms to offer resistance.

In contrast, the approaching Union infantry divisions were well drilled in ground combat and armed with the long-barreled Springfield rifles which could spit out destruction at twice the distance of the carbine. While well suited for skirmishing with infantry or even the hell-for-leather mounted charge against enemy cavalry, Rebel dismounted horsemen were no match for massed ground troops, particularly when so badly outnumbered. In short, the 2nd Alabama and her three sister regiments on the top of Bald Hill were asked to do the impossible. The only hope was that Hood could pull off a quick victory that afternoon at Peachtree Creek which might trigger a general halt to the fighting across the entire front.

The sun was unbearably hot that late July afternoon and the previous hours of desperate fighting had soaked the bodies of the 2nd Alabama troopers with sweat. Now, as they dug in on Bald Hill, the sight of so many Union troops below them in every direction only meant that it would soon be much, much hotter. While not that high, the solitary hill dominated the surrounding flattened countryside and provided a perfect vantage point where they watched off to their left as the Fifteenth Corps under Logan demonstrated vigorously on Cheatham's weak infantry line before inexplicably breaking off and pulling back. More importantly, they also watched with a sense of impending doom as Blair's Seventeenth Corps formed up to their immediate front, although Blair seemed sluggish in deploying his men for an assault. The culprit in the hesitation of action for both subordinate commanders Logan and Blair was General McPherson himself who had halted everything to access and mull things over. Uneasy about just how many Johnny Rebs were actually holding Bald Hill, he messaged Sherman by courier before granting permission for Blair to proceed anew to assault the hill.

> If we can soon dislodge the enemy from the hill [Bald Hill], I will press my whole line forward and ascertain the exact state of affairs.[643]

Like any officer worth his salt, Union General Blair was disappointed at the delay and most certainly understood the strategic importance of Bald Hill and the need to move quickly to capture it. Blair personally thought that the opposition he faced was only dismounted cavalry, but others on his staff insisted that it was surely regular infantry with artillery due to the almost fanatical resistance already encountered during the earlier day's fighting. In keeping with McPherson's cautiousness and perhaps recalling the slaughter at Kennesaw Mountain, Blair ordered Brigadier General Walter Gresham to move his division up and flush the Rebels off the place and then extend to the left and right to secure the hill. He would hold back his other divisions for now. Gresham saluted and returned to his command to make the necessary preparations.

In the meantime, Ferguson moved amongst his men with a poker face hiding as best he could a deep sense of foreboding, knowing that it was impossible for the cavalrymen to hold out against multiple waves of blue infantry should they press the matter. Still, as his brave men had done all day long, he was determined to make a respectable show of it, all the while praying for infantry support.

The fight opened when Gresham ordered in a brigade under Colonel Benjamin Potts to probe the Rebel positions. Potts marched forward and stopped his troops under the cover of a creek ravine about 400 yards from the rounded hill, sending a thick line of skirmishers to cautiously continue on ahead to better assess things. The blue line was easily within accurate firing range and Ferguson defiantly ordered his men to let loose. Sprays of lead rained down on the Yankees causing them to scramble for cover and return fire, sending back the disappointing news that angry Confederates were indeed intent on defending the knoll. Major Giles also described to his wife in real time the desperate combat of the day and the hope that friendly infantry would soon be there to assist as they now fought it out at Bald Hill.

> Well we have pitched into very heavy skirmishing & while I write the Cannons & musket balls are circulating around rapidly. I am in a safe place & can see some & hear all of it, we are driven back to within 1 mile of Atlanta [to Bald Hill] — fighting for every foot of ground — we have no Infantry on this line, but will have plenty here in one or two hours — more cannon .... I tell you again not to be uneasy about me, for I will take good care of myself.[644]

Given that the Rebels were furiously exchanging shots with his men and showing no signs of retreat, General Gresham concluded that if not regular infantry then several strong brigades of cavalry were defending the place.[645] Having already lost 50 men in killed and wounded moving against the Rebel cavalry earlier in the

day,[646] Gresham was also concerned that the heavily wooded base of the hill might conceal another ravine that could stall the main attack and produce even heavier losses if his men became bogged down. Indeed, because his skirmish line was stymied so quickly, the reconnaissance had been unable to either confirm or deny the topography in question or the enemy's strength, even though he received other positive reports that no Rebels could be found around to the far slope of Bald Hill, causing Gresham to ponder if perhaps a sweeping flank movement directed on that end rather than straight up the middle might be a better plan.

In order to personally satisfy himself of the true situation, Gresham trotted forward to Potts' location in the ravine to reconnoiter for himself. Under a brisk small-arms fire, all Gresham could discern was that resistance from Bald Hill was significant and that the Rebels handled their weapons with terrible effect. It was then that one of Ferguson's men ripped a Minnie ball straight through the Yankee general's left lower leg, shattering the tibia near the knee and ignominiously knocking him to the ground in great pain.[647] Anxious hands put the wounded general on a stretcher and hustled him back to the rear.

With Gresham down, the assault was again postponed and General Blair rode up to inspect things for himself. Confronted with the same conflicting intelligence, Blair determined that the best solution was to launch an overwhelming charge with two combined divisions and be done with it. He messaged his reserve division under Ohioan Brigadier General Mortimer Leggett to move into position next to Gresham's left (now temporarily commanded by Colonel William Hall) and point itself straight in front of Bald Hill.[648] Leggett would take the lead and Hall would follow. With a broad mouth and hot eyes, Leggett ordered up a fresh brigade to spearhead his division, aligned them in proper form, and waited for the final order to attack. In the interim, Leggett's skirmishers probed forward and opened up on Ferguson's men who were more than happy to return the favor. The bullets were now fast and furious and many who chronicled the fight for Atlanta noted

that the Rebel cavalrymen courageously stood their ground that afternoon inflicting great harm on the enemy.

> McPherson's XVII (17th) Corps under Major General Francis Blair, Jr., ran into determined Confederate resistance [Ferguson's brigade] on the [Union] left, south of the railroad [Georgia Railroad], where a small force of dismounted gray horsemen occupied a prominent knoll, cleared of timber and known to local folks as Bald Hill.[649]

While all this was transpiring, General McPherson and his staff appeared on the scene, requiring General Blair to once again signal a halt to his division commanders in order to discuss dispositions and progress. Strangely, instead of forcefully directing Leggett to launch the attack, Blair's response was measured, looking to McPherson for guidance. Indeed, no sooner had the generals dismounted to talk, did McPherson's cautiousness reassert itself. At this point, about an hour and a half of daylight remained and having fought a very stubborn dismounted cavalry all day long under the scorching rays of a sun that drained the life out of every living thing, McPherson postponed the attack until the next morning.

McPherson's lost golden opportunity on the late afternoon of July 20 perplexed both friend and foe. Not only had the doe-faced general halted the Fifteenth Corps in their movements against Cheatham's skeleton line, he had now also halted the Seventeenth Corps from taking Bald Hill. Ferguson could not fathom it and wrote:

> From the line of works occupied by my troops they could see masses of the enemy, fully 20,000 strong, all aligned and ready to attack .... I felt that any respectable effort on their part could easily dislodge my force and leave nothing between McPherson and the interior works which had been erected for the final defense of Atlanta.[650]

Later that early evening, it finally dawned on McPherson that he had been far too timid against the Confederates. Apparently, the primary obstacle that had stymied him was his obsessive belief that Hood actually intended to attack *his* army on July 20, and not General Thomas at Peachtree Creek.[651] McPherson was right about Hood attacking him, but off by two days — Hood would launch a major flank attack against McPherson on July 22, and around the very same ground the Union general was then standing upon. But on this day, instead of thinking about attacking, McPherson was worried about being attacked. In one of his last messages to Sherman (McPherson was shot dead off his horse on July 22) he informed Sherman that he had failed to take the pivotal high ground, blaming his lack of progress with an incredible statement about how Ferguson's use of "short Enfield rifles" had provided some sort of a supernatural advantage against his tens of thousands of infantry.

> We have had some pretty lively skirmishing and have driven the enemy from several pretty strong positions, though I do not think there has been much of anything but cavalry in front of us.... But they have had four pieces of artillery and are armed with short Enfield rifles, making it difficult to dislodge them.[652]

With only Wheeler's three brigades of worn out cavalry blocking McPherson that night, Hood finally responded to the extreme danger threatening the Confederate right and released General Pat Cleburne's crack infantry division, which had been his reserve force at Peachtree Creek, to move south and replace/assist the dismounted cavalry holding on for dear life. Cleburne's three brigades, consisting of the best 4,000 fighters in the Army of Tennessee, arrived a few hours after midnight and after marking out a line of defense, began entrenching.

Taking up fighting positions was difficult in the dark and Yankee sharpshooters made it even more so. Brigadier General James Smith was assigned to the far end of the Confederate defenses and

his 1,500 butternut infantry, mostly Texans, groped about in the dark digging as fast as they could. Unfortunately, Smith somehow failed to plant his troops at the top of Bald Hill and then on down the adjacent far slope. In fact, his actual line extended at its furthest point only up the near slope, far shy of the top of the hill. Brigadier General Mark P. Lowrey connected to Smith's left and Brigadier General Daniel C. Govan's brigade covered the remaining ground, so that the beefed-up Confederate reinforcements were solidly set from the Georgia Railroad all the way to the near slope of Bald Hill, but not to the top!

Inexplicably, Cleburne had somehow failed to ensure that the most important sector in the entire defensive line — Bald Hill — was sufficiently supplied with an extra heavy contingent of infantry and artillery. Instead of concentrating the necessary infantry force to hold the summit, which would most certainly be the pivotal contest come morning, the defense of both the top and the entire far side of Bald Hill was left solely to a handful of dismounted cavalry. Ferguson's frazzled troopers who had so valiantly held the entire hill the afternoon before were simply left alone at the top with Iverson's cavalry brigade placed from where Ferguson ended on down the far slope to the base of the hill, in case the Federals tried to sneak around. Once again, Ferguson's regiments were expected to stave off what would most certainly be the main attack from thousands upon thousands of Yankees. In retrospect, the otherwise brilliant General Cleburne should have saturated Bald Hill with artillery and infantry and placed the cavalry in reserve or as forward skirmishers.[653]

That same night of July 20, Sherman was fully aware that McPherson had missed out on a golden opportunity to blitz into Atlanta and sardonically instructed the commander of the Army of the Tennessee to shove his way forward on the morrow to occupy Bald Hill. Accordingly, General Leggett used the night hours to arrange his artillery and move up his forces to staging areas to conquer the summit by storm at first light on July 21.

The battle-hardened veterans of the 2nd Alabama had no illusions about their brutal assignment or about what awaited them at dawn. No doubt the Alabamians were stunned that none of Cleburne's infantry were sent to replace or at least to reinforce them. To make matters worse, in putting up such a valiant effort the day before, the Southern cavalrymen had expended much of their ammunition and had not yet been sufficiently resupplied. They all knew the importance of holding the high ground but given the disparity in numbers they also knew that if the Federal infantry came at them with a serious thrust there was no hope that they could stem the tidal wave. Nevertheless, whatever happened, they would put up a fight and few were unnerved by the prospect of being whipped.

Attention had already been given to the wounded with the seriously injured sent back to hospital and during the long night of July 20-21, shallow trenches were deepened as best as practicable, sentries doubled, and blazing fires lit to both deceive the Federals as to their true numbers and to help illuminate things should the enemy conduct a rare night attack. Finally, Ferguson had the men set up a second line of defense at the back base of the hill which could serve as a last stand, if necessary. Behind the precautionary second position, the horse holders lined up along Flat Shoals Road where they were instructed to keep the animals saddled and ready to receive their comrades for a rapid getaway. Few got any sleep and those that did were rousted from their bedrolls in the predawn darkness for a whispered roll call. The Yankees were about ready to "open the ball."

Preparatory to the attack, selected Union skirmishers crept forward in the darkness to the bottom of the hill just inside the wood line, so close that they could easily observe the individual campfires emanating from the crest. On the early dark morning of July 21, Major Giles paused long enough to pen his next letter home, even as thick ominous groups of blue infantry began maneuvering forward.

> We have fallen back to this place [Bald Hill] & have had heavy fighting last evening & this morning. Our Brig [Ferguson's] is doing good service — we are losing some men but not many as yet — none of our friends are hurt as yet. Our horses are all nearly a mile inside of the fortifications & the only danger we are in is from an occasional stray shell, which we have learned to dodge, so I tell you again not to be at all uneasy about me. I think we will have a very hard fight here.[654]

At 7 a.m. of July 21, Federal artillery fire consisting of ten-pounder Parrotts, pushed the gates of death open and raked the Confederates, blasting away from ranges not more than 800 yards off. Consisting of solid and exploding shells, the fire was directed at the near slope and center area of Bald Hill and went unanswered. In fact it was not until 8 a.m. that two batteries of Confederate artillery were finally unlimbered and placed on the near ridge to return fire.

The results of the Federal shelling were horrifying. Not only did the artillery signal that a major attack was imminent, but great damage was done, particularly to the gray infantry set out on the near side of Bald Hill — "[f]orty men were killed and 100 wounded in less than 300 seconds."[655] One shell tore into a group of 18 Confederates as they huddled in a freshly dug ditch, killing or wounding all except one.

After about an hour of intense firing the Federal bombardment mercifully ceased, signaling to the men that a ground assault was soon to follow. They were right. Arrayed in three brigades and one battalion, General Leggett's division of over 4,000 was ready. Leggett selected his largest and strongest brigade, commanded by Brigadier General Manning Force, to lead the assault and aimed it directly at the top of Bald Hill. To Force's right was Colonel Robert Scott's brigade and to Scott's left was Colonel Adam Malloy's brigade.

To support Leggett, General Blair ordered Brigadier General Giles Smith's division, who had succeeded the badly wounded Gresham, to launch a cooperating attack on Cleburne's infantry on the near side of Bald Hill. Two of Smith's brigades were also instructed to connect with Force's brigade as it moved forward.

The woody ground in front of Bald Hill made deployment difficult, but by 8:00 a.m. the color-bearers unfurled Union flags from their cases and a bravely mounted General Force gave the command, "Forward, March!" Like a gigantic ocean wave, the blue host lapped ahead and let out a hearty *huzzah*. "Line after line of the enemy came into sight," wrote a cavalryman on Bald Hill, "and as the blue columns advanced towards us in perfect formation with flags flying and bayonets flashing in the sunshine, they made a splendid appearance."[656]

The effects of the artillery barrage were shrugged off as every Rebel eye now took deadly aim. Like Cleburne's infantry, most of the Confederate cavalry had stayed awake all night either manning the freshly expanded rifle pits or sitting anxiously around campfires. Now that the Yankees were coming, the men of the 2nd Alabama wiped sweaty palms on pants and swung carbines to shoulder, they would soon have blood for breakfast. Officers gave the order to fire at will and in a matter of seconds the open terrain below was peppered by gunfire striking down many of the blue skirmishes. Behind them, however, came two densely packed parallel columns of blue, moving almost shoulder-to-shoulder, bits of metal clanking and gleaming in the bright morning sun. The regiments of the 12th and 16th Wisconsin formed the first line and the 20th, 30th, and 31st Illinois the second. Soon enough, the Wisconsin boys caught up to the skirmishes who seamlessly folded into formation with their comrades. It was now a double line of solid blue and steel.

Continuing forward, the Federals momentarily disappeared off the open ground and into a patch of forest where they wetted their feet across a shallow tributary of Sugar Creek. Climbing up the bank on the other side caused the alignment to veer off slightly to the

southwest so that when the Yankees tramped out of the woods and back onto open ground, their right flank was exposed to blasts of shot and shell from Confederate batteries. Almost by instinct, like a herd of buffalo, the very accurate artillery fire caused the entire body of Federals to shift further towards the far side of Bald Hill.

Ferguson's cavalrymen could clearly see that the Union attackers had diverted somewhat in their advance but not enough to cause the weight of the force to bypass them — the enemy was still going to encompass the top of the hill as well as hitting part of Smith's Texans on the near slope. The only cheering observation was that the closing range was now absolutely deadly. Along with her sister regiments, the 2nd Alabama fired as fast as they could reload, unleashing a lethal barrage which cut down scores of the enemy. The Wisconsin color bearers guiding the first line of infantry were particularly hard hit, so that when one was shot down another would grasp the wooden flagpole and hoist the Stars and Stripes anew.

For what seemed an eternity, a thunderstorm of lead missiles hissed and ripped gaping holes through the 12th Wisconsin, as screaming officers valiantly closed up the gaps and urged the men to follow the flag up the slope. Veering neither to the left nor to the right, the Union infantry kept moving, taking horrible casualties with each passing minute. "Our men fell in bunches," a member of the 16th Wisconsin recalled, "the Rebs kept firing volley after volley at us, and our boys kept dropping all the way up the hill."[657]

The only merciful break in the killing came about 400 yards from the summit when the leading elements were ordered to stop and take cover in the tall grass and brush while they waited for the second line to come up behind them and do the same. The 2nd Alabama troopers, still fanned out along the ridge line, saw the front row of Federals duck down in the grass, though the Rebels kept sweeping the ground as man after man shot away his last cartridge. With the Union masses now extending almost a full quarter mile across, the decision to halt and consolidate meant temporary safety of sort. "It was indeed refreshing and comforting to 'lie down' at such a time," one of the Union soldiers later wrote, "especially so

when we heard the little leaden messengers of death whizzing over us on their way to the rear."[658]

When all the Federals arrived at the designated stopping point and realigned themselves, General Force shouted out in a booming voice meant to both unnerve the Rebels as much as give much needed encouragement to his own troops: "Fix Bayonets!" For a few moments, the cling and clang of metal hitting metal rang out in unison as the Yanks attached the skinny knife-like tool onto the rifle barrel attachment. Then came the barking order: "Up Men!" "Forward, Double-Quick!" Fear of death gave way to strength of action and as if on parade a thick wall of Federals jumped to their feet, shifted rifled muskets to the hip, and rushed ahead to close the final distance as quickly as possible.

The onslaught could no longer be checked by Ferguson's outgunned troopers. Though some of the cavalrymen in the forward spots stood their ground and fought with clubbed rifles, knives, and pistol butts the majority sensed it was fruitless and made for the rear — they had already achieved the impossible, they could do no more. Ferguson ordered buglers to sound retreat and all went for the horses, deliberately passing right over the precautionary earthen trench-line scoped out at the downside of the hill. Those that stalled were bayonetted, shot, or captured. It was over.

Alarmed by the uproar on the top of Bald Hill, the other Rebel cavalry brigade on the far side, temporarily commanded by Colonel Crews (Iverson's brigade), discerned that Ferguson's position had been stormed and elected then and there to run for it as well. They fired a single ragged volley towards the Federal masses before scurrying to horse and galloping away.

The momentum was clearly with Force's blue infantry swarming over the hill, but shoving back Pat Cleburne who still held the near slope of Bald Hill was a different matter. In the race to the top, the far-right of Force's troops encountered the might of regular Rebel infantry and were stopped cold in their tracks. A witness recalled the resulting ferocity where "[b]ayonets and musket butts, sabers and revolvers, even fists and feet were used in that dreadful struggle."[659]

Having bounced off the brick wall of stalwart Confederate infantry, Force wisely pulled back all his men, some who were still pursuing Ferguson's retreating cavalrymen, and sent urgent requests to General Blair for immediate infantry and artillery support. Force no longer thought about attacking and now prepared himself to defend the hill just taken. It was well that he did. Cleburne realized his mistake in the initial deployment and began to marshal his troops for a swift counterattack to drive the Yankees off the top and roll them back down the hill.

The ensuing brief pause in no way meant that the blood-letting was over. First, Cleburne compensated for the loss of territory on Bald Hill by realigning his forces in a perpendicular formation to avoid being flanked. Second, fearing that he would not be able to stop McPherson's entire army should it now move forward to support Force's tenuous breakthrough, Cleburne sent urgent requests to Hood for more men. Third, Cleburne ordered blistering counterattacks.

Strangely, Union General McPherson never committed significant numbers of fresh infantry to Force until much later in the morning. Instead, realizing his grave error in not breaking apart Cheatham's weak line the previous day, he now foolishly sought to accomplish that very goal against Pat Cleburne and ordered Giles Smith to storm his brigades forward and hit the Confederate infantry directly on the level ground adjacent to Bald Hill.[660] Predictably, General Smith's men were decimated in the attempt to breach Cleburne's line, although the bloody effort did succeed in keeping the Irish general from sending sufficient reinforcements to retake the top of Bald Hill. Without more men, the Confederate counterattacks that morning were only able to recover about 200 yards of the positions formally held by Ferguson's dismounted cavalry[661] so that when Force finally received his own added reinforcements and artillery, General Cleburne was obliged to pull back. By 11:00 a.m. the hard fighting at Bald Hill had died down, only the sickening stench of death remained. At the end of the day, Cleburne was unable to retake the lost ground on the top causing him to abandon all of it, withdrawing to set up new and healthier fighting positions well beyond Fall Shoals road.

The Union had Bald Hill.⁶⁶² The fighting cost the Federals a staggering 700 men in killed, wounded, and missing to the Confederates 300.⁶⁶³ The exact number of Ferguson's losses are unknown, with estimates exceeding 100 probably not far off the mark.⁶⁶⁴ One of the captured cavalrymen recalled with customary Southern brashness that he and his fellows were forced to listen to a verbal reprimand from Francis Blair!

> They had a large flag over his tent [General Blair]. He made us a speech and told us what bad boys we were and that we should honor the flag, but I felt more like cutting his throat than listening to his speech.⁶⁶⁵

In a testament to the courage and determination of Ferguson's men who received the initial brunt of the attack,⁶⁶⁶ a goodly portion of the Union losses were suffered in taking the hill, although the bulk of the casualties were inflicted by Cleburne's spirited defense and counterattacks.⁶⁶⁷ Indeed, the 12th Wisconsin alone lost five color-bearers and 134 (killed or wounded) out of its 600-man regiment in helping their comrades wrestle the hill from Ferguson.⁶⁶⁸

With Bald Hill lost, all of Atlanta was in easy artillery range, now a mere mile and a half away. That afternoon, Blair ordered additional cannons hauled up the hill and began lobbing shells indiscriminately into the beleaguered city.

— Decatur —

If Sherman was frustrated with McPherson's timidity on July 20, he was delighted with the outcome of Hood's failed attacks at Peachtree Creek that very same day. On the other hand, where many saw only disaster as the blue noose tightened around Atlanta, Hood saw opportunity anew. Barely had the smoke cleared from the blood-soaked terrain of Peachtree Creek and Bald Hill before the crippled general hatched a second plan of attack, this time targeting the rear of McPherson's army which was still congregated

around Bald Hill. On the night of July 21, he pulled Hardee's corps off the line facing Schofield and sent it on a long night march right through the streets of Atlanta and then on further to the south before circling the men back up to the east towards Decatur so as to be prepared on July 22 to assault what he expected was the rear of the Army of the Tennessee. Since all the other Yankee infantry were off to McPherson's right and much of the Union cavalry was still gone raiding towards Stone Mountain, Hood sought a second chance to gain a stunning victory.

As was the case with Peachtree Creek, the concept of the operation looked good on paper but was far too ambitious in application. Hood had served admirably under the audacious Robert E. Lee, who executed similar bold movements, but he was no Robert E. Lee. After passing through town in a grueling night march, the already exhausted Confederates under the command of General Hardee took too long to then curve back up to the north and get into position for the next day's "sneak" attack. When the attacks were finally launched on July 22, they were once again piecemeal in nature and tragically "unlucky," for the Federals had surreptitiously taken precautionary defensive preparations which just so happened to face exactly at the very spot of the main Rebel attacks. For once, McPherson's cautiousness in constructing seemingly unnecessary obstructions to ward off imagined ghost assaults had paid off.

The initial plan called for Wheeler's cavalry along with Ferguson's troopers to join the infantry out of Atlanta as the guiding element of the combined force. However, when Hood saw the delays in the evening troop movements eating up the clock, he adjusted his original orders to attack McPherson from the rear and rerouted Hardee to attack him obliquely around Bald Hill, ordering Wheeler to proceed on to Decatur, now deserted but once a town of about 600 people, in order to destroy or threaten McPherson's immense wagon train of supplies parked in and around an old cemetery on the far side of town.

In obedience to orders, Wheeler linked up with Hardee's infantry after it emerged from Atlanta's perimeter and guided

them through thick tangles of heavy underbrush and thorns past Terry's Mill Pond where his scouts reported that they found no enemy infantry or cavalry to block the way ahead. This meant that the Confederate foot soldiers could now get into position to attack the Union left allowing Wheeler to part company from the blurry-eyed ground forces and proceed on the road to Decatur. The prospect of capturing large stores of Federal supplies invigorated the cavalrymen and there was little straggling.

Unfortunately for Wheeler, a brigade of New Jersey and Wisconsin troops had taken strong preparations to counter any sneak cavalry attacks. First, six cannons supported by riflemen were dug in on the Decatur road with several companies of skirmishers spread out into the woods ahead on both sides to alert on any Rebel horsemen. Second, should the artillery position be breached, the Federals constructed a strong barricade manned by a full regiment on a low ridge near a railroad cut. Third, behind all this, set up around the town center, another two regiments stood in reserve further shielding the hundreds of fully loaded supply wagons.

Once again, Federal vigilance paid off. Just before 1 p.m. Ferguson's brigade, which Wheeler had placed at the lead, made hard contact with the Yankee skirmishes and the fight was on. The other brigades quickly followed Ferguson's dismounted troopers who charged through the woods on foot, only to be stalled in the face of deadly canister blasts which badly mauled the gray troopers, forcing them to seek cover in the trees. Wheeler called up his own light artillery and through sheer grit the Confederates were able to storm over the cannons and hit the second barricade, taking it from two sides and driving the enemy back into the town.

Amazingly, it was not over. Desperate to buy additional time for the wagons to escape, large numbers of the retreating Federals reconstituted alongside their two reserve regiments who had already settled into firing positions all throughout the houses, sheds, and barns again slowing the Rebels and forcing bitter house-to-house fighting, mostly by squads. Death reigned supreme in the sweltering heat of July 22, as desperate men — blue and gray — shot each other

in fanatical close quarter fighting. With six-shooters ideal for such combat, explosions from hundreds of greasy hot barreled pistols quickly engulfing the city in acrid smoke.

After about 30 minutes of desperate fighting, the Yankees could stand no more and fled into the woods, leaving behind scores of dead, wounded, and prisoners. While the Confederates were victorious, the half-hour delay had allowed enough time for almost all of the wagons to harness up and race out the backdoor with a small escort of Federal horsemen. Still, the heavy wagons were easy targets for mounted pursuers and overtaking them would have been an easy and glorious finish to the day's work.

It was not to be. Much to Wheeler's dismay, three separate staff officers had appeared in rapid succession during the engagement in Decatur each directing him to immediately come to the aid of Hardee's embattled infantry. As much as Wheeler wanted to run down the Federal wagon train, with the enemy put to flight, he obeyed the orders and turned his troopers back towards Atlanta where he arrived just in time to help stabilize Hardee's Confederates who were fighting off a series of counterattacks.[669]

Ferguson's troopers were equally disappointed. Despite heavy losses at Bald Hill the previous day which had left many of the men dehydrated, tired, and hungry, they had once again been thrown into the very front of the fighting. Beginning with the hard contest to take out the Union artillery, where blasts of grapeshot sent shards of human flesh blowing into the woods, progressing on over the railroad cut, and then into the town frightful casualties[670] were taken, to include Company G's popular Captain William Ashley who suffered several gunshot wounds. As stated, the frenzied determination of the Union commanders to save their wagons obliged the Rebels to dislodge the enemy in street fighting, a thing that rarely occurred during the War. Ferguson wrote of the uniqueness.

> Other cavalry brigades joined in the attack but I made the direct attack fighting on foot through thick woods

and black oak. The resistance was stubborn, we were driving the enemy back slowly.... In a few minutes more we had driven the enemy from the woods and then advanced rapidly to the railroad cut. Here my horse was shot under me. The town was on the other side of the railroad and had to be taken house by house.[671]

Stained with sweat, smoke, vomit, and powder burns, those alive and unhurt were completely exhausted. The weather was so miserably hot and stifling that many of the over-heated Confederates simply collapsed from heat stroke, unable to move. Perhaps the most chilling testament to the horror of the struggle was recorded by a doctor in Ferguson's brigade regarding a trooper who had been shot in the head. "[He] had the front part of his skull shot off, but it did not break the membrane around the brain. I had to hold his hands to keep him from tearing out his brains."[672]

Wheeler's total losses in killed and wounded were about 150, with enemy losses consisting of 225 prisoners and another 125 killed and wounded. Of course, the Union losses would have been far greater, to include the certain capture and destruction of the wagons had Wheeler not been ordered to return to Atlanta.

While the 2nd Alabama was slugging it out in their own bloody killing fields at Decatur, the butternut and gray infantry situated around the Bald Hill battleground were fighting like crazed madmen. After being dropped off by Wheeler, the Confederate foot soldiers surged out of the woods as planned but instead of running into unprepared blue-coats lingering about bivouacs, they hit strong dirt and log defensive positions constructed by McPherson's engineers. The struggle that ensued degenerated into butchery. When it ended and Hood pulled his army inside the walls of Atlanta, the Rebels had suffered over 5,000 casualties while the Federals lost almost 4,000, to include the death of General McPherson who was shot off his horse by a skirmisher. Once again Sherman scored the victory, ironically, this time thanks to McPherson and a huge dose of luck.[673]

— Union Cavalry Strikes Atlanta's Railroad —

Sherman had now beaten back Hood's Confederates twice within the space of days, at Peachtree Creek and then outside of Atlanta itself. In both battles the Yankee general had simply pivoted his superior numbers to the defense to counter Hood's aggressive, yet tragic overreaches. Believing that Hood would not try a third assault anytime soon and having no desire to attack the fully manned Atlanta defenses to his front, Sherman's next move was to target the Macon & Western running south out from Atlanta to Macon, the only remaining railroad servicing Hood's badly bloodied army.

Sprawled outside the northern approaches of the city in a crude semi-circle, Sherman ordered his infantry to shift slowly to the right but his real design was to now make use of his tremendous cavalry advantage by sending out almost 10,000 superbly equipped horsemen in a double envelopment to go around both sides of Atlanta and cut the rail behind it. The two separate cavalry wings would converge at Lovejoy's Station, about 20 miles due south of Atlanta so that with the rail-line sufficiently destroyed, Hood might be forced to evacuate Atlanta.

Curiously, Sherman held a poor opinion of his horse soldiers and a great opinion of the Rebel cavalry and his decision to give them the chance to prove their worth did not sit well. "Somehow our cavalry is not good," he wrote to his wife in 1864, "the secesh with poor and mean horses make 40 & 50 miles a day, whereas our fat & costly horses won't average 10. In every march I have ever made our Infantry beats the Cavalry and I am ashamed of them."[674]

On July 27, General George Stoneman led 5,500 Federal horsemen from the east side of Atlanta semi-circling around the city and heading south where he was joined by an additional 1,000 men, while General Edward McCook took 3,500 cavalry from the western side of the city also semi-circling and heading south. Again, the plan was to rendezvous at Lovejoy's Station, a strong point that sat directly on the Macon & Western and obliterate both the depot and miles of the track in both directions. A secondary objective,

The Dalton/Atlanta Campaign

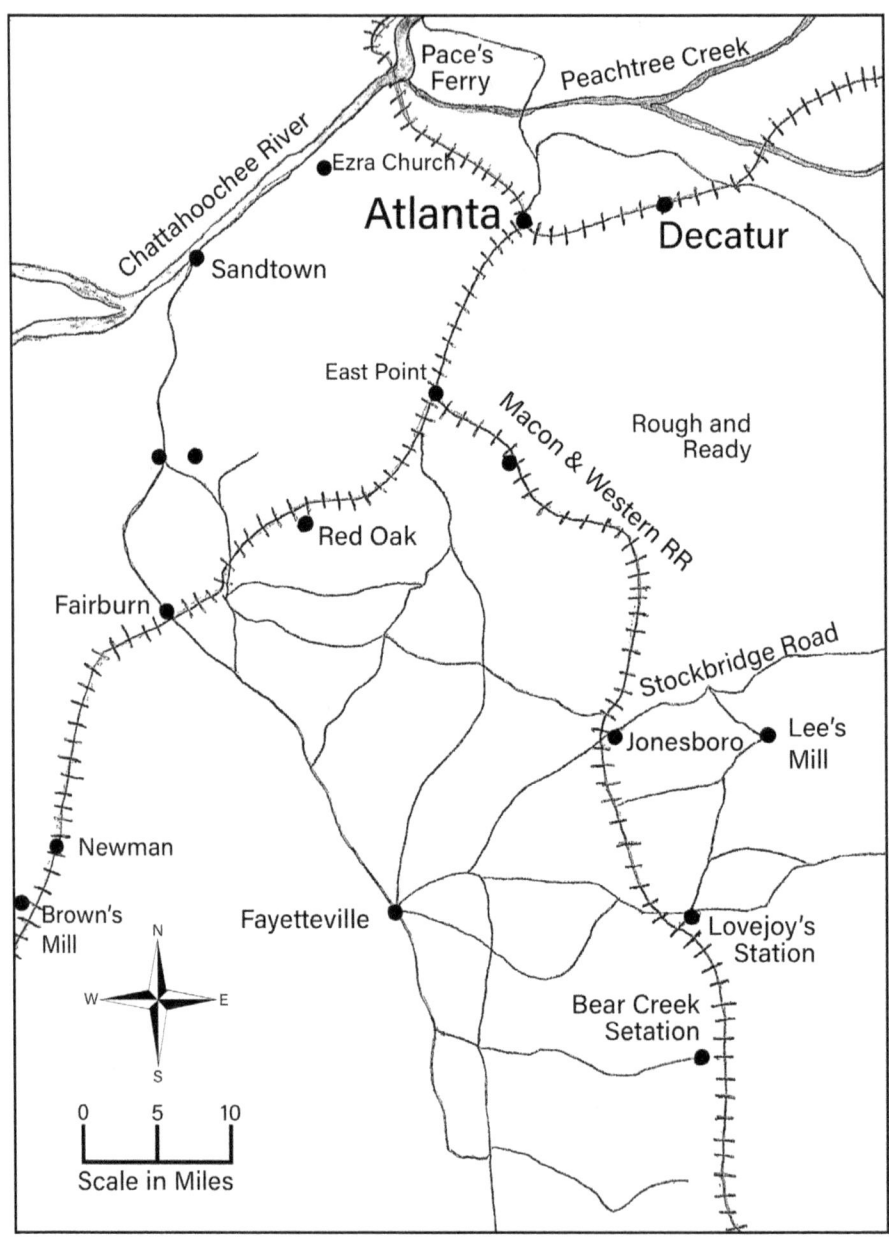

Area Map of Union Cavalry Raids.

requested by Stoneman and reluctantly approved by Sherman, was to then hit the Confederate POW camp at Macon in order to free some 1,500 Union officers and, if that went well, to next perhaps proceed on to Andersonville to liberate 30,000 starving Union enlisted prisoners. Wielding such large numbers in the combined cavalry force, the outlined objectives were certainly achievable.

Shortly after the Federals left their camps keen-eyed scouts sounded the alarm and the Confederate cavalry which numbered perhaps 3,800 ill-equipped riders scrambled to respond to the dual threat of over 10,000 Union cavalry. Easily guessing that the objective was to cut the Macon & Western railroad at some predetermined point, General Wheeler boldly split his inferior forces, directing one part to contend with Stoneman and the other to intercept McCook.

After some particularly rough skirmishing with Rebel cavalry at Campbellton, McCook reached Lovejoy's Station more or less on schedule. Stoneman, however, was nowhere to be found. Irrationally fearing that he would be encircled and cut off by Wheeler, McCook refused to set up a defensive perimeter and wait for Stoneman. He ordered his men to tear up some rail then saddled up to head back to his base at Marietta!

Sul Ross' small brigade of Texans was the first to find the retreating McCook at Fayetteville where they tore into the Federal rear so fiercely in a series of mounted charges that McCook was absolutely convinced that Wheeler's entire force was upon him. Abandoning all reason, McCook accelerated his retreat at break neck speed into the night. Smelling blood, the Rebels remained hot on his tail with the knock-out blow for McCook's command taking place on July 30, at Brown's Mill, where the Rebel cavalry, to include Ferguson, caught the Federals out in open fields and violently punished them, scattering the blue brigades like bowling pins and chasing the remnants all the way back to Marietta.

If McCook's raid was a dismal failure, Stoneman's fate was even worse. While McCook's contingent was soundly defeated, at least the majority were able to escape capture and make it back to

friendly lines. The fatal miscalculations about time and space were partly to blame for McCook's timidity, which often occurs in joint operations, but General Stoneman's defeat was caused by nothing less than a total loss of nerve. Not only did Stoneman not reach Lovejoy's Station as planned, he allowed his cavalry command to be completely surrounded, cut to pieces, and surrendered.

Riding out of their horse camps just below Decatur at 4:00 a.m. on the morning of July 27, Stoneman's 5,500 blue troopers linked up with Union General Garrard's division of horse soldiers giving him an unbelievable massive force of 6,500 troopers plus artillery. However, meeting spirited resistance from some small squadrons of Confederate cavalry, Stoneman incorrectly assumed, just as McCook did with Ross, that a superior Rebel force were gathering to his front. Instead of pushing his riders onward to cover the short distance to Lovejoy's Station where he would have the assurance of the added thousands from McCook's command, Stoneman unilaterally abandoned the agreed rendezvous and elected to proceed to far off Macon, the secondary objective and much deeper into Confederate territory. Leaving Garrard's 1,000 troopers behind to shield the move, Stoneman started swiftly towards Macon, only to slow to a crawl as the men were allowed to loot and plunder every person, home, and village along the way. Old men were robbed of their money, women of their rings and broaches, and homes smashed to pieces. The Yankees loaded their saddles with all sorts of stolen property, with whiskey and strong drink the most sought-after items. Disgraceful reports of Union cavalrymen sexually assaulting girls were also reported.[675]

By July 30, Stoneman at last reached the outskirts of Macon where he encountered a waist high dirt perimeter manned only by Georgia militia, some dismounted Confederates, and a handful of regular infantry, hardly a challenge to his superior numbers. Inexplicably, he again faltered and refused to move forward and take the place, deciding instead to push his now weary, rain-soaked command towards Andersonville another 60 miles deeper into Confederate territory.

Stoneman did not get far. On July 31, his rear was hit hard by Iverson's cavalry brigade of perhaps 1,400 at Sunshine Church where the Federals had no choice but to turn and fight, only to see things quickly disintegrate as more and more supporting Confederate cavalry arrived and pitched into the battle. After some rather desperate horse charges and counterattacks, Stoneman's confused cavalry was literally torn to pieces with General Stoneman and over 700 of his men taken prisoner and several thousand of their panic-stricken fellows scattered all across the countryside making for Atlanta as fast as possible. Ironically, instead of liberating POWs, Stoneman and hundreds of his men became POWs, a most fitting and satisfying end.

The 2nd Alabama's part in the grand Union cavalry forays was limited to tearing apart McCook's column and began on July 26, when Ferguson's brigade was on picket duty covering the Confederate left at Atlanta. Unaware that the two Union pincers were about to start their ambitious horse raid the next day, Hood had ordered Ferguson to prepare a day's rations and move out to the southwest to join General Kelly's cavalry division for a swift Rebel strike of their own behind Union lines. In obedience to orders, the 2nd Alabama and her sister regiments saddled up and by 11:00 p.m. they had made their way to the outskirts of East Point, where the men dismounted and caught some shut eye beside the road. At 3:00 a.m. boots and saddles were sounded and the cavalrymen mounted and proceeded to Campbellton on the Chattahoochee River, reaching that place just at daylight on July 27, the same day that McCook was heading in the opposite direction towards Lovejoy's Station. Still unaware of the ongoing Federal cavalry movements, Kelly's division and Ferguson's brigade halted on the riverbank as their engineers began work constructing a sturdy pontoon bridge for the horses to cross to the north bank. Shortly thereafter, a dust covered courier brought urgent orders for the troopers to return to Atlanta in response to excited reports that large bodies of Federal cavalry were on the move.

Ferguson's brigade was directed to fill the trenches all the way over to the east side of Atlanta which had been vacated that morning

by three brigades of Wheeler's cavalry to pursue Stoneman's raiders.[676] By order of General Hood, "General Ferguson's brigade will move to the right [arriving] to-night [27 July]."[677] In order to get to Atlanta with all speed, Ferguson was also instructed to take his dismounted brigade into town by train if possible and by 10 a.m. he marched off south to do so. Kelly's division was ordered to stand in place at Cobb's Mill on the Fayetteville Road, then later ordered to join Wheeler in chasing down the Federal cavalry.

By the late afternoon of July 27, Ferguson's troopers were manning the trenches on the east side of Atlanta vacated by Wheeler's three brigades. On the afternoon of July 28, however, Ferguson was again diverted. He was now sent to support S.D. Lee's retreating infantry corps which had suffered bloody losses that same day near Ezra Church, foolishly attacking superior numbers of Union infantry.

S.D. Lee's debacle unfolded as follows. When both wings of the Union cavalry departed on their serpentine movements, a large body of Federal infantry marched out from their camps on July 27, to provide both a diversion for the Union horsemen as well as test the Rebel infantry in that sector. Vigilant cavalry scouts alerted on the movement and Hood ordered S.D. Lee, just recently assigned from Mississippi to command Hood's old corps, to quickly shift his men forward to the strategic crossroads at Ezra Church and from there to look for an opportunity to crush any exposed column of the enemy infantry.

Hood envisioned that there might be a good chance to punch the Federals a significant blow, since they would be strung out on their march and could be caught out in the open. It was not to be. Unbeknownst to Hood or S.D. Lee, the Union troops had already seized Ezra Church and it was the entire Federal Army of the Tennessee that had maneuvered out across the ground, not just a single division. With most of the Confederate riders rapidly gathering to the south to thwart the Union cavalry raids, S.D. Lee had little reliable intelligence of enemy dispositions and was never fully aware of what really faced him. In any event, Lee was

desirous to prove himself in his new posting and disregarding at least the spirit of his instructions, he precipitously initiated a series of vicious, yet piecemeal assaults against what he assumed to be inferior numbers of enemy infantry. The bloody charges at Ezra Church cost almost 3,000 Confederate casualties with only 600 lost on the Federal side of the equation, the third major defeat for Hood's army. The only strategic achievement in the bloodletting was a temporary halt of the Army of the Tennessee's shift to the west, as Sherman decided to suspend all operations and wait for word on his cavalry's successes below Atlanta.

Ferguson arrived that evening shortly after the slaughter at Ezra Church ended. "I recall going to the tent of General S.D. Lee that night," Ferguson wrote, "and the agony he endured on account of the slaughter of his men that day."[678] Ferguson remained with S.D. Lee's corps the next day, until new orders on July 29, directed him to expeditiously turn his troopers south to assist in pursuing McCook's blue cavalry who were now hastily retreating from Lovejoy's Station and trying to reach the Chattahoochee.[679] In fact, when McCook left Lovejoy's Station at around 2:00 p.m. that day, Ferguson was headed south to join the swarm of angry Rebel's hunting him down. While Ross hit McCook hard at Fayetteville, other elements of cavalry under Red Jackson, Wheeler, and Ferguson also surged on the prey with running gun battles erupting well into the evening and early morning hours. At daylight, McCook managed to slip away at Newnan, although the thoroughly worn-out blue troopers would not be so lucky when cornered at Brown's Mill. The Yankees frantically attempted to break through the screaming Confederates to their front by means of some old-styled cavalry charges accompanied by spirited saber slashing and stabbing, and for a moment almost succeeded, before being beaten back with heavy losses. After McCook saw that he was hopelessly surrounded and cut-off, he wisely ordered his men to scatter in small groups and head to the Chattahoochee as best they could. In this way General McCook and the bulk of his troopers escaped, but well over 600 of them did not.

When the Union cavalry expedition was over, the combined Federal losses between Stoneman and McCook amounted to quite a

boon for the Rebels. Almost as precious as the victories themselves, the infusion of new arms, cavalry equipment, and fresh mounts provided a much-needed improvement in both the physical and mental well-being of the Confederate horsemen. The tally was truly staggering, it was Christmas morning in July! Official reports regarding Stoneman claimed:

> Three thousand two hundred prisoners [the number was actually about 2,000], including one major-general and five brigade commanders ... over four thousand horses, equipments and arms ... two batteries, two hundred pack-mules, their wagon train and several stands of colors.[680]

That McCook and Stoneman were so badly chewed up by the far smaller and irregularly armed Rebel cavalry did not greatly surprise Sherman, on the contrary, it simply confirmed his previous views. As punishment, he ordered most of the returning horsemen to dismount and fill the trenches to the front of Atlanta.

The only other Union cavalry commander that remained to be tested was Hugh Judson Kilpatrick, an insignificant looking man with reddish hair and a penchant for consorting with concubines he regularly carried along as his entourage.[681] Major Connolly on Sherman's staff famously described him as looking "like a monkey on horseback"[682] and his own men called him "Kill-Cavalry" Kilpatrick, for his reckless tactics that got many of them killed. Still recovering from wounds received in the opening days of the Atlanta campaign, Sherman also held Kilpatrick in low esteem referring to the twenty-eight-year-old as a braggart and "a damn fool,"[683] even though he clearly identified with him on a subliminal level, as both shared in the same vision of ruthlessly terrorizing Southern civilians.[684] Curiously, when posing for the camera, Sherman, Kilpatrick, and Colonel Spencer (1st Alabama Cavalry Union) shared the habit of arrogantly putting their right hand into their military overcoats at the stomach level, imagining themselves like the emperor Napoleon.

— Atlanta's End —

Already inherently prone to nervous outbursts, the news of the terrible mauling given to his 10,000-man cavalry momentarily stunned Sherman who was not quite sure what to do next. Indeed, both Grant in Virginia and now Sherman in Georgia were stymied and the autumn elections of 1864 loomed over Lincoln like the shadow of a jungle canopy. The people of the United States were tired and anxious for an end to the killing, one way or the other they just wanted peace.

Sherman decided to extend his infantry around the entire upper half of the city and, just like Vicksburg in July 1863, use his powerful artillery to pummel Atlanta into a surrender. Ignoring Article 18 of the Lieber Code, which required that Sherman first inform the enemy of his intent to bombard "so that the noncombatants, and especially the women and children, may be removed,"[685] the demented commander rolled his cannons up and began an indiscriminate bombardment. With 20-pounder Parrotts lobbing a shell every fifteen minutes, the city was scented with the presence of death so that the 4,000 civilians were not only forced to endure hours of confinement in crudely dug bunkers, but also the foulest of odors from the unburied dead animals and the occasional human body which emerged from rain-soaked graves. After being thwarted in three bloody battles, Hood's army also settled back into bombproofs built within the inner fortifications. Nevertheless, large Confederate flags still flew defiantly over Atlanta.

After a week of pelting the city with bombs, Sherman grew even more restless and ordered his infantry to try again to get at the Macon & Western by going further around to the west of Atlanta. With Confederate cavalry well posted, Hood was immediately informed of the new thrust and the Confederates were able to rapidly extend their trenches stretching an additional perimeter all the way to the south fork of Utoy Creek and then down to a mile or so below East Point. Expert at digging, the Rebels were ready and waiting when Sherman ordered repeated attacks against them.

Major General Hugh Judson Kilpatrick.

By the time the smoke cleared, the Union loss was 1,000 and the Confederates about 200.

It was now August 7, and the Federals once again fell back to their original encampments while Sherman employed the Union artillery with a renewed gusto, even bringing in heavy siege cannon from Chattanooga to further terrorize the population. He flippantly told General Howard, who had replaced the fallen McPherson, "Let us destroy Atlanta and make it a desolation."[686] Shells and their exploding fragments, called "blue-whistlers," now fell down like rain, sometimes at the astonishing rate of sixty per minute. Every home was damaged and scores of civilians killed or maimed.

In addition, sniping between the opposing armies made life very problematic for all concerned. The front lines on both sides

Porter House. Typical Result of Sherman's Bombardment. Photo by George N. Barnard.

boasted deep trenches equipped with steps and logs, in some spots a mere 300 yards apart. Anything exposed was shot all to pieces and field hospitals were rapidly filled with horribly wounded men hit predominately in the head and upper torso.

The stalemate was real even though Hood's front-line infantry and artillery was down to just 33,000[687] and replacements were nowhere to be had. In fact, the Confederates had lost over 12,000 in dead, wounded, or missing under Hood's short tenure.[688] By comparison, Sherman's losses since July had reached around 15,000, to include desertions and some due to expiration of their terms of service. Still, Sherman had a tremendous advantage with well over 85,000 well supplied men at his disposal and the ability to easily replace the losses.

Hood understood that he could not come out of the city to attack and that Sherman could not get into the city to dislodge him. Hood also understood that Sherman would keep trying to cut the Western & Atlantic below Atlanta. His foolish solution to the stalemate was to send out Wheeler and his 3,000 troopers to get behind Sherman

to do as much damage as possible to the Union's supply railroad, striking even into Tennessee. The time for that move had long since passed and Hood only further weakened his already anemic army.

It was August 11, 1864, when Wheeler departed Atlanta. It would be almost two months later before the much depleted cavalry command returned, entirely unsuccessful in its mission. By the time the gray cavalry linked up to the remnants of Hood's army at Cedartown (about 40 miles west of Marietta) on October 8, Atlanta had long since fallen.

With Wheeler's departure, Red Jackson's cavalry division remained to take up the slack, perhaps 1,800 effectives at best.[689] Ferguson, still technically assigned to Wheeler, was also left behind at Atlanta reflecting the fact that Wheeler had adopted Red Jackson's unwarranted prejudices. Wheeler childishly wrote:

> General Ferguson was insubordinate as a cadet, insubordinate as a lieutenant in the U.S. Army, and insubordinate as a brigadier under General [Red] Jackson.[690]

Desperately low on ground forces, much of Red Jackson's horsemen were dismounted and employed to supplement the Confederate infantry in the barricades and trenches around Atlanta. To be sure, Hood never seemed to grasp the real importance of cavalry, although at this point there was not much he could do even if he had. Only Ferguson's brigade was used to scout about on horseback outside the northern perimeter.[691] Sul Ross' small brigade was kept mounted as well and tasked as a ready reserve force to deal with everything else that might come up.

For his part, Sherman was absolutely delighted when he learned of Wheeler's precipitous departure. Even though the Yankee general sensed that his infantry would have to eventually perform the necessary task of taking Atlanta, if Hood was sending his primary cavalry general off, then Sherman would send his superior in number

blue cavalry out to take another shot at the Macon & Western. He gave the mission to the newly returned General Kilpatrick who proposed to hit the closer Jonesborough (later renamed Jonesboro) rail junction about 20 miles south of Atlanta as the main objective for destruction. Gathering his horsemen at Sandtown, Kilpatrick bragged that he could break 20 miles of rail.

In preparation for Kilpatrick's raid, demonstrations picked up in the no man's land between Decatur and Atlanta making it so hot that on August 16, Ferguson's men were forced to retreat inside the fortifications of Atlanta, only to bounce back the next day moving to scout as far east as Decatur.[692] The Rebels knew that something big was brewing and Kilpatrick ended the guessing game at sundown on August 18, when he rode out with 4,700 troopers and eight pieces of artillery.

As he had done with McCook, Sul Ross's 400-man cavalry brigade of Texans immediately responded and worked courageously to slow the Federals down while Hood guessed at where the Yankees were going to land along the Macon & Western. Ferguson's brigade was ordered to proceed to the small depot of Rough & Ready which also sat on the railroad about 13 miles south of Atlanta. Soon thereafter, Red Jackson pulled his troopers out of the trenches to saddle up and head south while Hood crammed a brigade of infantry onto trains and ran them down to Jonesboro.[693]

Hood's guess about Jonesboro was correct. As was often the case, however, miscommunications diverted the infantry train so that it passed straight through Jonesboro and on to Lovejoy's Station, another six miles down the track, where it ran into Armstrong's Confederate cavalry brigade which had just ridden out of their camps at Jonesboro to Lovejoy's Station! Apparently, both infantry and cavalry were deceived by a decoy regiment of Yankee riders that Kilpatrick had cleverly rushed out ahead of his main body to tear up some track near Lovejoy's Station.

Ferguson soon discovered Kilpatrick's true movement to Jonesboro and managed to join Ross to skirmish with the Federal rear, as the main body of blue bellies entered the place late on

August 19. Despite a heavy downpour which intensified into the night, the Yankee cavalry was able to pry up rails for about half a mile, burn the depot, and destroy a train. Ignoring the Jonesboro mayor who came out with a white flag to plea for fair treatment, those not assigned to destroying track fell upon the town, looting the hotels and houses of food and alcohol before setting everything on fire. The city of Jonesboro which was spread out along both sides of the tracks burned in the night to boisterous cheers and shouts accompanied by a mounted band which played "Yankee Doodle," and "The Star-Spangled Banner." But the malicious alcohol filled "fun" would soon turn to hard fighting.

Once it was established that Kilpatrick was at Jonesboro, the trains carrying the Confederate infantry commanded by the capable General Daniel Reynolds reversed and rushed backwards reaching the outskirts just after dark. Greeted by flames which lit up the night, Reynolds disembarked his regiments just south of the town and moved them forward in battle formation, skirmishers out front. First contact with the Federals came in the form of a murderous blast of gunfire aimed at the silhouettes of the unsuspecting men of the 10th Ohio.

What followed for the next five hours was a wild night of fighting between the blue dismounted cavalry and the gray infantry supported by Ferguson and Ross. Cognizant of the fate of his brethren McCook and Stoneman, Kilpatrick elected to stay dismounted and stay put. For one thing, he knew that without Wheeler to worry about that the Rebel cavalry he faced were no match for his robust numbers and he could also easily mount up and leave any Rebel infantry in the dust. For another, the ridiculous general sorely wanted to impress Sherman that he could accomplish the assigned mission of disabling the railroad when no one else could. So, as part of his dismounted troopers shot it out with Reynolds, the other part continued to tear up train track until the unmistakable wail of locomotive whistles coming from the north convinced Kilpatrick that he best ride away

However, instead of heading to the safety of Union lines, Kilpatrick thought to swing his column straight out to the east and then cut down to Lovejoy's Station, six miles to the south. At about 2:00 a.m., the Yankee general began pulling his mounted troopers out of Jonesboro. Positioning a strong rear guard behind a barricade of fences and timber to the south of town to keep up a steady fire with repeating rifles, by dawn of August 20, the last of the Yankee cavalrymen mounted up and rode away.

Division commander Red Jackson would later express great frustration that Kilpatrick had been able to escape in such a manner. Indeed, Jackson had devised an extremely ambitious trap which called for all three cavalry brigades, perhaps 1,800 effectives in total, and Reynolds' single infantry brigade to snare Kilpatrick's 4,300 men. The plan called for Armstrong to cover the southern entrance to Jonesboro, Ferguson to come in from the east, and Ross to come in from the west of Jonesboro. If Kilpatrick attempted to leave in the night, then the Confederate cavalry would hold him in place until Reynolds could rush forward and finish him off.

Of course, the plan had far too many moving parts to ensure a high probability of success. Not only did the night rains aggravate things tremendously, but all three cavalry brigades were moving about in the dark and relying on dumb luck as much as anything else to direct them to their proper staging areas.

Slogging out of Jonesboro, the Yankee cavalry moved in the dark due east towards the McDonough Road intending to later turn back towards Lovejoy's Station to destroy that place and then head to the safety of the left wing of the Federal army. Interestingly, the night march should have run the thousands of saddle-sore Federals smack into Ferguson's brigade — Red Jackson had ordered Ferguson to set up for the ambush about "a mile and a half or two miles east of Jonesboro."[694] Somehow, Ferguson was not there to confront the enemy when Kilpatrick's troopers marched past. In the darkness and continuing rain Ferguson had apparently taken the wrong road,[695] though Red Jackson would later falsely fume that Ferguson got drunk and halted his command.[696]

In any event, when the Confederates discovered in the morning that Kilpatrick had slipped away, Red Jackson initiated an immediate pursuit playing on a hunch that Kilpatrick was heading for Lovejoy's Station. For a second time Jackson attempted to trap Kilpatrick between converging bodies of Confederates. General Reynolds took his infantry back to where the tracks were intact and commandeered the first available train to Lovejoy's Station while Red Jackson gathered the rest of the Rebel cavalry and followed after Kilpatrick's column, sending Ross' brigade to the east of Lovejoy's Station. Only Ferguson was absent in the pursuit, having been ordered to proceed north to Rough & Ready, just in case Kilpatrick should move there and not to Lovejoy's Station.

Red Jackson was right in his initial guess. When Kilpatrick arrived at Lovejoy's Station around 11 a.m. on a hot August 20, Rebel cavalry were soon thereafter upon him. Winded riders altered Ferguson to immediately move to help close the trap and he rode fast arriving in time to join Jackson's men who were heavily skirmishing with Union cavalry pickets to the north, a troubling development that was relayed back to Kilpatrick.

For his part, Reynold's infantry along with a six-gun battery, were formed up and waiting in the town so that they smartly engaged the lead elements of Kilpatrick's men as they arrived. With Red Jackson and Ferguson pressing the Yankees hard from the north and west and Reynolds dug in to the south, Ross's 400 Confederates were arrayed as blocking force behind a large corn field on the nearby Nash Farm to the east. To bolster Ross, portions of Ferguson's brigade soon joined him, along with some regular infantry and State troops.[697]

The sudden appearance of so many Confederates on all sides spooked Kilpatrick who later exaggerated that he was facing 5,000 Rebel cavalry to his front and 10,000 of Patrick Cleburne's infantry to his rear. With visions of Andersonville racing through his mind, Kilpatrick imagined himself in a dire predicament — his only chance was to break out. Around 2 p.m., Kilpatrick ordered Colonel H.G. Minty to make a mounted charge to open a hole at the

weakest sector, which was to the east. Led by Minty, 1,200 mounted Federals lined up, drew sabers, and charged forward, decimating the primarily dismounted Rebels and allowing Kilpatrick to extract the rest of his command through the pathway and race back to the safety of Decatur. A tremendous rain that began around 4 p.m. and lasted until 4 a.m. helped ward off any pursuit, but also required the Yankees to discard most of their wagons and artillery.

Like Stoneman and McCook before him, the Kilpatrick raid was a failure. The Yankees had burned and looted much civilian property with little damage done to the military infrastructure or the railroad. Oblivious to his mediocre accomplishments, on August 22, Kilpatrick imperiously returned to his base camp riding in a stolen carriage loaded down with plundered silver and artwork. Confronted with a casualty list of over 300 killed, wounded, and missing, Kilpatrick had no problem bragging to Sherman that his troopers had destroyed enough of the Confederate railroad to disable it for ten days. Ironically, Kilpatrick's glowing report on his fantastic success was barely communicated before the Federal signal corps around Atlanta noted the far-off sound of whistles and the unmistakable plumes of locomotive smoke coming from an eleven-car train pulling into Atlanta on the morning of August 23. In less than two days the Confederates had repaired the Macon & Western. Ferguson with the 2nd Alabama was soon back patrolling the Decatur sector, taking their fair share of the Yankee equipment that Kilpatrick's men had abandoned.

— The Final Blow —

Frustrated with another failure, Sherman's next move was the one he had long contemplated and should have employed a month ago — completely disengage from Atlanta's front and make a grand sweep with his massive infantry force to the west and simply overrun the Macon & Western at multiple points below the city. Like Kilpatrick, Sherman decided that his primary target would be Jonesboro.

On August 25, the indiscriminate shelling of Atlanta abruptly stopped and civilians cautiously emerged from their bombproofs to see what it might mean. The next day, cavalry scouts reported that significant sections of the Union trenches had gone empty, only to the far north of the city did they find Henry Slocum's Twentieth Corps still in place protecting the incoming rail-line and attendant bridges.

The Yankee guns had fallen silent. Hood was not deceived. Having experienced Sherman's predilection for flanking moves, the Confederate general suspected more of the same and entertained no illusions that Sherman had given up and retreated. Red Jackson's troopers went out to find the disappearing Sherman and Hood simultaneously readied two of his three infantry corps so that a rapid concentration could be launched once Sherman was located. By August 28, a large body of Federal infantry reached the Atlanta & West Point spur some nine miles below East Point and began tearing it up. All doubt was now cast aside, Sherman was surely coming for the Macon & Western. Per usual, the only question was where along the line would his main force hit — Rough & Ready, Jonesboro, or Lovejoy's Station?

By August 29, Sherman himself was astride the railroad at Fairburn, enjoying the sight of his troops piling rails over blazing bonfires to then twist them around trees and telegraph poles, the so-called "Sherman's neckties." The next day, six Union army corps converged on Jonesboro and Hood raced out two infantry corps, Hardee and S.D. Lee, to stop them. The footsore Confederates arrived on the late night of August 30, and on into the early morning of August 31. Ferguson's brigade was left at East Port to help ward off any trouble and keep communications open between Hood, still headquartered in Atlanta, and Hardee and Lee.

For the first day the Confederates fanatically hurled themselves against strong Federal defenses accomplishing nothing and suffering over a thousand casualties. The second day saw Union troops counterattack a badly battered opponent forcing the Confederates

to fall back six miles under cover of darkness to Lovejoy's Station where they immediately entrenched.

Atlanta was now completely cut off and isolated. If Hood was to save the remainder of his army still there — Stewart's corps and the Georgia militia — he would have to abandon the city, and do it quickly. The problem, of course, was that between Hood's two shattered corps at Lovejoy's Station and Atlanta sat Sherman's huge and now thoroughly energized army. The only hope for Hood was to sneak them out of the city at night and then to carefully swing wide enough to bypass Sherman in order to reunite with the bulk of the army at Lovejoy's Station.

To cover the evacuation, Ferguson's undersized cavalry brigade was ordered to dismount and stretch out along the front-line fortifications to the north of Atlanta pretending to be infantry. Should the Federals send out a probe or launch an attack during the withdrawal, it was up to Ferguson's men to stalemate them. Ferguson was also ordered "to destroy the munitions and military stores that could not be removed" once the infantry soldiers "were fairly clear of the city."[698]

Since the Macon & Western was cut now in at least three places — Rough & Ready, Jonesboro, and an open spot halfway between the two — much government property had to be destroyed or simply given away to the remaining civilians in the city. The government warehouses were opened and bacon, clothing, blankets, flour, leather goods, and other items were eagerly carried off by a hungry population that did not know what was to befall them.

Around 5 p.m., on September 1, 1864, Hood ordered Stewart's corps and the Georgia militia to depart and to his great relief a less than alert enemy sat on their hands so that by 11 p.m. the very last of the foot soldiers had shuffled out of Atlanta's backdoor to the southeast, leaving Ferguson's troopers eerily alone.[699] An hour later, around midnight, huge thundering explosions lit up the night sky as munition stockpiles in the city were destroyed by

special engineer demolition details directly assisted by squads of cavalrymen. The rolling blasts consumed all to include 5,000 brand new infantry rifles and 3 million rolled paper cartridges stored at the Atlanta arsenal. Particularly galling was the loss of eighty-one boxcars containing Hood's reserve ordnance and five locomotives, all left stranded on the tracks, twenty-eight of them crammed with ammunition. As men of the 2nd Alabama helped set the charges at various locations throughout the city, others stood firm in the darkened trenches feeling the ground literally shake beneath their feet, signaling to every human being within 50 miles that the city was certainly being abandoned. The fantastic explosions that flamed high into the night sky flattened a nearby factory and left the remaining civilians in great amazement:

> The very earth trembled as if in the throes of a mighty earthquake. The houses rocked like cradles, and on every hand was heard the shattering of window glass and the fall of plastering and loose bricks. Thousands of people flocked to high places and watched with breathless excitement the volcanic scene on the Georgia Railroad.[700]

Ferguson was also amazed. His wonderment, however, was not about the explosions which he had expertly orchestrated, but over the fact that there were no Union movements of any kind against his forward positions as the demolition teams went about their work. Even after the earth-shattering events ceased, no Yankees appeared to reconnoiter. Ferguson later reflected with great satisfaction that his small force was eminently successful in their assigned mission to both demonstrate and then to destroy the abandoned military property, allowing Hood to pull off a complete evacuation of Atlanta, marching his men unmolested all the way to Lovejoy's Station.

> I was sent into the trenches [on September 1, 1864] to prevent the movement being discovered any sooner than possible. I did not really expect to remain in

*Hood's Destroyed Ordnance Cars in Atlanta.
Photo by George N. Barnard.*

them more than two or three hours for hardly had night set in when the bursting shells and explosion of ammunition of all kinds must have let the enemy know what was on foot, and what could a cavalry brigade with one fourth the men holding horses, accomplish against Sherman's Army? The night was simply infernal, the explosions were incessant and appalling.[701]

Finally, on the early morning of September 2, Union soldiers north of Atlanta began a strong yet cautious advance towards the outer fortifications. Seeing several hundred blue skirmishers making their way through the thick Georgia clay, Ferguson wisely pulled back his forward troopers into the city proper taking new positions behind hastily thrown up wooden barricades along Marietta Street, a move that greatly distressed Mayor James Calhoun who unsuccessfully pleaded with Ferguson to leave the city and spare any fur-

ther bloodshed.[702] It was not until 10 a.m. that Ferguson formally informed Mayor Calhoun that his men were departing. Calhoun immediately formed up a group of local citizens, to include a black Southerner, and rode out under a flag of truce where he surrendered to the first Federal officer he encountered.

To continue the deception as long as possible, General Ferguson's order to evacuate was communicated to his men verbally and not by bugle calls so that the troopers departed by groups, trotting their horses through the city streets heading east on the Decatur road. The chaos of the night before quickly gave way to an atmosphere of total anarchy as scoundrels of every description began to loot whatever and wherever they wished. To note that the temptation to grab personal property was contagious would be an understatement and not a few of Ferguson's men joined in by snatching up tobacco, bottles of liquor, or other items of fancy. Ferguson recalled the pandemonium on that last morning.

> Daylight came still no signs of the enemy. Finally after sunrise they appeared in three lines of battle. I called my men in from the trenches and advised the Mayor of the City to go out with a flag of truce and surrender the City, telling him he could assure the Federal general that there would not be any firing in the streets[703].... While riding out I saw the women who had broken into the warehouses of quarter master and commissary supplies, rolling barrels and carrying off supplies. This was all right but soon they began to break into private stores and what furies they proved as they warmed up to the work. I have now a much clearer conception of the women of Paris during the reign of terror.[704]

Some members of Ferguson's command took their general withdrawal more slowly than others, roaming about downtown, even as more and more triumphant Federals moved into the city.

One resident recalled seeing a sizable squadron of about "75 to 100 Confederate cavalrymen aligned at the public square, under an officers' command and ready for action ... seeking one last shot at the Yankee's coming down Marietta Street."[705] Another saw a band of Ferguson's cavalrymen taking cover behind "the granite columns of the Norcross building at Marietta and Peachtree"[706] also firing towards the Federals. While some of the troopers remained mounted and popped off their pistols before galloping away, it was only bravado and soon thereafter the remaining horse soldiers rode off in good order, the last of them directing their mounts onto the Car Shed Depots' wooden floor so that the "buckety buckety" sound of the horses hooves played a final "taps" for the doomed city. So it was that the 2nd Alabama Cavalry were the very last Confederate troops to exit Atlanta. By noon, the Union flag was raised over the city center.

Ferguson looped around to the south taking the McDonough Road where he made his way to join Red Jackson's cavalry picketed around Lovejoy's Station with Hood's army. The sights that greeted him on his twenty-plus mile journey spoke of a broken army, something that had never been the case under General Johnston's tactical retreats. Ferguson also had the opportunity to set fire to a final large train of cars left stranded on the tracks and filled with Confederate ammunition.

> When I reached [the road to] Decatur I found a large train of ammunition abandoned there. I had no means of moving it so set it on fire and continued my march to the sounds of exploding ammunition. The road in rear of our army [Hood's retreat from Atlanta to Lovejoy's Station] now presented a different sight from that to which I had been accustomed from Kingston to the Chattahoochee River. In all that distance I had brought up the rear on one of the main roads over which the Army had retreated, yet never

encountered a broken or abandoned wagon. Now the road was strewn with wrecks of all kinds.[707]

The fall of Atlanta was the death knell for the Confederacy. The months long battle had finally ended and Sherman's victory directly paved the way for Lincoln's reelection in November 1864, making it certain (absent a miracle) that it was no longer a question of if the Confederacy would be defeated, but when it would be defeated.

As part of Ferguson's brigade, from May 18, 1864, to September 2, 1864, the 2nd Alabama Cavalry participated in the following combat actions across the State of Georgia leading up to the surrender of Atlanta on September 2, 1864:

(1) Combat, near Kingston .... May 18-19, 1864

(2) Skirmish, Cassville .... May 22, 1864

(3) Combat, New Hope Church .... May 25, 1864

(4) Combat, Dallas .... May 26 - June 1, 1864

(5) Skirmish, Stilesborough .... June 9-10, 1864

(6) Combat, Brush Mountain .... June 15-17, 1864

(7) Combat, Powder Springs .... June 20, 1864

(8) Combat, Lattimer's Mills .... June 20, 1864

(9) Combat, Nickajack Creek .... July 2 to 5, 1864

(10) Combat, Ruff's Station .... July 4, 1864

(11) Combat, Smyrna Camp Grounds ..... July 4, 1864

(12) Combat, Chattahoochee River .... July 5-17, 1864

(13) Combat, Bald Hill .... July 20-21, 1864

(14) Combat, Decatur .... July 22, 1864

(15) Skirmish, Brown's Mill .... July 30, 1864

(14) Skirmish, Sandtown .... August 15, 1864

(15) Skirmish, Fairburn .... August 15, 1864

(16) Skirmish, Kilpatrick's Raid .... August 16-22, 1864

(17) Combat, Jonesboro .... August 19, 1864

(18) Combat, Lovejoy's Station .... August 20, 1864

(19) Skirmish, Atlanta .... 1-2 September, 1864 [708]

Chapter Eight

Terror March to the Sea

"To realize what war is, one should follow our tracks."[709] —William T. Sherman

WITH THE FALL OF ATLANTA, both armies spent the first part of September catching their breath. Having successfully reunited what remained of his forces at Lovejoy's Station, Hood shifted his shattered army to Palmetto about twenty-five miles southwest of Atlanta. Sherman did not challenge or go after Hood, content to pull his entire force back up to Atlanta to spread out like a nesting bird of prey stretching from Decatur to Marietta.

Sherman chose the grandest remaining house in Atlanta for his personal residence, expelling all the remaining civilians from their homes with a ten-day truce in order to send them as refugees south to Rough & Ready, ignoring Hood's strongly worded protest regarding the cruelty of the act. From September 12 to 27, a total of 709 white adults, most of them women, 867 children, and 79 enslaved people (Southern blacks who refused offers of liberation) were forced out of their houses with almost nothing except the clothes on their backs. Once in friendly territory, some of the refugees found shelter where they could, with most transported to Macon.

After acquiring much needed supplies, Hood met personally with President Davis who arrived at Palmetto on September 25. Davis reviewed the 35,000 troops and although he gave them a pep talk which included a strong promise that they would soon be "turned homeward and your feet pressing the soil of Tennessee," he was greeted by disheartening shouts from the threadbare ranks of, "Give us Johnston!" "Give us our old Commander!"[710]

Typical for Jeff Davis, who seemed impervious to good advice, he flatly refused to relieve Hood and instead listened approvingly to the crippled general's fanciful plan to go on the offensive, marching his army to the north of Atlanta to attack the Federal's attenuated supply line and draw Sherman's army out for a fight. In addition, the dour faced general specifically promised Davis that he would most certainly attack if the Yankee general should turn east into Georgia's interior. In short, Davis was told exactly what he wanted to hear and so he quickly agreed, only ordering the transfer of a disgruntled General Hardee to Charleston to take charge of the Department of South Carolina, Georgia, and Florida.

Flushed with the backing of Davis, Hood set about on a cat and mouse game with Sherman, maneuvering his army westward around Atlanta heading north, just out of reach of the enemy. Screened by Ferguson and Red Jackson, Hood easily crossed the Chattahoochee River eying Marietta as his first stop. With his own single rail-line threatened, Sherman had no choice except to pursue and as Hood correctly predicted sallied out after the Confederates with the bulk of his army. For the next two weeks Sherman chased the Rebels ever northward, generally along the same Western & Atlantic that the Yankees had fought their way down just a couple months ago. In the process of a full 50-mile trek, Sherman was unable to stop Hood's infantry as it struck numerous isolated Federal strong points and destroyed miles of rail hindering Union supply trains coming from Chattanooga to Atlanta. Sherman was greatly relieved, however, as he watched Hood soulfully leave the rail-line and shift his army west into Alabama. With his logistics no longer threatened, Sherman tired of the pursuit and dispatched

extra troops to General Thomas in Tennessee, to include all his cavalry divisions except for Kilpatrick, and returned to the Atlanta area to wait for final permission from Grant to execute his nefarious march of terror through Georgia.

On October 8, after an absence of two months, Wheeler finally returned to Hood, albeit in terrible shape. His horsemen were thoroughly fatigued and the horses broken down after the less than fruitful raid into Tennessee. By the middle of October 1864, Hood arrived at Gaylesville, Alabama, where he then embarked on a disastrous path that would devastate the once proud Army of Tennessee at the costly "victory" at Franklin and then obliterate his army at Nashville that December.[711] However, recalling his pledge to Davis about protecting the Georgia interior, Hood ordered Wheeler who was then off on a raid near La Fayette, to proceed back to Jonesboro.[712] Of course, Hood only agreed to give up Wheeler because he got Nathan Bedford Forrest's cavalry in exchange, plus he kept Red Jackson's troopers as well. Ferguson also went with Wheeler and his command was formally assigned on October 25, 1864, to Brigadier General Alfred Iverson's Division, Wheeler's Cavalry Corps. At the time, Ferguson's brigade consisted of the 2nd Alabama Cavalry; 56th Alabama Cavalry; 9th Mississippi Cavalry; 11th Mississippi Cavalry; and 12th Mississippi Cavalry.[713]

Because Ferguson had remained embedded with Hood's infantry and not with Wheeler who was absent on his latest raid, he was temporarily placed in charge of a division of cavalry, consisting of his brigade and two others. Before Ferguson headed to Jonesboro as ordered, he was obliged to investigate reports of a nearby Federal cavalry raid by a portion of Kilpatrick's division, to include the hated 1st Alabama Union, the Tory regiment Ferguson had soundly vanquished exactly one year ago at Vincents Crossroads. On October 28, Ferguson formed up his division at Terrapin Creek, about a mile north of Ladiga, Alabama, facing off against 1,500 Federals under the command of General Kenner Garrard. Starting at 10 a.m. and continuing for several hours, Ferguson's brigade carried the fight to the enemy sweeping the Yankees entirely off the field (the other two Rebel brigades saw no action that day). Ferguson noted with great

satisfaction that the victory resulted in the 1st Alabama Union being completely whipped and routed in confusion along the road leading to Rome, Georgia. Ferguson's losses were three privates and one officer, Lieutenant William H. Harris, of G Troop, 2nd Alabama, who died of his wounds four days later. The loss to the Federals were 25 killed and wounded and an elegant new stand of colors. This fight was the last engagement between Hood and members of Sherman's command and shortly thereafter Ferguson turned his horsemen to Jonesboro.

Able to reach Jonesboro long before Wheeler, who did not arrive until November 13, Ferguson recalled his final parting from Hood's army as well as the regrettable fact that fellow soldiers would often steal from one another when opportunity arose.[714]

> I accompanied him [Hood] to the Coosa River [a tributary of the Alabama River]. The night of our arrival there I slept in the tent of Lieutenant General S.D. Lee. He pulled off his boots and placed them by his feet. I placed mine by my head. In the morning, his were gone and mine were safe. I had a joke on him .... The next morning [October 26] I was ordered to turn back and command all the cavalry in Georgia until General Wheeler, then on a raid [at La Fayette] should return.[715]

— The Mythology of Sherman the Great —

The savagery and brutality visited on the South by Sherman and his hordes has never fully been admitted. Concentrated once more around Atlanta with a reopened rail-line, Sherman's soldiers were now poised to plunder and terrorize on a scale heretofore unseen on American soil in the March to the Sea. Disturbingly for truth-seekers, what are taken as unassailable facts — about the brave and brilliant William Tecumseh Sherman who dared go deep into enemy territory, cut off from friendly communications, and facing

Major General William T. Sherman.

destruction and ruin at any moment, all the while forced to "live off the land" — are all blatant fabrications. The truth is the antithesis.

First, there was no Confederate army to fight Sherman, Hood had long since moved into Tennessee and abandoned the State of Georgia. Only General Wheeler's small cavalry command supplemented by Ferguson's semi-independent brigade and the over-age men and under-age boys of the Georgia militia were there to at best harass the flanks of the Federal juggernaut. In other words, they were no match for 65,000 handpicked Yankees with 65 cannons, each drawn by eight-horse teams, bullying their way to the Atlantic Ocean. Badly outnumbered, cut off from infantry support, indifferently armed, without government rations, and in

very poor condition, it is a wonder that these handful of courageous Southern cavalrymen even dared to engage the Yankees at all. In fact, General Sherman faced no significant military opposition until he reached North Carolina the next year where part of his army was caught by surprise at Bentonville in March 1865.

Second, as previously discussed in *Union Terror*, Sherman carried enough rations in his 2,500 newly built wagons to easily feed every man in his command for well over a month, more than enough time to reach the coast of Georgia. There was absolutely no need to "requisition" food stuffs from the local civilians with the exception of perhaps some additional grain for his 25,000 horses. The entire narrative of "living off the land" was simply a duplicitous cover for thievery and arson. With the overt and tacit approval of his superiors, Sherman systematically and shamefully used his army to "make war" on civilians. Houses were looted and burned, farm animals not taken by the Yankees were killed, and any farming or manufacturing tools destroyed. All done in the name of spite.

As a military commander, Sherman was at best only average. The most positive comments that can be made about Sherman's military abilities involve his unflappable tenacity and careful planning. Tenacity, of course, can do great things when juxtaposed with a tremendous military establishment at ones disposal, such as was furnished to him by the industrialized North. Per usual, Sherman's plan was broad in the main and very low risk — he would forcefully roll his huge army to the east causing as much devastation to the civilian population as possible. In this vein, the Union troops were spread out like a raging river widening its banks and consuming all in its path. It was not an army operating under the rule of law, but a lawless infestation, a plague of locusts.

The *modus operandi* was the same as it had been during the Meridian terror march. In most instances, the homeowner's fields were torched, and the homes, barns, and sheds, looted and burned to the ground. The hogs, chickens, cattle, horses, and mules were either taken without payment or, if they were surplus, killed on the

Period Sketch of Sherman's Looters.

spot and left to rot; even the pets to include birds, dogs, and cats were killed. Clothing and bedding were destroyed or confiscated, leaving the innocents with only the garments on their backs. In short, when the marauders departed, the sight that greeted the eye was pitiful beyond belief — silhouetted across the charred remains of their homes, mothers and children were left in tears, instantly impoverished and destitute of any food or shelter. In some cases, scenes of depredation presented things even more shocking to the conscience, with black Southern women often suffering the worst abuses to include sexual assault.

And so, the mythology of Sherman's brave and risky march across enemy territory is a blatant lie, unless, of course, one suggests that "fighting" innocent unarmed civilians equates to heroism.

— Sherman's Terror March Begins —

As November arrived, so did the cold weather. The days were sometimes bright and warm in central Georgia, yet the nights were shivering and stark.

Sherman began preparations for his march by first recalling all the Federal troops garrisoned in the surrounding towns around Atlanta. As these soldiers streamed back to Sherman, they were ordered to burn to the ground the places they had recently occupied and to tear up the railroad track. Starting on November 10, Rome, Kingston, Cartersville, and all the towns in between were sacked and torched to the great amusement of the Yankees. The landscape was thoroughly devastated and the people driven away from their homes for miles on every side with everything in the way of cattle, forage, or provisions destroyed.

Once all had congregated around Atlanta, the great moment arrived to move out. Sherman drew up a dry and duplicitous institutional Special Order Number 120, authorizing the army to "*forage liberally* on the country [emphasis added],"[716] a despicable euphemism for laying waste to everything and inflicting suffering, fear, and terror on civilians.

To set the unmistakable tone for how Sherman *really* expected his army to behave, the once beautiful Atlanta was subjected to a final indignation. Sherman burned it to the ground. From November 14 to 15, the soldiers went on a rampage of looting and wanton arson and between 4,000 and 5,000 private homes went up in smoke. Like Nero's glee over a burning of Rome, Sherman winked and the great city burned. The only bright note was that he had already forcibly evacuated the civilian population so they did not witness the final desolation of their homes.

Accompanying the Fourteenth Corps, the last Federal troops to leave Atlanta, Sherman delighted in the fires and the party atmosphere. Interestingly, when Sherman rode out with his staff, the movement was kicked off by a queer incident which revealed much

about General Sherman's mental state. Major Henry Hitchcock, a young staff officer and aide to General Sherman recorded the following:

> Fellow very drunk, sitting on ground as we [Hitchcock and Sherman] passed troops ... cursed General [Sherman] loudly ... General rode quietly by him, not 10 feet off — heard all — no notice.[717]

Then, when the command party entered Marietta, Major Hitchcock was shocked by the wholesale vandalism and burning of personal property and, even more disturbing, General Sherman's manifest indifference to the gross violations of his own "official" orders restricting such actions.[718] Hitchcock soon understood, however, that all this destruction and terror was just as Sherman intended, even if the commanding general disavowed any responsibility for the depredations. Sherman wanted a scorched earth and his men knew it. In the words of one American general officer: "The most important thing I [General Colin Powell] learned is that soldiers watch what their leaders do. You can give them classes and lecture them forever, but it is your personal example they will follow."[719]

By the time Wheeler arrived in Jonesboro on November 13, General Ferguson had already gathered a great deal of valuable intelligence from recently taken Union prisoners and some escaped Confederates. All confirmed that Sherman intended to move a significant portion of his troops into the interior of Georgia. Two days later, on November 15, Rebel scouts reported that a massive exodus of Union infantry and wagons were rumbling south on the McDonough road preceded by five thousand cavalry under Judson Kilpatrick. The Federal horsemen attacked Wheeler's weary men at and around Jonesboro sweeping them all back down the railway, first to the strongpoint of Lovejoy's Station (the Georgia militia also retreated), then to Bear Creek, and finally to Griffin where the fighting ceased. In textbook fashion, the Union cavalry had wonderfully shielded the opening movements of Sherman's

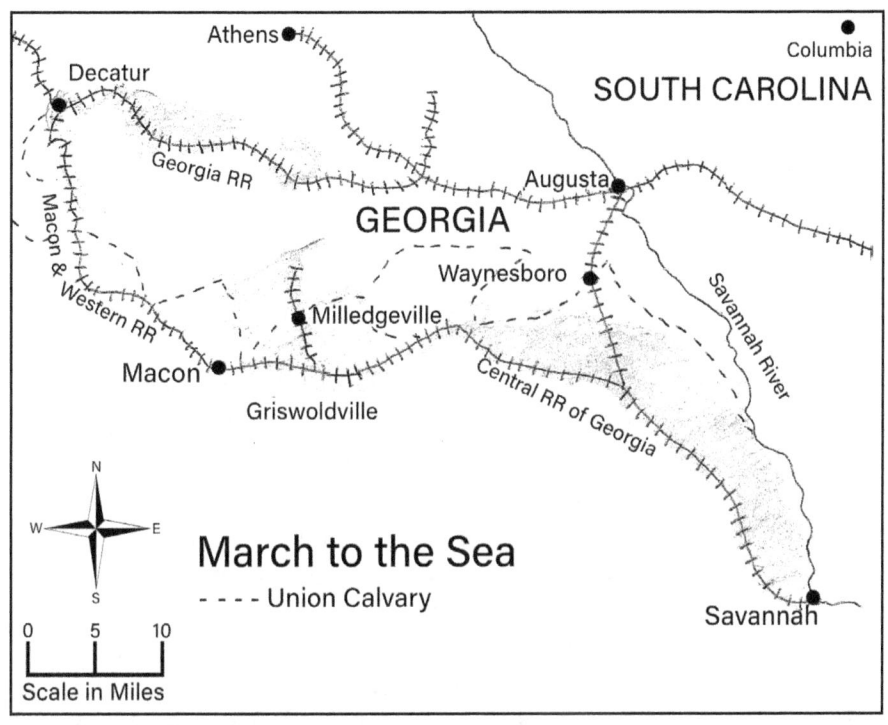

Sherman's March to Savannah.

move from Atlanta. Wheeler soon recovered his composure and on November 16, gave a very accurate assessment of Sherman's strength as "from sixty to seventy thousand"[720] in four corps arranged in two closely linked wings.

Sherman accompanied the left wing which was comprised of the Twentieth and Fourteenth Corps commanded by General Slocum. At first, most of the Federal cavalry traveled with the right wing, consisting of the Fifteenth and Seventeenth Corps, under General Howard, which was edging farther to the south toward Macon; later the cavalry shifted between and in front of the two wings as the need arose. By keeping the two wings in diverging directions — the right wing along the Macon railroad and the left wing east along the Augusta line — Sherman hoped to obscure the true nature of his movement which was the port city of Savannah where Federal ships could resupply his army.

Both bodies moved in a systematic manner under standard protocols, meandering more or less together while always keeping from 20 to 40 miles apart. Each wing would walk at a normal pace on and alongside the road making about 12 miles per day. While the widespread looting of civilian property made the over 2,500 fully stocked commissary wagons an unnecessary hindrance, the wagons were well guarded and located at or near the rear of each corps, 800 per corps. Each corps also carried along a 900ft section of pontoon bridges for river crossings. Finally, Sherman discouraged his commanders from allowing any enslaved people seeking their freedom to follow the army, only accepting able-bodied black Southerners to work in his pioneer battalions to help clear the roads.

General Hardee, stationed in Savannah, held temporary command of all Confederate troops in Georgia and along with other elements of the Confederate high command from General Hood (in Tuscumbia), to General Beauregard (on inspection tour in Mississippi), to General Cobb (in Macon), to General Richard Taylor (in Montgomery), to General Braxton Bragg (in Augusta), to Governor Brown of Georgia (in Milledgeville), the guessing game about Sherman's true objective began in earnest. Even Robert E. Lee in far off Virginia ordered Lieutenant General Taylor, son of the late President Zachary Taylor, to go to Georgia and prepare plans on how best to defend against Sherman. Regardless of where Sherman was ultimately heading — Lee at first suspected that Sherman would head straight to Richmond — all knew full well that he was no stranger to the use of terror and sadly understood that the Union army's march would be one of gross devastation. Wheeler's orders were to track the Federals, impede their movements, and keep them close to their columns in order to minimize, if possible, the swath of destruction.[721]

West Point, Miss., Nov. 20, 1864

General Wheeler:

General Hardee will for the present give orders for the defense of Georgia east of the Chattahoochee.

> My views are that positions should be defended only so long as not to risk safety of troops and materials required for active operations in the field. Meanwhile remove to safe locality all government property on line of enemy's march, and consume or destroy all supplies within his reach [emphasis added].
>
> P.G.T. Beauregard, General[722]

By November 19, Ferguson's cavalry and several thousand of the Georgia militia had consolidated at the important Confederate supply town of Macon to defend it at all costs. Wheeler sent another brigade of cavalry to help hold the place as well, while he personally directed his main focus to slowing the approaching Union infantry. That same day, elements of the two Rebel cavalry brigades accompanied by some regular infantry, probed out of Macon and engaged in sharp clashes with Kilpatrick's cavalry. But the danger to Macon had already passed. The enemy infantry skirted by just to the north of the city with the Federal horsemen soon following suit and headed to the nearby village of Griswoldville.

With Macon safe, Wheeler quickly recalled his detached brigade, stranding Ferguson's main force behind by request of Major General Howell Cobb, his superior at Macon. Ferguson recalled his frustration.

> At Macon I came across General Howell Cobb, who was my superior in rank and who, sorely against my will, kept me there idle for two or three days, fearing some detached force of the enemy might turn back from Sherman's column and burn the city.[723]

While Ferguson was held in Macon with a much depleted brigade of about 525 troopers,[724] Wheeler hit Kilpatrick's 5,000 horsemen at 2 a.m. on November 21, taking from 50 to 60 prisoners along with one hundred horses and arms[725] and 25 left "dead upon the field."[726] Unsure of the size of the Rebel cavalry, Kilpatrick hastened

out of the area under the cover of a light snowstorm. Nevertheless, Wheeler was too late by a day to bring up sufficient men to hinder Kilpatrick's cavalry from entering Griswoldville and destroying the manufacturing facilities to include the sturdy workshops that produced the famous Griswoldville Confederate revolver.

With Wheeler skirmishing Kilpatrick and heading in pursuit of Sherman's left wing to the north, the Georgia militia under the command of General Pleasant J. Phillips departed Macon to bolster the defenses of Augusta, leaving a fit to be tied Ferguson as the sole guardian of the city. Phillips was under direct orders to wait until he was certain that the Federal infantry in the right wing had passed through the area before proceeding in a direct route to Augusta. For whatever reason, some reported he was drunk, Phillips disregarded those extremely logical orders and chose to attack a nearby reinforced Federal brigade of 1,500 men armed with repeating rifles and four pieces of artillery.

The weather had been extremely cold and rainy for the last two days and at night the muddy potholes froze solid, capped by thin plates of ice. Nevertheless, on November 22, the inexperienced home guard uncased their battle flags and neatly lined up in four small brigades, about 4,000 teenage boys and old men. The charge would take them about 600 yards across an open corn field and down into a ravine where they planned to reorganize to then rush the final 100 yards to the Federal position which consisted of a sturdy barricade of rails. By this stage of the War, any competent commander would certainly know that such an attack across open ground was pure murder.

The charge was bravely made. The militia never reached the Union line. The Georgia militia suffered 523 casualties — 51 dead and 472 wounded — and the Union toll was 13 dead and 79 wounded, mostly the effects from long range artillery. After the attack, one Union Soldier walked the bloody field and saw scores of horribly wounded "old grey-haired and weakly-looking boys not over 15 years old."[727] Another Union participant heard groaning coming from a group of bodies piled up together and found a

fourteen-year-old boy with a broken arm and leg. "It was a terrible sight," he recorded, "cold in death, lay his Father, two Brothers, and an Uncle. It was a harvest of death.[728]

Apart from some small elements of troopers that Ferguson was able to send out to assist Wheeler, the gray cavalry did not directly participate in the tragic and unnecessary battle.[729] In fact, this "battle" with the Georgia militia was the only resistance that the right wing of Sherman's army faced throughout the march.

While the Union right wing was tramping past Macon, the left was edging straight towards Milledgeville, the capital of Georgia, then about 30 miles off. The defending force in the city were some regular infantry, the young teenage cadets from the Georgia Military Institute, and two poorly armed local home guard companies, about 650 men in total.[730] When Federal cavalry scouts entered the outskirts of Milledgeville on Sunday, November 20, to cut telegraph wires, the Governor, the military presence, and those civilians that could leave did so with great haste.

The first foot soldiers arrived on November 22, and on November 23, thousands of Federal infantry entered the town in dress parade style, cheered on with emotional wails and shouts by quite a number of enslaved people. Kilpatrick's cavalry, which had beat a hasty exit following Wheeler's thrashing the day before, also rode into the city and after consulting with Sherman, the decision was made to have Kilpatrick sweep northeast and make a convincing feint on Augusta, or, if practicable, to even attack the place. Not only was Augusta the site of the Confederacy's largest gun powder manufacturing mill, its foundry and ample government stores made it a logical target. However, Sherman's true intent was still Savannah, his plan was only to fool the Confederates into concentrating their limited forces at Augusta.

During their two day stay in Milledgeville, the Union troops were allowed to pillage the private dwellings and strip the homes of anything that would burn, using the furniture for their campfires. They also torched and looted several public structures to include the State's public library. Amazingly, and quite arbitrarily, on this

particular occasion, Sherman placed strong guards to prevent his men from burning down most of the private homes. By November 24, the army began to dutifully march out of the city. On November 25, Ferguson's brigade, who entered just as Sherman's rear guard was leaving, gave hot pursuit until the Federals crossed the Oconee River and set ablaze the main bridge behind them.

For his part, Ferguson recalled his welcomed release from Macon and subsequent arrival at the capital, just as the Federals were leaving.

> At last General Dick [Richard] Taylor arrived [at Macon] in a few minutes thereafter I interviewed him and got permission to go ahead [towards Augusta to assist Wheeler]. This I did in very short order before I caught up again with Sherman's rear [the left wing]. He had just entered and left Milledgeville, the Capital of Georgia. When some distance from that place I saw a column of black smoke rise suddenly. I judged that he had just left and was burning the bridge behind him. We marched [rode] faster and faster as we became more impatient and entered the city at a full gallop. The women ran out, knelt on the sidewalks, with hands joined in prayer, and tears streaming down their cheeks at the sight once more of Confederates. After their fearful experiences of the invaders these were tears of joy.[731]

Having been traumatized by Sherman's ruffians, the citizens of Milledgeville cheered and cried for joy when Ferguson's troopers came galloping in. However, as the townspeople got a closer look at their tattered saviors, attitudes changed. One woman wrote how tears of happiness turned to tears of sorrow when she saw the broken condition of the Southern cavalrymen up close.

A few ragged men came riding up and bowed and brandished their pistols, the tears streamed from our eyes — strong men wept — God bless our soldiers, our poor suffering soldiers.[732]

Cochrane wrote his sister Sophia about the 2nd Alabama's arrival into Milledgeville.

We charged into Milledgeville on last Friday, captured some Yankees but the army had crossed the Alconee [Oconee] river and burnt the bridge and delayed us a good deal as we had to swim our horses over the river. However we crossed 100 men over who took prisoners in every hour or so during the day and night.[733]

General Wheeler was now concerned about Augusta and since the Union cavalry had the most potential for ranging far and wide to plunder and destroy, he lit after them and left Ferguson the job of skirmishing the rear and flank of the slower moving infantry.[734] Although Kilpatrick's scoundrels absolutely reveled in robbing and burning homes at every opportunity, Wheeler was successful in keeping the blue vandals away from Augusta, thereby preventing a greater amount of terrorism than otherwise would have befallen the innocents.

The most notorious of the Union cavalry regiments was Colonel Spencer's 1st Alabama Union Cavalry, the same regiment that was soundly thrashed by the 2nd Alabama Cavalry at Vincents Crossroads in the fall of 1863. Instead of sending out squads of men (bummers) to pillage and fire civilian homes and farms, the entire regiment would ride out to commit the atrocities. Being mounted, they were able to commit their foul outrages with alacrity and then trot off to the next target. One member of the 1st Alabama Union wrote to his father concerning the standard procedure employed by the regiment, only hinting at the stark horror inflicted on civilian families.

> We take out the whole regt with our wagons, stop at a cornfield dismount and in a few minutes the boys have the wagons filled with corn. On the way home they have to defend themselves as well they can against the attacks of Hogs, Fowl, & Etc. & c.[735]

Stealing forage was one thing, but these Tories were so vicious towards women and children that even General Frank Blair, commander of the Seventeenth Corps, sent a strong admonishment to the regiment's commander, Colonel Spencer.

> [T]he outrages committed by your command during the march are becoming so common, and are of such an aggravated nature, that they call for some severe and instant mode of correction.[736]

Like the cries of innocent civilians for mercy, the complaint to Spencer from a superior commander fell on deaf ears. Given that General Sherman himself had obviously encouraged such conduct (Sherman had previously chosen the regiment to be his personal escort), neither Colonel Spencer nor anyone in his command were ever admonished, let alone disciplined, for their war crimes. Ironically, after the War, the then Union controlled newspaper, *Montgomery Advertiser*, extolled the humanity of Spencer in a February 1866 article:

> To Spencer's honor however, it may be said that he never made war on women and children, but on the contrary seemed to protect them from the brutality of his superior officers.[737]

Strangely, Wheeler communicated very little with Ferguson during this time frame.[738] Since Wheeler had generally considered Ferguson's brigade as semi-independent, he allowed Ferguson to use his own judgment in striking the Union infantry's rear and flanks

and/or sending out patrols to various points of concern. In keeping with that flexibility, on one occasion, Private Cochrane was assigned to accompany a small scout to Augusta to provide the most current intelligence to the authorities about the direction of Sherman's left wing. This dangerous mission well pleased Cochrane and provided him the chance to see Augusta firsthand, if only for a day.

> The next day [November 25] Gen. Ferguson told Lieut. Foster he wished him to take four well-mounted men and carry some very important dispatches to ... Augusta .... Lieut. Foster selected C. Martin, R. Hatten, R. Sutton and myself. Lieut. Foster went to Augusta and delivered his dispatches to Gen. Bragg who told him these dispatches came in the best time in the world for he did not know what we were doing.[739]

Cochrane was back with his unit three days later where he found the 2nd Alabama fully engaged in policing Sherman's left wing, picking off bummers and stragglers. Of course, the approximately 500+ effective Confederate horsemen of Ferguson's brigade were far too small to prove more than a nuisance to the infantry as it lumbered along. Still, the 2nd Alabama was kept busy day and night fighting numerous skirmishes to keep the Yankee raiding parties away from outlaying farms and villages.

Private Cochrane and his fellow troopers relished the task of nipping at the heels of Sherman. "We are in the rear, i.e. the brigade [Ferguson's], and on the left flank of Sherman's grand army," he wrote his family, "and are busily capturing the stragglers, beef cattle etc., keeping the rear closed up generally."[740]

Always the optimist, Ferguson noted that his brigade enjoyed some added benefits from their otherwise arduous duties. After all, Sherman had brought out of Atlanta 2,500 brand new supply wagons to haul rations.

> I soon overtook Sherman's army and was embarrassed with the number of prisoners we took for I had to detail men to take them all the way to Augusta. I captured also many wagons from parties sent out to collect forage and was then able to throw away all my old home made vehicles and use only the best made in Philadelphia for Uncle Sam and to have six good mules to each wagon.[741]

Although illness, wounds, and death had greatly thinned the ranks, the 2nd Alabama was proud of their brigade commander's leadership and understood that the much publicized riff between Jackson and Ferguson could not diminish the brigade's well-deserved reputation as hard fighters. "The whole command is in fine spirits," Cochrane wrote home on November 30, "Ferguson's name has at last been put in the papers. There is no Jackson [General Red Jackson] here to get the glory and you may expect to hear of us often."[742] Major Nugent agreed:

> We are constantly fighting the enemy, charging his Infantry in motion, his wagon trains & foraging parties. We keep them stirred up day and night & worry them no little. We have captured about 400 head of beef cattle from them; two or three wagons; a large number of horses & mules; 130 prisoners besides the killed and wounded not counted. Eight killed & wounded [in Ferguson's brigade]. On yesterday [Nov. 30, 1864] we charged through their skirmish line and went right into the camps of the 14th Corps. The whole skirmish line threw down their guns and surrendered .... Our men behave very gallantly and go in always with a rush.[743]

Indeed, if Wheeler still ignored Ferguson's proven accomplishments, General P.G.T. Beauregard held the South Carolinian's expert handling of the brigade in great esteem and on November 29, 1864, he recommended to Richmond that Ferguson be promoted to the rank of Major General. This would have advanced Ferguson over his nemesis Red Jackson, still a brigadier. Unfortunately, Richmond never took action.

November 29, 1864

> Wheeler's cavalry requires reorganization; one additional major general is needed. I recommend Brig. Gen. S.W. Ferguson for temporary appointment. Please answer by telegraph.[744]

General P.G.T. Beauregard

On December 1, the Union left wing swung out of Louisville to pivot sharply on Millen. During this movement, Kilpatrick's cavalry, accompanied by a full division of infantry, was pushed out towards Waynesboro with instructions to confront Wheeler and the next day in heavy fighting they drove the gray cavalry through the town. Both sides lost about 200 men.[745]

Having successfully screened Wheeler, the Union force abruptly shifted south to join the main column, signaling at last that Augusta was no longer at issue. Wheeler regrouped and followed, becoming so disgusted with Kilpatrick's wanton depredations on civilians that he sent a letter through the lines appealing to the Union officer's sense of honor as a fellow graduate of West Point.

> Since the commencement of this sad war I have used untiring efforts to maintain in my soldiers principles of chivalry and true soldierly honor. They have been

taught to despise and spurn the cowardly instincts which induce low men to frighten, abuse, and rob defenseless women and children .... I have only to ask, for the sake of these old associations [both were West Point graduates], for your own sake, and for the sake of the institution where military honor was taught, that you will offer some protection to the families left defenseless, and not leave them at the mercy of a brutal soldiery.[746]

The Confederate general's pleas for honorable observance of the law of war fell on deaf ears. On the contrary, as all criminals and culprits tend to do, Kilpatrick disingenuously charged Wheeler with doing the same thing! While it was true that Wheeler's cavalry increasingly relied on Southern civilians for forage and food in these desperate times, there was a vast difference in scope between Union *atrocities* and Wheeler's *requisitions*. Southerners did not burn down homes, slaughter stock, or commit outrages.

With the regular commissary depots in Georgia depleted or destroyed, not the least of Wheeler's problems was a desperate need to obtain adequate food for his soldiers and stock. If the Confederate cavalry was to stay active in the field, there was no other choice except to draw on the locals for help, willingly or otherwise. Besides, since April of 1863, Richmond had levied a one-tenth tax in kind on all agricultural produce from farmers and planters to include wheat, fodder, sugar, corn, oats, rye, buckwheat, rice, potatoes, hay, cotton, wool, tobacco, peas, beans, etc.[747] By the fall of 1864, with no reliable system in place to procure the food tax, the Confederate military was allowed to collect it on the spot and provide the applicable paper receipts.

In addition, confronted by extreme shortages of everything, Wheeler's men sometimes established their own "quartermaster department." One cavalryman described a "requisition" of fodder for the horses as follows:

My [cavalry] squad had some difficulty in finding forage, but finally we found a lot of wheat shocked in a field about two miles from camp. Without asking permission of anyone, we loaded our horses. No one but a cavalryman knows how much he can tie to his saddle. It is no job to carry seventy or eighty pounds of wheats or oats in the straw.[748]

In a letter to his father, Private O.D. Chester, a member of the 5th Georgia Cavalry that rode under Wheeler, described the predicament faced by all Confederate cavalrymen opposing Sherman.

[I]t is very hard on both horses and men. I have started at daybreak or sooner and ridden till after midnight without stopping long enough to unsaddle and then lying down with all my things on and without unrolling my blanket or un-saddling my horse and slept with my gun for a pillow. We have been separated from our wagons [quartermaster supplies] for some time and consequently have been very much in need of food. There are so many of us that the Citizens cannot supply us all, though they do a great deal.[749]

Then, in the same letter, Private Chester admits to helping himself to foodstuffs from a plantation that had recently been abandoned.

[Private] Proctor and I went out and found a very nice house and plantation that had been hurriedly abandoned by the owners …. We got as much as we wanted to eat [from the plantation's bee hives] but had no way of carrying any of it away. We then went

to the garden where we got a fine bagful of Irish potatoes and plenty of wheat for our horses which we brought off.[750]

Finally, as with all armies, some men in uniform will act in their individual capacity to commit crimes, particularly when discipline is wanting from their commanding officers. Without question, however, the vast majority of abuses that mirrored the practice of Union plundering were committed by various roving bands of deserters and renegades who covered their thievery when challenged by falsely claiming to be part of "Wheeler's cavalry."

As desperate as the Rebel horsemen were for food, which they did take as authorized by Richmond, they never robbed, burned, or destroyed personal property held by their own people,[751] unless the commander in the field determined that "supplies of all kinds useful to the enemy and not required for your use must be destroyed."[752] One eyewitness who put together a history of Wheeler's cavalry wrote:

> I have not forgotten the outcry against Wheeler's cavalry just prior to and after the close of the war; it was brought about in great measure, doubtless, by renegades from our armies who committed outrages which were charged by the people to the account of the cavalry.[753]

In his own report on Sherman's march, Wheeler noted the hardships:

> In closing this report I will state that during the last five months [July to December 1864] my command has been without wagons or cooking utensils, with orders to subsist upon the country [both on his raid into Tennessee and then opposing Sherman's march

to Savannah]. Its food has been limited to bread baked upon boards and stones and meat broiled upon sticks. It has not been paid in twelve months, and has not had regular issues of clothing ... the average traveling of each soldier [has been] at least twenty miles per day.... My troops have been continually in the immediate presence of the enemy, fighting nearly every day.[754]

In summary, all that stood between the Southern families and Sherman's terrorists were the brave cavalrymen of Wheeler's command. Again, while this small band of gray horsemen was not strong enough to stop Sherman, they snapped like hungry wolves on his flanks and rear, keeping thousands of foragers and outlying blue cavalry to much narrower limits of destruction than would otherwise have been the case.

— No Quarter —

The monstrous sights of looted and gutted homes coupled with the littered remains of thousands of decomposing farm animals slaughtered by Sherman's men shocked and enraged Southerners. The Yankee atrocities committed against women and children who were left starving, destitute, and homeless coupled with reports of rape, rubricated and energized a "no quarter for looters" policy. Since the Union's own General Order 100 listed death as the punishment for pillaging, the grim-faced Confederates had no qualms about carrying out that very sentence themselves, and with alacrity.[755] In turn, the knowledge that Sherman's soldiers would sometimes execute Confederate prisoners of war only added to a sense of vengeance. For instance, one of Sherman's undisciplined men wrote that he and his comrades had murdered 23 Confederate soldiers who had surrendered. "When there is no officer with us," the Wisconsin soldier confided in a letter home, "we take no prisoners."[756]

Accordingly, Yankees caught in the act of vandalism or other atrocities were executed where they stood and their mortal bodies dragged out by the feet to the nearest road to decay.[757] Then, hoping to deter further Union war crimes, large signs would be posted on or near the corpses reading: "Death to Foragers."

In other instances, it was not uncommon for the cavalry to boldly swoop down on an outlying Union squad and carry off a few. For instance, on November 28, four soldiers were snatched away from a Federal column by a hit and run cavalry charge that took advantage of a bend in the road. They were never heard from again.[758] The next day, Ferguson's cavalry captured three men of the Fourteenth Corps that had strayed to loot. Their bodies were discovered with the distinctive singe of gunshot residue on hair and clothing, indicating execution at close range.[759] On another occasion, Sherman was informed that four of his men had their throats cut and were left for dead. Miraculously, two of them were rescued as "the slashings had been bungled."[760]

One Confederate cavalryman dryly remarked that the tears of Southern women and flaming homes were far stronger concerns than the pleas of captured pillagers cowardly begging for their lives.[761] General Ferguson, who was given the primary task of following the blue infantry as closely as he thought prudent, openly acknowledged the policy of death to foragers and had absolutely no qualms about carrying it out. With grim resolve, his brigade most likely dealt summary justice to more of these criminals than any of their sister brigades. Again, added to Sherman's destruction of livestock and food that left women, children, the disabled, and elderly to starve or hurry away in pitiful refugee caravans, were numerous instances of Yankee "men who ... raped and killed with no compunction."[762] Ferguson recorded:

> I followed Sherman and picked up hundreds of prisoners many of them stragglers out plundering. I have no idea how many of the latter class were killed

on the spot for they were robbers and not entitled to the benefits of the rules of war.⁷⁶³

In his memoirs, General Ferguson also mentioned one such "cross-dressing" Yankee forager that was captured by Lieutenant Pettus and a small group of eight scouts who had crossed the swollen river near Milledgeville looking to ascertain the direction of march of the right wing of Sherman's army.

> A hail came from the other side to send the boat [back across the river], it was returned with a note from [Lieutenant] Pettus giving me the desired information and with a prisoner, who had been captured with a ladies handsome opera cloak, opera glass, and other plunder in his possession. I made use of some expression of disgust at such a fellow being taken prisoner. One of the men standing by said, "General, I will take him to the provost guard." I said very well and went on with my work, which just then was having a raft built. The next day was Sunday and a most lovely day, the population [of Milledgeville] came to the river bank to see the command crossing the stream. I noticed that groups would walk up the bank a short distance look at something and then come back. At last I asked what was the attraction and learned that it was a dead Yankee. I then remembered to have heard a shot in that direction the night before, [sic] soon after the prisoner had been started to the guard, and I did not doubt that he was the dead Yankee.⁷⁶⁴

Southern civilians were in total agreement to the policy. Major Nugent observed that the locals fully supported the cavalry's grim determination to get at the vandals and kill them.

> The people … welcome the little band of Confederate soldiers who are harassing the enemy. They divide the little remnant of their supplies with us, and bid us God's speed. As we were passing by … three beautiful ladies came out to see us pass and after blessing us, said they hoped we would "kill all the wretches" a very unchristian but by no means unnatural sentiment."[765]

On the other hand, Nugent also noted with dismay that some of the men sought retribution against *any* Federal that fell into their hands: "Our men can scarcely be restrained from killing them even after they surrender, and I have no doubt that several have been cruelly murdered."[766] For his part, Ferguson quickly moved to restrain his troopers from killing those not caught in the act of pillaging and he formed a "special guard detailed to prevent this outrage"[767] for the hundreds of regular prisoners of war taken into custody.

Of course, not all the officers in Ferguson's brigade were comfortable with the practice of executing renegade Union soldiers. Two months after the War ended, Captain Frank R. King, who commanded Company B, 2nd Alabama Cavalry, reported to Federal occupation authorities that his old boss Samuel Ferguson had ordered the regiment's provost marshal, Lieutenant William Muldrow, to murder a number of what King labeled as "Federal prisoners" captured during Sherman's march across Georgia. Captain King wrote on July 16, 1865:

> The crime which I charge against him is cold blooded and deliberate murder of Federal Prisoners, without even the shadow of a pretext. During the fall Campaign of Maj. Gen. Sherman through the State of Georgia, a number of Federal Soldiers fell into the hands of Genl. Ferguson who without any higher authority than his own, caused many of these Prisoners to be carried off in a close distant manner and cruelly shot

down. [N]o less than ten Federal Prisoners were thus inhumanely murdered by his orders on one occasion, while many other besides these mentioned met their fate in a similar manner.[768]

Shooting down marauders caught in the act of committing war crimes is far different than King's allegations of overt murder. Indeed, King's accusations were never substantiated by any other members of the command and were particularly suspect given the officer's extremely poor reputation in the brigade and with General Ferguson, as evidenced by an examining board's promotion evaluation recommendation, dated January 10, 1865:

> Hd Qr. Examining Board
>
> Ferguson's Brigade
>
> Robertsville, S.C. Jany 10th 1865
>
> Pursuant to "General Order No 2 Hd Qrs Ferguson's Brigade, Jan 7-8th 1865" the officers recited in paragraph III, to wit — Lt. Col. H.L. Muldrow, Maj. R.W. Carter and Maj Thos D. Hall, dully convened this day as a Board to examine all company officers in the Brigade not heretofore examined, or who may hereafter be promoted or elected, also all officers heretofore examined, discretionary with the Board....

Of Capt Frank King, Co B:

> Of his gallantry I can hardly speak. Has not a decided character in that respect. Is inattentive to his duty. Maintain his dignity. Morality & sobriety not good. Never saw him drunk, however, but once that I remember of. Has — 15 to 25 or 30 men [in the company]. Agg 78. Has no reputation for attention to orders. Absent sick considerably. Complains a good deal of bad health. Is not under arrest.[769]

Even more telling, on February 10, 1865, a month after the Board's negative report on King's character and ability, this same officer tried unsuccessfully to get his entire company to desert the 2nd Alabama Cavalry, an act of mutiny punishable by death under Article 7 of the Confederate Articles of War.[770] Though Ferguson did not pursue court-martial charges against him, King's cowardly conduct spoke volumes about his character and veracity. In any event, no criminal charges were ever filed against General Ferguson by the United States government after the War.

In turn, the notion that it was standard Confederate policy to murder Union soldiers who surrendered was not only false but it sadly contributed to unnecessary bloodshed in the conduct of combat activities. General Wheeler explained:

> The enemy had been falsely informed by their officers that we took no prisoners ... in the many fights which ensued, they continued to fly, refusing to surrender notwithstanding the demands of my men in close pursuit. Consequently, no alternative was left but to shoot or sabre them to prevent escape.[771]

In summary, the exact number of Union pillagers killed will never be known. One source reports that Sherman's men recovered 64 bodies in Georgia,[772] but it is certain that the mortal remains of the majority were never recovered and simply listed on the various company rosters as "missing." After reaching Savannah in December 1864, one source records that 500 of Sherman's men were recorded as captured or missing, in addition to 103 killed and 428 wounded.[773] Others place the Union casualties at far higher levels. When adding the Union losses associated with the fall of Savannah, one source assessed the aggregate as 2,800 — most of these in the "missing" category![774]

— Escape from Savannah —

By the evening of December 9, 1864, Sherman had reached the outskirts of Savannah. The 10,000-man garrison was now shut up behind the city defenses set out along a newly constructed western line which extended from the Savannah River on the right to the Little Ogeechee River on the left.[775] In command was "old reliable" General William Hardee, in appearance every inch a soldier and highly skilled at his craft.

Except for Lee's valiant army in Virginia, Hardee had amassed the largest Confederate force in the east and he had no intention of getting trapped in a losing contest against a numerically superior enemy. Using thousands of laborers operating from both sides of the mile-wide Savannah River connecting Georgia to South Carolina, Hardee constructed a long pontoon bridge consisting of rice flats taken from plantations, long shallow barges, and small boats which were all lashed together by ropes and chains, tied end to end in sections, and covered with planks. Heavy objects such as wheels stripped from railroad cars anchored the unsightly structure in the water. In this way, when the time was right, the entire army could escape into South Carolina and destroy the bridge behind them.

By December 14, with Sherman's march through Georgia over, most of Wheeler's cavalry, along with Ferguson's troopers, had crossed into South Carolina. Ferguson's brigade was barely settled at Sister's Ferry, when it was ordered to leave their horses and proceed to Savannah to reinforce Hardee's thin lines in the city. The troopers, who now numbered just over 500 effectives, greeted the new orders with great dismay, being converted to lowly "web-footers" was one thing, but with their horses being so far removed the Alabamians were extremely uncomfortable. Still, their displeasures were no longer the squawks of new recruits, they were the righteous grumblings of tough men who had "seen the elephant." Like all stout veterans, they would do their duty even though it seemed like Savannah would be Bald Hill all over again.

Hardee's Bridge from Savannah.

Reflecting Ferguson's continued state of autonomy from Wheeler, the unpleasant order went straight to Ferguson himself. On December 16, 1864,[776] the dismounted cavalrymen shuffled into Savannah where they would be divided up and sent in "small detachments all along the lines to points that were weakest."[777] Ferguson, made the best of it all and after entering the port city at the head of his brigade he cheered up his tight-lipped men with a bit of gallows humor. He wrote:

> It was a bitter pill to my men to be separated from their horse and they marched into Savannah in no good humor. I indulged in a little sport at their expense. When I had reached the [brigade's] camping ground in the park I gave the orders as if to mounted men, "Rear rank open order. Prepare to dismount, DISMOUNT." When they broke ranks they gave a cheer, showing that they appreciated the joke.[778]

The threadbare and faded gray or butter-nut colored uniforms stained with mud and begrimed by the soot of many camp fires, made quite a contrast to the outfits of the finely dressed and groomed garrison soldiers of Savannah. Ferguson recollected with

great affection the rough appearance of his troopers, which in stoic manliness they proudly wore as red badges of courage.

> There was a strong contrast in appearance between my old soldiers who had been marching and fighting for months and were ragged and smoke begrimed from the camp fires of pine, and the neatly dressed garrison of Savannah, which had access to the stores of blockade runners, and had some transactions even with the Confederate Quarter Masters.[779]

For his part, Hardee kept his powder dry and looked to the precise moment to exit. It was only when Sherman was within spitting distance of closing a loop around the entire city that Ferguson's brigade was pulled out of the trenches and crossed back over to the South Carolina side in order to provide cover for a night crossing of the entire army. Ferguson happily rushed out couriers to Barnwell County, South Carolina, to bring up the horses! They were the last Confederate soldiers to enter Savannah and now the first to exit by walking across Hardee's ingenious pontoon bridge.

On the dark night of December 20, 1864, Hardee's infantry gingerly moved out of Savannah under the booming sounds of covering artillery fire, right under the nose of Sherman. In addition to the entire army of 9,000 men of all arms, "forty-nine pieces of artillery, with limbers, caissons, forges, battery wagons, and baggage wagons, were safely transported over the pontoon bridges."[780] Just a couple hours after midnight, when all had departed, special engineers detached the flats and set them adrift. The next day Hardee rested at Hardeeville, South Carolina.

Like his failure at Atlanta to destroy Hood's army, Sherman would not be able to claim a military victory over Hardee either. The most he could do was to send a telegraph; messaging Lincoln that Savannah was a "Christmas present."

Chapter Nine

Davis' Cavalry Escort

"Duty is ours; results are Gods."[781]   — John Q. Adams

AS THE NEW YEAR OF 1865 dawned, the outlook was desperately bleak for the South. Food was scarce for soldiers and civilians alike and everything was now a luxury item. Only the spirit of resistance still burned bright.

With Sherman's hordes expected to move out of Savannah in the early spring and head north to aid Grant, Richmond strained to organize a force to try and block him. After escaping from Savannah, Hardee was headquartered in Charleston, with a little less than 9,000 infantry troops (the Georgia militia had returned to Georgia) and Wheeler's played out cavalry. The fighting aggregate was perhaps 13,000.

Not only were more men required to fill the ranks, but there was also the need to assess the condition of the cavalry. In late December 1864, the Inspector General's Office, Military Division of the West, dispatched Assistant Inspector General [IG], Lieutenant Colonel Alfred Roman to inspect Wheeler's command and provide a detailed assessment with recommendations for improvement/reorganization.[782]

On January 2, 1865, Hardee issued special orders reorganizing all the various cavalry forces under his authority. In the shakeup, General Iverson, who had previously commanded a brigade of Georgians, was officially promoted to command a division in Wheeler's cavalry corps and Ferguson's brigade was placed under his command, along with Lewis' Kentucky Orphan brigade, Anderson's Confederate brigade, Dibrell's Tennessee brigade, and Young's brigade.[783] At the time, Ferguson's brigade consisted of four regiments and one battalion:

2nd Alabama Cavalry, commanded by:
Lieut. Colonel John N. Carpenter

56th Alabama Cavalry, commanded by:
Col. William Boyles

9th Mississippi Cavalry, commanded by:
Col. Horace H. Miller

11th Mississippi Cavalry, commanded by:
Col. Robert O. Perrin

12th Mississippi Battalion, commanded by:
Col. William M. Inges[784]

It was unseasonably cold weather in January of 1865. Ferguson's brigade was dispatched to patrol the "low country" in South Carolina and he began writing a personal journal which he maintained until the end of the War. With no Yankees in sight at least things were quiet and the men and animals enjoyed a much needed respite. His first entry of January 1, 1865, records that the brigade was camped at Brighton, South Carolina, with "about eight hundred effective men for duty,"[785] a mere shell of a force structure that was more in keeping with the size of a regiment than a brigade.

Ferguson was painfully aware of the sorry state of his command, writing on January 3:

> I found many men without guns & many without cartridge boxes & c [cartridges]. Orders relative to the supply of ammunition to be kept on hand sadly neglected. Troops much in need of clothing & horse equipment.[786]

The same entry posted from Robertsville, also noted that Colonel Roman and Captain Ferry of "General Beauregard's staff arrived on a tour of inspection through Wheeler's Cavalry and are my guests."[787] The IG inspection took place from January 4-7, and Roman rendered his full report on January 22. At the start of his tour, the IG noted that "Ferguson's ... Brigade formed part of no division, [and] reported directly to Maj. Genl. Wheeler"[788] (Roman did not know that Hardee had already fixed this confused command problem, at least on paper, by putting Ferguson in Iverson's division). Roman described Ferguson's Brigade, as consisting of the five regiments:

> [The] 2nd and 56th Alabama Cavalry [Regiments], Inges' [12th Mississippi], Perrins' [11th Mississippi] and Miller's [9th Mississippi] Regiments — commanded by Brig. Genl. S.W. Ferguson, with a total [aggregate], exclusive of detached men, of 990.[789]

On the plus side, although an "aggregate number" of 990 was not the same as the "effective number," it was still far larger than what Ferguson was able to field on any given day in the nonstop fighting from Atlanta to Savannah when he was lucky to claim 550 effectives. While some of Ferguson's troopers had now returned to duty, having obtained either new or "rehabilitated" horses from one of the horse convalescent camps (to include a large "horse hospital" established at far away Carthage, Alabama),[790] perhaps close

to 1,000 members of his brigade had been kept back on various detached duty assignments in Mississippi and Alabama.[791] These absences were in addition to quite a few squadrons sent out to scout different areas in the region.

Furthermore, the deteriorating state of the War effort did nothing to convince those "missing" men from the brigade who had begun to melt away into the night in larger and larger numbers, such as half of Miller's Regiment, to now return to duty.[792] Ferguson wrote with some bitterness about the loss of these Mississippians who had deserted just after the fall of Savannah.

> One of the two Battalions of which Col. Millers Regiment [the 9th Mississippi] had been formed, the 17th Mississippi [Battalion], deserted in a body and returned to their homes in South Mississippi. This was due to the dislike they had for their Col. [Miller] more than to any other cause. In decrying the fight I had with the 1st Alabama Cavalry U.S.A. [in 1863] I described how I tried to have the gallant Bridges made Colonel of this Regiment [9th Mississippi] but Miller was forced to it. He was utterly worthless.[793]

The extreme lopsidedness in General Ferguson's five regiments was reflected in the IG's report which noted that Inge's Regiment had only 60 men and Miller's Regiment counted only 86.[794] Doing the math, this meant that a total of 850 men combined to make up the three remaining regiments, the 2nd Alabama, the 56th Alabama, and the 11th Mississippi. Fortunately, a more exact count for the 2nd Alabama can be gleaned from two surviving "Morning Report Effective Strength" reports signed off by General Ferguson. The first was taken at Matthew's Bluff, South Carolina, dated January 14, 1865,[795] and the second was conducted on the march and is dated January 16.[796]

On the morning of January 14, Ferguson's brigade left their camp at Old Martin and arrived at a new camp about one mile

outside of Matthew's Bluff, where the morning report showed a total of 990 men in the brigade, with an additional 115 recorded as sick or on extra duty (temporarily away from the command) for a total of 1,105. Horses numbered 1,209. At that time the 2nd Alabama Cavalry was counted as the largest of the five regiments with 27 officers, 44 non-commissioned officers, 302 privates, and 446 horses. With another 27 men listed as sick or on extra duty, the 2nd Alabama had an aggregate total strength of 373 men and an effective fighting strength of 346.[797]

The January 16 morning report presents an even more detailed accounting for the 2nd Alabama revealing that only one major, five captains, and five first lieutenants were present for duty, meaning that the colonel, lieutenant colonel, five captains, and five first lieutenants were on extended detached service away from the regiment. Basically, the Alabama regiment was split in half with five companies present with Ferguson and five companies on detached service at various locations in Alabama and Mississippi.

In total, Colonel Roman's IG report records that Wheeler's entire force consisted of ten brigades (Ferguson being one of the ten) with "7,670 men present, with and without serviceable horses."[798] The IG noted that the armament consisted of an astonishing variety of rifles and pistols, with only a merger "6,607 firearms in serviceable condition, comprising 3,896 rifles, 500 carbines, 123 shotguns and muskets, and 1,978 pistols."[799] To make matters worse, the arms were "of eight or nine different calibers, but mostly of calibers 57 and 54. The consequence was that, in many instances, ammunition for six or seven different calibers was required in the same company."[800] Roman explained that the want of uniformity was primarily because the weapons were "of guns captured by the men; and it often happens, that none but captured ammunition will fit those captured guns."[801]

Next, the IG recorded that the accouterments were inferior as well. With only 2,911 cap pouches, 3,772 cartridge boxes, and 3,000 waist belts, the men had no choice but to stuff ammunition into their pockets or saddle bags and hope that it would not spoil due to dampness.[802] Interestingly, by this stage of the War, cavalry

sabers were almost non-existent, the IG counting only "fifty or sixty" for the men and the "officers, in most cases, have no sabers."[803] Indeed, after the fighting in Georgia, it became painfully clear that sabers were no longer practicable weapons of war, dead weight best discarded or sent home as souvenirs.

Ragged and thinly uniformed, clothing was also deemed to be "very deficient" causing extreme suffering to the men. The IG saw the urgent need for "6,000 blankets, 7,000 suits of clothing, 5,000 hats, 8,000 pair [of] socks; and some 5,000 shoes."[804]

As it happened, the IG noted that although the men had received no pay for the past twelve or thirteen months, that some paper money had been delivered and was being paid out during his inspection. Still, not more than $160,000 in Confederate dollars had been issued of late with about one million and a half due on claims for horses killed or wounded in action.

In terms of military discipline and general appearance, the IG had nothing positive to write except that the men were always "respectful at inspection." He deemed the "military appearance as bad" with most of the troopers devoid of military bearing and "too much familiarity exist[ing] between officers and men."[805] "There seems to be an independent careless way about most of the officers and men," Roman noted, "which plainly indicates how little they value Army Regulations, and of tactics in general."[806] To be fair, the IG also observed that the commands of Forrest and Hampton had similar loose discipline but thought that Wheeler's leadership style no longer motivated the men to battle, whereas Forrest's always did.

The only bright news revolved around the horses, particularly for Ferguson's brigade. Allowed to rest and feed, the animals were "in very serviceable condition,"[807] even if many had crude saddles with ropes for bridles and stirrups. This was in stark contrast to other brigades, where the horses were so broken down that they could hardly pass for cavalry mounts. Curiously, the IG observed that the men took better care of their horses than they did of themselves with everyone now expert at producing homemade horse equipment. However, Colonel Roman raised the common

complaint concerning the government's policy of requiring all cavalrymen to supply their own war mounts. Since the government almost never paid for the death of the horse in combat as required, the IG concluded that troopers were less likely to risk harm to their mounts thereby contributing to a lack of aggressiveness in the field.

In concluding this section of his report, the IG marveled at how the men still kept faith to the Confederacy even though they were denied money and supplies by the nation they so loyally served. Nevertheless, the colonel was a realist and noted that without pay and no way to receive money from home, it was likely that the men "are very apt to take and carry away, what the government denies them the chance of buying."[808]

Addressing the widespread complaints and rumors that Wheeler's troopers were guilty of plundering Southern civilians for food and other items, the IG acknowledged that "bad men" who were a "disgrace to our service" were undoubtedly to be found, but he concluded that "they form only a small portion" of the command and that horse-thieves and other "mad dogs" engaging in depredations had no connection with Wheeler's troopers, even if many initially claimed to be part of that body. Instead, noting that the threat of famine permeated the entire country, the IG primarily faulted the quartermaster for dereliction of duty in failing to properly precede the "troops on a march, so as to prepare forage for the horses, and food for the men"[809] when they arrived at a predetermined point.

> When, after a long march, men and horses arrive at their camping ground, very often in a starving condition, it is almost natural, that, if no provisions are made to satisfy their hunger, they should endeavor to procure their food by their own exertions. Private details for forage and for supplies are then sent out, and men and horse are thus allowed to roam about the country in search of something to eat.[810]

The overall assessment ended with a recommendation that General Wheeler should be replaced due to his inability to control and motivate the men. Wheeler "is too gentle, too lenient; and we know how easy leniency can be made to degenerate into weakness."[811] "For the good of the cause"[812] Colonel Roman recommended that Wheeler had to go.

On the other hand, the IG was greatly impressed with two of the generals under Wheeler — Brigadier General Ferguson and Brigadier General Anderson — and recommended that both be immediately promoted to Major General. In fact, he could not understand why Wheeler's proposed plan for reorganization called for the promotion of junior brigadiers over the more senior General Ferguson, when such a move would obviously "deprive [Ferguson] of his rights," an outstanding officer "against whom no charge of inefficiency has ever been preferred."[813]

> General Ferguson has more system, more military experience than most of the General Officers of his years and rank. Both [Ferguson and Anderson] have been brought up as soldiers and would, no doubt, do honor to their commands.[814]

— Back in Georgia —

Besides worrying about the tremendous pressure placed on Lee's besieged army, President Davis was deeply concerned with Sherman's next move.[815] Davis was also worried about Federal cavalry raids in Georgia aimed to disrupt Confederate agents who struggled to reestablish at least a semblance of administrative control across the desolate countryside, to include Atlanta where herculean efforts were underway to repair a single rail-line through the city.[816] In addition, coupled with the burned-out homes, barren fields, and an alarming number of hungry women and children, was an increasing lawlessness throughout much of the State where

scalawags, draft dodgers, thieves, and assorted "ruffians" of all descriptions roamed about at will.

Partly in response to these concerns, Hardee gave Iverson's division the job of picketing all across the Savannah River region and Ferguson's brigade was set out on the southern-most part of the new line which had them patrolling up and down the center/eastern border region of Georgia, a bleak mission that did nothing except contribute to more desertions. Apart from a few minor skirmishes with Union cavalry in South Carolina and Georgia, the period from late January until early April 1865, saw Ferguson's troopers kept out of the real fighting. Interestingly, the chief complaint of the 2nd Alabama Cavalry when it was first formed in 1862, was one of idleness and now, as the Confederacy's time was coming to an end, that same complaint was on every lip.

In an August 1904, letter written from Greenville, Mississippi, Ferguson remembered the decisively negative impact of inaction on his men.

> In reading over my journal, I am as much puzzled, as I was at the time, to imagine what possible object was in view, when I was sent into Georgia [in late January 1865]. No enemy was there, and none expected, as far as I can see. The result was, that my brigade was kept in idleness from January until the better part of April; marching about in an aimless manner and receiving orders at one and the same time from several different Generals. The consequence was the men deserted in numbers, feeling that they were more needed at home, by their families, than in idle marches.[817]

Now more than ever, the men of the 2nd Alabama carried the worry of home and family in these desperate times as they patrolled the roads and river crossings. The winter terrain was empty of

forage and for much of the time the horses were reduced to eating bark, leaves, and old grass. Dirty, ragged, hungry, exhausted, sick, and short on everything, they too were wearing out, making it only natural that the desire of each man was to look to the safety of his family back home. The disintegration of the regiment was inevitable and they deserted, yes, but not to the enemy. Generally, in squad sizes marked along family relationships, many left Ferguson's brigade and made their way back to Alabama.

— Lee Takes Command of the Armies —

Too little, too late. Having been appointed by Congress in early 1865, as the supreme commander of all Confederate forces,, it was Robert E. Lee who was now making all the command and control military decisions for the Confederacy. Lee maintained his ever stoic demeanor and immediately set about reorganizing what was left of the force structure. On February 15, 1865, he replaced Joe Wheeler with Lieutenant General Wade Hampton, a native of South Carolina and a trusted subordinate. Lee also hurried along the remnants of Hood's army to reconstitute themselves in the Carolinas and on February 22, he called General Joe Johnston out of retirement from Macon and put him back in command of his old Army of Tennessee, as well as all the troops in South Carolina, Georgia, and North Carolina.[818] What remained of the Army of Tennessee was clad in rags and living on rations of worm-eaten peas, corn meal, and rancid pork, but they were glad to see their old commander.

Johnston's new "army" was a hodgepodge of disjointed pieces — the remnants of the Army of Tennessee, Hardee's untried soldiers, some militia, and various coastal forces in North and South Carolina — maybe 20,000 troops, including 3,000 effective cavalry. On the Union side of things, Sherman alone had over 80,000 heavily armed veterans, including 5,000 cavalry.

Only Ferguson's troopers were held back from Johnston due to earlier pleas from Major General Cobb for a cavalry brigade to go

even deeper into south Georgia to blunt Federal raids. On Christmas Day 1864, General Cobb messaged General Beauregard:

> The fall of Savannah thus closing that portion of Sherman's campaign, leads to the inquiry of the enemy's next movement .... Kilpatrick's cavalry, being now relieved from Sherman's army, can go in any direction, and already we have reports of its moving in that direction [central Georgia]. You are aware that I have no force to meet even a cavalry raid if made in any force, and hence I call your attention to the subject.[819]

Much to his dismay, about the middle of January 1865, Ferguson was ordered to depart his picket line and proceed to the mouth of the Altamaha River in Georgia. In desperation, Ferguson wrote two letters to friendly Congressmen in Richmond, both dated January 12, 1865, to enlist their help to return him to South Carolina so he could fight.[820]

> My Dear Friend January 12, 1865
>
> I have the misfortune to be placed in Wheeler's Corps .... I am ordered to the other side of the Savannah River to report to Genl Iverson .... As a Carolinian, I have more interest in fighting here, on my own soil, than any officer in Wheeler's Corps. Yet, I am selected to be sent away, while troops of the same command have to [be] kept here. Can you not aid me here? Since the War commenced I have done my duty faithfully, where ever sent and have asked nothing of the Government. All I ask now, that the crisis seems at hand, is to strike one blow on the soil of Carolina.[821]
>
> Gen. S.W. Ferguson

It was not to be. In obedience to orders, Ferguson moved his brigade to Augusta reaching that place by January 17, drawing rations and clothing. When he moved out from Augusta, the weather turned bitterly cold and Ferguson hurried ahead supply wagons to Macon to requisition additional heavy clothing and food. Strangely, even though the command quickly exhausted its supply of corn and entered a countryside so desolate that it could not sustain the animals, many of the troopers seemed content to be moving ever deeper into Georgia. They were getting closer to their homes and families in Alabama.

The situation became so dire that on January 29, when camped for the night near Mount Vernon, Ferguson summoned the regimental commanders to his tent to discuss the predicament. The commanders had faced much tougher obstacles and persevered, but this was 1865, not 1863, or even 1864. All agreed with the decision to turn around and march back to Augusta, yet rather than soothe the men, the desertions skyrocketed. For instance, one night shortly thereafter, February 10, a small portion of men belonging to Captain Whisanant's squadron, Co. B of the 2nd Alabama, simply left. Ferguson wrote in his diary:

> Feb. 11th. Rode back to Blackshaw's Ferry to see after the 2nd [Alabama Cavalry]; found that those who left, had done so, mostly at an early hour on the preceding night & were from [Captain] Wisenant's squadron. Sent the officers of that squadron after the men. Sent Dispatch to Genl [Daniel Harvey] Hill, informing him of the desertion.
>
> Feb. 12th. Made a speech to the 2nd Ala at parade. Heard of determination of some of 9th Mississippi to leave; took active steps to prevent it. Had roll called at night & made speech.[822]

Whole groups of troopers were leaving the ranks and taking their mounts with them. Still, one thing was certain, "the deserters were not cowards, or at least most of them were not."[823] The men all grew up in the same local communities and when they decided to quit the War, they generally all quit it together. Again, an individual who deserted was a coward, whereas a group that left viewed itself as having done all that duty required. What had bonded them so tightly was a common hostility toward the invading Yankees, but with defeat now obvious the "defense of home, fireside, wife and children" had the ultimate draw.[824] The true miracle is not that some in the 2nd Alabama Cavalry began to quit for home, but that they did not *all* leave! The only counter to the loss of manpower was that some troopers who had managed to find remounts were trickling back to the regiment.

In the interim, when the Federals slowly marched out of Savannah at the tail end of January 1865, not waiting for spring weather, the guessing game intensified. Where were they heading? Would it be to Columbia, Charleston, or perhaps Augusta? Since part of Sherman's command, the Army of the Tennessee, had already been shipped by boat some forty miles up the coast to Beaufort, South Carolina, Richmond was baffled.

By the middle of February 1865, Ferguson's brigade was once more in the neighborhood of Augusta, where feed for the animals was adequate. On February 15, their horses were watered in the river, fed, groomed, and picketed for the night and dinner was being prepared over the many small campfires when regimental buglers sounded "Boots and Saddles," which was half-smothered out by the groans of hundreds of disappointed troopers.[825] Ferguson was either going to join Lewis' cavalry brigade which was then dismounted and spread out in the breastworks of Augusta, or, in the alternative, the cavalrymen would fan out to fight a delaying action on horseback.

Luckily, it was a false alarm. Sherman was not coming their way after all. He was more intent on wreaking vengeance on the people of South Carolina than gaining any military advantage offered by capturing Augusta, even though it was a major manufacturing and

supply center for Lee's army. The State capital of Columbia and *all* of the surrounding homes in South Carolina would soon suffer ruthless acts of pillage and arson.

Sherman entered Columbia on February 17. Although the garrison surrendered the city without a fight, he allowed his drunken troops to loot and burn the public and private structures of the rich and the poor, black and white. Without sufficient forces to protect South Carolina, the old tactician Johnston had already abandoned the State entirely and retreated into North Carolina, calling to his side every available soldier he could find. Once again, it was Ferguson's brigade that was left behind.

With Sherman now razing his way across South Carolina, Ferguson sent mounted patrols into the State to help protect the food producing plantations and moved up his full brigade to Aiken and then to Hollow Creek where he was ordered to stand fast. His patrols probed the countryside for Federal cavalry resulting in both skirmishing and bringing back the latest news, but the relative inaction only contributed to more desertions. On March 7, when Ferguson moved to Richardsonville, South Carolina, fifty-five men of the 9th Mississippi saddled up in the dark and deserted. That same day, Ferguson issued a general order to keep closer watch on the horses.[826]

> HdQtrs Ferguson Brigade
>
> Edgefield Dist SC, 7 March 1865
>
> Hereafter Commanders of Regiments will be held responsible that a stable guard is half over the horses of each of their companies every night from retreat to reveille and that no animal is moved from their camp without their knowledge & permission during that period.
>
> By Command of Brg. Gen. Ferguson

On March 8, the brigade arrived at the Ninety-Six Railway depot and miraculously found in the surrounding sheds an abundance of hard yellow corn for the horses. On March 18, 1865, Ferguson recorded a typical entry:

> March 18th. Got sad news about Father & the ravages of the Yankees throughout our low country [South Carolina]. Learned that Lt. Bright and his party of scouts, had been surprised between Black Oak & Monks Corner, and that officer and two privates captured and two privates killed. Wrote to Hess & enclosed letter from Mrs. E. Holbrook. Wrote to May Lucas & to Richard Macbeth. Kate [Ferguson] and Miss Brooks went on a rabbit hunt. Invited to a dance at Mrs. Brooks but did not go.[827]

On March 23, Ferguson dispatched the 2nd Alabama to Newberry, along with Miller's regiment, "to arrest deserters about Pomaria."[828] Finally, on March 27, during heavy rain storms, Ferguson received welcomed orders to march his brigade north and report to General Joe Johnston at Raleigh. Even so, the more disturbing element that greeted the riders along the cold and muddy roads heading into Raleigh, were the throngs of desperate and heartbroken women and children sprawled out like clumps of leaves across the road. Females driving wagons or carts was an uncommon sight before the War, but now they filled the neglected countryside carrying crying and hungry children along with them. Tragically, within just over a week's time, the thousands who roamed about in the twilight zone of life and death would be joined by the remnants of Lee's heroic veterans, headed for home.

All the while desertions increased. On April 4, the stalwart general recorded in his journal that "about thirty men of the 2nd Alabama deserted"[829] in the night. By April 6, the brigade had made it to Dallas, North Carolina, after a "hard march of 27 miles"[830] that day. By April 9, 1865, the day Robert E. Lee surrendered the Army

of Northern Virginia at Appomattox Court House, the brigade passed through Saulsbury and then "camped at Lexington [North Carolina], after fording the Yadkin"[831] River.

The next day, Ferguson's men successfully brushed back Yankee horsemen belonging to the 10th Michigan Cavalry, chasing them as far away as High Point. On April 12, Ferguson reached Greensboro where he received the shocking news that "the Army of [Northern] Va had surrendered"[832] and after a meeting with Generals Cooper, Johnston, and Beauregard, the decision was made to put Ferguson in command of all the assorted cavalry then on the advanced line of Johnston's infantry. Ferguson moved his much-jaded horses three miles from Lexington and wondered, like everyone else, what would befall the nation with Lee now gone.[833]

Since the loss of Atlanta, the hope of the Southern Confederacy rested solely on the shoulders of R.E. Lee — if Lee fell, the South fell. He "was the head and front," one officer confirmed, "the very life and soul of the army."[834] He was also the life and soul of the South. Soldiers and civilians alike looked upon Robert E. Lee as something almost beyond other mortals. One Southern woman lamented in her diary: "What are we to do without him?"[835] This quality of unshakable dignity was perfectly illustrated just before the surrender at Appomattox, when Lee turned to Brigadier General Henry Wise and asked him what the army and country would think of him once he surrendered. Wise, a former Virginia governor, blurted out:

> General Lee, don't you know that you are the army .... [T]here is no country. There has been no country, for a year or more. You are the country to these men.[836]

Whether certain diehards acknowledged it or not, it was Lee's capitulation at Appomattox that signaled to all Southerners that the time had come to stop resisting the invaders. When Lee surrendered 28,000 emaciated men to Grant's 120,000, it was over. Providence had spoken and the gray-bearded general was perfectly content with the Lord God's perfect control of history. The evil of

slavery may not have directly cause the War, but the War had ended it. The ever stoic Lee who trusted in the Lord with all his being acknowledged:

> So far from engaging in a war to perpetuate slavery, I am rejoiced that slavery is abolished. I believe it will be greatly for the interest of the South. So fully am I satisfied of this ... that I would cheerfully have lost all I have lost by the war and suffered all I have suffered, to have this object attained.[837]

— Davis' Escort —

The constant rumors that Richmond was to be abandoned were finally fulfilled on April 2, 1865, when Lee advised Davis that his scarecrow army could no longer secure the city and was fleeing to the west. That same day, a Sunday, President Jefferson Davis and remnants of the government, hastily boarded a southbound train leaving the burning capital of the Confederacy to its sad fate. The cars also contained the Confederate treasury, assorted government papers, and a military escort consisting of 60 sharply-dressed midshipmen of the Naval Academy. Along with the now worthless paper currency, dozens of cloth sacks and wooden treasure boxes carried heavy loads of gold and silver specie, mostly coins minted in Mexico, mixed in with double-eagle gold coins, silver bricks, and gold ingots.

Davis chose Danville, Virginia, to set up a temporary surrogate capital since it was situated between Lee's then retreating army to the north and Johnston's army to the south in North Carolina. Waiting anxiously for news of Lee, Davis' immediate concern was to gather more soldiers to his side so that by April 9, the Confederate government in exile had accumulated a total of 3,000 armed men who had filtered into the city from all points of the compass, to include a large contingent of sailors.[838] Davis vowed to anyone that would listen that he intended to fight on even if it meant resorting to

guerrilla-type warfare or fleeing all the way to the trans-Mississippi into Texas, even though each passing day brought grim news of collapse and disaster for the nascent nation. In Alabama, the city of Selma fell on April 2, and Mobile soon followed suit on April 12.

When the paralyzing shock of Lee's surrender was confirmed on April 10, the panic in Danville was immediate. Predictably, the news that the heretofore indomitable Robert E. Lee had capitulated was hurrahed in the North. On April 10, 1865, the *New York Times* wrote quite correctly that the War was over:

> The great struggle is over .... The history of blood — the four years of war, are brought to a close .... The gigantic battles have all been fought. The last man, we trust, has been slain. The last shot has been fired.[839]

In the South, civilian and military morale plummeted. As if on cue, soldiers and their officers simply put down their weapons, to include the hodgepodge of military men in Augusta. Davis himself had no choice but to surrender or run and hasty preparations were made to board one of the few still functioning trains out of Danville to North Carolina where General Johnston's 16,000 infantry was still in the field, at least on paper. In addition, several thousand Confederate cavalrymen under various disjointed commands, to include Ferguson's brigade, were situated in the Carolinas.

Davis' train was lighter this time, as about $327,000 in silver and gold had been transferred to Charlotte. On April 11, the train chugged into Greensboro, North Carolina, and what remained of the government apparatus was forced to set up in smelly open boxcars at the depot. General Johnston met with Davis the next day and listened coldly as the president urged for the fight to continue. He advised Davis to surrender:

> My views are, sir, that our people are tired of the war, feel themselves whipped, and will not fight. Our country is overrun, its military resources greatly

Robert E. Lee.

diminished .... My small force is melting away like snow before the sun and I am hopeless of recruiting it. We may, perhaps, obtain terms [for surrender] which we ought to accept.[840]

Rebuffed by Johnston, the president and his staff left Greensboro and headed towards Charlotte. Since Federal cavalry had already cut the railroad, this leg of the journey was made by means of horseback and dilapidated wagons carrying the remaining treasury and official baggage. On the positive side, a cavalry escort of about 1,300 troopers from a mixed bag of Kentuckians, Tennesseans, Alabamians, and Mississippians agreed to accompany Davis and other cavalry, including Ferguson's, also joined up on the road so that the body swelled to about 4,000 troopers arranged in five brigades — S.W. Ferguson, J.C. Vaughn, W.C. Breckinridge, G. Dibrell, and Basil Duke.

By the time the party reached Charlotte on April 19, Davis took some comfort in the fact that he had a rather formidable cavalry command at his disposal. Unknown to any of them, however, was the assassination of President Lincoln on April 14, by John Wilkes Booth of Maryland, who had no connection whatsoever to the Confederacy. This news did not reach General Johnston until Sherman delivered it to him during the first of a series of surrender negotiations between the two on April 17 (Johnston would formally surrender on April 26 at the Bennett house), and reached Davis in Charlotte on April 19.[841] All knew that whatever magnanimous feelings that might exist in the North would soon turn to hatred and revenge[842] as evidenced by printed wanted signs offering fantastic sums of money for Davis' arrest. An April 28, 1865, posting by Union Major General J.H. Wilson's cavalry corps proclaimed:

> One Hundred thousand dollar's reward will be paid to any person or persons who apprehend and deliver Jefferson Davis to any of the military authorities of the United States. Several million dollars of specie

reported to be with him will become the property of the captors.

J.H. Wilson, Major General[843]

With Lee surrendered and Lincoln assassinated, the venture to protect Davis was not only a desperate one but a dangerous one, continued resistance could easily be viewed as criminal acts not covered by the law of war, making Davis' plea to Wheeler and Wade Hampton to withdraw any "volunteer" cavalry that they could from Johnston's army, an impossible order to reconcile with reality.[844] When Johnston formally surrendered on April 26, Davis packed up once again and left Charlotte for South Carolina.[845]

To avoid detection, Davis and his five brigades of cavalry now traveled in an erratic manner often backtracking and veering about as they made their way into South Carolina through the towns of York and Union, crossing the Broad River at Smith's ford and pressing on through until reaching the beautiful town of Abbeville on the early morning of May 2.

The dawning of a new month did nothing to boost morale and the president called his senior commanders together for what would be the Confederate chief's final council of War. All five long-faced generals unanimously pronounced that it was no longer possible to continue the conflict and that the morale of their respective commands was dismal. When a perplexed Davis drifted back from the brashness of their assessment, he asked why they had remained in the field at all. General Basil Duke answered for the group — it was for the sole purpose of helping President Davis evade the dishonor of capture.

> [W]e were desirous of affording him an opportunity of escaping the depredation of capture.... We said that we would ask our men to follow us until his safety was assured, and would risk them in battle for that purpose, but would not fire another shot in an effort to continue hostilities.[846]

The meeting ended with the agreement that by the next day or two that Davis should pursue his fantastic dream of reaching the trans-Mississippi with a smaller party in order to maximize his chances. The main Confederate column continued its march with Davis into Washington, Georgia, until May 3, when General John C. Breckinridge, the Secretary of War, ordered a halt and the treasury wagons were brought up to provide a final payment to the entire cavalry of just over 4,000 riders.

Lined up by brigades in the piney woods of Georgia, quartermasters doled out an average payout to each enlisted man of 26 dollars, for a total amount of about $108,000. It was not in old paper issue, or new paper issue, but good, hard, silver or gold. Interestingly, though each remaining trooper in the 2nd Alabama Cavalry received their pay,[847] a few of the men kept back one or two of the Mexican silver dollars as mementos. Private James Gould, Company B, 2nd Alabama Cavalry, placed one Mexican silver dollar in a cigar box, carefully wrapped in cloth and an old newspaper, where it passed down to his great-great grandson David E. Gould.[848] Another of those rare mint silver dollars is on permanent display at the Alabama Department of Archives and History, Montgomery, Alabama, with a placard that reads:

> James Madison Bullock, [Company C] adjutant for the 2nd Alabama Cavalry, received $30.00 as his final payment. Bullock used $28.00 in order to make his way home to Alabama, saving two silver dollars as souvenirs.

With this final renumeration, the men throughout all the brigades were done. On May 4, when Ferguson ordered his command to mount up, the majority, to include the officers, refused, believing they had no legal right to serve. This included most of the 2nd Alabama.[849] For his part, Ferguson was stunned and gave an impassioned speech in the middle of the camp urging them to remain.

> I had fine material in the rank and file but miserable Field Officers ... Col Boyles of the 56 Alabama demoralized his command as did Col Carpenter of the 2nd Alabama after the death of the brave Col Earle, who was killed leading a charge near Kingston, Ga.[850]

Gathering recollections from those that were then present, a 1908 article published in *The Montgomery Advertiser* noted that "passionate speeches were heard from many at an open air meeting" where "for the first time in its history, General Ferguson's cavalry was disorderly" with some refusing to surrender and others saying that they must — "they knew how to fight, these veterans, but they did not know how to surrender."[851] Lieutenant Burwell Lewis, who was then Acting Captain of Company B, 2nd Alabama, summed up the matter.

> He told them it was a soldiers duty to obey; when their commanders ordered them to fight, it was their duty to fight; when they ordered them to charge, it was their duty to charge, it mattered not what; when they ordered them to lay down their arms, it was their duty to lay down their arms. General Johnston had surrendered them they were a part of his army, they were surrendered.[852]

By May 6, Ferguson noted that only "eighty odd men of the Brigade had stuck with me [the number was 84] and that I had about ten wagons and teams left."[853] Again, the same phenomenon occurred throughout the other brigades — the men would not budge, insisting on an immediate surrender of arms. Davis himself departed with a tiny escort that same day and Breckinridge formally ordered all remaining cavalry to disband.

The troopers of Ferguson's command broke apart, seeking out and surrendering to the nearest Federal force they came upon, or, like what was left of Company B, of the 2nd Alabama,

May 4, 1865. Jefferson Davis Leaving the Cavalry Escort at Washington, GA. London Illustrated News, 1865.

Mexican Silver Dollar Paid to James M. Bullock from the Confederate Treasury. Photo Courtesy of the Alabama Department of Archives & History, Voices of Alabama Exhibit.

simply pointed their horses towards Shelby, Alabama, and rode off, Lieutenant Lewis leading them out. Curiously, according to one often quoted historical source, the 2nd Alabama surrendered as a unified command with 450 men on May 8, 1865, at Forsyth, Georgia, just a few miles north of Macon.[854]

While the date of May 8, 1865, for a surrender of a body of Confederate cavalry is undoubtedly correct — the May 20, 1865, edition of the *Charleston Daily Courier* records that a portion of Ferguson's brigade surrendered at Forsyth, making no reference to the numbers or regiments[855] — the preposterous number associated with the 2nd Alabama Cavalry is undoubtedly incorrect. The laying down of arms by "450 Rebel cavalry" at Forsyth, Georgia, on May 8 or 9, 1865, undoubtedly refers to either a remnant of Ferguson's brigade or perhaps to a roving body of Confederate cavalry of which some troopers from the 2nd Alabama had fallen in with to find a surrender location.

Another surviving source to shed light on the fact that only a portion of the 2nd Alabama surrendered at Forsyth, comes from a veteran of Company C, 2nd Alabama Cavalry, who recalled the entire regiment being paid, yet only mentions the surrender of twenty men from his company at Forsyth.

> My recollection is that either on the night of May the 5th or the morning of May 6th my regiment drew $37.00 dollars in silver ... and we [Company C] started off in the direction of Forsythe [sic], and some nine or ten miles from Washington we crossed a small river on a pontoon bridge, and were ordered by the Federals to deposit our arms on the bank of the river after we crossed over the bridge, that we went from there to Forsythe [sic], and disbanded. My recollection is there were only about twenty of my company there.[856]

Starting with Ferguson's Morning Report from January 14, 1865, which listed 373 men in the 2nd Alabama Cavalry less than

four months earlier, one must then subtract from that number: (1) the men from several large scouts now absent from the regiment, and (2) the large number of men that had deserted from that time until the present. Given those facts, the simple math refutes the claim that 450 men from the 2nd Alabama surrendered at Forsyth. Clearly, most of the remaining members of the regiment separated into familiar groups within their individual companies and either melted away to their homes in Alabama or surrendered to various Federal encampments here and there.

A wire sent to General Sherman on May 10, 1865, provides additional insight that the "450 number" most likely refers to the surrender of some chunk of Ferguson's entire brigade consisting of varied troopers from all his regiments[857] and not specifically to the remaining men of the 2nd Alabama Cavalry regiment.

> [T]wo brigades of 2,000 men were surrendered the day before [May 9] at Washington, Ga. consisting of [Confederate] General's Vaughn, Dibrell, Elzey, Williams, Lewis, Gilmer, and Lawton. And that [Union] General Croxton was presently [May 10] paroling *some of the men* of Brig. General Samuel Wragg Ferguson's Cavalry Brigade at Forsyth, Ga., [emphasis added].[858]

Another telegram sent by Major General Wilson to Sherman, dated May 10, 1865, confirms that troopers from the various regiments in Ferguson's brigade had surrendered at Forsyth:

> Captain (Lot) Abraham (4th Iowa Cavalry), of General Upton's division, yesterday received the surrender of two brigades of rebel cavalry 2,000 strong at Washington, Ga., including Generals Vaughn, Dibrell, Elzey, Williams, Lewis, Gilmer, and Lawton. General Croxton is *now engaged in paroling Ferguson's brigade at Forsyth*. The balance of the rebel cavalry which started as Davis' escort has either been paroled or gone home [emphasis added].[859]

Finally, when one adds all this to the fact that 30 of General Ferguson's 84 men who were willing to follow him were from the 2nd Alabama,[860] it is impossible that more than a handful of the surviving members of the regiment surrendered at Forsyth.[861] In the "Roll of Officers & Men of Ferguson's Cavalry Brigade, Honorable Discharge, near Washington, Ga., on May 6th 1865, by order of Genl John C. Breckinridge, Secretary of War," 84 members of the brigade are listed, 30 of the troopers being members of the 2nd Alabama Cavalry.[862] After receiving their honorable surrender discharges on May 6, at Washington, Georgia, the 30 holdouts of the 2nd Alabama quickly dissolved and also headed home.[863] They were:

Major Robert M. Hill (Surgeon)	Capt. Frank Richardson — Co. H.
Lt. F. Boykin — Co. H	Lt. E.K. Robbins — Co. H
Sgt. Maj. H.T. Cochrane	Sgt. G.W. Tunstall — Co. H
Sgt. W.A. Riley — Co. H	Sgt. G.W. Clements — Co. D
Sgt. C.D. McQueen — Co. G	Sgt. J.H. Tekill — Co. G
Sgt. Obediah Hester — Co. A	Prv. Aaron. H. Bradley — Co. H
Prv. Frank Feagin — Co. H	Prv. R.E. Hodges — Co.. H
Prv. E.R. Hodges — Co. H	Prv. W.R. Hodges — Co. H
Prv. J.J. Hodges — Co. H	Prv. W.A. Richardson — Co. H
Prv. William Turk — Co. H	Prv. Jesse Walker — Co. H
Prv. C.J. Martin — Co. D	Prv. J.W. Sanders — Co. D
Prv. J. Dockery — Co. D	Prv. N. Gore — Co. D
Prv. T. Carson — Co. D	Prv. T. Parish — Co. C
Prv. W. Laurence — Co. C	Prv. M.W. Lawrence — Co. C
Prv. H.H. Tekill — Co. G	Prv. William Prater — Co. A

Shortly thereafter, accompanied by a group of perhaps 40, Davis pressed south towards Madison, although he didn't get far. On May 10, 1865, President Davis, his wife, and a handful of followers were captured by a detachment of Federal cavalry near Irwinville, Georgia. Only $26,000 in coin was found with the party.[864]

For those Confederates that did formally disarm to Union forces, the parole passes they were issued "served as passports, tickets, and ration cards for the soldiers as they made their way home."[865] Of course, since most of the Southern rail systems were inoperable, the men walked or rode and given that the journey was long and the environment both desolate and hostile they traveled mostly by "ones or twos because it was easier to beg food."[866]

Once back in Alabama, all former Confederate soldiers — those that surrendered and had parole passes and those who went home without "surrendering" — were required to report in person to "the U.S. provost marshal in Montgomery," or other such official sites in Alabama"[867] where they would receive a printed "official parole." Then, in 1867, the Restoration Act of 1867 mandated that in order for citizenship to be restored that all former Confederate soldiers must take a "Loyalty Oath" — what Southerners called "swallowing the dog" — that they would not bear arms against the United States. One hundred and twenty Union officers were dispatched to all the counties in Alabama where they administered 50,000 oaths (by comparison 90,000 men voted in the 1860 elections). Without the oath, no one could vote, hold public office, or buy or sell property. This paper oath gave a general description of the soldier in terms of hair color, height, and complexion. While most of the former Rebels complied, a sizable number simply went to their farms and did not. The last loyalty oath was administered in 1898 in Winston County.

As for General Ferguson, he chose not seek out a formal surrender to nearby Union forces. The few remaining troopers that had remained to the very end, "clustered around him for the last farewell; he looked at them and for the first time they saw him quiver, he who had ridden at their head" followed by "tears that only come to the eyes of brave men."[868] Telling them "that parting

Loyalty Parole of Private Thomas Mosley, Co. E, 2nd Alabama Cavalry.

with them was sadder than death,"[869] Ferguson set out with a small party taking one or more of the remaining wagons and arrived at the Porcher home in Pendleton Village, South Carolina. Then, on May 22, 1865, he traveled with his wife to Columbia to have his name registered with the Union provost and receive a formal parole. While there, a Yankee cavalryman took a fancy to his wife's prized Arabian horse Juanita, "leveled his gun at Mrs. Ferguson and stole" the animal on the spot.[870] Ferguson later penned a heated letter of protest to General Sherman which was never answered.

Escorting Davis to Georgia was the last line in the last chapter for the 2nd Alabama Cavalry. At the beginning of the War the regiment was an imposing body of men, but three long years later the troopers were ill, thin, and used up, barely recognizable as flesh and blood. Stoop-shouldered from long rides in the saddle, their gray uniforms had long since been replaced by fragments of many tones and colors. Uncertain what the future would bring, at least the fighting had ended and they could go home.

Conclusion

THE END & THE BEGINNING

"The Lord has established His throne in the Heavens, and His sovereignty rules over all."[871] — Psalm 103:19

THE AMERICAN CIVIL WAR has long ended, yet understanding the underlying reasons for the conflict seems more controversial today than ever before. In large measure, this phenomena is due to nefarious forces that desperately seek to take full control over every aspect of American culture and history. Orwell's *1984* was penned as a dark warning about such things, but the so-called *progressive* movement in modern American society sees the book as a "how to manual" to advance a dystopian agenda where only one voice, the "Ministry of Truth" dictates its catechism of reality. Orwell wrote:

> Every record has been destroyed or falsified, every book rewritten, every picture has been repainted, every statue and street building has been renamed, every date has been altered. And the process is continuing day by day and minute by minute. History has stopped. Nothing exists except an endless present in which the Party is always right.[872]

Nevertheless, many Americans are truth-seekers who, as the old saying goes, "believe half of what they hear and nothing of what they see." Determined to think for themselves, truth-seekers acknowledge that a significant portion of America's historical DNA includes an understanding of the cruelty visited on innocent civilians by invading Union forces bent on wanton devastation. They reject the nonsensical thinking of myopic biographers of Sherman who bizarrely admit to "a considerable degree of admiration and respect for Sherman," then happily refuse to give any mention to the thing that forever marks him in the halls of infamy — his massive war crimes against civilians, actions both illegal under the laws of war and immoral under the laws of God.[873] Sherman and others of his ilk were terrorists and "terrorists harm their own cause, no matter how valid their concerns might be."[874] The brutal Union terror raids that desolated home after home and community after community did little to speed up the eventual defeat of the Confederacy. With vastly superior forces and resources, the United States in 1864, had only to grind down the Southern armies to win the war, pillaging and terrorizing their civilians was a vile, spiteful, and unnecessary evil that bore negative consequences for generations to come.

— Heroes of History —

As Union atrocities reached a zenith in 1864-1865, the 2nd Alabama Cavalry was uniquely positioned to see more than their fair share of the suffering and waste it produced. What they lacked in arms, equipment, and supplies to resist the terrorists, were made up for by an incredible sense of duty, courage, and perseverance. Serving under various commands, to include Ruggles and Ferguson, the 2nd Alabama Cavalry witnessed and fought the horrors and brutality of Union terror raids, to include Sherman's, more than any other regiment in the Confederacy. Many of the Alabamians that passed through this hard-fighting regiment poured out their life blood across the soils of Florida, Mississippi, Georgia, South Carolina, North Carolina, Tennessee, and Alabama, finding their final resting place in the ground they so valiantly defended.

Tragically, far too many also died of sickness, disease, starvation, and abuse at various POW camps in the North. One of those being Private Harry Harrison Mosley (1841-1865), who served in E Company with his cousin Private Thomas Mosley. Harry was captured on December 3, 1863, near Grand Junction, Tennessee, as part of the expedition to screen Forrest into Tennessee. He was sent to Fort Delaware and perished there of "hepatic dropsy" on June 18, 1865, well after the close of the War, marking him the last casualty of the 2nd Alabama Cavalry, still being in uniform, to have died in the War.

The death of the inspirational Captain Bill Allen, perfectly illustrates the story of these incredible men. Due to chronic illness, the highly esteemed leader of Company F was obliged to resign his position in January 1864, and return to his home in Pintlala (near Tuskegee), Alabama, to convalesce.[875] In keeping with his warrior ethos, Captain Allen kept busy recruiting new men for the regiment, but when he learned that the 2nd Alabama was encamped near Tuscaloosa, the physically jeopardized Allen left his one-month-old son and wife behind and traveled 140 miles to return to duty. The troopers were overjoyed to have their leader back in the saddle, even if all could see that he was a shadow of his former self. Within a few months his lingering illness spiked with a vengeance and this time it carried the flamboyant officer into his eternity. On June 13, 1864, Captain Allen succumbed to pneumonia in an Atlanta hospital, most certainly cared for in his dying days by Dr. John Augustus Baldwin, the acting assistant surgeon assigned to Allen's beloved F Troop.

When the news reached his wife, Mary Shackelford Allen, there was no hesitation about what to do. Both had long sensed the dark shadow of that awesome and fearful thing which awaits all mortals. Ignoring any personal jeopardy to herself, Mary packed up a few personal items and made the extremely dangerous journey to Atlanta bringing her husband's earthly remains back to Pintlala were she buried him in the Shackelford Cemetery beside their first son, Buster (Buster died in 1859 at the age of two).[876] Bill's passing was a blow from which Mary never recovered, nor did she wish to.

Strong in her Christian faithfulness and resting in the fragrance of those precious memories of love, Mary remained a widow for the next 43 years. The ever faithful companion died in 1907, and was gently interned next to her scandalous sweetheart, Captain William Lafayette "Hell-Roaring" Bill Allen.

For those of the 2nd Alabama who did survive, there was still the matter of dealing with the deep scars of war in their memories and bodies. In his own candid way, General Ferguson recounted a significant list of injuries and aliments he incurred:

> I was wounded in the arm when in a hand to hand encounter.... [I have] a stiffened almost useless right arm, irreducible hernia, right-side, locomotor Ataxia ... I drag the right leg in moving about due to original injury to my right side and arm.... Also, while convalescent, and on my return to Military Duty the horses to the vehicle I was riding in took fright and ran away down a hill upsetting the buggy. I was thrown out, rendered unconscious, my lip cut through from the nose down, and two teeth in front knocked out, my arm additionally injured and right side.[877]

And so, still wearing their tattered uniforms, the weather-beaten sons, brothers, and fathers of the 2nd Alabama returned to destitute families and homesites ravaged by the Yankees. An Alabama wife recalled the scenes.

> The return of our soldiers after the surrender, in their worn and ragged gray, as they tramped home by twos, threes, and sometimes in little squads of half a dozen or more, was pitiable in the extreme. Some were entirely without shoes or hats; others had only an apology for shoes and hats. They were coming home with nothing; and we could almost say, coming home to

nothing; for many verily found, when they reached the spot that had been to them a happy home, nothing save a heaped-up mass of ruins left to them.[878]

Times were desperate and the future clouded. Not only had Alabama suffered terribly from the Federal blockade and widespread atrocities across the countryside during the War years,[879] but neglected fields and loss of livestock meant hunger and starvation, and local governments possessed no resources to address the needs. Like his men, General Ferguson had lost everything. His family home was gone, his bank emptied, and no job to be had.

— Back in the United States —

The draconian provisions of the Reconstruction Act of 1867 did nothing to help and much to hinder recovery throughout the South. Under martial law, the former Confederate States were divided up into five military districts with over 50,000 Union soldiers stationed to enforce punishing rules that often worked to counter reconciliation.[880] As former Confederates tried to come to terms with the ravages of the War and the subsequent occupation, the region sank into even greater economic depression aggravated by the greed of so-called Northern carpetbaggers and Southern scalawags.[881]

Nevertheless, as time passed, these sons of Alabama and their families looked forward to better times. For instance, Sergeant Major Harden Perkins Cochrane came back to Tuscaloosa and like most ex-Confederates planted a spring crop working it with prayerful hands from dawn to dusk. Cochrane farmed for the next six years before going to medical college in New York where he graduated in 1874, and set up a practice in Franklin, Tennessee. Dr. Cochrane married his first wife in 1882, and his second in 1887. A member of the Episcopal church, he was very active in the Confederate Veterans fraternal organization and lived well into the new century, leaving this life at the ripe old age of 92.

Private James A. Gould, Co. B, 2nd Alabama Cavalry, circa 1865.

Other members of the regiment, like Private R.O. Simpson (1842-1925) of Wilcox County, Alabama, returned home penniless and took charge over a plantation belonging to his uncle where he later acquired several thousand acres of his own. What happened in Simpson's ensuing years caught the attention of the great Booker T. Washington who wrote approvingly how Simpson used his own personal wealth and effort to assist hundreds of black Southerners by establishing and building the "Snow Hill Institute" school, donating over 100 acres to the place, serving on its board of directors, and daily "going among the people encouraging them to buy land and homes, to be frugal, to educate their children and to live Christian lives."[882] Booker T. Washington wrote:

> Mr. Simpson is, as I have said, a modest and unassuming man of few words, but having made up his mind that a certain course is right, and having clearly

perceived his duty, he has pursued it steadfastly in spite of opposition or adverse criticism.[883]

Like Simpson and Cochrane, all the gray veterans would eventually join their comrades in death with not a few interned at State established Confederate old soldier homes. The mortal remains of Colonel Richard Earle rest on the grounds of the Woodlands in Georgia, and General Samuel Ferguson, who reached 82, is buried in Jackson, Mississippi. Dr. John Baldwin, who returned to the practice of medicine in Butler County, succumbed to an unspecified illness in 1885, and is buried in the family plot at the South Butler Cemetery, McKenzie, Alabama. Private Thomas Mosley returned to farming and died in 1891. He was laid to rest in the adjoining county. Private James Gould also went back to farming, siring four more children (seven in total). He was an active participant in numerous reunions of the veterans of the 2nd Alabama, the last known one for Company B being in September 1897. Gould passed away in 1905, at the age of 76 and is buried in Summer Hill Baptist Cemetery, in Shelby County, Alabama.

— Monuments Worth Celebrating —

With the War ended and the 13th Amendment adopted (December 1865) to abolish slavery in the pro-Union slave States, the cancer of slavery was finally extinguished and America could embark with renewed vigor on becoming a beacon of freedom for the world. Striding down this new path, Southerners would not soon forget the heroism, patriotism, and loyalty of their soldiers along the way. Before the century turned, the individual Southern States set up modest pensions for the widows and disabled veterans (to include veteran black Southerners) and also erected grand memorials to their heroes, although the greatest monuments would always be the innumerable graves of those who gave their lives.

Despite shrill voices that denigrate Confederate monuments as nothing more than symbols of racism, the truth-seeker understands that they are valuable reminders to each new generation of two

*Alabama Monument to Alabama's Confederate Cavalry,
State Capitol, Montgomery, Alabama.*

things: (1) the indomitable grit and courage which immortalized the Confederate soldier who did his duty; and (2) the basics of what it means to be a Southerner — "agrarianism, close family ties, fundamental religion, chivalry, the honoring of womanhood, [and] paternalism toward the less fortunate."[884] For instance, at the 1890 unveiling of a magnificent Confederate monument in Jackson, Mississippi, a Southern Senator spoke eloquently of irreducible Southern values.

> Which makes our people once practical and sentimental — makes them good soldiers and good citizens, sustains them in every trial, adapts them to every changed condition and anchors them upon their honor as a rock: something that makes the men knightly in their deference for women, and makes the gentle woman strong when trouble comes.[885]

While it is certainly a correct observation that Southern culture is marked by an allegiance to traditional conservative values, all Americans are made stronger by recalling a people who could not be terrorized by the specters of fear or terror. The eminent Civil War historian James M. McPherson's study on Confederate motivation concluded that the most powerful force that kept Southerners in the fight was not States' rights, maintaining the institution of slavery, or any other ideological purpose. It was "the defense of home and hearth against an invading enemy."[886]

In this vein, honoring the perseverance and sacrifice of these Southerners is not a brief objecting to the ultimate outcome of the conflict which was written long ago by the hand of Almighty God. At the time of the War, no one could know the future, it was enough to know *duty*. Much in line with the humility of modern combat soldiers who salute one another with an succinct understatement bound up in honor and duty — "Thank you for your service!" — General Lee, in his farewell address to the army closed by stating

that the men could take with them "the satisfaction that proceeds from the consciousness of duty faithfully performed."[887]

At the end of the day, as our country meanders along in paths measured by days, weeks, and months, it is efficacious that we do not fall into the twin traps of complacency and apathy when it comes to understanding the simple truths which fuel the blessings of freedom to a free people. In the profound words of novelist Rebecca West: "The trouble with man is twofold — he cannot learn truths that are too complicated and he forgets truths that are too simple."[888]

— THE 2ND ALABAMA CAVALRY REGIMENT —

Like any national entity that will ever exist in human history, it is true that the United States of America is not perfect (the postmodernist fixates on that fact) yet it is factually undeniable that Americans unabashedly stride upon this earth as the freest and most prosperous humans the world has ever seen. Whatever else we are in terms of culture, race, background, or geography, we are all Americans and share a common story that is made stronger by the courage and sacrifice that these Alabama cavalrymen set as part of our historical and national collective. The few particulars gathered and put on record herein will ensure to some small degree that this regiment's heroic story will not be distorted by the ignorance of those who seek to "reimagine" and "reinterpret" objective reality.

In conclusion, the 2nd Alabama Cavalry was composed of some of the best material that the South had to offer. After struggling through a first year of service marked by inaction and incompetent leadership, they proved themselves a sterling fighting regiment when assigned to independent duty in north Mississippi in the late spring of 1863. By the time that their incredible regimental commander, the gallant Colonel Richard Earle, was killed in action the next year, they had long since found their stride as the best regiment in Ferguson's brigade. Ferguson, himself a brave and skilled leader, who possessed no other ambition than to serve his

country, relied heavily on the 2nd Alabama until the very end. For their faithful duty, the troopers received nothing in return other than the right to be identified with one of the most outstanding cavalry regiments of the War.

The story of how well they fought and how great was their suffering will never be adequately told, yet it is without debate that these Southern heroes did their duty against overwhelming odds. No nation could have asked more. It was only fitting, then, that the 2nd Alabama Cavalry was present as the Confederacy drew her last gasping breath. They helped close her eyes and held her cold hand.

> Of what command were they who were thus faithful even unto the end, and who were to be the last Confederate soldiers into whose faces Mr. Davis was to look before he entered into his captivity? The answer is a matter of history of which they have a right to be forever proud![889]

2nd Alabama Cavalry Regiment

1862   1865

Confederate States of America

Colonel
Fountain W. Hunter

Colonel
Richard G. Earle

Lt. Colonel
John P. West

Lt. Colonel
Josiah J. Pegues

Alabama; Independent Now and Forever, 'Noli Me Tangere.'

2nd Alabama Cavalry Regiment

Alabama Cavalry
Confederate States of America

Captain
William L. Allen

Captain
Thomas R. Stacey

Captain
Felix Glackmeyer

Captain
Frank E. Richardson

Captain
Jacob W. Whisenant

Captain
Bethel J. Bonham

Captain
James A. Anderson

1st Lieutenant
Burwell B. Lewis

1st Lieutenant
Joseph Shackelford

Alabama Cavalry
Confederate States of America

1st Lieutenant
William P. Gaddis

1st Lieutenant
Walter Scott Stokes

2nd Lieutenant
Jefferson J. Beeland

2nd Lieutenant
Madison Shackelford

Sergeant Major
Hardin P. Cochrane

Sergeant
William M. Richards

Acting Asst. Surgeon
Richard Fowler

Private
Martin Van Buren Joiner

Private
Nipper A Teakell

Alabama Cavalry
Confederate States of America

Private
Mark L. McClammy

Private
Clifford D. McQueen

Private
Wesley R. Akridge

Private
Robert J. Hall

Private
James A. Gould

Private
Francis Marion Coker

Private
Tandy Walker Davis

Private
Jabez Wallace Hall

Private
George W. Weems

2ND ALABAMA CAVALRY REGIMENT

479

Alabama Cavalry
Confederate States of America

Private
James W. Foster

Private
W. H. Pate

Private
Isaac Newton Phillips

Private
Joseph Grizzard

Private
Lot W. Brantley

Private
Beverly W. Addison

Private
Henry B. Boddie

Private
James Coley Anthony

Private
George W. Roebuck

Alabama Cavalry
Confederate States of America

Private
Francis Shackelford

Private
Sampson F. Deavers

Private
Daniel M. Courtney

Private
Henry C. Fulcher

Private
Elias Richard Hodges

Private
John F. Capehart

Private
James William Bass

Private
Sterling Ramsey Kendrick

Private
Joseph S. Cushing

Alabama Cavalry
Confederate States of America

Private
Asa S. Kendrick

Private
James C. Parrish

Private
William T. Caddell

Private
James McInnis

Private
John A. Helton

Private
John W. McInnis

Private
Nathaniel M. Bayzer

Private
Edward F. Lee

Private
William W. Brown

ENDNOTES

[1] GEORGE ORWELL, 1984 (1949).

[2] JEFFREY F. ADDICOTT, UNION TERROR: DEBUNKING THE FALSE JUSTIFICATIONS FOR THE UNION'S USE OF TERROR AGAINST SOUTHERN CIVILIANS (2023).

[3] *See* Sherman's Civil War: Selected Correspondence of William T. Sherman 1860-1865 776 (1999), Brooks D. Simpson & Jean V. Berlin, eds.

[4] *See* Richard Shelly Hartigan, Lieber's Code and the Law of War 45—71 (1983) (citations to General Order 100 are referenced to the specific article contained within the Order).

[5] *See* Walter Kiaulehn, *Les Methodes de Guerre Americaines*, Signal, p. 12, No. 1, Deutscher Verlag Berlin, (1944). The German magazine was very similar in style and layout to LIFE Magazine (1883-1972) in the United States.

[6] *See* JAMES M. MCPHERSON, WHAT THEY FOUGHT FOR: 1861-1865 18 (1994).

[7] With over 30,000 members, the Sons of CONFEDERATE VETERANS was organized in 1896 and is "a historical, patriotic, and non-political organization" to honor the valor of the Confederate soldier. Membership is open to all male descendants of any veteran who served honorably in the Confederate armed forces, which includes black Southerners. *See* http://www.scv.org. The Combined Federal Campaign (CFC) includes the Sons of CONFEDERATE VETERANS as a qualified CFC charity.

[8] *See* BUTLER COUNTY ALABAMA MARRIAGE LICENSES VOL. 1865-1868. Thomas M. Mosley married Penelope V. Davis on February 11, 1867 and John Augustus Baldwin married Margaret Narcissus McPherson on July 30, 1867.

[9] *Id.* at Vol. 1898.

[10] *See* DAVID E. GOULD, *2nd Alabama Cavalry Regiment Facebook Group*. David Gould is a direct descendant of Private James A. Gould, Company B, 2nd Alabama Cavalry. Gould has amassed a great deal of valuable and detailed material on the regiment to include newspaper articles, books, diaries, period maps and first-hand accounts. *See also*, JOHN C. RIGDON, HISTORICAL SKETCH & ROSTER OF THE ALABAMA 2ND CAVALRY REGIMENT (2004). Well over two-thirds of the 252 page "book" is comprised of a roster of the soldiers that served in the regiment and a list of "mentions" and resources in surviving war period documents.

[11] U.S. War Department, WAR OF THE REBELLION: A COMPILATION OF THE OFFICIAL RECORDS OF THE UNION AND CONFEDERATE ARMIES (Washington D.C. 1880-1901) [HEREINAFTER OR]; *Civil War Records: Basic Research Sources*, NATIONAL ARCHIVES (Sept. 4, 2018), https://www.archives.gov/research/military/civil-war/resources#union.

[12] The number of 450 troopers of the 2nd Alabama Cavalry surrendering at Forsyth, Georgia, was first offered by Director of the Mississippi Department of Archives & History, Dunbar Rowland (1864-1937) in a short regimental history. *See*, CONFEDERATE MILITARY HISTORY EXPANDED EDITION, GEN. CLEMENT A. EVANS, ED., VOL. 7, 255 (1987). Drawing from materials "written by distinguished men of the South and edited by General Clement A. Evans of Georgia," the original 1899 book published by the Confederate Publishing Company consisted of 17 volumes and contained a series of brief regimental histories on Confederate regiments. In some instances the histories do not comport with other more accurate sources. [HEREINAFTER CONFEDERATE MILITARY HISTORY EXPANDED EDITION]. *See also*, DEBOSE DOCUMENT, August 23, 1905. On file with ALABAMA DEPARTMENT OF ARCHIVES & HISTORY [HEREINAFTER DEBOSE DOCUMENT]; JOSEPH H. CRUTE, JR. UNITS OF THE CONFEDERATE STATES ARMY (1987).

[13] THE LETTERS OF HARDEN PERKINS COCHRANE 1862-1864, arranged by Harriet Fitts Ryan, in the ALABAMA REVIEW, October 1954 [HEREINAFTER COCHRANE LETTERS]. The letters stopped in the late summer of 1864, most likely due to the smashing of the nation's infrastructure making mail delivery over great distances impossible.

[14] *See* GARY W. GALLAGHER, THE CONFEDERATE WAR 5 (1997) (arguing that the Confederacy was not doomed to defeat and that the Confederate people expected victory in spite of setbacks and Union terror tactics that targeted civilians).

[15] STEVEN PRESSFIELD, THE VIRTUES OF WAR: A NOVEL OF ALEXANDER THE GREAT (2004).

[16] MARK A. WEITZ, MORE DAMNING THAN SLAUGHTER: DESERTION IN THE CONFEDERATE ARMY 74-75 (2005).

[17] ALABAMA DEPARTMENT OF ARCHIVES & HISTORY; SERIES TITLE: CONFEDERATE MUSTER ROLL COLLECTION –– 2D ALABAMA CAVALRY REGIMENT, 1915 [sic 1913] MAY. Muster roll typewritten, submitted by L.M. Bashinsky, Troy, Alabama, April 23, 1862.

[18] *See* GLENDA MCWHIRTER TODD, FIRST ALABAMA CAVALRY U.S.A. (2006) [HEREINAFTER FIRST ALABAMA CAVALRY UNION]. Later in the War, the United States government also raised six regiments of Union infantry, composed of Northern white officers and former Alabama slaves. *See* WALTER L. FLEMING, CIVIL WAR AND RECONSTRUCTION IN ALABAMA (1905).

19   *See* OR, Series 1, Vol. 32, Pt. I, p. 393-394. Several contemporary newspapers report that a second regiment of Alabama Tories was raised late in the War. *See, e.g.*, CHICAGO DAILY TRIBUNE, February 27, 1864; ORLEANS INDEPENDENT STANDARD, February 19, 1864; MINERAL POINT WEEKLY TRIBUNE, June 1, 1864.

20   J.H. SEGARS & CHARLES KELLY BARROW, FORGOTTEN CONFEDERATES: BLACK SOUTHERNERS IN CONFEDERATE ARMIES: A COLLECTION OF HISTORICAL ACCOUNTS i (2012) [HEREINAFTER FORGOTTEN CONFEDERATES]; ERVIN L. JORDAN JR., BLACK CONFEDERATES AND AFRO-YANKEES IN CIVIL WAR VIRGINIA 34 (1995); Scott C. Williams, *Black Confederate Heritage* (1998); http://www.pricecamp.org/media.php?id=98.

21   *See, e.g.*, FORGOTTEN CONFEDERATES, at 17.

22   *See, e.g.*, KEVIN M. LEVIN, SEARCHING FOR BLACK CONFEDERATES, THE CIVIL WAR'S MOST PERSISTENT MYTH (2019). Levin argues that the number of blacks under arms in fighting combat roles for the Confederacy was insignificant.

23   ATLANTA HISTORY CENTER, http://www.atlantahistorycenter.com/.

24   FORGOTTEN CONFEDERATES, at 17, 22.

25   *Id.*

26   FREDERICK DOUGLAS, DOUGLAS MONTHLY, September, 1861.

27   PRIVATE ALEX K. HALL, COMPANY I, 2ND ALABAMA CAVALRY, LETTERS, AUGUST 15, 1862, ALABAMA DEPARTMENT OF ARCHIVES & HISTORY [HEREINAFTER HALL LETTERS].

28   *Id.*

29   FORGOTTEN CONFEDERATES, at 17, 39.

30   *See Id.*

31   COCHRANE LETTERS.

32   MICHAEL SCOTT ALEXANDER SMITH, THE HISTORY OF ST. PAUL'S EPISCOPAL CHURCH: A GOOD STORY OF SAINTS AND SINNERS (2016). The photo of Sergeant Major Cochrane was taken at a CONFEDERATE VETERANS reunion held in Nashville, Tennessee in 1925, and published in the *Banner* newspaper. Cochrane was a member of the McEwen Camp, CONFEDERATE VETERANS.

33   ERVIN L. JORDAN JR., BLACK CONFEDERATES AND AFRO-YANKEES IN CIVIL WAR VIRGINIA 186 (1995).

[34] *See* Jeffrey F. Addicott, *Contractors on the "Battlefield": Providing Adequate Protection, Anti-Terrorism Training, and Personnel Recovery for Civilian Contractors Accompanying the Military in Combat and Contingency Operations*, 28 HOUSTON JOURNAL OF INTERNATIONAL LAW 323 (2006).

[35] COCHRANE LETTERS, June 26, 1862.

[36] COCHRANE LETTERS, November 11, 1862. This was the winter camp built for Company D near Brewton, Alabama, in November 1862.

[37] *Id.* at 328.

[38] LIFE OF JOHNNY REB, at 328.

[39] COCHRANE LETTERS, June 14, 1864.

[40] COCHRANE LETTERS, June 23, 1863.

[41] COCHRANE LETTERS, July 5, 1862.

[42] COCHRANE LETTERS, December 27, 1862.

[43] COCHRANE LETTERS, November 26, 1863.

[44] COCHRANE LETTERS, July 21, 1862.

[45] COCHRANE LETTERS, June 1, 1862.

[46] COCHRANE LETTERS, July 5, 1862.

[47] COCHRANE LETTERS, September 6, 1862.

[48] COCHRANE LETTERS, November 30, 1862.

[49] DANIEL O'FLAHERTY, GENERAL JO SHELBY: UNDEFEATED REBEL 89 (1954).

[50] GARY R. MATTHEWS, BASIL WILSON DUKE, CSA: THE RIGHT MAN IN THE RIGHT PLACE 40 (2005).

[51] *Id.*

[52] *See, e.g.*, George Walsh, *Those Damn Horse Soldiers* (2006).

[53] *See* RON FIELD, CONFEDERATE CAVALRYMAN VERSES UNION CAVALRYMAN (2015).

[54] *See* ROBERT G. MCLENDON, JR., HISTORY OF THE 53RD REGIMENT ALABAMA VOLUNTEER CAVALRY AND M.W. HANNON'S CAVALRY BRIGADE ARMY OF TENNESSEE, C.S.A. XII (2007)

[HEREINAFTER HISTORY OF THE 53RD REGIMENT ALABAMA VOLUNTEER CAVALRY AND M.W. HANNON'S CAVALRY BRIGADE].

55   I. G., *Army Correspondence: Letter from Middle Tennessee*, MOBILE REGISTER & ADVERTISER, April 19, 1863, at 3.

56   CAMPAIGNS OF WHEELER AND HIS CAVALRY 1862-1865, INCLUDING THE SANTIAGO CAMPAIGN OF 1898, W.C. DODSON, ED., 295 (1899) [HEREINAFTER WHEELER AND HIS CAVALRY].

57   PHILIP KATCHER, CONFEDERATE CAVALRYMAN 1861-1865 17 (2002).

58   *See* LIEUTENANT COLONEL ALFRED ROMAN, INSPECTION REPORT OF WHEELER'S CAVALRY CORPS IN OBEDIENCE TO INSTRUCTIONS FROM HEADQUARTERS MILITARY DIVISION OF THE WEST, DECEMBER 28, 1864, JANUARY 22, 1865, ROMAN MSS, LIBRARY OF CONGRESS, WASHINGTON, DC [HEREINAFTER ROMAN INSPECTION REPORT].

59   SHEPHERD SPENCER NEVILLE BROWN, SR., WAR YEARS, C.S.A. 12TH MISSISSIPPI REGIMENT MAJOR S.H. GILES Q.M., ORIGINAL LETTERS, 1860-1865 219-220 (1998) [HEREINAFTER GILES LETTERS]. Major S.H. Giles was actually in the 11th Mississippi Cavalry Regiment, not the 12th Mississippi, and served for a time as the Brigade quartermaster for Ferguson's Brigade, of which the 11th Mississippi was assigned to from August 1863-May 1865.

60   GILES LETTERS, at 246.

61   COCHRANE LETTERS, July 8, 1862.

62   COCHRANE LETTERS, September 27, 1862.

63   MORNING TO MIDNIGHT IN THE SADDLE: CIVIL WAR LETTERS OF A SOLDIER IN WILDER'S LIGHTNING BRIGADE, CHRISTOPHER MCMANUS, THOMAS H. INGLIS, & JAMES HICKS, EDS., 180 (2012) [HEREINAFTER MORNING TO MIDNIGHT].

64   PEGUES LETTER.

65   DEBOSE DOCUMENT.

66   WILLIAM A. ALBAUGH III, CONFEDERATE EDGED WEAPONS (1993); *see also* COCHRANE LETTERS, May 7, 1862. Private Cochrane indicates that his camp is at the "Dog River Factory [near Mobile, Alabama] May 7, 1862."

67   Fred Edmunds, *Collecting Confederate Swords...The Mystique*, AMERICAN SOCIETY OF ARMS COLLECTORS (2013).

68   *See* ROMAN INSPECTION REPORT.

69   GILES LETTERS, at 245.

[70] William Warren Rogers, Jr., Confederate Home Front, Montgomery During the Civil War 47-59 (1999).

[71] Life of Johnny Reb, at 115-116.

[72] Cochrane Letters, July 21, 1862.

[73] Life of Johnny Reb, at 115-116.

[74] Cochrane Letters, January 25, 1863.

[75] *Id.* at 114.

[76] Cochrane Letters, September 27, 1862.

[77] Cochrane Letters, November 30, 1862.

[78] Cochrane Letters, December 27, 1862.

[79] John M. Coski, *"Company Business" in the Confederate Army Kept Paper Pushers Busy*, The Museum of the Confederacy Magazine, Spring 2009, at 7.

[80] Giles Letters, at 166-168.

[81] Articles of War For the Government of the Army of the Confederate States, Confederate States of America War Dept, Montgomery, AL, 1861 [hereinafter Confederate Articles of War].

[82] 2nd Alabama Cavalry Ledger Book, Company E, Alabama Department of Archives & History (Rare Book Room). The ledger details the number of men on extra camp duty and in the stockade. Note: A "Moseley" is on stockade guard duty over another "Moseley."

[83] Cochrane Letters, June 23, 1863.

[84] *See* Morning to Midnight, at 180.

[85] *Id.* at 67.

[86] Ron Field, Confederate Cavalryman verses Union Cavalryman 25 (2015).

[87] Cochrane Letters, July 5, 1862.

[88] Keith Miller, *Southern Horse*, Civil War Times, February 2006, at 31.

[89] *Id.*

[90] Giles Letters, at 178.

[91] *Id.* at 242-243.

[92] *Id.* at 201-202.

[93] Keith Miller, *Southern Horse*, CIVIL WAR TIMES, February 2006, at 32. The grain was either oats, barley, or corn. Smaller animals would be given less.

[94] PHILIP KATCHER, CONFEDERATE CAVALRYMAN 1861-1865 26 (2002).

[95] 2ND ALABAMA CAVALRY MUSTER ROLL, COMPANY F, April 3 to June 30, 1862. ALABAMA DEPARTMENT OF ARCHIVES & HISTORY.

[96] *Id.*

[97] *Id.*

[98] GILES LETTERS, at 214.

[99] WHEELER AND HIS CAVALRY, at 248.

[100] *See* R. PARKER, AN OFFICER'S NOTES (1917).

[101] HALL LETTERS, August 15, 1862.

[102] COCHRANE LETTERS, September 6, 1862.

[103] COCHRANE LETTERS, September 6, 1862.

[104] HALL LETTERS, June 23, 1864.

[105] PHILIP KATCHER, CONFEDERATE CAVALRYMAN 1861-1865 12 (2002).

[106] WHEELER AND HIS CAVALRY, at 310.

[107] *Id.*

[108] *Id.* at 311-312.

[109] COCHRANE LETTERS, December 27, 1862.

[110] COCHRANE LETTERS, June 6, 1864.

[111] Eric Wittenberg, *Rantings of a Civil War Historian, The Faithful Steeds*, Dec. 25, 2012, available at https://civilwarcavarly.com/?m=201212.

[112] COCHRANE LETTERS, June 14, 1864.

[113] SAM WATKINS, CO. "AYTCH": THE FIRST TENNESSEE REGIMENT OR A SIDE SHOW TO THE BIG SHOW 160 (2015).

[114] Keith Miller, *Southern Horse*, CIVIL WAR TIMES, February 2006, at 34.

[115] GILES LETTERS, at 381-382.

[116] SPENCER C. TUCKER, BRIGADIER GENERAL JOHN D. IMBODEN, CONFEDERATE COMMANDER IN THE SHENANDOAH 166 (2003).

[117] OR, Ser. 1, Vol 37, Pt. I, p. 544.

[118] COCHRANE LETTERS, July 8, 1862.

[119] WILLIAM H. DAVIDSON, WORD FROM CAMP POLLARD C.S.A. 24 (1978) [HEREINAFTER WORD FROM CAMP POLLARD].

[120] COCHRANE LETTERS, September 16, 1862.

[121] JOHN D. BILLINGS, HARDTACK & COFFEE 80 (1993).

[122] COCHRANE LETTERS, September 27, 1862.

[123] COCHRANE LETTERS, August 7, 1862.

[124] COCHRANE LETTERS, September 6, 1862.

[125] COCHRANE LETTERS, October 13, 1862. A vacant lot located on 211 Aber Lane, Riverview, Alabama, appears to encompass at least a part of the camp site of Company D's winter quarters.

[126] COCHRANE LETTERS, November 11, 1862.

[127] *See, e,g.*, Gary Fisher, Rebel Cornbread and Yankee Coffee (2001).

[128] "Voices of Alabama" Exhibit, ALABAMA DEPARTMENT OF ARCHIVES AND HISTORY, Montgomery, Alabama.

[129] *Id.*

[130] COCHRANE LETTERS, July 8, 1862.

[131] COCHRANE LETTERS, November 30, 1862.

[132] *Id.*

[133] *Id.*

[134] *Id.*

[135] *Id.*

[136] *See* ROBERT E. DENNY, CIVIL WAR MEDICINE (1995). Illness from poor food was phenomenally high.

137 Robert Hancock, *Soldier's Own Words Tell the Story in Between the Battles*, THE MUSEUM OF THE CONFEDERACY MAGAZINE, Spring 2009, at 13.

138 GILES LETTERS, at 136.

139 *Id.*, at 140.

140 TIMOTHY DAISS, IN THE SADDLE, EXPLOITS OF THE 5TH GEORGIA CAVALRY DURING THE CIVIL WAR 107-108 (1999).

141 Robert Hancock, *Soldier's Own Words Tell the Story in Between the Battles*, THE MUSEUM OF THE CONFEDERACY MAGAZINE, Spring 2009, at 10.

142 ROMAN INSPECTION REPORT.

143 *Id.*

144 SAMUEL WRAGG FERGUSON, BRIG. GENERAL, CSA, AND WIFE CATHERINE LEE: FEATURING SELECTIONS FROM THEIR WRITINGS, JAMES MARVIN LOWREY, ED., 245 (1994) [HEREINAFTER FERGUSON MEMOIRS/DIARY].

145 SAMUEL WRAGG FERGUSON, BRIG. GENERAL, CSA, UNPUBLISHED, DUKE UNIVERSITY SPECIAL COLLECTIONS LIBRARY 5-3 (1900) [HEREINAFTER FERGUSON DUKE LIBRARY].

146 COCHRANE LETTERS, September 6, 1862.

147 The CHORUS: Peas, peas, peas, peas, eatin'goober peas. Goodness, how delicious, eatin' goober peas.

Just before the battle, the general hears a row. He says "The Yanks are coming! I hear their rifles now!" He turns around in wonder, and what do you think he sees? The Georgia Militia eatin' goober peas! CHORUS. I wish this war was over, when free from rags and fleas We'd kiss our wives and sweethearts and gobble goober peas!

148 "CONFEDERATE LIFE" EXHIBIT, SOUTH CAROLINA STATE MUSEUM, COLUMBIA, SOUTH CAROLINA.

149 A.E. PENDLETON, PENDLETON PAPERS, LETTER TO GENERAL PENDLETON, dated November 6, 1864.

150 W.G. BEAR, STONEWALL'S MAN: SANDIE PENDLETON 7 (1959).

151 LIFE OF JOHNNY REB, at 50-51.

152 *See* Michael R. Bradley, *Tullahoma*, BLUE & GRAY MAGAZINE, p. 48, XXVII, #1 (2010).

153 LIFE OF JOHNNY REB, at 53.

[154] WILLIAM WARREN ROGERS, JR., CONFEDERATE HOME FRONT, MONTGOMERY DURING THE CIVIL WAR 9 (1999). Eliza Coppinger was a well-known *madam* in Montgomery, but the 1860 census listed her "as the proprietor of a boardinghouse." *Id.*

[155] *Id.* at 54.

[156] COCHRANE LETTERS, April 12, 1862.

[157] MOBILE REGISTER & ADVERTISER, April 19, 1863, at 3.

[158] COCHRANE LETTERS, November 30, 1864.

[159] J. WILLIAM JONES, CHRIST IN THE CAMP (1887).

[160] *See e.g.*, MICHAEL KORDA, CLOUDS OF GLORY: THE LIFE AND LEGEND OF ROBERT E. LEE 160-161 (2014).

[161] Ron Gragg, *The Quotable Robert E. Lee*, SOUTHERN PARTISAN, Fourth Quarter 1989, at 29. *See* Eph. 2:8-9. By bearing the sins of all humanity — past, present, and future — in His own body on the Roman cross, Jesus Christ accomplished all the work necessary so that God's perfect essence would not be compromised by human sin and He could thereby provide an eternal and irrevocable relationship (salvation) to any human who desired it by expressing faith alone in Christ.

[162] J. WILLIAM JONES, CHRIST IN THE CAMP 268-270 (1887).

[163] JAMES W. SILVER, CONFEDERATE MORALE & CHURCH PROPAGANDA 64 (1957).

In the South there existed no agency nor any group of leaders as likely as the church to exercise a direct and guiding influence on the conduct of the individual citizen. If he looked anywhere for counsel, it was the church. *Id.*

[164] 25 CONFEDERATE VETERAN 261-264 (1917).

[165] *See, e.g.*, STEPHEN V. ASH, A YEAR IN THE SOUTH: 1865 (2002).

[166] CONFEDERATE ARTICLES OF WAR, at Article 2.

[167] EDWARD J. STACKPOLE, THEY MET AT GETTYSBURG 27 (1956).

[168] J. WILLIAM JONES, CHRIST IN THE CAMP 77 (1887).

[169] JAMES C. NISBET, FOUR YEARS ON THE FIRING LINE 44 (1987) [HEREINAFTER FOUR YEARS ON THE FIRING LINE].

[170] *Id.* at 43

[171] Moxley Sorrel, Recollections of a Confederate Staff Officer 87 (1987).

[172] *See* My Dear Nellie: The Civil War Letters of William L. Nugent to Eleanor Smith Nugent, William M. Cash & Lucy Somerville Howorth ed., 178 (1977) [hereinafter Nugent Letters].

[173] Four Years on the Firing Line, at 23 (1987).

[174] Charles Walker, Memorial Virginia Military Institute 44 (1871).

[175] Four Years on the Firing Line, at 44.

[176] The Bible teaches that all Christians continue to sin after salvation. Further, although no future sin can cause a Christian to become "unsaved," he is still commanded to stay in "fellowship" with God the Holy Spirit. This is accomplished by naming privately to God any known sin that the Christian commits at which point God puts that Christian back in a fellowship relationship called "filling of the [Holy] Spirit." *See* Jeffrey F. Addicott, Christian Doctrines, 2nd Ed. 515-528 (2023). 1 John 1:9 states:

If we [Christians] confess our sins [a known sin], He is faithful and righteous to forgive us our sins and to cleanse us from all unrighteousness [all unknown sins]. *Id.*

[177] Life of Johnny Reb, at 115-116.

[178] Hall Letters, March 6, 1863.

[179] Moxley Sorrel, Recollections of a Confederate Staff Officer 87 (1987).

[180] *Id.*

[181] Cochrane Letters, October 13, 1862.

[182] Dr. J.W. Jones, Life and Letters of Gen. Robert Edward Lee 379 (1906).

[183] The Bible identifies three interlocking categories of Divine Will: (1) The Directive Will of God, e.g., it is His will that all humans should be saved per 1 Jn. 3:23; 1 Tim. 2:4; (2) The Permissive Will of God, God allows the free will decisions of humans to operate in time; and (3) The Overruling Will of God, God keeps the results of human free will within His overall control of human history, e.g., Balaam was not permitted to curse the Hebrews per Numbers 23:5. *See* Jeffrey F. Addicott, Christian Doctrines, 2nd Ed. 473-484 (2023).

[184] Edward J. Stackpole, They Met at Gettysburg 322 (1986).

Endnotes

185 H.H. Cunningham, Doctors in Gray 5 (1993) [hereinafter Doctors in Gray].

186 Cochrane Letters, July 8, 1862.

187 Michael R. Bradley, With Blood and Fire 42 (2003).

188 Robert E. Denny, Civil War Medicine 3 (1995).

189 Cochrane Letters, November 11, 1862.

190 Perry Andrews Letter, June 28, 1862, Alabama Department of Archives & History. Written by Private Perry Andrews, Company C, 2nd Alabama Cavalry, to his father Warren Andrews from Bluff Springs, Florida [hereinafter Andrews Letter].

191 Robert F. Reilly, MD, *Medical and Surgical Care During the American Civil War, 1861-1865*, Baylor University Medical Center Proceedings (2016).

192 *See* No Soap, No Pay, Diarrhea, Dysentery & Desertion, Jeff Toalson, ed., (2006).

193 Robert E. Denny, Civil War Medicine 3 (1995).

194 C. Kenneth McAllister, *The Heart of the Lion*, Blue & Gray Magazine, Vol. XXVIII #1, at 31.

195 Doctors in Gray, at 185. "No matter what else a patient had, he had diarrhea." *Id.*

196 Life of Johnny Reb, at 257.

197 *Id.* at 11.

198 Thomas Eans, *Medical Care During the War for Southern Independence*, Confederate Veteran, July/August 2016, p. 19.

199 *Id.* at 57.

200 *Id.* at 11. By 1861, there were only twenty-one medical schools in all of the Southern States.

201 Doctors in Gray, at 107.

202 Terry G. Scriber & Theresa Arnold-Scriber, The Fourth Louisiana Battalion in the Civil War 250 (1988).

203 Alabama Department of Archives & History, J.A. Baldwin, Co. F, 2 Reg't Alabama Cavalry Company Muster Role, Oct. 31 to Dec. 31, 1862.

204 Dr. Richard Fowler assigned to Company H, 2nd Alabama Cavalry, was also appointed as an assistant surgeon from his camp in South Alabama and put on extra duty serving thereafter at various Confederate hospitals. Although placed in charge of a small hospital in Tennessee, he too was denied an officers rank.

205 DOCTORS IN GRAY, at 133.

206 Lee Peacock, *Butler County's John Augustus Baldwin Served as Confederate Assistant Surgeon*, EVERGREEN COURANT, Mar. 23, 2017.

207 ALABAMA DEPARTMENT OF ARCHIVES & HISTORY, J.A. BALDWIN, CO. F, 2 REG'T ALABAMA CAVALRY, 1ST MISSISSIPPI C.S.A. Hospital, Jackson, MS.

208 *Id.*

209 COCHRANE LETTERS, July 8, 1862.

210 COCHRANE LETTERS, June 26, 1862.

211 *Id.*

212 *See, e.g.*, KATE: THE JOURNAL OF A CONFEDERATE NURSE, RICHARD BARKSDALE HARWELL, ED. (1959).

213 RICHARD LOWE, A TEXAS CAVALRY OFFICER'S CIVIL WAR 296-297 (1999).

214 E.H. Robinson, *Reminiscences of Ferguson's Cavalry*, 12 CONFEDERATE VETERAN 62 (1904),

215 *Id.*

216 E.H. Robinson, *Strange and Fatal Freak of Lightning*, 15 CONFEDERATE VETERAN 360 (1907).

217 FERGUSON MEMOIRS/DIARY, at 299.

218 FERGUSON DUKE LIBRARY, at 5-1.

219 E.H. Robinson, *Strange and Fatal Freak of Lightning*, 12 CONFEDERATE VETERAN 360 (1907).

220 *Id.* at 360.

221 COCHRANE LETTERS, July 8, 1862.

222 LIEUTENANT COLONEL J.J. PEGUES, LETTER TO HONORABLE THOMAS OWEN, APRIL 15, 1903, ALABAMA DEPARTMENT OF ARCHIVES & HISTORY [HEREINAFTER PEGUES LETTER].

Endnotes

[223] DeBose Document. *See also*, Joseph H. Crute, Jr., Units of the Confederate States Army (1987); Stewart Sifakis, Compendium of The Confederate Armies — Alabama 29-30 (2007).

[224] Word From Camp Pollard, at 24.

[225] Confederate Muster Roles 2nd Alabama Cavalry: The following companies were mustered into the 2nd Alabama Cavalry Regiment in Montgomery, Alabama: Company A — March 8, 1862; Company B — March 21, 1862; Company C — March 22, 1862; Company D — March 22, 1862; Company E — April 23, 1862; Company F — April 26, 1862; Company G — April 30, 1862; Company H — April 21, 1862; Company I — April 14, 1862; Company K — April 23, 1862.

[226] Stewart Sifakis, Compendium of The Confederate Armies — Alabama 29 (2007) [hereinafter Compendium — Alabama].

[227] DeBose Document.

[228] *See* Compendium — Alabama, at 29.

[229] *See* http://www.archives.state.al.us/referenc/alamilor/mil_org.html.

[230] *See* Word From Camp Pollard, at 4. After about ten months in service the Second Alabama Cavalry Regiment is said to still number "nearly a thousand." *Id.*

[231] Montgomery Daily Advertiser, March 8, 1863. On file: *History of the 2nd Alabama Cavalry*, Alabama Department of Archives & History.

[232] *Id.* at 29-30.

[233] 2nd Alabama Cavalry Muster Roll, Alabama Department of Archives & History.

[234] Pegues Letter.

[235] Compendium — Alabama, at 29.

[236] Pegues Letter.

[237] *Id.*

[238] Robin Young, For Love and Liberty: The Untold Civil War Story of Major Sullivan Ballou & His Famous Love Letter 299 (2006).

[239] Hall Letters, August 15, 1862.

[240] The Daily Selma Reporter, August 14, 1862.

[241] Word From Camp Pollard, at 105.

²⁴² *Id.* at v.

²⁴³ *Id.*

²⁴⁴ WORD FROM CAMP POLLARD, at 15. "On the Tensas [River] there was a ferry for passengers, troops and military goods bound to and from Mobile. Two steamers left daily for Tensas Landing."

²⁴⁵ ARTHUR W. BERGERON, JR., CONFEDERATE MOBILE 15 (1991).

²⁴⁶ WORD FROM CAMP POLLARD, at 18.

²⁴⁷ *Id.* at 19.

²⁴⁸ *Id.* at 15.

²⁴⁹ *See, e.g.*, ARTHUR W. BERGERON, JR., CONFEDERATE MOBILE 92-103 (1991).

²⁵⁰ *Id.* at v.

²⁵¹ *Id.* at 27. Brigadier General James Cantey commanded the Confederate forces at Pollard.

²⁵² *Id.* at 21.

²⁵³ WORD FROM CAMP POLLARD, at v.

²⁵⁴ PEGUES LETTER.

²⁵⁵ *Id.* at 25.

²⁵⁶ COCHRANE LETTERS, January 5, 1863.

²⁵⁷ WORD FROM CAMP POLLARD, at 27.

²⁵⁸ COCHRANE LETTERS, December 27, 1863.

²⁵⁹ MOBILE EVENING TELEGRAPH, October 24, 1862.

²⁶⁰ COCHRANE LETTERS, July 8, 1862.

²⁶¹ *See "Damn The Torpedoes!" The Campaigns for Mobile 1864-1865*, ALABAMA GULF COAST CONVENTION & VISITORS BUREAU (2003).

²⁶² COCHRANE LETTERS, November 30, 1862.

²⁶³ COCHRANE LETTERS, June 8, 1862.

²⁶⁴ WORD FROM CAMP POLLARD, at 187-188.

Endnotes

265   THE HERITAGE OF MONTGOMERY COUNTY ALABAMA 98 (1998).

266   *See* PINTLALA HISTORICAL ASSOCIATION, Vol. 25, No. 2, April 2011 at 8.

267   *Id.*

268   *On Alabama and Florida Railroad*, Mobile Register & Advertiser, June 16, 1862.

269   COCHRANE LETTERS, June 8, 1862.

270   *Id.*

271   *On Alabama and Florida Railroad*, Mobile Register & Advertiser, June 16, 1862.

272   *Id.*

273   *Id.* at 290.

274   2ND ALABAMA CAVALRY MUSTER ROLL, COMPANY F, APRIL 3 TO JUNE 30, 1862. ALABAMA DEPARTMENT OF ARCHIVES & HISTORY.

275   *Id.*

276   ANDREWS LETTER.

277   PEGUES LETTER.

278   HALL LETTERS, August 15, 1862.

279   PEGUES LETTER.

280   *See "Origin of Company K, 2nd Alabama Cavalry,"* ALABAMA DEPARTMENT OF ARCHIVES & HISTORY.

281   Confederate Military History, Alabama Troops (Confederate) — Cavalry; Supplement — Records of Events, Vol. 1, 41 (2008) [hereinafter ALABAMA TROOPS — CAVALRY.]

282   *Id.*

283   *"Origin of Company K, 2nd Alabama Cavalry,"* ALABAMA DEPARTMENT OF ARCHIVES & HISTORY.

284   ALABAMA TROOPS — CAVALRY, at 42.

285   OR, Ser. 1, Vol. 16, Pt. 2, pp. 767-768.

286   ANDREWS LETTER.

287 *See generally*, Bertram Wyatt-Brown, Southern Honor: Ethics & Behavior in the Old South (1982).

288 *Id.* at 53.

289 Eric Foner, *The Making and Breaking of the Legend of Robert E. Lee*, NY Times (Aug. 28, 2017).

290 Bertram Wyatt-Brown, Southern Honor: Ethics & Behavior in the Old South 105 (1982).

291 *Id.*

292 Cochrane Letters, November 25, 1862.

293 Alabama Department of Archives & History, Mathew R. Marks, 2 Reg't Alabama Cavalry.

294 Pegues Letter.

295 Montgomery Weekly Mail, December 10, 1862.

296 Confederate Articles of War, at Article 6.

297 Adjutant and Inspector General's Office, Richmond, Gen. Order 35, April 4, 1863.

298 *Id.*

299 Hall Letters, December 8, 1862.

300 Weekly Advertiser, June 17, 1863. *See also*, undated letter, Alabama Department of Archives & History, Mrs. M.L. Kirkpatrick, volume ii, at 73.

301 Letter from the Director, Alabama Department of Archives & History to Colonel Thomas Spencer, dated January 3, 1951, Alabama Department of Archives & History.

302 Mary E. Kellogg, Army Life of an Illinois Soldier 243 (1906) [hereinafter Army Life of an Illinois Soldier].

303 The Heritage of Calhoun County, Alabama 112-113 (1998).

304 *Id.* at 112-113.

305 *Id.* at 113.

306 *Id.* Tom Walker was a personal friend of Earle and was one of the men that signed the promotion request to President Davis.

307 HALL LETTERS, December 8, 1862.

308 2ND ALABAMA CAVALRY MUSTER ROLL, COMPANY F, Oct. 31 to Dec. 31, 1862. ALABAMA DEPARTMENT OF ARCHIVES & HISTORY.

309 *Pursuit and Defeat of the Enemy by Our Cavalry — Gallantry of the 2nd Alabama*, G.H.A. Letter, June 22, 1863, ALABAMA DEPARTMENT ARCHIVES & HISTORY, Mrs. M.L. Kirkpatrick's Scrapbook, vol. ii, p. 75 [hereinafter G.H.A. Letter].

310 OR, Ser. I, Vol 25, Pt. I, p. 1069.

311 R.O. Simpson, 24 CONFEDERATE VETERAN 107 (1916).

312 MARK LARDAS, ROUGHSHOD THROUGH DIXIE, GRIERSON'S RAID 1863 20 (2010).

313 *Id.* at 107.

314 WORD FROM CAMP POLLARD, at 27.

315 COCHRANE LETTERS, April 7, 1863.

316 Private Robert Wardroper, April 11, 1863 letter (on file with author).

317 *Id.*

318 PEGUES LETTER.

319 OR, Ser. 1, Vol. 24, Pt. I, p. 972-973.

320 PEGUES LETTER.

321 *Id.*

322 Report of General Daniel Ruggles, SOUTHERN HISTORICAL SOCIETY PAPERS, VOL. VIII, JANUARY TO DECEMBER, 1880, AT 534 [HEREINAFTER RUGGLES REPORT].

323 PEGUES LETTER.

324 OR, Ser. 1, Vol. 24, Pt. 3, p. 972-973.

325 *Id.*

326 OR, Ser. 1, Vol. 24, Pt. 3, p. 972-973.

327 FERGUSON MEMOIRS/DIARY, at 25.

328 TIMOTHY B. SMITH, THE REAL HORSE SOLDIERS 82 (2018).

329 OR, Ser. 1, Vol. 36, Pt. I, p. 530.

330 R.R. Hancock, Hancock's Diary: A History of the Second Tennessee Confederate Cavalry 240 (1999) [hereinafter Hancock Diary].

331 James A. Ramage, Rebel Raider 60 (1986).

332 Timothy B. Smith, The Real Horse Soldiers 139 (2018).

333 OR, Ser. 1, Vol. 36, Pt. I, p. 530.

334 Hancock Diary, at 240.

335 OR, Ser. 1, Vol. 36, Pt. I, p. 536.

336 Mike Phifer, *Wrecking on the Railroad*, Civil War Quarterly, Early Winter 2016, at 84.

337 *Id.*

338 George F. Hager, Military Annals of Tennessee 613 (1886).

339 *Second Alabama Cavalry Capsule History*, Hill College, Texas Heritage Museum, Hillsboro, Texas. Undoubtably, if this number is anywhere close to correct, most of the 70 losses for the regiment in the Grierson campaign were most likely in the "missing" category giving chase to the 2nd Iowa Cavalry Regiment over many miles of territory. *See also*, Letter to Mr. Steve Hamilton, Alabama Department of Archives & History, July 26, 1963: "The Second Alabama fought Grierson at Okolona, with a loss of about 70 men killed and wounded ...." *Id.*

340 OR, Ser. 1, Vol. 24, Pt. I, p. 535.

341 Confederate Articles of War, at Article 62.

If upon marches, guards, or in quarters, different corps shall happen to join, or do duty together, the officer of highest rank, according to the commission by which he is mustered, in the army, navy, marine corps, militia, there on duty by orders from competent authority, shall command the whole, and give orders for what is needful for the service .... *Id.*

342 OR, Ser. 1, Vol. 24, Pt. I, p. 692-964.

343 OR, Ser. 1, Vol. 24, Pt. I, p. 691.

344 OR, Ser. 1, Vol. 23, Pt. I, p. 535.

345 OR, Ser. 1, Vol. 24, Pt. I, p. 691.

346 *Id.*

[347] *Id.*

[348] *Id.* at 692. Report of Major W.A. Hewlett.

[349] *Id.*

[350] OR Ser. 1, Vol. 24, Pt. I, p. 692-694.

[351] W. Brewer, Alabama: Her History, Resources, War Record, and Public Men: From 1540 to 1872 678 (1872). The skirmish at Kings Creek is also known as Mud Creek, which was the name given to a nearby smaller creek running parallel to Kings Creek.

[352] OR, Ser. 1, Vol. 36, Pt. I, p. 694.

[353] The Heritage of Calhoun County, Alabama 13 (1998).

[354] The Weekly Advertiser, May 15, 1863. Captain John P. West is recorded as "Commanding Regiment."

[355] Hancock Diary, at 248.

[356] G.H.A. Letter.

[357] G.H.A. Letter.

[358] The Weekly Advertiser, June 17, 1863.

[359] G.H.A. Letter.

[360] Ruggles Report, at 529.

[361] Marion Morrison, A History of the Ninth Regiment, Illinois Volunteer Infantry (1864) [hereinafter Ninth Regiment, Illinois Volunteer Infantry].

[362] *Id.* at 56.

[363] *Id.*

[364] *Id.*

[365] *Id.*

[366] *Id.*

[367] *Id.*

[368] Hancock Diary, at 254.

[369] *Id.* at 254-255.

370 RUGGLES REPORT, at 533.

371 *See* G.H.A. Letter.

372 *Id.*

373 *Id.*

374 Ross Massey, *General Joe Johnston and the Atlanta Campaign*, CONFEDERATE VETERAN, July/August 2010, p. 57.

375 *Id.*

376 NINTH REGIMENT, ILLINOIS VOLUNTEER INFANTRY, at 58.

377 *Id.* at 57.

378 G.H.A. Letter.

379 RUGGLES REPORT, at 532.

380 G.H.A. Letter.

381 HANCOCK DIARY, at 255.

382 ALABAMA TROOPS — CAVALRY, at 42.

383 GEORGE F. HAGER, MILITARY ANNALS OF TENNESSEE 613 (1886).

384 *Id.*

385 *Id.*

386 COCHRANE LETTERS, July 18, 1863.

387 RUGGLES REPORT, at 533.

388 ALABAMA TROOPS — CAVALRY, at 42-52.

389 2ND ALABAMA CAVALRY MUSTER ROLL, COMPANY F, Dec. 31 to June 30, 1863. ALABAMA DEPARTMENT OF ARCHIVES & HISTORY.

390 G.H.A. Letter.

391 HANCOCK DIARY, at 255.

392 *Id.*

393 Ninth Regiment, Illinois Volunteer Infantry, at 58.

394 *Id.* at 58.

395 *Id.*

396 Hancock Diary, at 256.

397 G.H.A. Letter.

398 *Id.*

399 Ruggles Report, at 533.

400 G.H.A. Letter.

401 *Id.*

402 Giles Letters, at 267.

403 Ferguson Memoirs/Diary, at 334.

404 *Id.* at 52-53.

405 Letter to President Jefferson Davis, July 12, 1863 (copy on file with author).

406 OR, Ser. 1, Vol. 32, Pt. I, p. 333. *Gen. Steven D. Lee Reports on Condition and Alignment of His Cavalry, August 1863.*

407 *Id.* at 231.

408 OR, Ser. 1, Vol. 32, Pt. I, p. 333.

409 Ferguson Memoirs/Diary, at 141.

410 Cochrane Letters, November 26, 1863.

411 Nugent Letters, at 134.

412 *Id.* at 152.

413 OR, Ser. 1, Vol. 43, Pt. I, pp. 833-835. Letter written by General James Chalmers, December 15, 1863.

414 *Id.*

415 Ferguson Duke Library, at 4-33.

416 *See* J. Gary Laine & Morris M. Penny, Law's Alabama Brigade in the War Between the Union and the Confederacy 201 (1996).

417 Ferguson Duke Library, at 4-35.

418 Hancock Diary, at 274.

419 *Ferguson's Report, Headquarters Brigade, Near Courtland, Ala., October 31, 1863*, available at www.mycivilwar.com/battles/631026.html (last visited April 9, 2016); OR, Ser. 1, Vol. 23, Pt.1, pp. 37-38 [HEREINAFTER VINCENTS CROSSROADS — FERGUSON].

420 ALABAMA: A DOCUMENTARY HISTORY 423 (1900).

421 FERGUSON DUKE LIBRARY, at 4-35.

422 COCHRANE LETTERS, November 26, 1863.

423 VINCENTS CROSSROADS — FERGUSON.

424 *See* VIRGINIA O. FOSCUE, PLACE NAMES IN ALABAMA 117 (1989). Located where Alabama State highways 19 and 24 intersect in Franklin County. "First named Vincents Crossroads for a local family ... renamed for the red berries of the bay bushes in the area." *Id*.

425 COCHRANE LETTERS, November 26, 1863.

426 FIRST ALABAMA CAVALRY UNION, at 104-105.

427 *See* MICHAEL L. BRADLEY, WITH BLOOD AND FIRE 165-197 (2003).

428 FIRST ALABAMA CAVALRY UNION, at 104-105.

429 *Id*.

430 *See* KENNETH W. NOE, THE YELLOWHAMMER WAR: THE CIVIL WAR AND RECONSTRUCTION IN ALABAMA 202-203 (2013).

431 FIRST ALABAMA CAVALRY UNION, at 105-106.

432 VINCENTS CROSSROADS — FERGUSON.

433 HANCOCK DIARY, at 276.

434 FERGUSON DUKE LIBRARY, at 4-35.

435 HANCOCK DIARY, at 277.

436 FERGUSON DUKE LIBRARY, at 4-35.

437 VINCENTS CROSS ROAD — FERGUSON.

438 HANCOCK DIARY, at 277.

439 FIRST ALABAMA CAVALRY UNION, at 106.

440 *See generally*, DOUGLAS SOUTHALL FREEMAN, LEE'S LIEUTENANTS: A STUDY IN COMMAND (1945). Because Southern officers led

from the front, the Confederate armies achieved more victories but suffered significantly higher losses in their officer corps.

[441] FIRST ALABAMA CAVALRY UNION, at 105-106.

[442] Id.

[443] Id.

[444] See JOHN R. PHILLIPS, THE STORY OF MY LIFE (1923) [HEREINAFTER PHILLIPS MEMOIRS].

[445] Id.

[446] FIRST ALABAMA CAVALRY UNION, at 105-106.

[447] COCHRANE LETTERS, November 26, 1863.

[448] FIRST ALABAMA CAVALRY UNION, at 106.

[449] COCHRANE LETTERS, November 26, 1863.

[450] FERGUSON MEMOIRS/DIARY, at 152-154.

[451] HANCOCK DIARY, at 276-277.

[452] Id.

[453] PHILLIPS MEMOIRS.

[454] Id. "About dark we, fifteen or twenty of us, who had been engaged in these skirmishes came up with a bunch of our comrades. There were perhaps fifty of them huddled together looking at something." Id.

[455] FIRST ALABAMA CAVALRY UNION, at 106.

[456] VINCENTS CROSS ROAD — FERGUSON.

[457] Id.

[458] HANCOCK DIARY, at 277.

[459] PHILLIPS MEMOIRS.

[460] FIRST ALABAMA CAVALRY UNION, at 106.

[461] Id. at 106.

[462] FERGUSON MEMOIRS/DIARY, at 152-154.

463 2ND ALABAMA CAVALRY MUSTER ROLL, COMPANY F, Aug. 31 to Oct. 31,1863. ALABAMA DEPARTMENT OF ARCHIVES AND HISTORY.

464 *Id.*

465 2ND ALABAMA CAVALRY MUSTER ROLL, COMPANY B. ALABAMA DEPARTMENT OF ARCHIVES AND HISTORY.

466 VINCENTS CROSS ROAD — FERGUSON.

467 FERGUSON MEMOIRS/DIARY, at 154.

468 *Id.* at 155.

469 MOBILE ADVERTISER AND REGISTER, October 31, 1863.

470 *Id.*

471 COCHRANE LETTERS, December 10, 1863.

472 SAMUEL W. MITCHAM, JR., BUST HELL WIDE OPEN, THE LIFE OF NATHAN BEDFORD FORREST 62 (2016) [HEREINAFTER BUST HELL WIDE OPEN].

473 EDWARD G. LONGACRE, A SOLDIER TO THE LAST 138 (2007) [HEREINAFTER SOLDIER TO THE LAST].

474 *Id.*

475 HANCOCK DIARY, at 287.

476 FERGUSON MEMOIRS/DIARY, at 166-167.

477 *Id.* at 168.

478 *Id.*

479 *Id.* at 169.

480 *Id.* at 170.

481 HANCOCK DIARY, at 291-292.

482 COCHRANE LETTERS, December 10, 1863.

483 HANCOCK DIARY, at 295.

484 FERGUSON MEMOIRS/DIARY, at 171.

485 HANCOCK DIARY, at 296-297.

486 *Id.* at 297.

487 FERGUSON MEMOIRS/DIARY, at 166-167.

488 *Id.*

489 FERGUSON MEMOIRS/DIARY, at 166-167.

490 HANCOCK DIARY, at 297.

491 BUST HELL WIDE OPEN, at 144.

492 NUGENT LETTERS, at 154.

493 A&E Television Networks, *Nathan Bedford Forrest*, HISTORY CHANNEL (2018).

494 SELECTED CORRESPONDENCE OF SHERMAN, at 600.

495 *The Present Aspect of the War — Causes for Hope*, NEW YORK TIMES, March 16, 1864, at 4.

496 MARC WORTMAN, THE BONFIRE — THE SIEGE AND BURNING OF ATLANTA 208-209 (2009) [HEREINAFTER THE BONFIRE].

497 *Id.* at 93.

498 *See* SAMUEL W. MITCHAM, JR., THE GREATEST LYNCHING IN AMERICAN HISTORY: NEW YORK 1863 (2020).

499 HISTORY OF 53RD REGIMENT ALABAMA VOLUNTEER CAVALRY AND M.W. HANNON'S CAVALRY BRIGADE, at 161.

500 FORGOTTEN CONFEDERATES, at 7. Signed by Davis and passed into law on March 13, 1865, the act was entitled: "An Act to Increase the Military Force of the Confederate States." Under the new law, each State was to furnish a quota of "volunteering" slaves, enrolling a total of 300,000 men who could then secure their freedom after honorable service to the nation. *Id.*

501 BONFIRE 201 (1970).

502 *Id.* at 601.

503 MERIDIAN EXPEDITION, at 283-288.

504 OR, Ser. 1, Vol. 56, Pt. I, p. 728.

505 *Id.* at 67.

506 FERGUSON DUKE LIBRARY, 4-37.

507 MERIDIAN EXPEDITION, at 89.

508 FERGUSON MEMOIRS/DIARY, at 178-179.

509 OR, Ser. 1, Vol. 32, Pt. I, p. 250.

510 *Id.* at 380. Ferguson's report written from Calhoun Station, March 31, 1864.

511 MERIDIAN EXPEDITION, at 121.

512 *Id.* at 134-135.

513 *Id.*

514 OR, Ser. I, Vol. 32, Pt. II, p. 723.

515 MERIDIAN EXPEDITION, at 140-142.

516 WEEKLY PIONEER AND DEMOCRAT, Mar. 25, 1863.

517 FERGUSON MEMOIRS/DIARY, at 178.

518 *Id.* at 298.

519 OR Ser. 1, Vol. 32, Pt. II, p. 723.

520 OR Ser. 1, Vol. 32, Pt. I, p. 378.

521 MERIDIAN EXPEDITION, at 147.

522 OR, Ser. 1, Vol. 32, Pt. I, p. 380.

523 Letter from William T. Sherman to Gen. J.A. Rawlins (March 7, 1864) *in* OR, Ser. 1, Vol. 32, Pt. I, p. 176.

524 MERIDIAN EXPEDITION, at 304-306.

525 LUCIAS W. BARBER, ARMY MEMOIRS OF LUCIUS W. BARBER, COMPANY D, 15TH ILLINOIS VOLUNTEER 138 (1894).

526 MERIDIAN EXPEDITION, at 227.

527 R.A. (Robert Alonzo) Brock, *Sherman's Advance on Meridian — Report of General W.H. Jackson,* SOUTHERN HISTORICAL SOCIETY PAPERS, Volume 9, January to December, 1881, 158.

528 OR, Ser. 1, Vol. 32, Pt. I, p. 380.

529 *Id.* at 158.

530 MEMPHIS DAILY APPEAL, April 2, 1864. "[T]he bodies of over twenty negro children have been taken out of Chunky Creek since

the Yankees left, who were thrown in by the inhuman scoundrels to get them out of the way [the infantry was crossing over the body of water]. We have heard of other cruelties in the neighborhood of Meridian, which are too horrible to publish." *Id.*

[531] OR, Ser. 1, Vol. 32, Pt. II, p. 498.

[532] BUCK T. FOSTER, SHERMAN'S MISSISSIPPI CAMPAIGN 169 (2006).

[533] MERIDIAN EXPEDITION, at 244.

[534] JACKSON REPORT, at 159.

[535] OR, Ser. 1, Vol. 32, Pt. I, p. 380.

[536] *Id.*

[537] "VOICES OF ALABAMA" EXHIBIT, ALABAMA DEPARTMENT OF ARCHIVES AND HISTORY, MONTGOMERY, ALABAMA.

[538] OR, Ser. 1, Vol. 32, Pt. 3, p. 825.

[539] *Id.* at 785.

[540] RICHARD LOWE, A TEXAS CAVALRY OFFICER'S CIVIL WAR 293 (1999).

[541] *Id.* at 288.

[542] *Id.* at 290.

[543] J. Clemens to W.H. Seward, May 5, 1864, ABRAHAM LINCOLN PAPERS, LIBRARY OF CONGRESS, WASH. D.C., available at http://hdl.loc.gov/loc.mss/ms000001.mss30189a.3285700.

[544] STEPHEN DAVIS, ATLANTA WILL FALL 3 (2001). This quote is from a Southern journalist published in the MOBILE ADVERTISER AND REGISTER, May 29, 1864.

[545] For an excellent discussion of the Battle of Atlanta, *see* GARY ECELBARGER, THE DAY DIXIE DIED: THE BATTLE OF ATLANTA (2010) [HEREINAFTER THE DAY DIXIE DIED].

[546] WEEKLY ADVERTISER, July 25, 1864.

[547] CONFEDERATE MILITARY HISTORY EXPANDED EDITION, VOL. 8, at 256.

[548] OR, Ser. 1, Vol. 38, Pt. 4, p. 691. Aggregate Present and Absent: 3,827; Aggregate Present: 1,949; Present for Duty: 142 Officers and 1,579 men (1,721); Total Effective: 1,575.

549 OR, Ser. 1, Vol. 47, Pt. 2, pp. 1012-1013. General Wheeler complained in a January 14, 1865, communication to General Braxton Bragg: "General Ferguson had, I am informed, 1,700 effective men when he arrived at Rome [Georgia] last year [May 1864], and when he reported to me [July 1864] his report showed 547 effective men and 3,400 on the rolls, showing a want of care which no command under my orders ever yet exhibited." *Id.*

550 Charles C. Jones, THE SIEGE OF SAVANNAH in December 1864 and the Confederate Operations in Georgia and the Third Military District of South Carolina During General SHERMAN'S MARCH from Atlanta TO THE SEA 89-90 (1874).

551 OR, Ser. 1, Vol. 32, Pt. 3, p. 246.

552 *Id.* at 313.

553 *Id.*

554 *See* STEPHEN DAVIS, ATLANTA WILL FALL 198 (2001).

555 ARMY LIFE OF AN ILLINOIS SOLDIER, at 245.

556 *See* MICHAEL R. BRADLEY, WITH BLOOD & FIRE xi (2003). Provides an excellent discussion of what life was like for Southerners occupied by Union forces. "Life was far more harsh and occupation much more brutal than has been generally conceived." *Id.*

557 DAVID EVANS, SHERMAN'S HORSEMEN 57 (1996) [HEREINAFTER SHERMAN'S HORSEMEN].

558 *See, e.g.*, TERRY G. SCRIBER & THERESA ARNOLD-SCRIBER, THE FOURTH LOUISIANA BATTALION IN THE CIVIL WAR 55 (2008).

559 *See* Marion B. Lucas, *William Tecumseh Sherman v. The Historians*, PROTEUS, Fall 2000, at 16.

560 AUDACITY PERSONIFIED: THE GENERALSHIP OF ROBERT E. LEE, PETER S. CARMICHAEL, ED., 142 (2004). Responding to Lee's victory at Fredericksburg in December 1862, Johnston stated: "What luck some people have. Nobody will ever come to attack me in such a place." *Id.*

561 OR, Ser. 1, Vol. 38, Pt. 4, p. 680.

562 BRET W. WEATHERFORD, WEATHERFORDS IN THE CIVIL WAR at 32 (on file with author).

563 SOLDIER TO THE LAST, at 51.

564 MORNING TO MIDNIGHT, at 180.

565 *Id.*

566 Giles Letters, at 267.

567 Jim Miles, Fields of Glory 61 (1995).

568 Army Life of an Illinois Soldier, at 243.

569 Clent Coker, Barnsley Gardens at Woodlands 118 (2000).

570 Letter by Colonel Thomas Spencer, *War Brings Tragedy to Historic Old Barnsley*, January 6, 1951. Alabama Department of Archives & History.

571 Author interview with Clent Coker, historian and chief curator of Woodlands museum, March 12, 2019.

572 *Id.* at 120.

573 Cochrane Letters, June 6, 1864.

574 William Ray Jewell, History of the 72nd Regiment Indiana Volunteer Infantry of the Mounted Lightning Brigade 298-299 (1882).

575 OR, Ser. 1, Vol. 38, Pt. 2, p. 806.

576 Cochrane Letters, June 6, 1864.

577 Alabama Reporter, September 22, 1864, Vol. 25, No. 38, at 2.

578 *Id.*

579 Frances Thomas Howard, In and Out of The Lines (1905).

580 *Id.* at 9.

581 *Id.*

582 *Id.* at 10.

583 *Id.*

584 Ferguson Memoirs/Diary, at 37.

585 Morning to Midnight, at 180.

586 Pegues Letter.

587 Cochrane Letters, June 14, 1864.

588 Clent Coker, Barnsley Gardens at Woodlands 118 (2000).

589 ARMY LIFE OF AN ILLINOIS SOLDIER, at 243.

590 Letter by Colonel Thomas Spencer, *War Brings Tragedy to Historic Old Barnsley*, January 6, 1951. ALABAMA DEPARTMENT OF ARCHIVES & HISTORY. Additional details about the death of Colonel Earle can be gleaned from the research of Colonel Spencer who was able to obtain an interview with a member of the Barnsley family (her mother witnessed the burial of Colonel Earle on the Woodland property) and view the personal effects found on the body of Colonel Earle to include "a small memo book" and a daguerreotype of "Mary L. Quim the housekeeper for the Barnsley's." *Id.*

591 *Id.*

592 Letter by Colonel Thomas Spencer, *War Brings Tragedy to Historic Old Barnsley*, January 6, 1951. ALABAMA DEPARTMENT OF ARCHIVES & HISTORY.

593 JIM MILES, FIELDS OF GLORY 61 (1995).

594 COCHRANE LETTERS, June 14, 1864.

595 ALABAMA DEPARTMENT OF ARCHIVES & HISTORY; SERIES TITLE: CONFEDERATE MUSTER ROLL COLLECTION — 2D ALABAMA CAVALRY REGIMENT, 1915 [sic 1913] May. Muster roll typewritten, submitted by L.M. Bashinsky, Troy, Alabama; April 23, 1862.

596 FERGUSON DUKE LIBRARY, at 4-38.

597 *Id.* at 4-39.

598 DENNIS KELLY, BLUE & GRAY MAGAZINE'S HISTORY AND TOUR GUIDE OF THE ATLANTA CAMPAIGN 119 (1996) [HEREINAFTER HISTORY AND TOUR GUIDE OF THE ATLANTA CAMPAIGN].

599 T.D.R., *Letter to the Editor*, MONTGOMERY DAILY ADVERTISER, June 5, 1864. Also on file: ALABAMA DEPARTMENT OF ARCHIVES AND HISTORY, HANNON'S CAVALRY BRIGADE.

600 *Id.*

601 *Id.* at 119.

602 COCHRANE LETTERS, June 6, 1864.

603 COCHRANE LETTERS, June 14, 1864.

604 GILES LETTERS, at 300.

605 GEORGE L. GRISCOM, FIGHTING WITH ROSS' TEXAS CAVALRY BRIGADE, CSA, HOMER L. KERR, ED., (1976).

606 BUST HELL WIDE OPEN, at 2.

607 SHERMAN'S HORSEMEN, at 433.

608 NUGENT LETTERS, at 209.

609 CONFEDERATE ARTICLES OF WAR, at Article 25.

610 NUGENT LETTERS, at 209.

611 HENRY PUTNEY BEERS, THE CONFEDERACY: A GUIDE TO THE ARCHIVES OF THE GOVERNMENT OF THE CONFEDERATE STATES OF AMERICA 143 (2004). *See also*, CONFEDERATE ARTICLES OF WAR, at Article 65.

612 Special Orders No, 220, Secretary of War, Adjutant and Inspector General's Office, Richmond, Sept 16th 1864.

613 HISTORY AND TOUR GUIDE OF THE ATLANTA CAMPAIGN, at 100.

614 *See* RICHARD A. BAUMGARTNER & LARRY M. STRAYER, KENNESAW MOUNTAIN: JUNE 1864 29 (1998).

615 SAM WATKINS, CO. "AYTCH": THE FIRST TENNESSEE REGIMENT OR A SIDE SHOW TO THE BIG SHOW 160 (2015).

616 *See, e.g.*, SHERMAN'S HORSEMEN, at xxxiii.

617 BRET W. WEATHERFORD, WEATHERFORDS IN THE CIVIL WAR at 34 (on file with author).

618 FERGUSON DUKE LIBRARY, at 4-38.

619 *See, e.g.*, WILLIAM R. BROOKSHER & DAVID K. SIDER, GLORY AT A GALLOP 114-126 (1993).

620 *Id.* at 126.

621 SHERMAN'S HORSEMEN, at 434.

622 GILES LETTERS, at 337.

623 FERGUSON DUKE LIBRARY, at 4-38, 39.

624 *See* LAWRENCE KRUMENAKER, WALKING THE LINE (2014).

625 STEPHEN DAVIS, WHAT THE YANKEES DID TO US: SHERMAN'S BOMBARDMENT AND WRECKING OF ATLANTA 22 (2012).

626 RUSSELL S. BONDS, WAR LIKE THE THUNDERBOLT 28-33 (2009) [HEREINAFTER WAR LIKE THE THUNDERBOLT].

627 The BONFIRE, at 298.

628 *See* CLIFFORD DOWDEY, LEE'S LAST CAMPAIGN, 45 (1960).

629 FERGUSON DUKE LIBRARY, at 4-39.

630 HISTORY AND TOUR GUIDE OF THE ATLANTA CAMPAIGN, at 194.

631 GILES LETTERS, at 343.

632 ARMY LIFE OF AN ILLINOIS SOLDIER, at 282.

633 WAR LIKE THE THUNDERBOLT, at 106. Sherman's grossly inflated estimate was almost 5,000 casualties for the Confederates.

634 GILES LETTERS, at 345.

635 THE DAY DIXIE DIED, at 32.

636 *Id.* at 27.

637 WHEELER AND HIS CAVALRY, at 209.

638 THE DAY DIXIE DIED, at 27.

639 HISTORY AND TOUR GUIDE OF THE ATLANTA CAMPAIGN, at 211.

640 For an excellent description of the back and forth messages, *see* WHEELER AND HIS CAVALRY, 205-213.

641 SOLDIER TO THE LAST, at 61.

642 JOHN P. DYER, "FIGHTIN" JOE WHEELER 178 (1941).

643 OR, Ser. 1, Vol 52, Pt. 3, p. 569.

644 GILES LETTERS, at 345.

645 *See* SOLDIER TO THE LAST, at 611. Longacre incorrectly asserts that Ferguson's brigade was in the woods and not atop Bald Hill.

646 THE DAY DIXIE DIED, at 29.

647 ALBERT CASTEL, DECISION IN THE WEST 379 (1992) [HEREINAFTER DECISION IN THE WEST].

648 OR, Ser. 1, Vol. 38, Pt. 3, p. 579-580.

649 WAR LIKE THE THUNDERBOLT, at 115.

650 JOHN LUNDBERG, THE COLOR BRIGADE OF THE ARMY 242 (2016).

[651] DECISION IN THE WEST, at 377-379.

[652] OR, Ser. 1, Vol 37, Pt. 4, p. 208.

[653] OR, Ser. 3, Vol. 38, Pt. 3, pp. 746, 752; THE DAY DIXIE DIED, at 32-35.

[654] GILES LETTERS, at 345.

[655] THE DAY DIXIE DIED, at 35.

[656] JAMES TURNER, JIM TURNER CO. G. 6TH TEXAS INFANTRY, C.S.A., FROM 1861-1865, TEXANA, NO. 2 (1974).

[657] THE DAY DIXIE DIED, at 38; Taken from Gilbert D. Munson, "*A Matter of War History. The Capture and Fortification of Leggett's Hill.*" CINCINNATI DAILY GAZETTE, September 12, 1879.

[658] *Id.* at 38.

[659] THE DAY DIXIE DIED, at 40.

[660] HISTORY AND TOUR GUIDE OF THE ATLANTA CAMPAIGN, at 212.

[661] OR, Ser. I, Vol 37, Pt. 3, p. 753.

[662] STEVEN E. WOODWORTH, NOTHING BUT VICTORY 535-537 (2005).

[663] HISTORY AND TOUR GUIDE OF THE ATLANTA CAMPAIGN, at 212.

[664] *See* THE DAY DIXIE DIED, at 252.

[665] *See* STRAYER & BAUMGARTNER, ECHOES OF BATTLE 219 (1991).

[666] *See*, SOLDIER TO THE LAST, at 161. In order to deflect criticism from himself for not holding Bald Hill, General Wheeler placed all the fault on General Ferguson.

[667] WAR LIKE THE THUNDERBOLT, at 124.

[668] OR, Ser. 1, Vol. 37, Pt. 3, p. 571.

[669] WHEELER AND HIS CAVALRY, at 210-211.

[670] W. BREWER, ALABAMA: HER HISTORY, RESOURCES, WAR RECORD, AND PUBLIC MEN FROM 1540 TO 1870 678 (1975).

[671] FERGUSON MEMOIRS/DIARY, at 25.

[672] *See* MAMIE YEARY, REMINISCENCES OF THE BOYS IN GRAY 223-224 (2018).

673 DECISION IN THE WEST, at 412.

674 SELECTED CORRESPONDENCE OF SHERMAN, at 738-739.

675 SHERMAN'S HORSEMEN, at 297.

676 History of 53rd Regiment Alabama Volunteer Cavalry and M.W. Hannon's Cavalry Brigade, at 204.

677 WHEELER AND HIS CAVALRY, at 219.

678 FERGUSON DUKE LIBRARY, at 5-3. Ferguson mistakenly penned that it was Peachtree Creek.

679 DECISION IN THE WEST, at 438.

680 WHEELER AND HIS CAVALRY, at 233.

681 BURKE DAVIS, SHERMAN'S MARCH 194 (1980). *See also*, E.L. DOCTOROW, THE MARCH 226-227 (2006).

682 DAVID SMITH, SHERMAN'S MARCH TO THE SEA 1864: ATLANTA TO SAVANNAH 19 (2007).

683 JAMES HARRISON WILSON, UNDER THE OLD FLAG; RECOLLECTIONS OF MILITARY OPERATIONS IN THE WAR FOR THE UNION, THE SPANISH WAR, THE BOXER REBELLION VOL. I 371 (1912).

684 *See* EDWARD G. LONGACRE, WORTHY OPPONENTS: WILLIAM T. SHERMAN & JOSEPH E. JOHNSTON 295 (2006).

685 *See* RICHARD SHELLY HARTIGAN, LIEBER'S CODE AND THE LAW OF WAR 49 (1983)

686 Stephen Davis, *A Very Barbarous Mode of Carrying on War: Sherman's Artillery Bombardment of Atlanta*, GEORGIA HISTORICAL QUARTERLY 89, No. 1 (Spring 1995) at 68.

687 DECISION IN THE WEST, at 438.

688 *Id.* at 438.

689 RICHARD LOWE, A TEXAS CAVALRY OFFICER'S CIVIL WAR 293 (1999).

690 SHERMAN'S HORSEMEN, at 434.

691 HISTORY OF 53RD REGIMENT ALABAMA VOLUNTEER CAVALRY AND M.W. HANNON'S CAVALRY BRIGADE, at 207.

692 DECISION IN THE WEST, at 471.

693   *Id.* at 471.

694   SHERMAN'S HORSEMEN, at 433.

695   DECISION IN THE WEST, at 472.

696   *Id.* at 472.

697   SMITH D. ATKINS, ATLANTA PAPER NO, 25, WITH SHERMAN'S CAVALRY 55, 613-614 reprinted from Military Recollections, Illinois Commandery, Vol, 11, Chicago, 1894.

698   DAILY NATIONAL REPUBLICAN, September 16, 1864. This article was published in the Washington City newspaper and was sourced to captured Confederate soldiers from Atlanta.

699   *See* HISTORY AND TOUR GUIDE OF THE ATLANTA CAMPAIGN, at 298.

700   *Id.* at 298-299.

701   FERGUSON DUKE LIBRARY, at 5-2.

702   The BONFIRE, at 313.

703   FERGUSON DUKE LIBRARY, at 5-3.

704   *Id.*

705   STEPHEN DAVIS, WHAT THE YANKEES DID TO US: SHERMAN'S BOMBARDMENT AND WRECKING OF ATLANTA 263 (2012).

706   *Id.*

707   FERGUSON DUKE LIBRARY, at 5-2.

708   *Second Alabama Cavalry Capsule History*, Hill College, Texas Heritage Museum, Hillsboro, Texas.

709   *See* Nick Overby, *Supplying Hell: The Campaign for Atlanta*, QUARTERMASTER PROFESSIONAL BULLETIN, at 4-7, Winter 1992. "We have devoured the land and our animals eat up the wheat and cornfields close. All the people retire before us and desolation is behind. To realize what war is one should follow our tracks."

710   TO THE SEA, at 23.

711   SHERMAN'S MARCH, at 48-63.

712   SOLDIER TO THE LAST, at 179.

713 HISTORY OF THE 53RD REGIMENT ALABAMA VOLUNTEER CAVALRY AND M.W. HANNON'S CAVALRY BRIGADE, at 259.

714 LIFE OF JOHNNY REB, at 46.

715 FERGUSON DUKE LIBRARY, at 5-2.

716 SHERMAN'S MARCH, at 33.

717 TO THE SEA, at 55.

718 NOAH ANDRE TRUDEAU, SOUTHERN STORM 63-64 (2008).

719 COLIN POWELL, THE CONTRAILS LEADERSHIP, https://www.usafa.af.mil/News/Features/Article/738571/the-contrails-leadership/.

720 WHEELER AND HIS CAVALRY, at 285.

721 *Id.* at 286-289.

722 *Id.* at 288.

723 FERGUSON DUKE LIBRARY, at 5-2.

724 EDWIN L, DRAKE, THE ANNALS OF THE ARMY OF TENNESSEE AND EARLY WESTERN HISTORY, VOL. 1, 346 (1878).

Sherman's columns were all in motion southward on November 15th and General Wheeler was able to oppose him with but about 1,500 men, and he hurried on his troops en route, and was joined by General Ferguson's Brigade with 525 men, and on November 20th (1864), near Macon, General Wheeler`s force was 3,026. *Id.*

725 WHEELER AND HIS CAVALRY, at 289, 293.

726 SOLDIER TO THE LAST, at 180.

727 THE SEA AND BEYOND, at 161.

728 TO THE SEA, at 176.

729 THE DAILY CONFEDERATE, December 5, 1864. This article was taken from information provided by members of Ferguson's brigade who reported on Wheeler's involvement at Griswoldville.

730 DAVID SMITH, SHERMAN'S MARCH TO THE SEA 1864: ATLANTA TO SAVANNAH 41 (2007).

731 FERGUSON DUKE LIBRARY, at 5-2.

732 SOLDIER TO THE LAST, at 181.

733 COCHRANE LETTERS, November 30, 1864.

734 *See* CHARLES C. JONES, JR., THE SIEGE OF SAVANNAH 57-72 (1874) [HEREINAFTER THE SIEGE OF SAVANNAH].

735 THE SEA AND BEYOND, at 121.

736 *Id.* at 150.

737 MONTGOMERY DAILY ADVERTISER, February 24, 1866.

738 JOHN P. DYER, "FIGHTIN" JOE WHEELER 179-186 (1941).

739 COCHRANE LETTERS, November 30, 1864.

740 *Id.*

741 FERGUSON MEMOIRS/DIARY, at 217.

742 COCHRANE LETTERS, November 30, 1864.

743 NUGENT LETTERS, at 224.

744 OR, Ser. 1, Vol. 44, Pt. I, p. 905.

745 NOAH ANDRE TRUDEAU, SOUTHERN STORM 243 (2008).

746 OR, Ser. 1, Vol. 44, Pt. I, at 637.

747 HENRY PUTNEY BEERS, THE CONFEDERACY: A GUIDE TO THE ARCHIVES OF THE GOVERNMENT OF THE CONFEDERATE STATES OF AMERICA 166 (2004).

748 TIMOTHY DAISS, IN THE SADDLE, EXPLOITS OF THE 5TH GEORGIA CAVALRY DURING THE CIVIL WAR 58 (1999).

749 *Id.*

750 *Id.*

751 WHEELER AND HIS CAVALRY, at 211.

752 *See* JOHN DYER, FROM SHILOH TO SAN JUAN, THE LIFE OF "FIGHTIN JOE" WHEELER 161 (1961).

753 WHEELER AND HIS CAVALRY, at 231.

754 *Id.* at 215.

755 TO THE SEA, at 116-117.

756 OR, Ser. 1, Vol. 39, Pt. 2, p. 713.

757 LEE KENNETT, MARCHING THROUGH GEORGIA: THE STORY OF SOLDIERS AND CIVILIANS DURING SHERMAN'S CAMPAIGN 263 (1995).

758 TO THE SEA, at 116.

759 *Id.* at 117.

760 *Id.* at 110.

761 THE SEA AND BEYOND, at 128.

762 *See* TO THE SEA, at 8; Burke Davis, SHERMAN'S MARCH 186-187 (1980).

763 FERGUSON DUKE LIBRARY, at 5-2.

764 *Id.*

765 NUGENT LETTERS, at 224.

766 *Id.*

767 *Id.*

768 Letter of Captain Frank R. King, Montevallo, Alabama, July 16, 1865, ALABAMA DEPARTMENT OF ARCHIVES & HISTORY.

769 GILES LETTERS, at 406.

770 CONFEDERATE ARTICLES OF WAR, at Article 7:

Any officer or soldier who shall begin, excites, cause, or join in any mutiny or sedition in any troop or company in the service of the Confederate States, in any party, post, detachment, or guard, shall suffer death, or such other punishment as by a court-martial shall be inflicted. *Id.*

771 THE SIEGE OF SAVANNAH, at 68-69.

772 THE SEA AND BEYOND, at 128.

773 TO THE SEA, at 289.

774 THE SIEGE OF SAVANNAH, at 174.

775 *See* STANLEY WEINTRAUB, GENERAL SHERMAN'S CHRISTMAS, SAVANNAH 1864 (2009).

776 THE SIEGE OF SAVANNAH, at 135.

777 FERGUSON MEMOIRS/DIARY, at 217.

778 *Id.*

779 *Id.*

780 THE SIEGE OF SAVANNAH, at 153-154.

781 JOHN Q. ADAMS. *See* https://www.kingsburyjournal.com/stories/duty-is-ours-results-are-gods,5558?.

782 ROMAN INSPECTION REPORT; *see also,* HISTORY OF 53RD REGIMENT ALABAMA VOLUNTEER CAVALRY AND M.W. HANNON'S CAVALRY BRIGADE, at 288-289. A second inspection was done of Iverson's Division by Major John G. Devereux, Assistant Adjutant and Inspector General in late January 1865, but Ferguson's brigade was separated from the Division and not inspected. Interestingly, Major Devereux noted:

Attention is attracted to the large proportion of mules in the cavalry; fully one-quarter of the division is mounted on them. Permit me to strongly recommend mounting all cavalry on public horses, and the retention of these mules for transportation purposes. *Id.*

783 OR, Ser. I, Vol. 59, Pt. I, p. 979.

784 *Id.*

785 FERGUSON MEMOIRS/DIARY, at 237.

786 *Id.*

787 *Id.*

788 ROMAN INSPECTION REPORT.

789 *Id.*

790 OR, Ser. I, Vol. 38, Pt. IV, p. 691.

791 *See* OR, Ser. I, Vol. 49, Pt. I, p. 946.

792 *See* MARK A. WEITZ, MORE DAMNING THAN SLAUGHTER: DESERTION IN THE CONFEDERATE ARMY (2005).

793 FERGUSON MEMOIRS/DIARY, at 228.

794 *Id.*

795 MORNING REPORT, EFFECTIVE STRENGTH, Jan. 14, 1865, FERGUSON'S BRIGADE AT MATTHEWS BLUFF, S.C., (copy on file with David Gould).

796 MORNING REPORT, EFFECTIVE STRENGTH, Jan. 16, 1865, FERGUSON'S BRIGADE (copy on file with David Gould). The report listed 1 officer and 28 enlisted men as prisoners of war and 90 being absent due to illness.

797   *Id.*

798   ROMAN INSPECTION REPORT. Company B of the 9th Alabama Cavalry in Hagan's Brigade had only one officer and one enlisted man. Company D of the 9th Alabama Cavalry had only one man present for duty.

799   *Id.*

800   *Id.*

801   *Id.* When a Rebel would capture a Henry or Spencer rifle, for example, the Confederate Quartermaster had no ammunition to supply and it became worthless once all the captured cartridges were used.

802   *Id.* The IG noted that the command needed at a minimum 1,471 cartridge boxes, 1,455 cap pouches, and 1,290 waist belts in order to allow the soldiers to carry the required amount of caps and cartridges.

803   *Id.*

804   *Id.* Amazingly, the IG noted that the general health of the men was very satisfactory, "though camp itch prevails extensively in several brigades." The IG recommended that the Chief Commissary should issue soap so that regular washing would be encouraged.

805   *Id.* The IG noted that orders were not properly obeyed and inspections of arms were at best made on a weekly basis even though Army Regulations required daily inspections. In turn, roll calls were largely neglected.

806   *Id.*

807   *Id.*

808   *Id.*

809   *Id.*

810   *Id.* The IG noted that the men would provide "certified accounts" which were pieces of script promising payment.

811   *Id.* "General Wheeler's men like him, but do not appear to be proud of him."

812   *Id.* Although not willing to recommend who should replace Wheeler, the IG urged prompt action from Richmond: "We have no time to lose at this juncture of our affairs." *Id.*

813   *Id.*

814   *Id.*

815   OR, Ser. 1, Vol. 59, Pt. I, p. 1002.

816   THE SIEGE, at 343. In March 1865, a single rail-line was operational from Alabama to Atlanta.

817   FERGUSON MEMOIRS/DIARY, at 269.

818   JOSEPH E. JOHNSTON, NARRATIVE OF MILITARY OPERATIONS 587 (1874).

819   OR, Ser. 1, Vol. 44,, Pt. I, p. 989.

820   FERGUSON MEMOIRS/DIARY, at 240-241.

821   *Id.* at 241.

822   FERGUSON MEMOIRS/DIARY, at 249.

823   MARK A. WEITZ, MORE DAMNING THAN SLAUGHTER: DESERTION IN THE CONFEDERATE ARMY xvii (2005).

824   *Id.* at 26.

825   OR, Ser. 1, Vol. 47, Pt. 2, p. 1199.

826   GILES LETTERS, at 418.

827   FERGUSON MEMOIRS/DIARY, at 253.

828   *Id.* at 254.

829   FERGUSON MEMOIRS/DIARY, at 255.

830   *Id.*

831   *Id.* at 256.

832   *Id.*

833   *Id.*

834   *See* ROBERT AUGUSTUS STILES, FOUR YEARS UNDER MARSE ROBERT 267 (1904).

835   THE DIARY OF EMMA LECONTE: WHEN THE WORLD ENDED, EARL SCHENCK MIERS, ED. 96 (1957).

836   Joseph B. Mitchell, *You Are the Army,* CIVIL WAR MAGAZINE, July-Aug. 1991, at 25. When General Lee surrendered the Army of Northern Virginia in April 1865, all military forces throughout the South quickly followed suit. The identification with Lee was so

great that much of the Confederate military followed Lee rather than President Jefferson Davis who advocated continued resistance.

[837] Douglas Southall Freeman, R.E. Lee: A Biography Vol, 1V, 401 (1934).

[838] Michael B. Ballard, A Long Shadow 62 (1986) [hereinafter A Long Shadow].

[839] New York Times, April 19, 1864.

[840] Burke Davis, The Long Surrender 71 (1985).

[841] A Long Shadow, at 99.

[842] Jefferson Davis, The Rise and Fall of the Confederate Government 682-684 (1958).

[843] Ina Woestemeyer Van Noppen, Stoneman's Last Raid 99 (1961).

[844] A Long Shadow, at 109. Wade Hampton could only "muster his personal staff and a small escort." *Id.*

[845] Wheeler and His Cavalry, at 209.

[846] A Long Shadow, at 123.

[847] 2nd Alabama Cavalry Muster Roll, Company K, Alabama Department of Archives & History, Private W.I. Stokes notes that the entire regiment was paid in Mexican coin on the night of May 7, 1865. However, the actual date of payment was May 3, 1865.

[848] The "Gould" Mexican Silver dollar coin is in the possession of his direct descendant, David Gould of Lake, Mississippi.

[849] Thomas M. Owen, Dictionary of Alabama Biography, Vol. 4, at 1339 (1998). Records that Lt. Col. Pegues was in command of the regiment, although other sources state that Colonel Cunningham was the commander.

[850] Ferguson Memoirs/Diary, at 269.

[851] The Montgomery Advertiser, March 9, 1908.

[852] *Id.*

[853] Ferguson Memoirs/Diary, at 262.

[854] Confederate Military History Expanded Edition, Vol. VIII, at 255.

[855] Charleston Daily Courier, May 20, 1864.

[856] FERGUSON MEMOIRS/DIARY, at 340. Letter from J.H. Steele to Gen. Ferguson, dated Dec. 20, 1911.

[857] *See*, OR, Ser. 1, Vol. 24, Pt. I, p. 555. A report from Brigadier General William J. Palmer states that "Ferguson's brigade, consisting chiefly of Georgians and numbering about 1,000, after crossing the Savannah was allowed to march to Macon, where it surrendered to General Wilson." *Id.*

[858] FRANCIS TREVELYAN MILLER, THE PHOTOGRAPHIC HISTORY OF THE CIVIL WAR 34 (1911).

[859] OR, Ser. 1, Vol. 49, Pt. 2, p. 702.

[860] Hd Qrs Ferguson's Brigade, Lincoln Co ,Ga, May 5, 1865,

I hereby certify that the within list [84 members of Ferguson's Brigade] of officers and men, comprises all those that remained with Genl Ferguson and were HONORABLY discharged by the Secretary of War.

    T.K. Irwin, Capt & A.A.A. Genl.

[861] FERGUSON MEMOIRS/DIARY, at 262-268. Of the 26 members of the 2nd Alabama, 13 were from Company H and 6 from Company D. Sergeant Major Cochrane is listed in this final role.

[862] *Id.*

[863] *Id.* at 266-268.

[864] THE DAY DIXIE DIED, at 60.

[865] JOHN M. COSKI, *GOING HOME*, THE MUSEUM OF THE CONFEDERACY MAGAZINE, Winter 2012, at 6.

[866] THE DAY DIXIE DIED, at 111.

[867] *Id.* at 7.

[868] THE MONTGOMERY ADVERTISER, March 9, 1908.

[869] *Id.*

[870] FERGUSON MEMOIRS/DIARY, at 285.

[871] Psalm 103:19.

[872] GEORGE ORWELL, 1984 (1949).

[873] *See e,g.*, JAMES LEE MCDONOUGH, WILLIAM TECUMSEH SHERMAN: IN THE SERVICE OF MY COUNTRY, A LIFE xii (2016).

874 Quotes About Terrorism, HEARTS AND MINDS, https://www.heartsandminds.org/inspire/terrorism/.

875 THE HERITAGE OF MONTGOMERY COUNTY, ALABAMA 98 (2001).

876 *Id.* at 98.

877 FERGUSON MEMOIRS/DIARY, at 299.

878 PARTHENIA ANTOINETTE HAGUE, A BLOCKADED FAMILY: LIFE IN SOUTHERN ALABAMA DURING THE CIVIL WAR 164(1888).

879 *Id.* at 25. Recalling before the War: "Often have we sat on the colonnade of that lovely Alabama home, and wondered if any part of the world could be more beautiful."

880 JOSEPH BERNARDO & EUGENE H. BACON, AMERICAN MILITARY POLICY 235-237 (1957). By the start of 1866, the Union Army had gone from a force of 1,000,516 in May 1865, to a volunteer force of 11,043 men.

881 *See* WALTER L. FLEMING, CIVIL WAR AND RECONSTRUCTION IN ALABAMA (1905).

882 BOSTON EVENING TRANSCRIPT, May 20, 1905.

883 *Id.*

884 A LONG SHADOW, at 166.

885 4 CONFEDERATE VETERAN 71 (1896). Address by Senator E.C. Walthall, remarks at the unveiling of the Confederate soldier statute in Jackson, Mississippi.

886 *See* JAMES M. MCPHERSON, WHAT THEY FOUGHT FOR: 1861-1865 18 (1994).

887 DR. J.W. JONES, LIFE AND LETTERS OF GEN. ROBERT EDWARD LEE 376 (1906).

888 REBECCA WEST (CICELY ISABEL FAIRFIELD), THE MEANING OF TREASON 311 (1949).

889 WHEELER AND HIS CAVALRY, at 370.

890 *See* SHANNON PRITCHARD, CONFEDERATE FACES IN COLOR 323 (2013).

About the Author

JEFFREY F. ADDICOTT is a Professor of Law and the Director of the Warrior Defense Project at St. Mary's University School of Law, San Antonio, Texas, where he teaches a variety of courses to include National Security Law and Terrorism Law. An active duty Army officer in the Judge Advocate General's Corps for twenty years (he retired in 2000 at the rank of Lieutenant Colonel), Professor Addicott spent a quarter of his career as the senior legal advisor to the United States Army's Special Forces. An internationally recognized authority in terrorism law and the law of war, Professor Addicott not only lectures and participates in professional and academic organizations both in the United States and overseas, he is also a frequent contributor to national and international media outlets.

Foreign presentations on terrorism and national security law include numerous lectures at universities and government institutions in India, China, Sultanate of Oman, Colombia, Peru, Ukraine, Germany, France, Austria, Canada, Thailand, Japan, Honduras, Haiti, Egypt, Kuwait, Panama, Guatemala, Albania, Okinawa, Cuba, South Korea, England, Mexico, Sweden, Ireland, Scotland, Greece, Israel, Russia, and Uruguay. Presentations in the United States include over 1,000 appearances at universities and government institutions, as well as more than 5,000 appearances on radio, print, and television broadcasts to include the *Wall Street Journal, New York Times, Washington Post, Miami Herald, Dallas Star-Tribune, San Antonio Express-News, Los Angeles Times, Chicago Tribune, Washington Times, Washington Examiner,* FOX NEWS Channel, MSNBC, CNN, ABC, PBS, NBC, CBS, NPR, BBC, Voice of Russia, and al-Jazeera.

Professor Addicott is a prolific author, publishing over one hundred books, articles, and monographs on a variety of legal topics. Among his many contributions to the field, Professor Addicott pioneered the teaching of law of war and human rights courses to the militaries of numerous nascent democracies in Eastern Europe and Latin America. For these efforts he was awarded the Legion of Merit, named the "Army Judge Advocate of the Year" and honored as a co-recipient of the American Bar Association's Hodson Award.

Dr. Addicott served as the Associate Dean for Administration and Finance at St. Mary's University School of Law (2006-2007). He is also the 2007 recipient of St. Mary's University Alumni Association's "St. Mary's University School of Law Distinguished Faculty Award." Addicott also founded "Bible Doctrine Ministries" where he teaches non-denominational Bible classes (under categorical, isagogical, and exegetical teaching) at St. Mary's University School of Law, San Antonio, Texas.

Lieutenant Colonel Addicott (U.S. Army, Ret.) served in senior legal positions in Germany, Korea, Panama, and throughout the United States. Professor Addicott holds a Doctor of Juridical Science (SJD) and Master of Laws (LLM) from the University of Virginia School of Law. He also received a Master of Laws (LLM) from the Judge Advocate General's School, a Juris Doctor (JD) from the University of Alabama School of Law and a bachelor of arts with "Honors in Government" (BA) from the University of Maryland.

SOUTHERN BOOKS. NO APOLOGIES

OVER 90 TITLES FOR YOU TO ENJOY
SHOTWELLPUBLISHING.COM

JEFFERY ADDICOTT
Union Terror: Debunking the False Justifications for Union Terror

MARK ATKINS
Women in Combat: Feminism Goes to War

JOYCE BENNETT
Maryland, My Maryland: The Cultural Cleansing of a Small Southern State

GARRY BOWERS
Slavery and The Civil War: What Your History Teacher Didn't Tell You

Dixie Days: Reminiscences Of a Southern Boyhood

JERRY BREWER
Dismantling the Republic

ANDREW P. CALHOUN
My Own Darling Wife: Letters From A Confederate Volunteer

JOHN CHODES
Segregation: Federal Policy or Racism?

Washington's Kkk: The Union League During Southern Reconstruction

WALTER BRIAN CISCO
War Crimes Against Southern Civilians

JOHN DEVANNY
Continuities: The South in a Time of Revolution

JOSHUA DOGGRELL
Doxed: The Political Lynching of a Southern Cop

JAMES C. EDWARDS
What Really Happened?: Quantrill's Raid On Lawrence, Kansas

TED EHMANN
Boom & Bust In Bone Valley: Florida's Phosphate Mining History 1886-2021

JOHN AVERY EMISON
The Deep State Assassination of Martin Luther King Jr.

DON GORDON
Snowball's Chance: My Kidneys Failed, My Wife Left Me & My Dog Died...

JOHN R. GRAHAM
Constitutional History of Secession

PAUL C. GRAHAM
Confederaphobia

When The Yankees Come: Former Carolina Slaves Remember

Nonsense on Stilts: The Gettysburg Address & Lincoln's Imaginary Nation

JOE D. HAINES
The Diary of Col. John Henry Stover Funk of the Stonewall Brigade, 1861-1862

CHARLES HAYES
The REAL First Thanksgiving

V.P. HUGHES
Col. John Singleton Mosby: In the News 1862-1916

Terry Hulsey
25 Texas Heroes

The Constitution of Non-State Government: Field Guide to Texas Secession

Joseph Jay
Sacred Conviction: The South's Stand for Biblical Authority

Suzanne Johnson
Maxcy Gregg's Sporting Journals 1842-1858

James R. Kennedy
Dixie Rising: Rules For Rebels

Nullifying Federal and State Gun Control: A How-To Guide For Gun Owners

When Rebel Was Cool: Growing Up In Dixie, 1950-1965

Walter D. Kennedy
The South's Struggle: America's Hope

Lincoln, The Non-Christian President: Exposing The Myth

Lincoln, Marx, and the GOP

J.R. & W.D. Kennedy
Jefferson Davis: High Road to Emancipation and Constitutional Government

Yankee Empire: Aggressive Abroad and Despotic at Home

Punished With Poverty: The Suffering South

The South Was Right! 3rd Edition

Lewis Liberman
Snowflake Buddies; ABC Leftism For Kids!

Philip Leigh
The Devil's Town: Hot Springs During The Gangster Era

U.S. Grant's Failed Presidency

The Causes of the Civil War

The Dreadful Frauds: Critical Race Theory And Identity Politics

Jack Marquardt
Around The World In 80 Years: Confessions of a Connecticut Confederate

Michael Martin
Southern Grit: Sensing The Siege at Petersburg

Samuel Mitcham
The Greatest Lynching In American History: New York, 1863

Confederate Patton: Richard Taylor and The Red River Campaign

Charles T. Pace
Lincoln As He Really Was

Southern Independence. Why War? The War To Prevent Southern Independence

James R. Roesch
From Founding Fathers To Fire Eaters

Kirkpatrick Sale
Emancipation Hell: The Tragedy Wrought By Lincoln's Emancipation Proclamation

Joseph Scotchie
The Asheville Connection: The Making of a Conservative

ANNE W. SMITH

Charlottesville Untold: Inside Unite The Right

Robert E. Lee: A History for Kids

KAREN STOKES

A Legion Of Devils: Sherman In South Carolina

The Burning of Columbia, S.C.: A Review of Northern Assertions and Southern Facts

Fortunes of War: The Adventures of a German Confederate

A Confederate in Paris: Letters of A. Dudley Mann 1867-1879

JACK TROTTER

Last Train to Dixie

JOHN THEURSAM

Key West's Civil War

H.V. TRAYWICK, JR.

Along The Shadow Line: A Road Trip through History and Memory on the Old Confederate Border

LESLIE TUCKER

Old Times There Should Not Be Forgotten: Cultural Genocide In Dixie

JOHN VINSON

Southerner Take Your Stand!

MARK R. WINCHELL

Confessions of a Copperhead: Culture and Politics in the Modern South

CLYDE N. WILSON

Calhoun: A Statesman for the 21st Century

Lies My Teacher Told Me: The True History of the War For Southern Independence

The Yankee Problem: An American Dilemma

Annals Of The Stupid Party: Republicans Before Trump

Nullification: Reclaiming The Consent of the Governed

The Old South: 50 Essential Books

The War Between The States: 60 Essential Books

Reconstruction and the New South, 1865-1913: 50 Essential Books

The South 20th Century And Beyond: 50 Essential Books

Southern Poets and Poems, 1606-1860: The Land They Loved, Volume 1

Looking For Mr. Jefferson

African American Slavery in Historical Perspective

JOE WOLVERTON

What Degree Of Madness?: Madison's Method To Make American States Again

WALTER KIRK WOOD

Beyond Slavery: The Northern Romantic Nationalist Origins of America's Civil War

Green Altar (Literary Imprint)

CATHARINE BROSMAN
An Aesthetic Education and Other Stories (2nd Ed)

Chained Tree, Chained Owls: Poems

Aerosols and Other Poems

RANDALL IVEY
A New England Romance: And Other Southern Stories

JAMES E. KIBBLER, JR.
Tiller : Clayback County Series, Vol. 4

THOMAS MOORE
A Fatal Mercy: The Man Who Lost The Civil War

PERRIN LOVETT
The Substitute, Tom Ironsides 1

KAREN STOKES
Belles

Carolina Love Letters

Carolina Twilight

Honor in the Dust

The Immortals

The Soldier's Ghost: A Tale of Charleston

WILLIAM THOMAS
Runaway Haley: An Imagined Family Saga

Gold-Bug
(Mystery & Suspense Imprint)

BRANDI PERRY
Splintered: A New Orleans Tale

MARTIN WILSON
To Jekyll and Hide

Free Book Offer

DON'T GET LEFT OUT, Y'ALL.
Sign-up and be the first to know about new releases, sales, and other goodies
—plus we'll send you TWO FREE EBOOKS!

Lies My Teacher Told Me:
The True History of the War for Southern Independence
by Dr. Clyde N. Wilson

When The Yankees Come
Former Carolina Slaves Remember Sherman's March From the Sea
by Paul C. Graham

FreeLiesBook.com

Southern Books. No Apologies.
We love the South — its history, traditions, and culture — and are proud of our inheritance as Southerners. Our books are a reflection of this love.